Lecture Notes in Computer Science　　　10213

Commenced Publication in 1973
Founding and Former Series Editors:
Gerhard Goos, Juris Hartmanis, and Jan van Leeuwen

More information about this series at http://www.springer.com/series/7412

Simone Bianco · Raimondo Schettini
Alain Trémeau · Shoji Tominaga (Eds.)

Computational Color Imaging

6th International Workshop, CCIW 2017
Milan, Italy, March 29–31, 2017
Proceedings

 Springer

Editors
Simone Bianco (iD)
University of Milan-Bicocca
Milan
Italy

Raimondo Schettini (iD)
University of Milan-Bicocca
Milan
Italy

Alain Trémeau
University Jean Monnet
Saint-Etienne
France

Shoji Tominaga
Chiba University
Chiba
Japan

ISSN 0302-9743   ISSN 1611-3349 (electronic)
Lecture Notes in Computer Science
ISBN 978-3-319-56009-0   ISBN 978-3-319-56010-6 (eBook)
DOI 10.1007/978-3-319-56010-6

Library of Congress Control Number: 2017935019

LNCS Sublibrary: SL6 – Image Processing, Computer Vision, Pattern Recognition, and Graphics

Printed on acid-free paper

This Springer imprint is published by Springer Nature
The registered company is Springer International Publishing AG
The registered company address is: Gewerbestrasse 11, 6330 Cham, Switzerland

Preface

We welcome you to the proceedings of CCIW 2017, the Computational Color Imaging Workshop, held in Milan, Italy, during March 29–31, 2017.

This sixth CCIW was organized by the University of Milan-Bicocca, with the endorsement of the International Association for Pattern Recognition (IAPR), the Gruppo Italiano Ricercatori in Pattern Recognition (GIRPR), and the Gruppo del Colore (GdC).

The aim of the workshop was to bring together engineers and scientists of various imaging companies and research laboratories from all over the world, to discuss diverse aspects of their latest work, ranging from theoretical developments to practical applications in the field of color imaging, as well as color image processing and analysis.

Since the First Computational Color Imaging Workshop organized in 2007 in Modena, Italy, CCIW has been an inspiration for researches and practitioners in the fields of digital imaging, multimedia, visual communications, computer vision, and consumer electronics who are interested in the fundamentals of color image processing and its emerging applications.

For CCIW 2017 there were many excellent submissions of high scientific level. Each paper was peer reviewed by at least two reviewers. Only the 20 best papers were selected for presentation at the workshop. The final decision for the paper selection was based on the criticisms and recommendations of the reviewers, and the content relevance of papers to the goals of the workshop. In addition to the submitted papers, four distinguished researchers were invited to this sixth CCIW to present keynote speeches.

In this 6th Computational Color Imaging Workshop, challenging issues and open problems not sufficiently addressed in the state of the art were addressed. In the following, we summarize issues and problems that were covered by the papers accepted for CCIW 2017, the invited speeches, and the tutorials.

CCIW 2017 started on March 29, 2017, with four tutorials:

- Material Appearance by S. Tominaga
- Color Texture Analysis and Classification by F. Bianconi, C. Cusano, and P. Napoletano
- Review of Systems Coupling Multispectral Imaging and 3D Imaging by A. Tremeau
- Color Vision Is a Spatial Process: The Retinex Theory by M. Lecca [11]

The three invited talks were hosted over the next two days:

- On Gloss and the Appearance of Color by A. Gijsenij
- Fourier Multispectral Imaging: Measuring Spectra, One Sinusoid at a Time by K. Hirakawa [6]
- Computational Print Control by J. Morovic [14]

In the Color Image Processing session, S. Yamaguchi et al. [22] presented a method for smoke removal based on a smoke imaging model and a space-time pixel compensation. E. Provenzi [17] presented the similarities and differences in the mathematical formalizations of the Retinex models and its variants. M. Lecca et al. [12] presented a new Milano Retinex implementation, based on an intensity thresholding strategy.

In the Color Image Quality session, B. Ortiz-Jaramillo et al. [16] presented a software for image fidelity assessment. S. Corchs and F. Gasparini [4] presented a multidistortion database to be used for image quality assessment, and G. Ciocca et al. [3] presented an image analysis based on image complexity to investigate interference between distortions and image contents in image quality assessment.

In the Color in Digital Cultural Heritage session, J.A. Toque et al. [19] presented a method for the visualization of subsurface features in oil paintings using a combination of high-resolution visible and near-infrared scanned images. K. Yoshida et al. [23] presented a scanner for high-resolution imaging of wall paintings. M. Tsuchida et al. [20] presented a technique for visualizing lost design of degraded early modern tapestry using infrared images. R. Kanai et al. [7] presented a novel scanning technique for imaging of gold and silver foils used in art works. T. Komiyama et al. [9] presented a transmission type scanning system to be used for ultra high-resolution scanning. T. Vitorino et al. [21] showed the importance of hyperspectral imaging applied to the investigation of paintings.

In the Spectral Imaging session, P. Lapray et al. [10] presented a database of spectral filter array images that combine both visible and near-infrared bands. H.A. Khan et al. [8] presented an analytical survey of highlight detection in color and spectral images.

In the Color Characterization session, M. Hebert et al. [5] presented a method for the characterization of structural color prints by hyperspectral imaging and hypercolor gamut estimation. S. Mazauric et al. [13] presented a fast calibration reflectance-transmittance model to compute multiview recto-verso prints. J.-B. Thomas et al. [18] presented the use of an image contrast measure as a gloss material descriptor.

In the Color Image Analysis session, S. Bianco et al. [1] presented the recognition of artistic photo filtering using Convolutional Neural Networks. P. Napoletano [15] presented a comparison between hand-crafted and learned descriptors for color texture classification. F. Bianconi et al. [2] presented an improved opponent-color local binary patterns for color texture classification.

March 2017

Simone Bianco
Raimondo Schettini
Shoji Tominaga
Alain Trémeau

References

1. Simone Bianco, Claudio Cusano, and Raimondo Schettini. Artistic photo filtering recognition using cnns. *Proceedings of the 6th International Workshop CCIW 2017.*
2. Francesco Bianconi, Raquel Bello-Cerezo, Paolo Napoletano, and Francesco Di Maria. Improved opponent colour local binary patterns for colour texture classification. *Proceedings of the 6th International Workshop CCIW 2017.*
3. Gianluigi Ciocca, Silvia Corchs, and Francesca Gasparini. A complexity-based image analysis to investigate interference between distortions and image contents in image quality assessment. *Proceedings of the 6th International Workshop CCIW 2017.*
4. Silvia Corchs and Francesca Gasparini. A multidistortion database for image quality. *Proceedings of the 6th International Workshop CCIW 2017.*
5. Mathieu Hebert, Juan Martinez-Garcia, Thomas Houllier, Hayk Yepremian, Nicolas Crespo-Monteiro, Francis Vocanson, Alain Tremeau, and Nathalie Destouches. Characterization by hyperspectral imaging and hypercolor gamut estimation for structural color prints. *Proceedings of the 6th International Workshop CCIW 2017.*
6. Keigo Hirakawa. Fourier multispectral imaging: Measuring spectra, one sinusoid at a time. *Proceedings of the 6th International Workshop CCIW 2017.*
7. Ryo Kanai, Ari Ide-Ektessabi, Tatsuya Komiyama, Kyohei Yoshida, Masahiro Toiya, Peng Wang, Yoshiharu Kowada, and Jay Arre Toque. A novel scanning technique for imaging of gold and silver foils used in art works. *Proceedings of the 6th International Workshop CCIW 2017.*
8. Haris Ahmad Khan, Jean Baptiste Thomas, and Jon Yngve Hardeberg. Analytical survey of highlight detection in color and spectral images. *Proceedings of the 6th International Workshop CCIW 2017.*
9. Tatsuya Komiyama, Ari Ide-Ektessabi, Daichi Tsunemichi, Peng Wang, Yusuke Isobe, Ryo Kanai, and Kyohei Yoshida. A transmission type scanning system for ultra high resolution scanning. *Proceedings of the 6th International Workshop CCIW 2017.*
10. Pierre-Jean Lapray, Jean-Baptiste Thomas, and Pierre Gouton. A database of spectral filter array images that combine visible and nir. *Proceedings of the 6th International Workshop CCIW 2017.*
11. Michela Lecca. Color vision is a spatial process: The retinex theory. *Proceedings of the 6th International Workshop CCIW 2017.*
12. Michela Lecca, Carla Maria Modena, and Alessandro Rizzi. T-rex: A milano retinex implementation based on intensity thresholding. *Proceedings of the 6th International Workshop CCIW 2017.*
13. Serge Mazauric, Thierry Fournel, and Mathieu Hebert. Fast-calibration reflectance-transmittance model to compute multiview recto-verso prints. *Proceedings of the 6th International Workshop CCIW 2017.*

14. Jan Morovic, Peter Morovic, Jordi Arnabat, Xavier Farina, Hector Gomez, Joan Enric Garcia, and Pere Gasparin. Computational print control. *Proceedings of the 6th International Workshop CCIW 2017.*
15. Paolo Napoletano. Hand-crafted vs learned descriptors for color texture classification. *Proceedings of the 6th International Workshop CCIW 2017.*
16. Benhur Ortiz-Jaramillo, Ljiljana Platisa, and Wilfried Philips. ifas: Image fidelity assessment software. *Proceedings of the 6th International Workshop CCIW 2017.*
17. Edoardo Provenzi. Similarities and differences in the mathematical formalizations of the retinex model and its variants. *Proceedings of the 6th International Workshop CCIW 2017.*
18. Jean-Baptiste Thomas, Jon Yngve Hardeberg, and Gabriele Simone. Image contrast measure as a gloss material descriptor. *Proceedings of the 6th International Workshop CCIW 2017.*
19. Jay Arre Toque, Koji Okumura, Yashuhide Shimbata, and Ari Ide-Ektessabi. Visualization of subsurface features in oil paintings using high-resolution visible and near infrared scanned images. *Proceedings of the 6th International Workshop CCIW 2017.*
20. Masaru Tsuchida, Keiji Yano, Kaoru Hiramatsu, and Kunio Kashino. Visualizing lost designs of degraded early modern tapestry using infra-red image. *Proceedings of the 6th International Workshop CCIW 2017.*
21. Tatiana Vitorino, Andrea Casini, Costanza Cucci, Marcello Picollo, and Lorenzo Stefani. When it is not only about color: the importance of hyperspectral imaging applied to the investigation of paintings. *Proceedings of the 6th International Workshop CCIW 2017.*
22. Shiori Yamaguchi, Keita Hirai, and Takahiko Horiuchi. Video smoke removal based on smoke imaging model and space-time pixel compensation. *Proceedings of the 6th International Workshop CCIW 2017.*
23. Kyohei Yoshida, Peng Wang, Ryo Kanai, Tatsuya Komiyama, Masahiro Toiya, and Ari Ide. A simple scanner for high resolution imaging of wall paintings. *Proceedings of the 6th International Workshop CCIW 2017.*

Organization

CCIW 2017 was organized by the University of Milan-Bicocca, Italy, in cooperation with Jean Monnet University, Saint-Etienne, France, and the Graduate School of Advanced Integration Science, Chiba University, Japan.

Executive Committee

Conference Chairs

Simone Bianco — University of Milan-Bicocca, Italy
Raimondo Schettini — University of Milan-Bicocca, Italy
Shoji Tominaga — Chiba University, Japan
Alain Tremeau — Jean Monnet University, Saint-Etienne, France

Program Committee

Jan Allebach, USA
Ide-Ektessabi Ari, Japan
Francesco Bianconi, Italy
Franck Boochs, Germany
Graham Finlayson, UK
Brian Funt, Canada
Francesca Gasparini, Italy
Jon Hardeberg, Norway
Markku Hauta-Kasari, Finland
Mathieu Hebert, France
Javier Hernandez-Andres, Spain
Takahiko Horiuchi, Japan
Po-Chieh Hung, Japan
Francisco Imai, USA
Michela Lecca, Italy
Linsday MacDonald, UK

Yoshitsugu Manabe, Japan
Jan Morovic, Spain
Damien Muselet, France
Paolo Napoletano, Italy
Sergio Nascimento, Portugal
Juan Luis Nieves, Spain
Jussi Parkkinen, Finland
Alessandro Rizzi, Italy
Maurizio Rossi, Italy
Gaurav Sharma, USA
Bogdan Smolka, Poland
Sabine Susstrunk, France
Joost Van De Weijer, Spain
Maria Vanrell, Spain
Stephen Westland, UK
Geoff Woolfe, Australia

Keynote/Invited Talks

Arjan Gijsenij — AkzoNobel, The Netherlands
Keigo Hirakawa — University of Dayton, Ohio, USA
Jan Morovic — HP Inc., Sant Cugat del Valles, Spain
Michela Lecca — Fondazione Bruno Kessler (FBK), Trento, Italy

Sponsoring Institutions

University of Milan-Bicocca, Italy
Jean Monnet University, Saint-Etienne, France
Graduate School of Advanced Integration Science, Chiba University, Japan
International Association for Pattern Recognition (IAPR)
Gruppo Italiano Ricercatori in Pattern Recognition (GIRPR)
Gruppo del Colore (GdC)

Contents

Invited Talks and Tutorials

Fourier Multispectral Imaging:
Measuring Spectra, One Sinusoid at a Time

Keigo Hirakawa[✉]

Electrical and Computer Engineering, University of Dayton,
300 College Park, Dayton, OH, USA
khirakawa1@udayton.edu
http://issl.udayton.edu

Abstract. We recently introduced the notion of Fourier Multispectral
Imaging (Fourier MSI), a novel technique for undersampling spectral
images without significant sacrifices to the spectral features that may be
useful for material identification. The idea originated in Fourier transform spectroscopy, where multiple interferometric measurements are used
to take spectral samples while varying optical path difference (OPD).
Since interference is equivalent to spectral modulation by a filter with
sinusoidally shaped transmittance function, we designed a sinusoidal filter using thin film Fabry-Perot to acquire OPD samples at every pixel.
Owing to the rapid decay of OPD samples, Fourier MSI is an ideal multispectral imaging modality for preserving spectral features with the fewest
spectral samples. We detail our prototyping efforts and demonstrate the
advantages of such multispectral imaging configurations.

Keywords: Fabry-Perot · Fourier transform spectroscopy ·
Multispectral imaging

1 Introduction

In spectroscopy, the interaction between light and matter is used to study the
properties of the reflecting surface materials. The absorption of electromagnetic radiation depends on the material composition, penetration depth, photon
energy conversion to heat, etc. Spectrally narrowband electromagnetic radia-
tions called emission lines also correspond to the difference in energy between
two active atomic/molecular states. Hence, the spectral attenuation of reflected,
transmitted, or scattered light (or the presence of spectral emission lines) can
be useful for detecting the composition of chemicals or inferring the state of the
materials. The applications are wide ranging, including material identification,
biopsy, geophysical surveying, and target tracking/detection/recognition.

In human visual system, a light in the visible range is observed by three types
of photon receptors known as cones. The spectral responses of the three photon
receptor types are different, giving rise to the notion of perceived "color." Hence
one may interpret human color vision as a type of *undersampling* on the light

© Springer International Publishing AG 2017
S. Bianco et al. (Eds.): CCIW 2017, LNCS 10213, pp. 3–12, 2017.
DOI: 10.1007/978-3-319-56010-6_1

spectra by the three spectral samples summarizing the spectral characteristics of
the material. However, it is impossible to recover the full light spectra from the
color tristimulus values (e.g. red, green, blue). As such, utility of color imaging
as means of material/chemical identification is severely limited.

Full spectral description of light can also be useful in color imaging. An
accurate color rendering and material appearance require modeling of light
and reflectance spectra. For example, consider the problem of computational
"relighting"—rendering a scene captured under one illuminant as if it were lit
by another illuminant. The relighting is a function of a full spectrum, meaning it cannot be performed with only tristimulus values. An accurate imaging
and color rendering of objects containing fluorescent agents (or ordinary objects
illuminated by fluorescent illumination) is difficult also because the underlying
spectral features are extremely narrow. Hence, most color imaging applications
involving these difficult scenarios rely on crude approximations in a three dimensional subspace that clearly have limitations.

The complexity of hyperspectral imaging (dense spectral sampling at every
pixel) hardware is very high and its acquisition speed is very slow. The color imaging sensors on the other hand are fast and simple, but they do not have the dis-
criminating features for detection/recognition tasks. As an alternative to hyperspectral imaging, multispectral imaging (MSI) systems make N finite spectral
measurements using N predetermined filters to reduce the hardware complexity. Conventional MSI configurations use narrowband filters whose center wavelengths were chosen to satisfy the needs of the imaging applications (example
shown in Fig. 1(b)) [1–4]. Although this approach indeed helps reduce the hardware complexity, a given sensor configuration is optimized for the detection of
one or two specific materials only (e.g. a filter transmittance is aligned with the
emission line). Undersampling with narrowband filters does not yield a "general-
puropose" MSI hardware that is application-agnostic or multipurpose. MSI-based

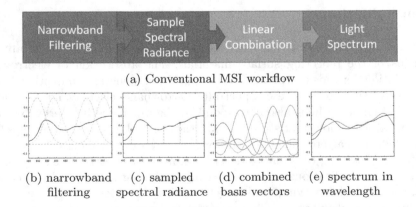

(a) Conventional MSI workflow

(b) narrowband   (c) sampled   (d) combined   (e) spectrum in
filtering   spectral radiance   basis vectors   wavelength

Fig. 1. Conventional multispectral imaging leverages narrowband filtering to sample
spectral radiance. Basis vectors are linearly combined to reconstruct the spectrum.
(Color figure online)

surveillance/security/biometry systems are particularly prone to spoofing attacks if there is an overreliance on certain spectral features or filter center wavelengths.

Our goal for MSI is to develop a novel foundation for undersampling spectra that best preserves the spectral features of materials. Towards this goal, we recently introduced the notion of Fourier multispectral imaging [7]. We leverage the direct correspondences between Fourier sampling theories and the Fabry-Perot thin film filters that have sinusoidal shaped spectral transmittance functions. As we detail below, the sinusoidally shaped filters have advantages over the narrowband filtering in preserving spectral features that are critical for tracking/detection/recognition tasks. Fourier MSI is also general purpose, allowing the detection of multiple materials/chemicals/objects by a single detector. In this paper, we review key details of the Fourier MSI and describe the ongoing prototyping efforts at the University of Dayton towards verifying its viability.

2   Fourier Multispectral Imaging

2.1   Interferometric Spectroscopy

By "spectrum of light" we refer to the spectral radiance, or surface radiance (watts per steradian per square meter) as a function of wavelengths per unit of wavelengths (meter). In physics and optics, the spectral radiance is equivalently be expressed in terms of wavenumber (radians per meter), which describes the number of periodic wave cycles per distance (reciprocal of wavelengths, which is the distance per cycle). Among techniques available to measure the spectral radiance is the Fourier transform spectroscopy.

Consider measurements in the Fourier transform spectroscopy made by a well-known device known as Michelson interferometer, shown in Fig. 2. The two light paths (via the mirrors A and B, as indicated by green and blue arrows)

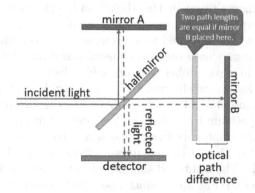

Fig. 2. Michelson interferometer. The two light paths (via the mirrors A and B) are combined at the detector. The difference of the path lengths determines the phase difference of the combined beams that interfere destructively/constructively. (Color figure online)

are combined at the detector with the help of the half mirror. The difference in the path lengths (referred to as the optical path difference, or OPD) determines the phase difference of the combined beams that interfere destructively/constructively, which can be inferred from the light intensity measured by the detector. The spectral radiance of the light can be recovered by taking a Fourier transform of the interferogram, acquired from repeating the measurements with varying OPDs.

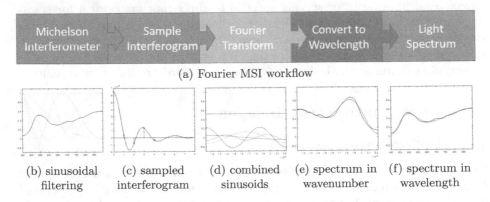

(a) Fourier MSI workflow

| (b) sinusoidal | (c) sampled | (d) combined | (e) spectrum in | (f) spectrum in |
| filtering | interferogram | sinusoids | wavenumber | wavelength |

Fig. 3. Fourier multispectral imaging samples interferogram, which is effectively same as filtering with a sinusoidal transmittance. Forward Fourier transform recovers the spectra in wavenumber domain, which may subsequently be converted to wavelength.

It is clear from the Fourier transform relations that the interferogram and the spectral radiance represent equivalent information. We proposed in [5–7] the notion of Fourier MSI, or the undersampling of the interferogram, whose workflow is summarized in Fig. 3(a). The example in Fig. 3(c) shows five interferometric measurements taken by the Michelson interferometer in Fig. 2. Each of these five measurements corresponds to the coherence strength at varying optical path lengths. The acquired measurements are also equivalent to filtering the light with filters whose spectral transmittance function are sinusoidally shaped—sinusoidal in wavenumber domain, which looks like a skewed sinusoid in the wavelength domain as shown by Fig. 3(b). Unlike the narrowband filter counterparts, the sinusoidal "filters" have broadband transmittance.

To recover the spectrum from the sampled interferogram, we take its Fourier transform by linearly combining five cosine waves together. The cosine's periodicity is reciprocal of the OPD, and its amplitude is scaled by the measured values—see Fig. 3(d). The combined sinusoids reconstruct the light spectrum in the wavenumber domain (Fig. 3(e)), which may also be converted into wavelength in Fig. 3(f). The recovered spectrum closely approximates the light spectrum, albeit slightly smoother than the actual spectrum. With only five interference measurements, spectral features such as peak heights and locations are accurately preserved.

2.2   Narrowband MSI v.s. Fourier MSI

We now contrast the proposed Fourier MSI to the conventional MSI approach of using narrowband filters, which is effectively an undersampling of the spectral radiance. We compare Figs. 1 and 3 to illustrate the profound differences between undersampling interferogram and spectral radiance. As illustrated in Fig. 1(b), the center wavelength of the five narrowband filters may or may not coincide with the spectral peak of the light (by chance). As a result, the peak of the recovered spectrum in Fig. 1(e) coincides with the one of five filter transmittance functions (and not with the light spectrum). Mitigating this problem by increasing the number of spectral samples also increases the hardware complexity; in an application-specific MSI hardware, we may also tune the center wavelengths of the filter transmittance to coincide with the spectral features of interests.

Appealing to the fact typical light spectra lives in a low dimensional subspace, one may improve the performance of the conventional MSI by projecting the measurements to a vector spaces (e.g. principal component analysis) that best models the light—see Fig. 4. Fourier MSI is expected to benefit from such approach also. However, although model-based recovery is useful for imaging natural scenes, it is less effective in applications such as anomaly detection or chemical/material analysis, and less desirable for target detection where the underlying models confound the detection rates. Clearly, an accurate multispectral imaging without invoking models (the so-called "nonparametric" techniques) are more desirable in many applications.

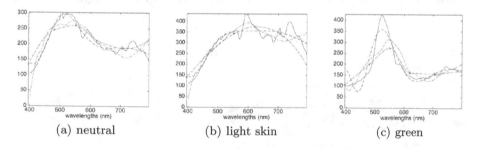

(a) neutral   (b) light skin   (c) green

Fig. 4. Simulated reconstruction from five spectral samples. Blue = ground truth. Red = Fourier MSI. Pink = Monno MSI with cubic interpolation. Green = Monno MSI with PCA reconstruction. (Color figure online)

From the sensing point of view, the Fourier MSI is a far more efficient than the conventional MSI. The energy of the interferogram in Fig. 3(c) decays rapidly with the increasing OPD, and the N spectral samples should correspond to short coherence lengths to maximize the captured signal energy. In this sense, interferogram is an ideal sensing modality for MSI—each successive interferometric measurement of longer OPD is a refinement to the signal reconstructed with the shorter OPD samples. Compare this to the undersampled spectral radiance—as illustrated in Fig. 1(c), the signal energy is spread evenly throughout the wavelengths ranges, meaning it is difficult to determine the N center wavelengths that maximizes the overall signal fidelity.

However, one disadvantage to the Fourier MSI is the Gibbs phenomenon. For example, the presence of narrow spectral feature near 520 nm in Fig. 4(c) cause the unwanted oscillation in 400–500 nm region. The Gibbs phenomenon can be suppressed by increasing the number of OPD measurements.

2.3   Filter Designs for Fourier MSI

In the previous sections, we showed the advantages to undersampling the interferogram. However, the hardware configuration in Fig. 2(a) does not preserve spatial location, meaning Michelson interferometer is appropriate for spectroscopy but not spectral imaging. In [5, 7], we proposed to replace the hardware design by leveraging Fabry-Perot thin film filter. As illustrated in Fig. 5(a), an etalon is a three dimensional structure where partial reflections occur at the interfaces. The detector sees a linear combination of multiple reflected light, resulting in an interference caused by the path length differences among the reflections. One major advantage to Fabry-Perot thin film filters over the Michelson interferometer is that it preserves the spatial location (i.e. appropriate for imaging).

Consider a Fourier MSI system where the same scene is imaged using multiple Fabry-Perot filters of varying thicknesses, as shown in Fig. 5(a). Since the path lengths differences are integer multiples of the etalon thicknesses, the light combined at the detector is a linear combination of equally spaced OPD samples, as shown in Fig. 5(b–f). In addition, the path differences of the light combined

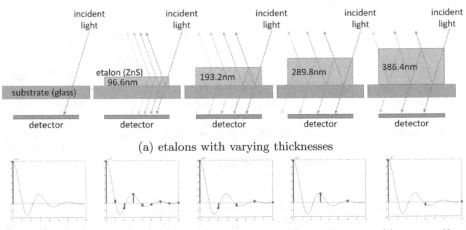

(a) etalons with varying thicknesses

(b) no filtering   (c) 96.6nm filter   (d) 193nm filter   (e) 290nm filter   (f) 386nm filter

Fig. 5. Fabry-Perot filter with varying etalon thicknesses. (b) If unfiltered, we measure the zero coherence light. (c–f) Each filtered light is a combination of discrete OPD samples that must be linearly uncombined in post-processing.

by multiple etalons whose thicknesses are integer multiples of each other are also integer multiples of a common OPD length. We conclude, therefore, that each etalon measurement is a linear combination of the OPD samples in Fig. 3(c) we are after. Thus by linearly uncombining the acquired data, we can recover the desired interferometric values.

3 Prototyping and Results

Prototyping efforts are being carried out at the University of Dayton to verify the effectiveness of Fourier MSI. The "Prototype #1" configuration is shown in Fig. 6(a) [7]. The selected operating range is 450–900 nm, which is one octave in the wavenumber. We used a grayscale image sensor (OptiTrack V120 Slim), with a CMOS detector responding from 380–1000 nm. A 450 nm longpass filter and a 900 nm shortpass filter were added to restrict the range of incoming light that the detector responds to.

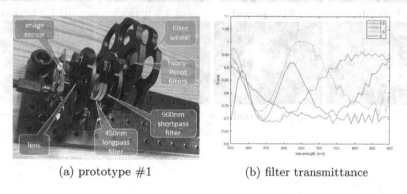

(a) prototype #1   (b) filter transmittance

Fig. 6. (a) Bulk filter-based Fourier multispectral imaging prototype system. (b) Spectral transmittance of the Zinc Sulfide filters of varying thicknesses.

For the sinusoidal filters, we fabricated six Fabry-Perot thin-film bulk filters on a glass substrate, using Zinc Sulfide thin film [7,8]. Zinc Sulfide is ideal for our application because of relatively small dispersion over 450–900 nm. Dielectric filters form almost perfect sinusoids, as shown in Fig. 6(b). The cavity thicknesses were chosen so that the sinusoid spans 0.5, 1.0, 1.5, 2.0, 2.5, and 3.0 periods over 450 nm–900 nm. Images were taken by time multiplexing using filter wheels to exchange the fabricated filters.

Figure 7 shows examples of LED spectra imaged and recovered by Prototype #1. LEDs emit very narrowband light, which are precisely the type of spectra that is difficult to capture with conventional MSI systems. The spectral peaks recovered by the Fourier MSI are at (or very near) the emission wavelengths, albeit the presence of the Gibbs phenomenon and the recovered spectral peaks that are wider than the actual spectra. This confirms the claim made in [7] that

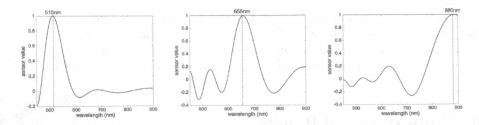

Fig. 7. Narrowband LED spectra reconstructed from by the Prototype #1. The reconstructed peaks (blue) coincide with the LED emission wavelengths (red) fairly accurately. (Color figure online)

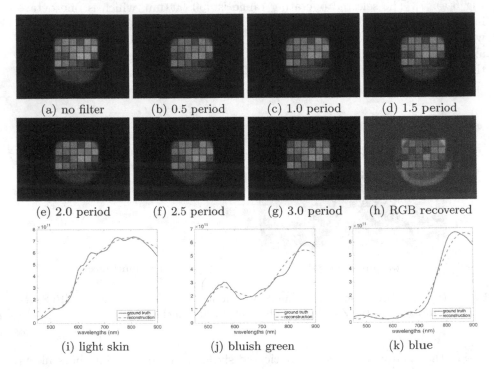

Fig. 8. Example of the Prototype #1 measurements. (a)–(g) Raw sensor data. (i–k) Recovered spectra. (h) RGB rendering of the recovered spectral scene. The ground truth spectra shown here is the combination of the spectral reflectance (measured by a contact spectrometer), illuminant and the quantum efficiency (measured using a monochrometer). (Color figure online)

the Fourier MSI systems have near-infinite resolution in detecting the wavelengths of a single wavelength peak.

Shown in Fig. 8 are example OPD measurements from the Prototype #1. The actual spectral measurements in Fig. 8(a–g) are linearly combined to yield the spectral reconstruction in Fig. 8(i–k), yielding a per-pixel recovery of the

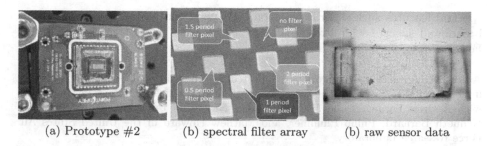

(a) Prototype #2   (b) spectral filter array   (b) raw sensor data

Fig. 9. (a) Spectral filter array-based single-shot Fourier multispectral imaging prototype system. (b) Filter array is comprised of four types of Zinc Sulfide thin-film filters of varying thicknesses. (c) Raw sensor data captures the spatially multiplexed OPD measurements. Post-processing "demosaicking" step recovers a full four-filtered interferogram.

spectrum. The RGB rendering of the recovered spectra is shown in Fig. 8(h). The ground truth spectra in Fig. 8(i–k) was rendered by taking the reflectance data measured by a field contact spectrometer, which was combined with the spectral radiance of the illuminant and the quantum efficiency of the sensor, both measured by a monochromenter. While the reconstructions are not perfect, the recovered spectra accurately represented the features such as the narrowband spectral peaks and sharp transitions.

Another ongoing prototyping effort at the University of Dayton include fabrication of pixelized Fabry-Perot Zinc Sulfide filters [9]. As shown in Fig. 9(b), we fabricated a spectral filter array comprised of four types of filters (0.5–2.0 period filters) spatially multiplexed over the substrater [5,11]. In our "Prototype #2," the spectral filter array is attached to the CCD sensor surface directly (Fig. 9(a)), where each filter is designed to occupy multiple pixels so that the filter-pixel misalignments can be handled in post-processing (Fig. 9(c)). The spectral filter array configuration enabling a single-shot Fourier MSI, where the "demosaicking" is used to interpolate the missing filtered values to recover a full four-filtered interferogram from its spatially multiplexed version [6,10,11].

4 Conclusion

In this paper, we reviewed the novel concept of Fourier multispectral imaging—undersampling of interferogram intended to reduce the complexity of the spectral imaging—and the practical implementation using Fabry-Perot thin-film filters that yield periodic spectral transmittance functions while preserving the pixel/spatial integrity. We showed by simulated examples that the Fourier MSI captures spectral features such as peaks far more accurately than the conventional MSI approach of using narrowband filtering. We described the ongoing prototyping efforts at the University of Dayton to verify the feasibility of Fourier MSI. Our Prototype #1 demonstrated the ability to recover very narrowband spectral features such as LED emission, and yield acceptable reconstruction of broadband spectra. Our Prototype #2 enables a single-shot capability to the Fourier MSI.

Acknowledgments. This work is supported by the National Science Foundation under Grant No. 1307904. The work presented in this article represents a joint effort with Andrew Sarangan, Jie Jia, and Chuan Ni of the University of Dayton, and Kenneth Barnard, Philip Plummer, and Mathew Howard of the United States Air Force Research Laboratory.

References

1. Monno, Y., Kitao, T., Tanaka, M., Okutomi, M.: Optimal spectral sensitivity functions for a single-camera one-shot multispectral imaging system. In: 2012 IEEE International Conference on Image Processing (ICIP). IEEE (2012)
2. Miao, L., Qi, H.: The design and evaluation of a generic method for generating mosaicked multispectral filter arrays. IEEE Trans. Image Process. **15**(9), 2780–2791 (2006)
3. Miao, L., Qi, H., Ramanath, R., Snyder, W.E.: Binary treebased generic demosaicking algorithm for multispectral filter arrays. IEEE Trans. Image Process. **15**(11), 3550–3558 (2006)
4. Shrestha, R., Hardeberg, J.Y., Khan, R.: Spatial arrangement of color filter array for multispectral image acquisition, Society of Photo Optical Instrumentation Engineers (2011)
5. Hirakawa, K., Barnard, K.J.: Fourier spectral filter array design for multispectral image recovery. In: Imaging Systems and Applications. Optical Society of America, paper IM1C-5 (2014)
6. Jia, J., Barnard, K.J., Hirakawa, K.: Fourier spectral filter array for optimal multispectral imaging. IEEE Trans. Image Process. **25**, 1530–1543 (2016)
7. Jia, J., Ni, C., Sarangan, A., Hirakawa, K.: Fourier multispectral imaging. Opt. Express **23**, 22649–22657 (2015)
8. Ni, C., et al.: Design and fabrication of sinusoidal spectral filters for multispectral imaging. International Society for Optics and Photonics, SPIE Nanoscience+Engineering (2015)
9. Ni, C., Jia, J., Hirakawa, K., Sarangan, A.: Design and fabrication of Fourier spectral filter array for multispectral imaging. In: Proceedings of the SPIE 9927, Nanoengineering: Fabrication, Properties, Optics, and Devices XIII, 99270W (2016)
10. Jia, J., et al.: Guided Filter Demosaicking For Fourier Spectral Filter Array. Electronic Imaging (2016)
11. Jia, J., Hirakawa, K.: Single-shot fourier transform multispectroscopy. 2015 IEEE International Conference on Image Processing (ICIP). IEEE (2015)

Computational Print Control

Ján Morovič[✉], Peter Morovič, Jordi Arnabat, Xavier Fariña, Hector Gomez,
Joan Enric Garcia, and Pere Gasparin

HP Inc., Sant Cugat del Vallés, Spain
jan.morovic@hp.com

Abstract. Printing may seem like a dinosaur among today's imaging technologies, since its roots stretch back to Becquerel's work that lead to the first color
photographs and the first mechanical color reproduction at the end of the nineteenth century. Ten years ago, we then made the fundamental discovery of a new
print control domain, where instead of choices about colorant amounts that are
akin to the effect of color filters used since the beginning of color printing, print
can be specified by the probabilities of colorant combinations, the Neugebauer
Primaries. This has led to the ability to print patterns that were previously inac-
cessible and consequently, by using large-scale computational optimization, to
delivering more color gamut, greater ink use efficiency and greater sharpness and
detail in print, while using the same materials and printing system as before. This
keynote will present the basic principles of the HANS print control paradigm,
review the highlights of results obtained using it to date and indicate its potential
future developments.

Keywords: Printing · Imaging · Pipeline · Color · Optimization · HANS

1 Introduction

Printing is among the oldest imaging technologies used today. Its roots lie in the use of
stamps to transfer patterns onto clay, as used since 3000 BC, which then lead to the use
of woodblocks for printing images and text onto textiles as early as 200 AD and then
via Guttenberg's invention of moveable type in the 15th century to the digital printing
of the late 20th century, via the invention of photomechanical color reproduction in the
19th century. Until these last two developments, printing was wholly in the realm of the
crafts and relied on the individual craft person's skills and experience for success.

It was then the invention of automated color printing at the end of the 19th century
that enabled an engineering solution for printing and the advent of digital printing technologies like inkjet and laser printing that opened the doors to the introduction of
computation into the process. However, for decades, little has changed in terms of how
printing was performed, in spite of the new potential that digital processing enabled.
Even today, the printing systems used from the home, via the office and into commercial
and industrial production apply the same mindset as was first introduced in the late 19th
century. The key question that printing pipelines ask is: how much of each of the available colorants to use for matching each printable color. Once colorant quantities are
determined, whether they be inks, dyes, toners or waxes, a pattern-building process (i.e.,

© Springer International Publishing AG 2017
S. Bianco et al. (Eds.): CCIW 2017, LNCS 10213, pp. 13–25, 2017.
DOI: 10.1007/978-3-319-56010-6_2

halftoning, dithering) is performed largely on a per-colorant basis and the end result is sandwiched together. This, in principle, is a computational equivalent of the photomechanical process, where colorant amounts are determined by filters and pattern formation is the result of glass "screens" where dots are formed on a photosensitive material when light is reflected from an original image and passes through filters and then screens. Even though that process today is the result of computation performed by a digital image processing pipeline, it follows the photomechanical sequence and inherits many of its fundamental constraints.

Here, the foremost limitation is that for each combination of colorant amounts, there is precisely one printed pattern that the pipeline can generate. While this may seem like no constraint at all, in this paper it will be shown that it is, in fact, a dramatic limit on an otherwise much vaster control domain.

To arrive at that insight, it is worth considering a question that, at first sight, might appear unrelated and extraneous: "Is the set of all possible spectra convex?" In other words, if we were to carry a telespectroradiometer around, measuring spectra all around the world, what would their gamut look like. Would it have concavities or not? It might seem like this is an unanswerable question, until Maxwell's spinning top experiments are remembered [1]. There, Maxwell colored segments attached to a spinning top with different colors and found that the color that resulted from spinning it was a convex combination of the segments' colors, with their areas as convex weights. Going back to the question about the set of all possible spectra, it can be seen that, if the spectra that occur individually in nature can be applied to segments on a spinning top, then the resulting set can be made convex. Even if the spinning top mechanism has restrictions in terms of being most directly suited for surface colors, it turns out that there is another, more universal mechanism that has the same convex properties. When viewing a scene from a certain distance, variation below a certain angular subtense cannot be resolved by the human visual system, and its content is convexly combined by optical additive mixture. Also from the perspective of measurement, the variation within the angular subtense delimited by an instrument's aperture is equally optically added.

Positively answering the question about whether the gamut of all spectra is convex then leads to asking why the gamuts of all printing systems are not. A defining feature of print color gamuts are their concavities, typically as the darkest printable color is approached, resulting in a characteristic funnel shape. Why is it that prints, whose colors are the result of colorant combinations being printed in patterns and then viewed such that those patterns are combined optically, end up having gamut concavities? Looking at print color formation, as understood already in the 1930s by Hans Neugebauer [2], it can be seen that it too is fundamentally convex and that it depends on the color of colorant combinations – the Neugebauer Primaries – and on the relative, local areas that they each occupy in print, where these relative local area coverages add up to one (since they are relative) and therefore constitute convex weights (Fig. 1). From first principles, print gamuts ought to be convex, but today they aren't.

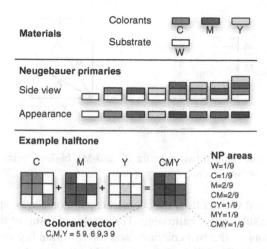

Fig. 1. Colorants and substrate (top), Neugebauer Primaries (center) and an example of how colorant amounts and Neugebauer Primary area coverages relate in a halftone (bottom).

This is the thought process that lead to the discovery of a new print control paradigm – HANS – in November 2007, whose details, properties, benefits and applications will be set out in the remainder of this paper and which has lead to a change in print control that also allows for taking full advantage of computational optimization.

2 HANS Basics

The discovery of missing convexity in print has led to a new print control paradigm, where it is no longer colorant amounts but the relative area coverages of Neugebauer Primaries that are an image processing pipeline's control domain. This new paradigm is called Halftone Area Neugebauer Separation – HANS [3] and its basic principles will be set out next.

2.1 Colorant Versus Neugebauer Primary Space

In a two–colorant printing system, e.g., using cyan (C) and magenta (M) colorants, a colorant-based approach results in some part of the two–dimensional CM colorant space being accessible. The constraints here are the maximum total colorant amount (mT) that avoids colorant–substrate interaction artifacts (e.g., bleeding, coalescence, etc. for ink; peeling, etc. for toner) and the maximum amounts (mC and mM) of the two colorants by themselves that result in a colorant amount – color relationship that is usable (e.g., monotonic) when forming colorant vectors (Fig. 2).

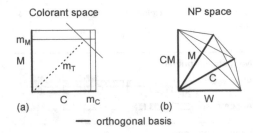

Fig. 2. Print control spaces for a two–colorant (C and M), bi–level printing system: (a) the colorant space and (b) the Neugebauer Primary space.

Each of the colorant vectors from the accessible polygon can be specified at a pixel that is an input to the subsequent halftoning. The combined result of the available colorant space, the halftoning, the two colorants and the substrate is a curved surface in a color space (e.g., CIE XYZ, CIE LAB, etc.), to which input colors need to be gamut mapped [4].

However, these two inks result in four NPs: W (the blank substrate), C, M and the CM overprint. If more than two levels of ink can be specified at each halftone pixel, then the space is of higher dimensionality still. Without constraints from colorant–media interactions, the accessible part of the NP space is a k^n–dimensional simplex – i.e., in the bi–level, CM case it has the 100% area coverages of the W, C, M and CM NPs as its vertices (Fig. 2b). The effect of colorant–substrate imposed constraints is the intersection of this simplex with half–spaces defined by mC, mM and mT. The use of the NP space gives access to any pattern made up of a system's NPs and printed output becomes analogous to mosaics assembled from individual NP tiles.

To illustrate the increased range of patterns accessible via HANS, a particular ink vector: [cC, cM] = [0.5, 0.5] can be considered. From the point of view of the NP space, each ink vector corresponds to a continuum of NP area coverage vectors, which satisfy the following constraints:

$$aC + aCM = cC \tag{1}$$

$$aM + aCM = cM \tag{2}$$

where aX represents the area coverage of NP X and cY represents the area coverage of ink Y.

Figure 3 shows halftone patterns that match the example ink vector but differ in their NPac vectors and colors when printed on a HP Designjet Z3100 printer on Hahnemühle Smooth Fine Art paper. The extremes of the NPac range differ by 26 ΔE2000 color difference units [5].

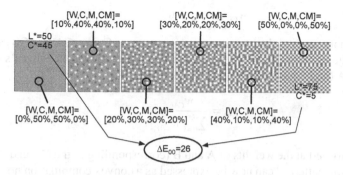

Fig. 3. Continuum of halftone patterns corresponding to a single ink vector: [cC,cM] = [0.5, 0.5]. (Color figure online)

For an ink space approach, halftoning results in one of the patterns shown in Fig. 3, while HANS can access the entire continuum. Since even a two colorant system already has 4 dimensions in the HANS domain, this direct NP control gives access to metamers (i.e., halftone patterns that differ from one another but result in the same color under given viewing conditions) because colorimetry is 3 dimensional (leaving one degree of freedom), while ink–based color separation only attains this possibility with four or more inks.

2.2 The Neugebauer Primary Area Coverage Vector

An NP is a discrete combination of colorant units (e.g., ink drops) and an NPac expresses a convex combination of multiple NPs, with weights having a [0,1] range and expressing relative area coverages. Such k^n-dimensional vector notation is convenient since multiple NPacs can be further convexly combined thanks to the domain's associativity [6].

In its most basic instantiation, halftone print color formation consists of the convex combination of the colors of the Neugebauer Primaries (NPs). E.g., a pattern C that is formed by combining some of a printing system's NPs, can be characterized by its NP area coverage (NPac) vector – $NPac_C$, which is of the following form:

$$T(NPac_C) = \sum_{i=1}^{k^n} \left(w_{Ci} * T(NP_i) \right) \tag{3}$$

where k is the number of colorant levels per colorant per pixel, n is the number of colorants, $\sum_{i=1}^{k^n} w_{Ci} = 1$ (i.e., the weights are convex), NP_i is the i-the NP, and T() is color (in this case its Yule-Nielsen corrected colorimetry).

The key insight here is that this convex combination of relative area coverage weighted NP colors can also be seen as the convex combination of constituent sub-patterns – for example CA and CB (e.g., a pair of patterns that were individually determined and that can give rise to a continuum of patterns between them in the way laid out below) – such that:

$$w_{Ci} = w_{CBi} + w_{CAi} \tag{4}$$

Furthermore, each of the constituent sub-patterns of C (i.e., CA and CB) also has an equivalent, full pattern (A and B), whose weights relate to the sub pattern's weights as follows for A (and equivalently for B):

$$w_{Ai} = \frac{w_{CAi}}{\sum_{j=1}^{k^n} w_{CAi}} \tag{5}$$

Having arrived at the weights of A and B (corresponding to the CA and CB constituents of C), the pattern C can now be expressed as a convex combination not of NPs but of the NPacs A and B:

$$T(NPac_C) = x * T(NPac_A) + y * T(NPac_B) \tag{6}$$

where

$$x = \sum_{j=1}^{k^n} w_{CAi}, x = \sum_{j=1}^{k^n} w_{CBi} \text{ and } x + y = 1 \tag{7}$$

As a consequence of associativity, it is possible to perform convex combinations not only of at-pixel states (i.e., the Neugebauer Primaries), but also of a pattern's subpatterns (Fig. 4), which is going to be important both for transitioning and optimization.

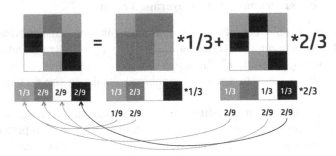

Fig. 4. Associativity of pattern convex combination.

2.3   NPac Metamer Sets

The concept of metamers – i.e., stimuli that under one set of circumstances result in the same visual response, but under another differ from each other – is key to HANS, since it allows for the grouping of NPacs that result in the same color into metamer sets [7] as follows (Fig. 5):

1. Given a set of p NPs and their colorimetries (measured or predicted), form all polyhedra with up to n vertices (n∈ [4, p]) in the colorimetric space.

2. For a given color S, whose metamer set is to be found, compute its barycentric coordinates with respect to each of the polyhedra from step 1. In the case of tetrahedra with V_i ($i \in [1, 4]$) vertices it is done as follows:

$$
\begin{pmatrix} b_1 \\ b_2 \\ b_3 \\ b_4 \end{pmatrix}^T = \begin{pmatrix} S_X \\ S_Y \\ S_Z \\ 1 \end{pmatrix}^T \times \left(\begin{pmatrix} V_{1X} & V_{2X} & V_{3X} & V_{4X} \\ V_{1Y} & V_{2Y} & V_{3Y} & V_{4Y} \\ V_{1Z} & V_{2Z} & V_{3Z} & V_{4Z} \\ 1 & 1 & 1 & 1 \end{pmatrix}^T \right)^{-1}
\tag{8}
$$

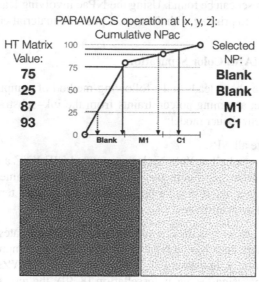

Fig. 5. (Top) PARAWACS halftoning by comparing selector matrix values with cumulative NPac intervals and (bottom) example of using a blue-noise matrix (left) with the same NPac to give a halftone (right) that honors NPac area coverages and has the spatial structure of the chosen matrix.

Equation 8 is the inverse of the system formed by three equations expressing how S is the convex combination of V_1 to V_4 and the equation of b_1 to b_4 summing to one. If all members of b are from [0,1], S is inside the tetrahedron. Furthermore, since b represents normalized volumes of sub-tetrahedra formed by sets of three original vertices and S (for the original vertex that S substitutes), they are also the relative area coverages with which tetrahedron vertex NPs need to be combined. For practical purposes, up to 16 vertex polyhedra are typically considered, but this number could be increased to form more complex patterns. The result of step 2 is the set of all metamers formed by different sets of four NPs.

3. The set of NPacs obtained from step 2 delimits the metamer set of color S in NPac space. Note that due to the convexity of the NPac space, the metamer set can be further sampled by generating convex combinations of NPacs obtained from step 2, thanks to the associativity of the NPac domain.

2.4 Optimization of Print Attributes

Given metamer sets for a set of colors sampling the available convex hull, color separation can be optimized by deciding which of the available metamers to choose for each color. Here any print attribute that can be determined or predicted from NPacs, can be explicitly taken into account and multiple attributes can be directly weighted depending on the needs of particular applications.

A simple attribute to consider is how much ink is used. Knowing the amount of ink involved in the NPs and by them using the metamer NPacs' area coverages, the minimum within each metamer set can be found. Using the NPac involving least ink for all available colors then leads to printing with the lowest possible material costs.

2.5 Summary of HANS Color Separation

Bringing together the above leads to the following method of computing a color separation to NPac space, assuming no constraints from the ink–substrate interaction and using the original Neugebauer model:

1. Print and measure all NPs.
2. Compute NP convex hull in Yule-Nielsen corrected CIE XYZ and sample it.
3. For each sample from step 2 compute the corresponding metamer set.
4. From each metamer set select the NPac that is optimal in terms of the chosen (combination of) print attributes.

The result of the above process is a set of CIE XYZ coordinates that span the full color gamut and where each has an NPac assigned to it. To compute the NPac color separation for an arbitrary, in–gamut CIE XYZ input, the CIE XYZs from step 2 need to be tessellated (e.g., using Delaunay tessellation [8, 9]), the tessellating tetrahedron enclosing the input color needs to be found and barycentric coordinates for the vertex NPacs can be computed. These barycentric coordinates then form an NPac with the vertex NPacs as its members, which can finally be re-expressed as an NPac with NP members, thanks to associativity. Applying this algorithm to an entire, in-gamut CIE XYZ image will result in a corresponding NPac image, which is then the input to the next, halftoning stage. Note also that this transformation can be performed by first computing a look-up table indexed in XYZ, which for each node contains NPacs.

2.6 From NPac to Halftone

The HANS halftoning maps NPacs to at-halftone-pixel NPs (e.g., drops per ink) and two categories of halftoning approaches apply: device-state error diffusion [3] or PARA-WACS matrix-based halftoning [10]. In both cases, the role of halftoning is that for a sufficiently large area of a constant NPac, it needs to result in a placement of individual NPs such that when counting their frequency over the area, the original area coverage is obtained and that the resulting pattern meets expectations in terms of pleasingness, robustness, detail preservation, etc. At halftone-pixel level, halftoning becomes the selection of a single NP from the NPac specified for that pixel.

To simplify this selection in the matrix halftoning case, called PARAWACS (Parallel Random Weighted Area Coverage Selection), an NPac can be expressed cumulatively. I.e., the NPac: [Blank (white) 80%, 1 drop M 10%, 1 drop C 10%] becomes [W = 80%, M = 90%, C = 100%] in cumulative terms, which in turn defines intervals for each of the NPs such that [0 to 80] corresponds to the Blank state, [80 to 90] to one drop of M and [90 to 100] to one drop of C. Using this representation, what is needed next is a uniform distribution of values between 0% and 100%, for example in the form of a pre-computed matrix of a desired pattern, where the matrix values then act as NP selectors. Here, matrix values are categorized according to cumulative intervals so that if the value at [x, y] is in the range [0 to 80] the halftone pixel is left blank, if it is in the range [80 to 90] a drop of the M NP is placed and if the random number is in the interval [90 to 100], a C NP is used. The diagram in Fig. 5 shows this process for four random values (corresponding to four [x, y] locations) and using a blue-noise matrix [11].

3 Applications and Results

While the above has focused on setting out the basic principles and mechanisms of the HANS computational print control paradigm, this section will provide an overview of some of the key applications and results obtained to date.

3.1 CMY Metamers

Since the HANS domain is of significantly higher dimension than the colorant domain, it changes even the basic constraints of print color reproduction. A significant result here is the ability to form metamers even in three-colorant systems, which previously were considered to lack the ability of forming metamers. When controlling such printing systems in colorant terms, it is the case that for each within-gamut color there is precisely one colorant combination that results in it.

Instead, with HANS, even in a binary, three-colorant printing system there are $2^3 = 8$ NPs, which in turn can be combined in multiple ways to match in-gamut colors. As a result, even with three colorants there is redundancy and it is possible to choose from a variety of alternatives [12]. Applying HANS to a printer with only CMY inks still resulted in 115 distinct metamers for a mid-gray color (Fig. 6) and gave access to a range of ink use where the maximum was 13% greater than the minimum for a system where colorant domain control yields no metamers. The optimization that resulted in metamers for a sampling of the CMY system's color gamut used 244 "base" NPacs with known colorimetry that involved the system's NPs and a sampling of the gamut surface. Over this set, a search was performed, resulting in the evaluation of 14,4 million tetrahedra.

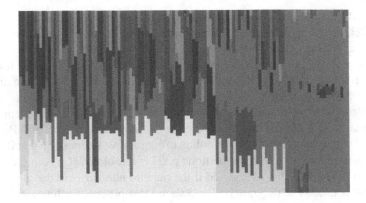

Fig. 6. A visualization of 115 metamers: each column represents an NP area coverage vector where constituent color block lengths heights are proportional to the corresponding base NPac color's relative area coverage.

3.2 Gamut and Ink Use Optimization

Among the first results of using a HANS printing pipeline was its application to a *HP Designjet L65500* printer using CMYKcm latex inks on a self–adhesive vinyl substrate [3]. Computing a mapping to NPacs, following the process outlined in Sect. 2 of this paper, resulted in 20% less ink use than the minimum achievable in a colorant domain pipeline (where that was the result of using maximum gray component replacement) with less grain than previous minimum. At the same time as delivering a reduction in ink use, the HANS pipeline also gave access to 10% more color gamut (Fig. 7).

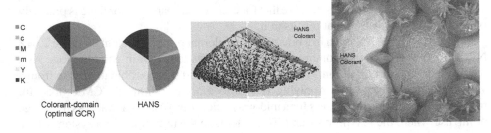

Fig. 7. (Left) Ink use of colorant-domain and HANS pipelines, (center) corresponding color gamuts and (right) scanned prints.

3.3 Hand-Building of Color Separations

Instead of being confined only to complex, computational solutions, the HANS NPac domain also lends itself to dramatic simplification and the hand-building of printing system resources. An extreme example here is the possibility of defining a color separation by hand-selecting only eight NPacs – one for each vertex of a device RGB cube and then having NPacs computed for the entire color space by interpolation in an analytical tessellation of the eight vertices, using tetrahedra that all share the black to white long diagonal of the RGB cube. The result is a printing pipeline that, for each printed color combines up to four of a set of eight NPacs [6]. This results both in a high degree of simplicity when generating printing resources and in a system that can be characterized and calibrated on the basis of a very small number of measurements (Fig. 8).

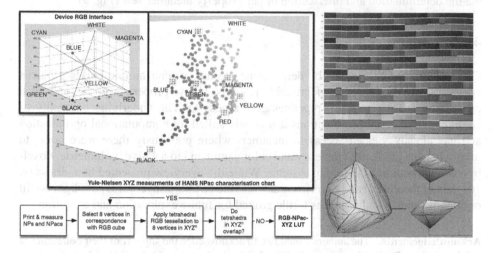

Fig. 8. Hand-building node selection putting RGB vertices and NPacs in direct correspondence. (Color figure online)

Fig. 9. 3D object printed using HANS3D pipeline to control voxel-by-voxel volumetric material composition (Model: Klein Bottle by krasul, published on July 22, 2013, www.thingiverse.com/ thing:121871 under Creative Commons – Attribution license).

3.4 HANS3D

Finally, the HANS paradigm of controlling the use of at-pixel states by assigning relative area coverages to them can also be extended to the control of 3D printing systems. There, it is the set of all possible voxel contents that are the atomic building blocks of a print control pipeline and their use is governed by assigning relative volumetric coverages to them. Since in 3D printing, color is only one of many properties that can be controlled, the equivalent there of NPs are material vectors (Mvecs) and instead of NPacs, it is material vector volume coverages (Mvocs) that determine local printed object composition. The resulting HANS3D pipeline [13] can take advantage of the breadth of HANS benefits and can further deliver control over volumetric material use (e.g., tuning layer-to-layer complementarity) and allow for a co-optimization of multiple object properties via the determination and intersection of per-property metamer sets (Fig. 9).

4   Summary

Controlling printing systems by determining the use of their atomic building blocks opens up a vast new space of printable patterns, whose properties go beyond what conventional, colorant-space pipelines give access to. The underlying convexity of colorant and material combinations is uniquely suited for computational optimization and has already yielded access to metamers where previously there were none, to improvements in ink use efficiency and color gamut and to a native, volumetric, voxel-by-voxel control of 3D printing systems. While the overview presented here draws on 10 years of theoretical and experimental work, the HANS print control paradigm is still only in its infancy and promises fertile ground for future exploration and evolution.

Acknowledgements.   The authors would like to acknowledge the support of their colleagues at HP Inc.: Africa Real, Albert Serra, Andrew Fitzhugh, Annarosa Multari, David Gaston, Gary Dispoto, Jay Gondek, Juan Manuel Garcia Reyero, Lihua Zhao, Rafa Gimenez, Ramon Pastor, Sascha de Peña, Tsuyoshi Yamashita, Virginia Palacios and Yan Zhao.

References

1. Maxwell, J.C.: Experiments on colour, as perceived by the eye, with remarks on colour blindness. Trans. Roy. Soc. Edinb. **21**(2), 275–298 (1855)
2. Neugebauer, H.E.J.: Die theoretischen Grundlagen des Mehrfarbenbuchdrucks. Zeitschrift für wissenschaftliche Photographie, Germany **36**(4), 73–89 (1937)
3. Morovič, J., Morovič, P., Arnabat, J.: HANS – controlling inkjet print attributes via neugebauer primary area coverages. IEEE Trans. Image Process. **21**(2), 688–696 (2011)
4. Stollnitz E.J.: Reproducing Color Images with Custom Inks, Ph.D. thesis, University of Washington (1998)
5. CIE: CIE 142:2001: Improvement to industrial colour difference evaluation, CIE Central Bureau, Vienna (2001)
6. Morovič, J., Morovič, P., Rius, M., García–Reyero, J.M.: 8 vertex HANS: An ultra-simple printer color architecture, In: IS&T/SID 21st Color and Imaging Conference, Albuquerque, NM, pp. 210–214 (2013)
7. Finlayson, G.D., Morovic, P.: Metamer sets. J. Opt. Soc. Am. A: **22**(5), 810–819 (2005)
8. Delaunay, B.: Sur la sphère vide. Izvestia Akademii Nauk SSSR, Otdelenie Matematicheskikh i Estestvennykh Nauk **7**, 793–800 (1934)
9. Preparata, F.P., Shamos, M.I.: Computational Geometry: An Introduction. Springer, New York (1985)

10. Morovič, P., Morovič, J., Gondek, J., Ulichney, R.: Direct pattern control halftoning of neugebauer primaries. IEEE Trans. Image Process. (2017) (submitted for publication)
11. Ulichney, R.: Dithering with Blue Noise. Proc. IEEE **76**(1), 56–79 (1988)
12. Morovič, P., Morovič, J., García–Reyero, J.M.: HANS: Meet The CMY Metamers, In: IS&T/SID Color and Imaging Conference 2011, San Jose, CA, 7–11 November 2011, pp. 229–233 (2011)
13. Morovič, P., Morovič, J., Tastl, I., Gottwals, M.: HANS3D: a volumetric voxel-control print content processing pipeline, In: ACM SIGGRAPH 2017, July 2017, Anaheim, CA (2017) (submitted for publication)

Color Vision Is a Spatial Process:
The Retinex Theory

Michela Lecca[✉]

Center for Information and Communication Technology, Technologies of Vision,
Fondazione Bruno Kessler, 38123 Trento, Italy
lecca@fbk.eu

Abstract. Born through the work of Edwin H. Land and John J.
McCann more than 40 years ago, Retinex theory proposes a computational model to explain and estimate the human color sensation, i.e.
the color perception that human vision system produces when oberving
a scene. Retinex is founded on a series of experiments, evidencing that
the human color sensation at any observed point does not depend merely
on the photometric cues of that point, but also on those of the surrounding regions and on their spatial arrangement. Indeed, human color vision
is a spatial process. This paper presents the conceptual framework of
Retinex, the main challenges it faced and solved, and some algorithmic
procedures implementing it.

1 Introduction

Developed by Edwin H. Land and John J. McCann, Retinex [22,23] is an interesting theory proposing a computational model to estimate the human *color
sensation*, i.e. the color perception produced by the human vision system when
observing a scene. More precisely, in "The Science of Color" [32], the Committee on Colorimetry of the Optical Society of America defines the human color
sensation as a "mode of mental functioning that is directly associated with the
stimulation of the organism".

Retinex originated in the late 1950 s from a series of experiments, evidencing
that the process of the color formation performed by the human vision system
strongly differs from that performed by a camera. In particular, experiments
carried out on sets of colored patches, called Mondrians, showed that the color
appearance as reported by humans looking a scene does not correlate with the
radiances of the observed scene. This means that the human color sensation
may differ from the color computed from the quanta catches coming from the
observed scene and acquired by the eye photo-receptors. Therefore, the color of
an object under a given light as reported by a human may differ from the color
of the same object under the same conditions as detected by a camera. This
phenomenon is at the basis of the human *color constancy*, that is the human
capability to discount a color cast due to the light illuminating the scene, so
that a same object viewed under different light conditions is perceived as the
same entity [11].

© Springer International Publishing AG 2017
S. Bianco et al. (Eds.): CCIW 2017, LNCS 10213, pp. 26–39, 2017.
DOI: 10.1007/978-3-319-56010-6_3

Land and McCann hypothesized that when looking a scene, the human vision system processes independently the long, medium and short wavelengths coming from the scene and acquired by the retina photo-receptors, and produces a novel scene, whose wavebands, termed the *lightnesses*, have color constancy [22,23].

To understand the mechanism of the lightness formation, Land and McCann developed new experiments, that showed the importance, in the color formation, of the edges and of the relative spatial relationships among the reflectances of the observed regions. They definitely proved that color sensation and thus color vision are *spatial processes*, related to the *local* color distribution of the image. The empirical evidences they collected lead to a computational model able to estimate the color sensation from a RGB stimulus, i.e. the *Retinex algorithm*.

The outcomes of their research were also supported by biological studies on human vision, e.g. [3,6–9,19], that revealed the existence of a mechanism of spatial interaction among the responses of the eye photoreceptors, taking place both in the retina and in the primary visual cortex of the brain. Inspired by some of these works, in 1963, Land named its theory Retinex, from the contraction of the words RETina and cortEX.

From its first announcement, the Retinex theory continuously attracts the attention of the research world. A complete understanding of how humans see colors is still an open problem. The human vision system is a complex machine, much efforts are necessary to have a complete knowledge about it. Retinex represents a significant step in this direction, and it still attracts the interest of researches from different areas, such as computer scientists, biologists, psychologists. Many variants of the original Retinex algorithm of Land and McCann and of its spatial color sampling have been proposed, with the main aims of further investigating the mechanism of spatial color interaction, proposing more efficient computational algorithmic solutions, and/or solving practical problems of machine vision, such as color image enhancement, color rendition, dynamic range compression, image retrieval based on human color constancy. e.g. [4,14,16,18,25,34–36,38–40].

This works introduces in Sect. 2 the conceptual framework of Retinex the main challenges it faced and solved, and the original algorithm. In addition, this paper presents some algorithms of the Milano Retinex family, a special class of Retinex inspired implementations, mainly employed for image color enhancement (Sect. 3). Final conclusions are drawn in Sect. 4.

2   The Original Retinex Algorithm

This Section describes the experiments at the basis of the Retinex theory and the algorithm proposed by Land and McCann and its algorithmic implementation. More details are available in [22,23,27,28].

2.1   The Experiments

The evidences at the basis of the Retinex theory have been collected by a series of experiments, that can be classified in two groups: experiments on color patches (color Mondrians) and experiments on gray level patches (gray Mondrians).

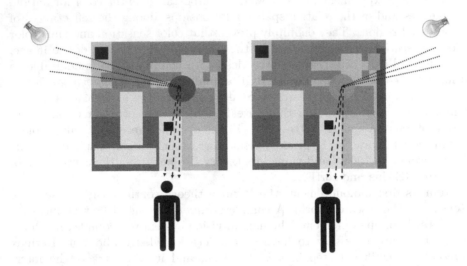

Fig. 1. Two Mondrians are illuminated by two lights (on top), tuned so that the green circle on left and the red circle on right have the same radiance. An observer looks at them. Despite the identical quanta catches, the observer reports green color on left and red color on right. The experiment shows that color sensation does not correlate with radiance. (Color figure online)

Experiments on Color Mondrians: the color constancy - Retinex theory was born from some experiments Land was carried on at the late of 1950 s at the Polaroid Corporation, of which he was a con-founder. A colleague projected on a screen a mixture of two monochromatic pictures, one through a red filter and the other one through a simple white light: in the final picture, he observed more than the white, black and reddish colors that were expected. Land explained this phenomenon by supposing the existence of a sort of color *adaptation* performed by the human vision system.

To better understand this phenomenon, Land prepared other tests by using panels of colored patterns, that he named a *Mondrian*, because of its similarity with the artworks of the Dutch painter Pieter Cornelis Mondriaan (1872–1944), known as Mondrian. The Mondrians were built up and used under controlled conditions, e.g. specularities of highlights were avoided.

In an experiment, he considered two identical Mondrians, positioned side/by-side. He attached respectively on the left Mondrian a circular green paper, and on the right Mondrian a circular red paper. Then he illuminated each Mondrian uniformly with a light source, tuned so that the radiance from the green and red circles was the same (see Fig. 1). If the human vision system works as a standard photo-camera, then an observer should say that the green and the red circles have the same color: on the contrary, the green and the red circles appeared to the observers still green and red. Land repeated the experiments by changing the time of fixation and the color of the patches, but again, the result was the same: the observers were able to detect the actual color of the patches. The color as reported by the humans did not correlate with the physical radiances.

This experiments suggested that the human vision system performs a sort of color adaptation, that discount color casts due to the illumination. This mechanism is at the basis of the color constancy, that is the human capability to recover the reflectance of an observed object inspite the color of the light.

Land arrived to the following, first, important conclusion: when the human vision system observes a scene, the long, medium and short wavebands are processed by the human vision system in order to be color constant. Land hypothized that, for any observed scene, the human vision system produces a new image, whose long, medium and short wavebands, named *lightnesses*, are computed independently from the long, medium and short wavebands of the observed scene, acquired by the retina photo-receptors, i.e. by cones and rods.

According to biological studies, that revealed that the human vision takes place in the retina and in the visual primary cortex of the brain [3,6–9,19], Land named its theory Retinex from the words RETina and cortEX.

Experiments on Gray-Level Mondrians: edge importance and spatial issues - The experiments of Land proceeded with the help of other colleagues of the Polaroid Corporation and in particular of John J. McCann, which joint the Vision Research Laboratory of the company in 1961.

To understand the mechanism of the lightness computation, Land and McCann took into account some visual phenomena suggesting a spatial character of the vision, i.e. simultaneous contrast and edge importance in color vision.

The simultaneous contrast is a phenomenon studied by the French chemist Michel Eugène Chevreul in the 19th century and illustrated in Fig. 2: the same gray square is positioned at the center of two squares with different colors. The square appears darker when it is shown on the left background.

This observation leads to the following, second result: the color sensation at a point depends on the surrounding colors, thus in the lightness, the color at a point is modified *relatively* to the colors in its surround.

Expressing a quantity relatively to an other quantity implies a comparison process, that can be accomplished through the computation of the ratio between these quantities. Therefore, Land and McCann arrived to the conclusion that the lightness depends on ratios between the reflectances of near-by areas, as suggested by the phenomenon illustrated in Fig. 3: the adjacent squares on left appear differently colored, but this does not happen when the central edge is occluded (right). The importance of the edges in color sensation was deeply investigated by a series of experiments on a gray level Mondrian illuminated by a smooth gradient. Again, observers were asked to report their sensation on the different Mondrian patches, leading to the following outcomes: (1) the ratio

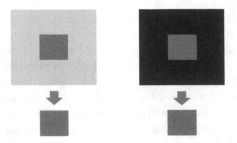

Fig. 2. Simultaneous Contrast: the gray square shown on different background appears differently colored. This phenomenon suggests the existence of a spatial interaction among the colors.

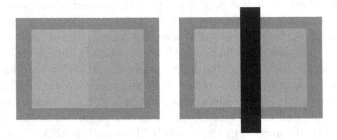

Fig. 3. The picture on left appears composed by two rectangles with two slightly different gray intensities, displayed on a dark background. When the central edge is occluded by a black rectangle, the gray levels of the two rectangles appears equal to each other.

between points located across an edge correlates with the appearance; (2) slight edges are irrelevant to color sensation. Finally, the analysis of edges implies a *local* image processing: the color sensation does not depend on global properties, like for instance the color distribution over the whole image represented by histograms [29].

Finally, another spatial issue had to be considered in color sensation: according to the study in [5], the color sensation at a point is influenced more by the colors of the regions closer to that point that by those of regions located far way.

To sum up, the Retinex theory states that the human color sensation is a complex process, that involves a *local, spatial* comparison among different areas of any observed scene.

2.2 The Algorithm

The different outcomes of the experiments lead to an algorithm for the prediction of the color sensation. The general workflow of this algorithm applied to a RGB image consists of three main steps: (1) pre-calibration; (2) color filtering; (3) post-calibration.

The pre-calibration step matches the digital values of the device used for image acquisition with the actual luminance of the observed scene. The pre-calibrated image undergoes to the spatial comparison which at the basis of the lightness computation: this phase, that we call color filtering, is the main core of the Retinex algorithm. The output image is the input of the post-calibration step, which remaps the digits into a scale of appearance. Pre- and post-calibrations are fundamental steps for modeling the human color vision [27, 30].

According to the experiments carried out on color and grey Mondrians, the Retinex algorithm proposed by Land and McCann processes any input image channel by channel as follows. For each channel, a set of paths randomly chosen over the image is used to explore and compare the image intensities of different regions. Given a path connecting two image regions, the algorithm computes the lightness by the so-called *chain ratio*, i.e. the product of the ratios between the intensity values of adjacent pixels. Ratios are a way to measure the image gradient, thus to detect the edges, that, according to the experiments described before, play an important role in color sensation. The multiplication of the ratios allows to spatially relate the color information among distant regions without loosing the information along the bridges system [27]. When the ratio product along a path exceeds the value 1.0, a *reset mechanism* is implemented: the cumulative product is set to 1.0 and the ratio chain restarts from this value. Reset is a fundamental operation: it implements a normalization process that is performed by our vision system and that allows to express the color we perceive at a point relatively to the other, i.e. as a percentage of a *local white* detected in its surround (see Chaps. 21 and 33 in [27]). When a ratio is close to one, its contribution is cast to 1.0: this operation reproduces the experimental evidence that slight edges do not contribute to the color sensation. An example of the ratio-product-reset procedure is given in Fig. 4.

The original Retinex algorithm is iterative, i.e. the paths are computed each after the other, and it is *destructive*, i.e. the digital values of the input image are overwritten with the values output by the ratio-reset procedure computed along the path. Many paths are computed over the image to guarantee an accurate exploration of the color distribution around each region and to reduce the chromatic noise due to the random path sampling. Finally, the lightness at a point is computed by averaging the partial results over the total number of paths.

The whole mechanism implemented by Retinex is called *ratio-product-reset-average* from its main steps.

The work in [33] provides the equation of the ratio-product-reset-average mechanism for the computation of the color filtering. Let I be a color channel of a pre-calibrated RGB image and let x be an image pixel. Hereafter, the intensity levels of I are supposed to be normalized in order to range over $(0, 1]$. The neighborhood of x is explored by a set of n paths $\gamma_1, \ldots, \gamma_n$, each of them ending at x and starting from a pixel y_k ($k = 1, \ldots, n$) randomly selected over the image. Each path $\gamma \in \{\gamma_1, \ldots, \gamma_n\}$ is modeled as a function defined on a set of natural numbers $\{1, \ldots, l_k\}$ such that $\gamma(1) := x$, $\gamma(l_k) = x_{l_k} := y_k$, while

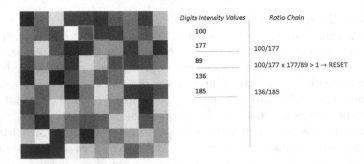

Digits Intensity Values	Ratio Chain
100	
177	100/177
89	100/177 x 177/89 > 1 → RESET
136	
185	136/185

Fig. 4. Example of the ratio-reset mechanism of the Retinex algorithm. See text for more explanation.

$\gamma(t_{k-1}) = x_{k-1}$ and $\gamma(t_k) = x_k$ are subsequent pixels over γ ($k = 2, \ldots, l_k$). The parameter l_k denotes the length of the path γ_k.

The lightness at x (before post-calibration) is given by

$$L(x) = \frac{1}{n} \sum_{k=1}^{n} \prod_{t_k=1}^{l_k} \delta_k(R_{t_k}) := \frac{1}{n} \sum_{k=1}^{n} \prod_{t_k=1}^{l_k} \delta_k\left(\frac{I(x_{k+1})}{I(x_k)}\right) \qquad (1)$$

Here R_{t_k} is the ratio of the intensities of two adjacent pixels on γ i.e. $R_{t_k} = \frac{I(\gamma(t_{k+1}))}{I(\gamma(t_k))}$, and $\delta_k : \mathbf{R}^+ \to \mathbf{R}^+$ is the function such that

$$\delta_k(R_{t_k}) = \begin{cases} R_{t_k} & \text{if } 0 < R_{t_k} \leq 1 - \varepsilon \\ 1 & \text{if } 1 - \varepsilon < R_{t_k} \leq 1 + \varepsilon \\ R_{t_k} & \text{if } 1 + \varepsilon \leq R_{t_k} \leq \frac{1+\varepsilon}{\prod_{m_k}^{t_k-1} \delta_k(R_{m_k})} \\ \frac{1}{\prod_{m_k}^{t_k-1} \delta_k(R_{m_k})} & \text{if } R_{t_k} > \frac{1+\varepsilon}{\prod_{m_k}^{t_k-1} \delta_k(R_{m_k})} \end{cases} \qquad (2)$$

The threshold ε is a positive parameter ranging over $[0, 1]$ and introduced to model the insensitivity of the color sensation to slight gradients.

The path-based approach proposed in the pioneer works [22,23] is not the unique possible spatial color sampling for estimating color sensation. In 1986, Land presented an alternative version of the Retinex algorithm, where the path based color sampling is replaced by a sort of high-pass filter [20,21]. Precisely, in this work, Land computed the value $L(x)$ as the ratio between the intensity value at x and the average value of a set of pixels located in a surround of x, having density proportional to the Euclidean distance from x, i.e.

$$L(x) = \frac{I(x)}{(I * G_\sigma)(x)} \qquad (3)$$

where G_σ is a convolution kernel, usually a Gaussian one, e.g. $G_\sigma(x) = \frac{1}{\sqrt{2\pi}\sigma} e^{-\frac{\|x\|}{\sigma^2}}$, $\forall x \in \mathbf{R}^2$, and σ is a real, strictly positive number. This Retinex version attracted the interest of many researchers, that investigate the properties and the mathematical form of this implementation [17]. This algorithm, also called *Single-Scale Retinex*, has been then extended to a multi-scale version, termed *Multi-Scale Retinex*. This latter has been proved to perform better that the Single-Scale version in many applications, such as dynamic range compression, color rendition, contrast enhancement in medical imaging, e.g. [13,15,16,35,37,41]. The Multi-Scale Retinex modifies the Eq. (3) by computing a weighted average of many Single-Scale Retinex outputs, generally in a logarithmic space:

$$\log L(x) = \frac{1}{n} \sum_{i=1}^{n} w_i (\log I(x) - \log((I * G_{\sigma_n})(x))) \qquad (4)$$

where the w_is are parameters weighting the different single-scale Retinex outputs, and $n > 1$.

Many different spatial color sampling inspired by the Retinex principles have been (and still are) proposed in the literature to solve many different computer vision problems, as those listed above. The next Section presents some algorithms of the so-called Milano Retinex family [33], a special class of Retinex-inspired color filtering implementions mainly used for color enhancement. This family is of interest because its members perform a color filtering based on an approximated version of Eq. (2) and exploit different spatial exploration schemes, including path-based, 2D, and probabilistic spatial color sampling.

3   Alternative Spatial Color Sampling: Examples from Milano Retinex Family

The Milano Retinex algorithms differ from the original Retinex in three main points. First, they propose alternative ways for the spatial exploration of the image. Second, the computational color filtering procedure is not destructive. Third, they compute the lightness L by an approximation of Eq. (2), obtained by setting $\varepsilon = 0$. This choice is justified both by mathematical and empirical issues, showing that the threshold mechanism is in general unessential [33]. When $\varepsilon = 0$, Eq. (2) becomes simpler, precisely, for any color channel I, the lightness at a pixel x (named *target*) is given by:

$$L(x) = \frac{1}{n} \sum_{i=1}^{n} \frac{I(x)}{I(m_i)} \qquad (5)$$

where m_i is a pixel with maximum intensity over the path γ_i, i.e.

$$I(m_i) = \max\{I(y) : y \in \gamma_i(\{1, \ldots, l_i\})\}. \qquad (6)$$

Equation (5) expresses the lightness at each point as the average of the ratios between the intensity at x and a local maximum, that becomes the local white reference (see Chap. 33 in [27]).

The color filtering algorithms of the Milano Retinex class differ to each other in the way the spatial analysis is performed. The different spatial color sampling

Fig. 5. Examples of spatial color sampling of an input image (left) performed by the Milano Retinex approaches ETR (middle) and RSR (right) on the red channel of the input. This samples are around the barycenter of the image support (indicated respectively by a red, filled circle in the middle picture, and by a blue, empty circle in the right picture. (Color figure online)

procedures of this family can be categorized in path-based, 2D, and probabilistic approaches.

Examples of Path-Based Milano Retinex Spatial Color Sampling. The works in [26,31] are the pioneer Milano Retinex approaches. The spatial sampling is performed in the first one by lines, and in the second one by Brownian paths.

Image aware paths have been recently introduced by the methods Termite Retinex (TR) [39], Energy-driven Termite Retinex (ETR) [24] and its light version Light-ETR [40]. The approaches are of interest because they explicitly model the importance of the edges in color sensation. In fact, in these methods, the paths are not randomly selected over the image nor constrained a priori by geometric features (e.g. for instance, they are not lines), but they are built up so

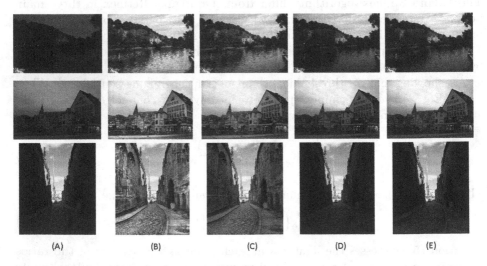

(A)   (B)   (C)   (D)   (E)

Fig. 6. Examples of color enhancement performed by some algorithms of the Milano Retinex family. (A) Input image and outputs of (B) TR, (C) ETR, (D) RSR, (E) QBRIX (distance-weighted version).

that to adhere as much as possible to the edges of each image color channel. Specifically, the paths are thought as the traces of termites (i.e. white ants), each of them exiting one after the other from the nest (i.e. the target) in search for a local white reference (i.e. a pixel with the maximum intensity over the path).

In TR, each path is determined by a sort of contrast follower, that starts from the target and proceeds pixel by pixel by maximizing a function f proportionally to the contrast value and to the squared Euclidean distance between adjacent pixels. The distance term was introduced to spread the termite swarm across the image in order to take into account the color spatial distribution accurately. A penalty term is introduced to avoid the over-exploration of the image, so that f decreases over pixels already traveled by a termite.

ETR inherits from TR the general, swarm-inspired exploration scheme, but it computes each termite route as the local minimum of an energy functional, designed to favor the visit of pixels having high gradient magnitude, with the preference for pixels close to the target and never traveled before. Differently from the Brownian path scanning and from TR, ETR provides a global mathematical condition for describing the paths. The computational issues of ETR have been analyzed in [40], which presents an approximated, computationally more efficient version of ETR. Figure 5 (middle) shows an example of ETR spatial exploration: flat regions are explored less than the others. TR exhibits a similar behaviour, but its paths become random over image areas with null values of f. In this respect, ETR provides a more deterministic procedure to compute a path connecting two pixels.

The number of the paths and the penalty value are user inputs. TR also requires a value for the maximum length of the path.

Examples of 2D Milano Retinex Spatial Color Sampling. Random Spray Retinex (RSR) [?] replaces the path based exploration scheme with a 2D sampling, leading to a faster computation of the lightness. This new scheme has been introduced mainly to solve some problems of the path-based sampling, mainly related to the redundancy of the information collected by random paths and to the chromatic noise due to their randomness. For each chromatic channel, RRS scans the neighborhood of each target x by a 2D set of random pixels randomly selected around x from a radial distribution, according to the fact that the colors of the pixels closest to x influence more its color sensation than those of the pixels located far away. The lightness at x is computed as the ratio between the intensity $I(x)$ and the maximum intensity over the spray. The chromatic noise due to the random samples is reduced by generating many sprays. The final lightness is obtained as the average value of the lightnesses computed over each spray. The numbers of sprays and the number of samples per sprays are input user.

Many different versions of RSR have been published. In particular the works in [1,2] propose computationally more efficient implementations of RSR. An example of RSR sampling is reported in Fig. 5 (right).

Examples of Probabilistic Milano Retinex Spatial Color Sampling. The works QBRIX [12] and RSR-P [10] present respectively a probabilistic approximation and an exact formulation of RSR. These last two methods avoid the random sampling and thus output an image free of chromatic noise.

QBRIX (from Quantile-Based approach to RetIneX) relies on the fact that the color sensation at any image pixel is poorly influenced by (1) colors rarely occurring in the image and (2) colors of pixel located far from. Issues (1) and (2) lead to two different implementations of QBRIX. Both of them computes the lightness at any pixel of any color channel as the intensity level of a quantile, that the user selects on the probability density fucntion (pdf) of the channel intensities. The first implementation does not use any information about the spatial arrangement of the color, while the second one accounts for this information by weighting the contributions of the channel intensities to the pdf through a function of the distance of the pixels from the target. Thus, this "spatially weighted intensity pdf" must be re-computed for any pixel.

RSR-P (where P stands for Population) is an exact mapping of RSR in to a population based approach, that completely avoids the random sampling and the related chromatic noise. It bases on the estimation of the probability to sample, around each target, n pixels with intensity higher than that of the target and radially distributed around the target. In this framework, RSR results to be an approximated version of RSR-P.

Figure 6 shows some examples of color enhancement provided by some algorithms of this family. In particular, the results obtained by RSR-P and by the first implementation of QBRIX are omitted respectively for the high similarity with RSR and for the distance-free color processing that is not in line with the spatial principles of Retinex.

As visible from this figure, all these algorithms produce a new, enhanced image, where the details are more visible and the mean image brightness is higher. The path-based approaches perform similarly, and provide a better contrast enhancement in the dark areas with respect to the 2D and probabilistic methods.

The difference between the path-based methods and the others are mainly due to the different ways to spatially explore each target neighborhood. These examples point out the importance of the spatial exploration scheme. The use of this or that method depends on the applications, that can be to improve the global or local image visibility, to remove a color cast due to the illuminant or simply making a picture more pleasant.

4   Conclusions

Despite developed many years ago, Retinex is still an attractive research field, as proved by the wide range of recent conferences and publications on it. The Retinex theory nurtured the first mathematical model of the human color sensation and is nowaday inspiring new advanced efforts both in biology and computer vision.

References

1. Banic, N., Loncaric, S.: Light random sprays retinex: exploiting the noisy illumination estimation. IEEE Signal Process. Lett. **20**(12), 1240–1243 (2013)
2. Banić, N., Lončarić, S.: Smart light random memory sprays retinex: a fast retinex implementation for high-quality brightness adjustment and color correction. JOSA A **32**(11), 2136–2147 (2015)
3. Barlow, H.B.: Summation and inhibition in the frog's retina. J. Physiol. **119**(1), 69 (1953)
4. Ciocca, G., Marini, D., Rizzi, A., Schettini, R., Zuffi, S.: Retinex preprocessing of uncalibrated images for color-based image retrieval. J. Electron. Imaging **12**(1), 161–172 (2003)
5. Creutzfeldt, O., Lange-Malecki, B., Wortmann, K.: Darkness induction, retinex and cooperative mechanisms in vision. Exp. Brain Res. **67**(2), 270–283 (1987)
6. Daw, N.W.: Goldfish retina: organization for simultaneous color contrast. Science **158**(3803), 942–944 (1967)
7. De Valois, R.L., De Valois, K.K.: Spatial vision. Ann. Rev. Psychol. **31**(1), 309–341 (1980)
8. De Valois, R.L., Morgan, H., Snodderly, D.M.: Psychophysical studies of monkey vision-iii. spatial luminance contrast sensitivity tests of macaque and human observers. Vision Res. **14**(1), 75–81 (1974)
9. Dowling, J.E.: The Retina: An Approachable Part of the Brain. Harvard University Press (1987)
10. Gabriele, G., Lecca, M., Rizzi, A.: A population-based approach to point-sampling spatial color algorithms. J. Opt. Soc. Am. A **33**(12), 2396–2413 (2016)
11. Geusebroek, J.-M., van den Boomgaard, R., Smeulders, A.W.M., Gevers, T.: Color constancy from physical principles. Pattern Recogn. Lett. **24**(11), 1653–1662 (2003)
12. Gianini, G., Manenti, A., Rizzi, A.: Qbrix: a quantile-based approach to retinex. JOSA A **31**(12), 2663–2673 (2014)
13. Hanumantharaju, M.C., Ravishankar, M., Rameshbabu, D.R., Ramachandran, S.: Color image enhancement using multiscale retinex with modified color restoration technique. In: 2nd Conference on Emerging Applications of Information Technology (EAIT), pp. 93–97. IEEE (2011)
14. Islam, A., Farup, I.: Enhancing the output of spatial color algorithms. In: 2nd European Workshop on Visual Information Processing (EUVIP), pp. 7–12. IEEE (2010)
15. Jang, J.H., Kim, S.D., Ra, J.B.: Enhancement of optical remote sensing images by subband-decomposed multiscale retinex with hybrid intensity transfer function. IEEE Geosci. Remote Sens. Lett. **8**(5), 983–987 (2011)
16. Jobson, D.J., Rahman, Z., Woodell, G.A.: A multiscale retinex for bridging the gap between color images and the human observation of scenes. IEEE Trans. Image Process. **6**(7), 965–976 (1997)
17. Jobson, D.J., Rahman, Z., Woodell, G.A.: Properties and performance of a center/surround retinex. IEEE Trans. Image Process. **6**(3), 451–462 (1997)
18. Kolås, Ø., Farup, I., Rizzi, A.: Spatio-temporal retinex-inspired envelope with stochastic sampling a framework for spatial color algorithms. J. Imaging Sci. Technol. **55**(4), 40503-1–40503-10 (2011)
19. Kuffler, S.W.: Discharge patterns and functional organization of mammalian retina. J. Neurophysiol. **16**(1), 37–68 (1953)
20. Land, E.: Recent advances in retinex theory (1985)

21. Land, E.H.: An alternative technique for the computation of the designator in the retinex theory of color vision. Proc. Nat. Acad. Sci. U.S.A. **83**(10), 3078–3080 (1986)
22. Land, E.H., McCann, J.J.: Lightness and retinex theory. J. Optical Soc. Am. **1**, 1–11 (1971)
23. Land, E.H.: The retinex theory of color vision. Sci. Am. **237**(6), 108–128 (1977)
24. Lecca, M., Rizzi, A., Gianini, G.: Energy-driven path search for termite retinex. J. Opt. Soc. Am. A **33**, 1 (2016)
25. Lu, H., Yang, S., Zhang, H., Zheng, Z.: A robust omnidirectional vision sensor for soccer robots. Mechatronics **21**(2), 373–389 (2011)
26. Marini, D., Rizzi, A.: Colour constancy and optical illusions: a computer simulation with Retinex theory. In: Proceeding of ICIAP, pp. 657–660, Monopoli, Italy, September 1993
27. McCann, J., Rizzi, A.: The Art and Science of HDR Imaging. Wiley (2011)
28. McCann, J.J.: Retinex algorithms: many spatial processes used to solve many different problems. Electron. Imaging **2016**(6), 1–10 (2016)
29. McCann, J.J., Savoy, R.: Measurements of lightness: dependence on the position of a white in the field of view. In: Electronic Imaging 1991, San Jose, CA, pp. 402–411. International Society for Optics and Photonics (1991)
30. McCann, J.J., McKee, S.P., Taylor, T.H.: Quantitative studies in retinex theory a comparison between theoretical predictions and observer responses to the color mondrian experiments. Vision Res. **16**(5), 445–IN3 (1976)
31. Montagna, R., Finlayson, G.D.: Constrained pseudo-Brownian motion and its application to image enhancement. J. Opt. Soc. Am. A **28**(8), 1677–1688 (2011)
32. Optical Society of America: Committee on Colorimetry. The Science of Color. Crowell, New York (1953)
33. Provenzi, E., De Carli, E., Rizzi, A., Marini, D.: Mathematical definition and analysis of the Retinex algorithm. J. Opt. Soc. Am. A: Opt. Image Sci. Vis. **22**(12), 2613–2621 (2005)
34. Provenzi, E., Fierro, M., Rizzi, A., De Carli, L., Gadia, D., Marini, D.: Random spray retinex: a new Retinex implementation to investigate the local properties of the model. Trans. Img. Proc. **16**(1), 162–171 (2007)
35. Rahman, Z., Jobson, D.J., Woodell, G.A.: A multiscale retinex for color rendition and dynamic range compression. In: SPIE International Symposium on Optical Science, Engineering and Instrumentation, Applications of Digital Image Processing XIX, vol. 2847, pp. 183–191 (1996)
36. Rahman, Z., Jobson, D.J., Woodell, G.A.: Retinex processing for automatic image enhancement. J. Electron. Imaging **13**(1), 100–110 (2004)
37. Rahman, Z., Woodell, G.A., Jobson, D.J.: Retinex image enhancement: application to medical images. In: NASA Workshop on New Partnerships in Medical Diagnostic Imaging (2001)
38. Schettini, R., Ciocca, G., Zuffi, S., et al.: A survey of methods for colour image indexing and retrieval in image databases. In: Color Imaging Science: Exploiting Digital Media, pp. 183–211 (2001)
39. Simone, G., Audino, G., Farup, I., Albregtsen, F., Rizzi, A.: Termite Retinex: a new implementation based on a colony of intelligent agents. J. Electron. Imaging **23**(1), 013006-1–013006-13 (2014)
40. Simone, G., Cordone, R., Lecca, M., Serapioni, R.P.: On Edge-aware path-based color spatial sampling for retinex: from Termite Retinex to light-energy driven Termite Retinex. J. Electron. Imaging (to appear). Special Issue, Retinex at 50

41. Vázquez, S.G., Barreira, N., Penedo, M.G., Saez, M., Pose-Reino, A.: Using retinex image enhancement to improve the artery/vein classification in retinal images. In: Campilho, A., Kamel, M. (eds.) ICIAR 2010. LNCS, vol. 6112, pp. 50–59. Springer, Heidelberg (2010). doi:10.1007/978-3-642-13775-4_6

Color Image Processing

Video Smoke Removal Based on Smoke Imaging Model and Space-Time Pixel Compensation

Shiori Yamaguchi$^{(\boxtimes)}$, Keita Hirai$^{(\boxtimes)}$, and Takahiko Horiuchi

Graduate School of Advanced Integration Science, Chiba University,
Yayoi-cho 1-33, Inage-ku, Chiba 263-8522, Japan
acda2711@chiba-u.jp, hirai@faculty.chiba-u.jp

Abstract. This paper presents a novel video smoke removal method based on a smoke imaging model and space-time pixel compensation. First, we develop an optical imaging model for natural scenes that contain smoke. Then, we remove the smoke in a video, frame-by-frame, based on the smoke imaging model and conventional dehazing approaches. Next, we align the smoke-removed frames using corresponding pixels. To obtain the corresponding pixels, we use SIFT and color features with distance constraints. Finally, to reproduce clear video appearance, we compensate pixel values by utilizing the space-time weightings of the corresponding pixels between the smoke-removed frames. Validation experiments show our method can provide effective smoke removal resulting in dynamic scenes.

Keywords: Smoke removal · Dehazing · Dark Channel Prior · Smoke imaging model · Pixel compensation

1 Introduction

Natural and artificial disasters often critically damage our lives. In such disaster situations, we have a critical need for quick lifesaving actions, disaster investigations, and post-disaster monitoring. In these situations, it is often difficult to enter disaster areas because of unstable footing and poisonous gases. Thus, the uses of machines, such as drones or small robots, is effective in dealing with such disasters. Drones, particularly, are useful investigation tools for disaster scenes [1,2]. They make it possible to obtain a large amount of information by flying over the affected area. Rescue robots can take many forms for searching through rubble and water [3,4]. In such machines, on-board compact cameras are employed for scene recognition and autonomous actions. However, the performance of these cameras and machine vision algorithms are degraded because of smoke and other gases in the disaster areas. Because fog and haze as well as smoke reduce scene visibility, many dehazing methods have been proposed [5–11]. Tan proposed a single-image dehazing method to enhance the contrast [5]. Fattal presented an image dehazing method based on a haze imaging model [6]. He et al. restored haze image visibility based on the above haze imaging model and Dark

© Springer International Publishing AG 2017
S. Bianco et al. (Eds.): CCIW 2017, LNCS 10213, pp. 43–54, 2017.
DOI: 10.1007/978-3-319-56010-6_4

Channel Prior algorithm [7] (see next section). Gibson and Nguyen evaluated He's approaches by using principal component analysis and minimum volume ellipsoid approximations [8]. Fattal proposed a dehazing method using colorlines [11], which realized better clarity than his previous method [7]. Video dehazing methods for video are often realized by extending previous single-image dehazing techniques [12–14]. Tarel et al. presented a fast dehazing algorithm based on a median filter, and applied it for video dehazing in vehicle cameras [12]. Zhang et al. used spatial and temporal coherence based on a Markov random field (MRF) model for reducing spatial veiling and temporal flicker [13]. Kim et al. presented video dehazing based on block-based restoration [14].

However, there are two problems in applying conventional approaches to video smoke removal. One is the spatial non-uniformity of smoke density. The conventional dehazing techniques assume that uniform scene haze covers all parts of an image. Moreover, it is assumed that conventional haze imaging models depend only on scene distance and do not take into account non-uniform haze and density that do not depend on distance. Further, single-image dehazing approaches cannot sufficiently remove partially covered strong fog and smoke in each frame. Another problem is the inappropriate reuse of the haze imaging model. Even though a smoke imaging model is actually different from the haze imaging model, some conventional methods have applied the haze imaging model not only for dehazing, but also smoke removal. For proper image/video smoke removal, a smoke imaging model should be constructed in the same way as the haze imaging model.

In this study, we propose a smoke imaging model and smoke removal method for video sequences. In our approach, the video camera moves freely, and partially covered smoke areas are temporally shifting. The scene and smoke do not keep relative positions. First, we remove the smoke from each frame. Next, we calculate corresponding pixels between the frames. For this calculation, we use SIFT and color features with distance constraints. Then, we compensate each pixel color by space-time weighting of adjacent frames. This paper is organized as follows: We describe the haze imaging model and a conventional dehazing approach in Sect. 2. The model and approach are the basis of our proposed method. Then, we propose a smoke imaging model and our smoke removal method in Sect. 3. In Sect. 4, we show experimental results and discussions. Moreover, we compare our method with conventional methods. Finally, conclusions and future research are discussed in Sect. 5.

2   Dehazing Model and Conventional Approach

Figure 1 shows transmission of light in a natural scene containing haze. In general, the haze imaging model is given by the following equation:

$$\mathbf{I}(\mathbf{x}) = \mathbf{J}(\mathbf{x})t(\mathbf{x}) + \mathbf{A}(1 - t(\mathbf{x})), \tag{1}$$

where $\mathbf{x}$ is pixel coordinates in camera image is pixel coordinates in camera image $\mathbf{I}$, $\mathbf{J}$ is scene radiance, $\mathbf{A}$ is global atmospheric color, and t is medium

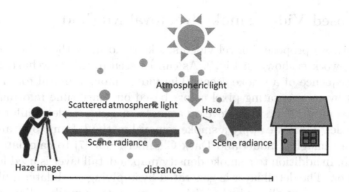

Fig. 1. Haze imaging model.

transmission of scene radiance. If an image does not contain scene haze, light from the scene objects reach the camera directly without any diffusions in the air. On the other hand, when haze is present in the air, the scene radiation is diffused by the haze prior to reaching the camera. In this situation, light scattered by the particles in the atmosphere also reach, as shown in Fig. 1. The transmission value t is defined by

$$t = \exp(-\beta \cdot d(\mathbf{x})),\qquad(2)$$

where β is a diffusion coefficient, and d is the distance between objects and a camera. As shown in Eq. (2), haze is uniformly distributed in scenes, and depends only on distances. Input image I could be restored by estimating t, $\mathbf{A}$, and $\mathbf{J}$. He et al. found that at least one of the RGB values in a patch was very low (almost zero) when using an image under clear daylight [7]. This phenomenon, called Dark Channel Prior, is as follows:

$$J^{dark}(\mathbf{x}) = \min_{c \in r,g,b} (\min_{y \in \Omega(\mathbf{x})} J^c(\mathbf{y})) \simeq 0,\qquad(3)$$

where Ω is a patch region of a pixel $\mathbf{x}$, and c is an RGB channel. Then, based on Eqs. (1) and (3), a transmission map is estimated:

$$\bar{t}(\mathbf{x}) = 1 - \omega \min_{c \in r,g,b} (\min_{y \in \Omega(\mathbf{x})} (\frac{I^c(\mathbf{y})}{A^c})),\qquad(4)$$

where ω is a parameter for keeping some amount of haze for far-distant objects. In order to estimate atmospheric color $\mathbf{A}$, it is necessary to find a pixel of $t(\mathbf{x}) = 0$. Based on Eq. (2), the transmission value $t(\mathbf{x})$ will be 0 at the pixel of infinite distance $d(\mathbf{x}) \to \infty$. Assuming that the distance in the sky area will be infinite, they employ the brightest pixel in an input image as the sky area. The estimated transmission map $\bar{t}$ generally contains block noise due to the patch-based processing. After the refinement of noisy transmission map $\bar{t}$ by soft matting, scene radiance $\mathbf{J}$ is estimated by

$$\mathbf{J}(\mathbf{x}) = \frac{\mathbf{I}(\mathbf{x}) - \mathbf{A}}{\max(t(\mathbf{x}), t_0)} + \mathbf{A},\qquad(5)$$

here t_0 is a lower limit transmission threshold for noise reduction.

3   Proposed Video Smoke Removal Method

In this study, we propose a novel video smoke removal method. The flow chart of our framework is shown in Fig. 2. As can be seen in this flowchart, the input is a video sequence of a smoke scene. The video smoke removal for the output is executed by compensating pixel colors based on space-time information. For realizing this purpose, first, we develop a smoke imaging model similar to a haze imaging model. Then, we apply a smoke removal method, frame by frame, based on the smoke imaging model and Dark Channel Prior [7] to calculate a smoke density map. In addition to a smoke density map, a detail layer is used for precise pixel selection. The detail layer is generated by applying the bilateral filter to an input frame. Then we align pixel positions between temporally-adjacent frames. Finally, we synthesize video frames using pixel selection maps based on smoke density maps and detail layers.

In the conventional method discussed in Sect. 2, there are several issues regarding video smoke removal. He et al.'s method assumed spatial uniformity of haze density. Their approach cannot sufficiently remove partially covered thick fog and smoke in each frame. Moreover, the haze imaging model was applied to smoke removal, in spite of the fact such a model was different from a smoke imaging model. Instead, we developed a smoke imaging model and a video smoke removal framework for addressing the above issues.

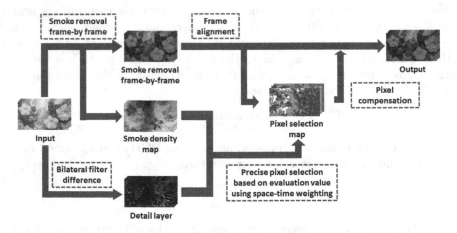

Fig. 2. Flowchart of the proposed algorithm.

3.1   Smoke Imaging Model

Figure 3 shows the imaging model for a scene containing haze and smoke. If input videos contain smoke, each frame can be represented by the sum of scene radiance, global atmospheric light, and light scattered by particles of smoke. Here, the smoke imaging model is given by

$$\mathbf{I}(\mathbf{x}) = (1 - \psi(\mathbf{x}))\left(\mathbf{J}(\mathbf{x})\,t(\mathbf{x}) + (1 - t(\mathbf{x}))\,\mathbf{A}\right) + \psi(\mathbf{x})\mathbf{S}, \qquad (6)$$

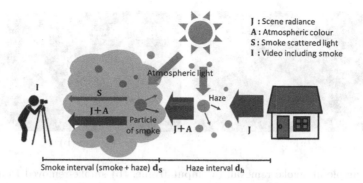

Fig. 3. Smoke imaging model. In a scene containing smoke, the three components (scene radiance, atmospheric light and light through smoke) reach the camera.

where $\mathbf{x}$, $\mathbf{I}$, $\mathbf{J}$, $\mathbf{A}$, and t are the same as Eq. (1). $\mathbf{S}$ is smoke-scattered light color, and ψ is smoke density. This is a typical smoke imaging model containing both haze and smoke. Here, we assume that the smoke density ψ does not depend on distance d_s between objects and smoke. In addition, if the distance between objects and camera is sufficiently short, I is not affected by the global atmospheric color $\mathbf{A}$ due to scene haze. In other words, we can ignore the transmission ($t(\mathbf{x}) \approx 1$). In this situation, Eq. (6) can be rewritten as

$$\mathbf{I}(\mathbf{x}) = \mathbf{J}(\mathbf{x})\,(1 - \psi(\mathbf{x})) + \psi(\mathbf{x})\mathbf{S}. \tag{7}$$

Here, let be $\rho(\mathbf{x}) = 1 - \psi(\mathbf{x})$, Eq. (7) can be formed as

$$\mathbf{I}(\mathbf{x}) = \mathbf{J}(\mathbf{x})\,\rho(\mathbf{x}) + \mathbf{S}\,(1 - \rho(\mathbf{x})). \tag{8}$$

When setting the smoke density $\psi(\mathbf{x}) = 0$, scene radiance is not affected by smoke. On the other hand, when $\psi(\mathbf{x}) = 1$, camera image $\mathbf{I}$ is equal to smoke color $\mathbf{S}$. Comparing Eq. (1) with Eq. (8), the smoke imaging model and haze imaging model can be substantially given by an equivalent expression. Thus, we estimate ψ and $\mathbf{S}$ from $\mathbf{I}$ for recovering the scene radiance $\mathbf{J}$. We can solve Eq. (8) by the same manner described in Sect. 2. In this method, we apply the Dark Channel Prior algorithm [7] in each frame. After the frame-by-frame smoke removal process, smoke remains in several regions. Figure 4 shows an example of smoke removal. As can be seen in this example, the visibility of the smoke-removed frame is better than that of the input frame. However, regions with smoke still remain. Thus, in the next step, we address a method to recover better visibility by using temporally-adjacent frames (See Sect. 3.3).

3.2   Frame Alignment with Distance and Color Constraints

SIFT features are often used to detect corresponding points between frames. However, in frames containing smoke, it is difficult to achieve accurate alignment

(a)   (b)

Fig. 4. Example of smoke removal; (a) input frame. (b) smoke-removed frame based on a smoke imaging model. This smoke removal is executed frame-by-frame (not using temporal information).

by using only SIFT features. Therefore, we add two constraints to SIFT for detecting robust corresponding points between smoke frames.

One constraint is to set a limitation on detection ranges. The amount of movement between frames can be assumed to be small. Thus, searching a feature point $k_{n'}$, which is corresponding to a feature point k_n is limited within the surrounding $h \times h$ pixels of the feature point k_n.

The other constraint is to use the color information of a patch. The corresponding points obtained by only SIFT features are few, because the pixel values affected by smoke are different in each frame. We use the RGB information of surrounding $l \times l$ pixels of a feature point. Then we employ the Euclidean distances of SIFT feature and color information for evaluating correspondences. The evaluation value E_{Align} is given by

$$E_{Align} = (1 - w)\varphi(\mathbf{v}^{k_n}, \mathbf{v}^{k_{n'}}) + w\varphi(\mathbf{p}^{k_n}, \mathbf{p}^{k_{n'}}), \tag{9}$$

$$\varphi(\mathbf{v}, \mathbf{v}') = \|\mathbf{v} - \mathbf{v}'\|_2, \tag{10}$$

where $\mathbf{v}^{k_n}, \mathbf{v}^{k_{n'}}$ are the SIFT features (128 dimensions) of points $k_n, k_{n'}$, respectively, in the frame n, n'. $\mathbf{p}^{k_n}, \mathbf{p}^{k_{n'}}$ are the RGB features ($3l^2$ dimensions), represented by the surrounding $l \times l$ pixels of feature points $k_n, k_{n'}$. w is a parameter containing the ratio of the Euclidean distance of SIFT features to color features. It is possible to obtain correct corresponding points by using smaller evaluation values $E_{Align} < th_{Align}$. Then, we calculate a homography matrix using RANSAC. When the number of the obtained corresponding points is too small, the homographic transformation cannot be correctly performed. In such situations, we do not use the frame for the pixel compensation. Figure 5 shows an example of corresponding point detection. As can be seen in Fig. 5, we obtain a correct homography matrix by using SIFT with the above two constraints.

3.3   Pixel Compensation with Space-Time Weighting

After frame alignment, we compensate pixel values by space-time weightings of corresponding pixels in smoke-removed frames. For using a precise pixel, we

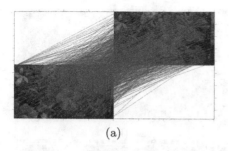 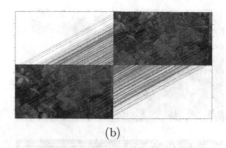

(a)   (b)

Fig. 5. Corresponding point detection of adjacent two frames; (a) SIFT features only. (b) SIFT features with distance and color constraints.

apply smoke density maps $\psi(\mathbf{x})$ as same as $t(\mathbf{x})$ in He et al.'s method [7]. In addition to smoke density maps, we use detail layers to evaluate the decrease of component detail caused by smoke. This is because smoke reduces details, as well as color saturations of a scene. We generate a detail layer by calculating the difference between the input frame and bilateral filtered frame as follows:

$$Y_D = Y - Y_B, \tag{11}$$

where Y_D, Y, and Y_B are a detail layer, an input frame and filtered frame, respectively. Then, we compensate pixel values based on the combinations of the smoke density maps and detail layers. The evaluation value E is given by

$$E(\mathbf{x}) = \lambda \rho(\mathbf{x}) + (1 - \lambda) Y_D(\mathbf{x}), \tag{12}$$

where λ is a parameter to control the weighting between a smoke density map and detail layer.

Pixel correspondence reliability is affected by spatial and temporal distances. Thus, we add spatial and temporal weights for compensating precise pixel values. The weighted evaluation value E_{weight} is given by

$$E_{weight}(\mathbf{x}, n, n') = G_t(n, n') \cdot G_s \cdot E(\mathbf{x}), \tag{13}$$

where $G_t(n, n')$ is the temporal Gaussian weight given by

$$G_t(n, n') = \frac{1}{2\pi\sigma_t^2} \exp(-\frac{|n' - n|}{2\sigma_t^2}), \tag{14}$$

and $E_s(\mathbf{x})$ is $E(\mathbf{x})$ in Eq. (12) with the spatial Gaussian weight given by

$$G_s \cdot E(\mathbf{x}) = \sum_{\mathbf{y} \in \Omega(\mathbf{x})} \lambda \cdot \rho(\mathbf{y}) \cdot g(\mathbf{y}, \sigma_s) + (1 - \lambda) \cdot Y_D \cdot g(\mathbf{y}, \sigma_s), \tag{15}$$

$$g(\mathbf{y}, \sigma_s) = \frac{1}{2\pi\sigma_s^2} \exp(-\frac{\|\mathbf{x} - \mathbf{y}\|_2^2}{2\sigma_t^2}), \tag{16}$$

Fig. 6. Example of a pixel selection map; (a) input frame, (b) smoke density map, (c) detail layer, (d) pixel selection map (red: $n - 3$, green: $n - 2$, blue: $n - 1$, yellow: n, white: $n + 1$, cyan: $n + 2$ and magenta: $n + 3$ frame, respectively). (Color figure online)

where Ω is a patch of pixel $\mathbf{x}$, and σ_s, σ_t are parameters that control the space and time weightings. By selecting the pixel with the maximum evaluating value, we replace a pixel value of a current frame with one from temporally adjacent frames. We store selected frame numbers, which have precise pixel values in a pixel selection map. Figure 6 shows a pixel selection map using a smoke density map and detail layer. As described above, the pixel selection map is actually generated by using smoke density maps and detail layers of temporally adjacent frames. Finally, we synthesize smoke-removed frames via the pixel selecting maps.

4   Results and Discussion

In this study, we captured videos containing smoke by using a Drone camera (Parrot's Bebop Drone). Smoke in a scene was generated using commercial fireworks. The drone is freely flown in the scene with smoke. When we executed the proposed method, the videos were resized from original 1920 × 1080 to downsampled 800 × 450 pixels, in order to shorten the processing time. Parameters were set as shown in Table 1.

Figure 7 shows an example of our experimental results. In this figure, we used seven adjacent frames in the synthesis. As shown in Fig. 7(a), an input frame is fully covered by smoke. In particular, we cannot see a part of the tree on the right. As shown in Figs. 7(b) and (c), a smoke density map and a detail layer enable

Table 1. Parameter setting.

Smoke removal of frame-by-frame		
ω	Parameter in Eq. (4)	0.95
t_0	Transmission lower limit	0.1
Frame alignment with constraints		
h	Limit of detection range	61
l	Patch size	5
w	Weight of corresponding point	0.5
th_{Align}	Evaluation of corresponding point	1.0
Frame select and pixel compensation		
λ	Parameter for space-time weighting	0.7
σ_t	Parameter of temporal weighting	10
σ_s	Parameter of spatial weighting	0.64

(a)   (b)

(c)   (d)

(e)   (f)

Fig. 7. Our input and result example; (a) input frame, (b) smoke density map, (c) detail layer, (d) pixel selection map (red: $n-3$, green: $n-2$, blue: $n-1$, yellow: n, white: $n+1$, cyan: $n+2$ and magenta: $n+3$ frame, respectively), (e) frame-by-frame smoke removal, (f) our final result. (Color figure online)

precise smoke detection. Then, a pixel selection map in Fig. 7(d) was generated based on smoke density maps and detail layers of temporally-adjacent frames. As shown in Fig. 7(d), we can see that pixel colors can be restored from temporally-adjacent frames. The result of smoke removal, frame-by-frame, in Fig. 7(e) has better visibility than that in Fig. 7(a). However, Fig. 7(e) still presents a dull appearance. On the other hand, as shown in Fig. 7(f), our method can restored a clear appearance in the tree on the left and fallen leaves on the ground. A part of the tree on the right was not fully restored because scene radiance information is almost lost in this dense smoke region.

Further, we recorded videos with and without smoke for comparing the ground truth with the smoke-removed results. The videos were recorded using a camera with constant motion and a panel in front of the camera. Figure 8 is a

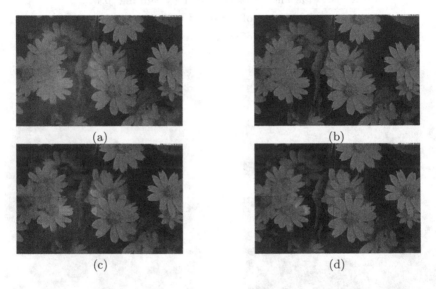

Fig. 8. Comparison of each method; (a) input frame containing the smoke, (b) ground truth, (c) He et al. [7], (d) our method.

Fig. 9. Failure case of the proposed method; (a) result frame with smoke remaining, (b) pixel selection map using our algorithm.

comparison of the conventional dehazing methods and our result. In this figure, we used five adjacent frames in the synthesis. As can be seen in Fig. 8(c), smoke in the lower left corner was not completely removed by He et al.'s method [7]. Moreover, smoke in the other region was similarly not removed well by their method. Figure 8(d), using our pro-posed method, achieves removal of almost all the smoke. Figure 9 shows a smoke-removed frame and its frame selection map in a failure case. The smoke region remains in this result. This is because the number of detected corresponding points is too small. In this case, only two frames were used for pixel compensation.

5   Conclusion

In this paper, we have proposed an algorithm to remove smoke in a video by combining multiple frames. We described optical phenomena for natural scenes contain smoke. Then, we developed a smoke imaging model. Moreover, we applied dehazing methods in each frame, detected the corresponding point using SIFT with two constraints, and aligned frames. Finally, we selected the clearest pixels without smoke using the smoke density map and detail layer for synthesizing the smoke-removal frame. In our experiment, some smoke still remained in the video frame, because of the wrong correspondence of feature points between frames. We should improve the matching technique by brightness adjustment and additional image information.

References

1. Flyability. Introducing Gimball, the collision-tolerant drone, May 2016. http://www.flyability.com/product/
2. Search and Rescue with UAVS, May 2016. https://www.microdrones.com/en/applications/areas-of-application/search-and-rescue/
3. Popular Science. Watch google's humanoid robot learn the world is a harsh place, May 2016. http://www.popsci.com/watch-googles-humanoid-robot-learn-world-is-harsh-place
4. IEEE Spectrum. DARPA's Rescue-Robot Showdown, May 2016. http://spectrum.ieee.org/robotics/humanoids/darpas-rescuerobot-showdown
5. Tan, R.T.: Visibility in bad weather from a single image. In: Computer Vision and Pattern Recognition, pp. 1–8. IEEE Press, Alaska (2008)
6. Fattal, R.: Single image dehazing. ACM. Trans. Graph. **27**(3), 1–9 (2008). (Proceeding SIGGRAPH 2008)
7. He, K., Sun, J., Tang, X.: Single image haze removal using dark channel prior. In: Computer Vision and Pattern Recognition, pp. 1956–1963. IEEE Press, Miami (2009)
8. Gibson, K.B., Nguyen, T.Q.: On the effectiveness of the dark channel prior for single image dehazing by approximating with minimum volume ellipsoids. In: IEEE International Conference on Acoustics, Speech and Signal Processing, pp. 1253–1256. IEEE Press, Prague (2011)

9. Yang, S., Zhu, Q., Wang, J., Wu, D., Xie, Y.: An improved single image haze removal algorithm based on dark channel prior and histogram specification. In: 6th International Conference on Model Transformation, pp. 279–292, Budapest (2013)

10. Tan, Z., Bai, X., Wang, B., Higashi, A.: Fast single-image defogging. FUJITSU Sci. Tech. J. **50**(1), 60–65 (2014)

11. Fattal, R.: Dehazing using color-lines. ACM. Trans. Graph. **34**(1), 1–14 (2014). (Proceeding SIGGRAPH 2015)

12. Tarel, J.P., Hautiere, N.: Fast visibility restoration from a single color or gray level image. In: 20th IEEE International Conference on Computer Vision, pp. 2201–2208. IEEE Press, Kyoto (2009)

13. Zhang, J., Li, L., Zhang, Y., Yang, G., Cao, X., Sun, J.: Video dehazing with spatial and temporal coherence. Vis. Comput. **27**(6), 749–757 (2011)

14. Kim, J., Jang, W., Sim, J., Kim, C.: Optimized contrast enhancement for real-time image and video dehazing. J. Vis. Commun. Image R. **24**(3), 410–426 (2013)

Similarities and Differences in the Mathematical Formalizations of the Retinex Model and Its Variants

Edoardo Provenzi$^{(\boxtimes)}$

Laboratoire MAP5 (UMR CNRS 8145), Université Paris Descartes,
45 rue des Saints-Pères, 75006 Paris, France
edoardo.provenzi@parisdescartes.fr

Abstract. Edwin H. Land and John J. McCann introduced the Retinex model as a computational theory of color vision. However, they specified the details of Retinex rather algorithmically and not mathematically and this opened the way to a multitude of different interpretations of their model, many times even contradicting ones. The aim of this paper is to present a systematic and self-contained overview about these different interpretations and the corresponding mathematical formalizations in terms of variational principles and partial differential equations.

1 Introduction

The most popular paper about the original Retinex formulation is [19]. Retinex stands for 'Retina plus Cortex', which refers to the fact that the mechanisms underlying human color vision depend both on the retinal photoreceptors catches and on the cortex interpretation of this signals. The original Retinex is a computational model with the aim of finding a perceptual correlate of reflectance, called 'lightness' by Land, to be tested with psychophysical measurements.

Through a series of groundbreaking experiments, mostly performed with the famous 'Mondrian tableaux', Land and McCann proved that human perception of a surface's color is much more influenced by the spatial distribution of the surrounding surfaces than by the spectral distribution of the light used to illuminate the Mondrian tableau. As underlined by McCann in many papers and conference speeches, spatial locality of color perception is the central concept in the whole Retinex theory. Thus, at least in its original form, the aim of Retinex is not to discard illumination and recover the intrinsic reflectance of surfaces, as several authors claim in their paper even nowadays, but to quantify how the points of the spatial surround cooperate to modify color perception.

In spite of their innovative and important experimental achievements, neither Land nor McCann 'carved their model into stone' through a rigorous mathematical formulation. In this paper, we are going to discuss the two major classes of Retinex that can be found in the literature: ratio-reset Retinex and Horn's Retinex [11]. We will underline how profound is the difference between these two interpretations thanks to variational principles and partial differential equations.

© Springer International Publishing AG 2017
S. Bianco et al. (Eds.): CCIW 2017, LNCS 10213, pp. 55–67, 2017.
DOI: 10.1007/978-3-319-56010-6_5

Before entering in the mathematical details of variational formulations, it is worth introducing, in the following section, the basic formalization of the original Retinex formula developed in [25]. This will help us fix the ideas and the notation about many concepts and notations that will be discussed in the following sections.

2 Land and McCann's Original Retinex Model

As previously commented, the original Retinex model of Land and McCann [19] is based on the assumption that the HVS operates with three retinal-cortical systems, each processing independently the low, middle and high wavelengths of the visible electromagnetic spectrum. Every independent process forms a separate image determining a quantity that they called *lightness* and denoted with L. Land and McCann found a computational way to reproduce lightness for their Mondrian tableaux by introducing spatial comparisons among intensities, calculated over *paths*. The comparison is performed through a multiplicative chain of ratios, subjected to these non-linear operations: *Threshold mechanism*: if the ratio does not differ from 1 more than a fixed threshold value, then it is set to be unitary; *Reset mechanism*: if the cumulated product of ratios overcomes the value 1 in a certain point of the path, then it is forced to 1, so that the computation restarts from it. In this way, this point becomes a local white reference, so hat the reset mechanism is responsible for the white-patch behavior of Retinex.

Let us now present the mathematical formalization of Land and McCann ratio-threshold-reset Retinex computation provided in [25]. Given a discrete digital image function with normalized range, $I : \Omega \subset \mathbb{Z}^2 \to [0,1]$, consider a collection of N oriented paths $\gamma = \{\gamma_1, \ldots, \gamma_N\}$ composed by ordered chains of pixels starting in y_k and ending in x, $k = 1, \ldots, N$. Let n_k be the number of pixels traveled by the path γ_k and let $t_k = 1, \ldots, n_k$ be its parameter, i.e. $\gamma_k : \{1, \ldots, n_k\} \to \Omega \subset \mathbb{R}^2$, $\gamma_k(1) = y_k$ and $\gamma_k(n_k) = x$. Write, for simplicity, two subsequent pixels of the path as $\gamma_k(t_k) = y_{t_k}$ and $\gamma_k(t_k + 1) = y_{t_k+1}$, for $t_k = 1, \ldots, n_k - 1$. Consider, in every fixed chromatic channel $c \in \{R, G, B\}$, their intensities $I(y_{t_k})$, $I(y_{t_k+1})$ and then compute the ratio $R_{t_k} = \frac{I(y_{t_k+1})}{I(y_{t_k})}$ with the initial condition $R_0 = 1$.

With this notation in mind, the value of lightness provided by the ratio-threshold-reset Retinex algorithm for a generic pixel $x \in \Omega$, in every fixed chromatic channel c (that we avoid specifying for the same of a clearer notation), is given by:

$$L_{\varepsilon,\gamma}(x) = \frac{1}{N} \sum_{k=1}^{N} \prod_{t_k=1}^{n_k-1} \delta_k(R_{t_k}) \tag{1}$$

where $\delta_k : \mathbb{R}^+ \to \mathbb{R}^+$, $k = 1, \ldots, N$, are functions defined in this way: $\delta_k(R_0) = 1$ and, for $t_k = 1, \ldots, n_k - 1$,

$$\delta_k(R_{t_k}) = \begin{cases} R_{t_k} & \text{if } 0 < R_{t_k} \leq 1 - \varepsilon \\ 1 & \text{if } 1 - \varepsilon < R_{t_k} < 1 + \varepsilon \\ R_{t_k} & \text{if } 1 + \varepsilon \leq R_{t_k} \leq \dfrac{1+\varepsilon}{\prod_{m_k=0}^{t_k-1} \delta_k(R_{m_k})} \\ \dfrac{1}{\prod_{m_k=0}^{t_k-1} \delta_k(R_{m_k})} & \text{if } R_{t_k} > \dfrac{1+\varepsilon}{\prod_{m_k=0}^{t_k-1} \delta_k(R_{m_k})} \end{cases} \qquad (2)$$

being $\varepsilon > 0$ a fixed threshold. The second option is the mathematical implementation of the threshold mechanism while the fourth implements the reset mechanism (and so the white patch behavior) of the algorithm.

It is useful to write the contribution of the single path γ_k to $L_{\varepsilon,\gamma}(x)$ as:

$$L_{\varepsilon,\gamma_k}(x) = \prod_{t_k=1}^{n_k-1} \delta_k(R_{t_k}), \qquad (3)$$

so that formula (1) reduces simply to the average of these contributions, i.e. $L_{\varepsilon,\gamma}(x) = \frac{1}{N} \sum_{k=1}^{N} L_{\varepsilon,\gamma_k}(x)$.

2.1   The Limit Behavior $\varepsilon \to 0$

The analytical formula to describe the ratio-threshold-reset Retinex algorithm just introduced allowed making predictions about the model. As explained in [25], this can be done if the threshold mechanism is disregarded, or, equivalently, by considering the case $\varepsilon \to 0$.

As $\varepsilon \to 0$, the functions δ_k become much simpler:

$$\delta_k(R_{t_k}) = \begin{cases} R_{t_k} & \text{if } 0 < R_{t_k} \prod_{m_k=0}^{t_k-1} \delta_k(R_{m_k}) \leq 1 \\ \dfrac{1}{\prod_{m_k=0}^{t_k-1} \delta_k(R_{m_k})} & \text{if } R_{t_k} \prod_{m_k=0}^{t_k-1} \delta_k(R_{m_k}) > 1 \end{cases} \qquad (4)$$

hence, when $\varepsilon \to 0$, δ_k behaves either as the identity or the reset function.

In [25] it was proven that this implies the following formula:

$$L_{0,\gamma}(x) = \frac{1}{N} \sum_{k=1}^{N} \frac{I(x)}{I(y_{H_k})}, \qquad (5)$$

where y_{H_k} is the pixel with highest intensity traveled by γ_k. From now on, we will refer to formula (5) as describing the 'ratio-reset Retinex algorithm'.

Notice that he presence of paths makes the ratio-reset Retinex a *local* algorithm, where locality is intrinsically represented by the geometry of paths used. However, when $n_k \to |\Omega|$ or $N \to \infty$, the ratio-reset Retinex loses its local properties and reduces, see [25], to the global diagonal von Kries model [16]. On the other hand, if we use small values of n_k or N, the resulting lightness images are affected by a lot of noise, see again [25].

Finally, it is important to underline that, since intensity values are normalized, $0 < I(y_{H_k}) \leq 1$ for every $k = 1, \ldots, N$ and then $\sum_{k=1}^{N} \frac{1}{I(y_{H_k})} \geq N$. It follows that $L(x) \geq I(x)$ for every pixel i and this proves that an image filtered with the ratio-reset Retinex is always brighter or equal to the original one. This shows an important limitation of this algorithm: an over-exposed picture can only be worsened by the application of the ratio-reset Retinex used as a color corrector.

2.2   From Paths to Pixel Sprays: RSR and Related Algorithms

The information obtain thanks to the mathematical formulation of Retinex has important consequences on the structure of $\mathcal{P}_x(\Omega)$, the set of paths embedded in the image domain Ω and ending in the point x. After formula (5), on this set it is natural to define the following equivalence relation: given $\gamma, \eta \in \mathcal{P}_x(\Omega)$,

$$\gamma \sim \eta \quad \Leftrightarrow \quad \max_{y \in \gamma^*}\{I(y)\} = \max_{y \in \eta^*}\{I(y)\} \tag{6}$$

where γ^* and η^* are the co-domains of the paths, i.e. the collections of pixels traveled by γ and η, respectively.

Paths belonging to different equivalence classes give different contributions to the lightness computation, while every path in a given equivalence class gives rise to the same value of $L_{0,\gamma_k}(x)$. It follows immediately that $\mathcal{P}_x(\Omega)$ contains redundant paths and that the correct set of paths to consider is given by the quotient set $\mathcal{P}_x(\Omega)/\sim$, whose elements are the equivalence classes of paths with respect to the equivalence relation defined in (6).

In each equivalence class one can choose a single representative path to compute $L_{0,\gamma_k}(x)$, in particular, the more efficient one is the two-points path whose co-domain is simply given by $\{y_{H_k}, x\}$. Thus, the ordering operations needed to generate the paths are totally unnecessary for the final lightness computation. Moreover, by a mathematical point of view, paths are topological manifolds of dimension 1 embedded in the image, which is a topological manifold of dimension 2, so paths do not really scan local neighborhoods of a pixel, rather *particular directions* in these neighborhoods. This directional extraction of information can lead to halos or artifacts in the filtered image, see e.g. [7].

These considerations led the authors of [26] to consider 2-dimensional objects such as *areas* instead of 1-dimensional paths to analyze image locality for an efficient color correction. Roughly speaking, their idea is to implement spatial locality by selecting a fraction of pixels from these areas with a density sample that changes according to a given function of their distance with respect to the target pixel x. Each function generates a different kind of pixel selection around x, leading to different kind of 'sprays', each of which shows different local filtering properties. The new implementation of the ratio-reset Retinex that follows this idea is called RSR for 'Random Sprays Retinex'.

In RSR the role of a path γ_k traveling n_k pixels and *ending* in the target x is played by $S_k(x)$, a spray with n_k pixels *centered* in x. Actually, once the number of points per spray is chosen, there is no need to vary it with k, hence, from now on, we will write n instead of n_k to denote the number of pixels per spray. The ratio-reset operation along a path is substituted by the search of the pixel with highest intensity in the whole spray. The functional expression of formula (5) to compute the lightness remains exactly the same in both algorithms, so the ratio-reset Retinex and RSR share the same intrinsic properties.

In [1,2] two techniques have been proposed to reduce noise generation also decreasing the computational time of RSR.

In [27] the spray technique was used to fuse RSR with ACE [28], another perceptually-inspired color correction algorithm that makes use of the gray-world hypothesis [5]. The hybrid algorithm is called RACE and it is able to color correct both under and over exposed images.

A more recent proposal to fuse WP and GW features in a single algorithm is that presented in [15] and called STRESS for Spatio-Temporal Retinex-like Envelope with Stochastic Sampling. As Retinex, STRESS computes, for each pixel, the local white reference, but also the black reference in each chromatic channel. This is done through calculating the maximum and minimum envelope functions, denoted as $E_{\max}(x)$ and $E_{\min}(x)$, respectively.

Finally, let us mention that, in [9], the RSR sampling technique has been studied from a probabilistic point of view, resulting in the algorithm QBRIX and, in [10], further comparisons among Retinex models are discussed.

3   A Variational Framework for the Ratio-Reset Retinex

The similarities between the ACE formula [28] and the gradient descent equations for histogram equalization obtained in [29], led to the discovery of a variational interpretation of ACE in the paper [4]. The framework were further extended in [23] and, finally, in [3] a variational framework for (an anti-symmetric version of the) ratio-reset Retinex has been discussed. In order to understand how this is possible, let us come back to the lightness formula (5).

Land and McCann proposed a further Retinex mechanism, the scaling, implemented via a strictly increasing function $f : (0,1] \to (0,1]$ such that $f(r) \geq r$ for all $r \in (0,1]$ applied to the ratio $r = \frac{I(x)}{I(y_{H_k})}$, so that the Retinex lightness formula becomes:

$$L_{0,\gamma,f}(x) = \frac{1}{N} \sum_{k=1}^{N} f\left(\frac{I(x)}{I(y_{H_k})}\right). \tag{7}$$

The reset mechanism of Retinex and the scaling operation can be merged: in fact, we can extend f to $(0,+\infty)$ preserving its continuity by defining

$$\hat{f}(r) = \begin{cases} f(r) & \text{if } r \in (0,1] \\ 1 & \text{if } r \in [1,+\infty). \end{cases}$$

It is clear that applying this new scaling function $\hat{f}$ to the ratios $I(x)/I(y)$, with x fixed and y that varies in Ω, jointly implements the scaling and the reset mechanism.

Now we have all the elements to introduce the continuous version of the Retinex algorithm presented in [3] under the name 'Kernel-Based Retinex', or KBR for short. Given $x \in \Omega$, let $Y_{w,x}$ be the random variable modeling the selection of a pixel in the neighborhood of x according to the density $w(x,y)$.

The output $L_w^{\text{KBR}}(x)$ of the KBR algorithm at the pixel x is defined as the conditional expectation of $\hat{f}\left(\frac{I(x)}{I(Y_{w,x})}\right)$ with respect to the distribution w of pixels around x, i.e.

$$L_w^{\text{KBR}}(x) = \mathbb{E}_{Y_{w,x}}\left[\hat{f}\left(\frac{I(x)}{I(Y_{w,x})}\right)\right]. \tag{8}$$

This formula is used independently for each color channel and can be written more explicitly as

$$L_w^{\text{KBR}}(x) = \sum_{\{y\in\Omega:I(y)\geq I(x)\}} w(x,y)\, f\left(\frac{I(x)}{I(y)}\right) + \sum_{\{y\in\Omega:I(y)<I(x)\}} w(x,y). \tag{9}$$

All the basic properties of the ratio-reset Retinex are faithfully implemented in (9): KBR is founded on the propagation of a two-pixel ratio comparison between the fixed target x and the generic pixel y that runs across the image; these comparisons are then subjected to the reset and scaling performed by $\hat{f}$ and, finally, locally averaged with weight w, in order to produce the value of $L_w^{\text{KBR}}(x)$.

To study the action of KBR of pixel intensities, it is useful to rewrite (9) introducing the functions

$$\text{sign}^+(\xi) := \begin{cases} 1 & \text{if } \xi > 0, \\ \frac{1}{2} & \text{if } \xi = 0, \\ 0 & \text{if } \xi < 0, \end{cases} \qquad \text{sign}^-(\xi) = 1 - \text{sign}^+(\xi),$$

so that Eq. (9) can be re-written as

$$L_w^{\text{KBR}}(x) = \sum_{y\in\Omega} w(x,y)\, f\left(\frac{I(x)}{I(y)}\right)\text{sign}^+(I(y)-I(x)) + \sum_{y\in\Omega} w(x,y)\,\text{sign}^-(I(y)-I(x)). \tag{10}$$

Thanks to Eq. (10) we can verify that KBR always increases brightness as the original Retinex implementation. In fact, since $f(r) \geq r$ for all $r \in (0,1]$, then $f\left(\frac{I(x)}{I(y)}\right) \geq \frac{I(x)}{I(y)} \geq I(x)$, so

$$L_w^{\text{KBR}}(x) \geq \sum_{y\in\Omega} w(x,y)\, I(x)\,\text{sign}^+(I(y)-I(x)) + \sum_{y\in\Omega} w(x,y)\,\text{sign}^-(I(y)-I(x)) \tag{11}$$

moreover, being $I(x) \leq 1$, we can write

$$L_w^{\mathrm{KBR}}(x) \geq \sum_{y \in \Omega} w(x,y)\, I(x)\, \mathrm{sign}^+(I(y) - I(x)) + \sum_{y \in \Omega} w(x,y)\, I(x)\, \mathrm{sign}^-(I(y) - I(x))$$

$$= I(x) \sum_{y \in \Omega} w(x,y)\, [\mathrm{sign}^+(I(y) - I(x)) + \mathrm{sign}^-(I(y) - I(x))]$$

$$= I(x) \sum_{y \in \Omega} w(x,y) = I(x), \tag{12}$$

having used the fact that the kernel is normalized. As in the original formulation, this property implies that over-exposed pictures could not be enhanced with Retinex unless we use a post-processing stage and that further iterations of Retinex keep on increasing the intensity until a white image is reached.

This equation of KBR does not correspond to the minimization of an energy functional. However, let us consider the sum of the function $f\left(\frac{I(x)}{I(y)}\right) \mathrm{sign}^+(I(y) - I(x))$ and of its the anti-symmetrized version on the region $\{x \in \Omega : I(y) \leq I(x)\}$, i.e.

$$L_w^{\mathrm{aKBR}}(x) = \sum_{y \in \Omega} w(x,y)\, f\left(\frac{I(x)}{I(y)}\right) \mathrm{sign}^+(I(y) - I(x))$$

$$- \sum_{y \in \Omega} w(x,y)\, f\left(\frac{I(y)}{I(x)}\right) \mathrm{sign}^-(I(y) - I(x)) \tag{13}$$

where aKBR stands for anti-symmetrized KBR.

In [3] it was proven that the right-hand side of the previous equation can be interpreted as the minimization of the energy functional given by:

$$C_w^f(I) = \sum_{x \in \Omega} \sum_{y \in \Omega} w(x,y) f\left(\frac{\min(I(x), I(y))}{\max(I(x), I(y))}\right). \tag{14}$$

Minimizing $C_w^f(I)$ corresponds to maximizing the contrast in a local (due to the presence of the weight w) and non linear way (due to the ratio and to the presence of f). This explained in a quantitative and qualitative way how and why the somewhat involved ratio-reset mechanism of Retinex allows for a *unilateral contrast enhancement*, always directed towards the highest intensity.

KBR, ACE, RACE and STRESS corrected this unilateral behavior. In [24] the spatially-based variational framework was translated into a wavelet-based setting.

4   Retinex: A 'melody' that Everyone Plays Differently

In image processing it is hard to find a model whose name has been interpreted in so many different ways as 'Retinex'. In this section, we present a synthetic description of the evolution of the Retinex interpretation.

Path-wise Retinex share a local WP nature and mostly differ from each other by the path geometry used to explore spatial locality: Land and McCann used piecewise linear paths in [19]. In [6], [21], and [30] those paths were substituted by double spirals, Brownian paths and traces of a specialized swarm of termites, respectively.

Center/surround Retinex are local GW algorithms originated from [18], where Land noticed that he could reproduce Mach bands originated by a spinning white square on a black background by using a different Retinex formulation. Precisely, for every image point, the intensity of the center x is replaced by the ratio between $I(x)$ and the average value of the surround, sampled with a density that decays as the inverse of the square distance from the center. Writing with L^{CS} this 'center/surround lightness', we have: $L^{CS}(x) = I(x)/<\{I(y), y \in \text{Surround}\}>$, where $< \cdot >$ represents the average operator. Comparing this last formula with (5), it can be seen that there is a fundamental difference between this formulation and the original one: there the ratio is performed over the pixel with highest intensity, while in this formulation it is implemented over the mean value of the surround. In practice, this last formulation can be seen as a gray-world method to remove the illuminant component of the image [5].

In 1997, Johbson, Rahman and Woodell [13] re-elaborated Land's idea presented in [18]: they worked with logarithmic data, approximating the average of the surround by convolving the image function I with a normalized kernel function F, usually a Gaussian. If we use again, for simplicity, the symbol L^{CS}, we can write this model as follows: $L^{CS}(x) = \log(I(x)) - \log((F*I)(x)), \forall x \in \Omega$.

Multilevel Retinex algorithms were pioneered by Frankle and McCann in [7] and further refined in [8]. In these works a multilevel version of the original local WP Retinex is presented, the authors abandon paths and consider a computation that takes into account all pixels. The input image is progressively sub-sampled averaging a number of pixel that grows as increasing powers of 2. On each sub-sample level a ratio-reset computation (without threshold) is operated a certain number of times, from the coarser sub-sample level to the finest one. Because of the sub-sampling, as we go far from the target pixel, we do not consider actual pixel values, but average values of macroareas of increasing size. A rigorous mathematical formulation of these multilevel algorithms is still lacking.

Based on this idea, Marini, Rizzi and De Carli [21] constructed a local WP multilevel version of Brownian path Retinex that reduced the amount of noise in the output images. A different multilevel proposal has been pointed out by Johbson, Rahman and Woodell in [12]: they introduced a certain number S of scales where performing the convolutions with normalized Gaussian functions F_s, $s = 1, \ldots, S$. Each scale is associated to a suitable weight w_s, which gives more importance to finer scales than to coarser ones.

Finally there are WP Retinex versions based on solving a Poisson equation. They rely on a work of Horn [11], in which he remarkably pointed out, for the first time, the need for a spatially isotropic two-dimensional version of Retinex. Horn considered, as Land, only Mondrian tableaux illuminated by a smoothly varying light. However, differently from Land, he explicitly tackled the ill-posed problem of inverting the equation $I_c(x) = S_c(x)L_c(x)$, $c \in \{R, G, B\}$, with respect to $S_c(x)$, the reflectance of the point x, knowing only the image intensity $I_c(x)$ and not the illumination $L_c(x)$. If we pass to logarithmic values, i.e. $\log I_c(x) = \log S_c(x) + \log L_c$ or, equivalently, $\log S_c(x) = \log I_c(x) - \log L_c$ and we apply a differential operator D to both sides, then $D(\log L_c(x))$ will be small but finite everywhere, while $D(\log S_c(x))$ will be different from zero only if x is close to sharp edges.

If we apply a threshold operator δ_T defined as follows:

$$\delta_T(s) = \begin{cases} s & \text{if } |s| > T \\ 0 & \text{elsewhere,} \end{cases}$$

for all $s \in \mathbb{R}$ and if the threshold $T > 0$ is small enough, then we obtain $D(\log S_c(x)) = \delta_T(D(\log I_c(x)))$. Horn insisted on the choice of the Laplacian for D instead of the gradient, arguing that first order derivatives are one-dimensional, while the second order derivatives involved in the Laplacian are isotropic and thus more suited for the topology of an image. By substituting D with the Laplacian operator Δ, the last formula becomes a Poisson equation:

$$\Delta(\log S_c(x)) = \delta_T(\Delta(\log I_c(x))), \tag{15}$$

whose solution allows to recover the logarithmic reflectance $\log S_c(x)$. It is clear that Horn's method is based on quite restrictive hypotheses: smoothness of illumination (violated by scenes with deep shadows, for instance) and a Mondrian-like world (violated each time edges are not sharp).

5   Mathematical Formalizations of Horn's Interpretation

Besides the variational framework described in Sect. 3, in the literature there exist alternative variational models of Retinex-like algorithms and also formalizations based on partial differential equations (PDE). The aim of this section is not to give an exhaustive list, rather to discuss the main features of the most famous alternative mathematical formalizations of Retinex-like algorithms present in the literature.

The first authors to embed a Retinex-like algorithm in a variational framework were Kimmel and colleagues in [14]. They did not considered the original Land's ratio-threshold-reset Retinex, but Horn's interpretation. In fact, they started from the logarithmic equation $\log I_c(x) = \log S_c(x) + \log L_c(x)$, $c \in \{R, G, B\}$ and tried to solve it with respect to $\log L_c(x)$ by imposing the hypothesis of smoothness on the illuminant part of the logarithmic image. Once obtained an estimation of the illumination, they could infer the reflectance information $S_c(x)$. This one then undergoes suitable transformations and gives an illuminant-invariant version of the original image.

It is important to underline a fundamental difference between this variational technique and the one presented in the previous sections: *here contrast enhancement of the original image* $\log I_c(x)$ *is obtained by decreasing the contrast of the illuminant image* $\log L_c(x)$. In fact, $\log I_c(x)$ is measured by the camera and so it is a fixed data, $\log L_c(x)$ is estimated by using a smoothness prior, thus the estimated reflectance $\log S_c(x) = \log I_c(x) - \log L_c(x)$, or $S_c(x) = I_c(x)/L_c(x)$ is forced to have a stronger contrast than the original image data. Instead, the variational principles previously discussed *act directly on the contrast of the original image*, without taking into account the separation between reflectance and illuminant and related approximations and priors.

Avoiding the subscript c, the functional proposed in [14], with the notations of this paper, can be expressed as follows:

$$E_{\alpha,\beta}(\log L) = \sum_{x\in\Omega}[|\nabla\log L(x)|^2 + \alpha(\log L(x) - \log I(x))^2 + \beta|\nabla(\log L(x) - \log I(x))|^2]$$
(16)

with the constraints $\log L(x) \geq \log I(x)$, because the reflectance $S(x)$ is always between 0 and 1, and the boundary condition $\langle\nabla\log L, n\rangle = 0$ on $\partial\Omega$, i.e. $\log L$ orthogonal to the normal n to the boundary $\partial\Omega$ of Ω.

The first term of the functional forces spatial smoothness on the illumination L. The authors chose that particular analytical form because the Euler-Lagrange equation associated to $\sum_{x\in\Omega}|\nabla\log L(x)|^2$ is the Laplace PDE $\Delta\log L = 0$, whose steepest descent solution is equivalent to a Gaussian smoothing. The second penalty term forces a proximity between $\log L$ and $\log I$, so that their difference $\log S$, the logarithmic reflectance, tends to 0, i.e. the reflectance R tends to 1, or white. The authors declare that the principal objective of this term is to regularize the problem, so that it is better conditioned in view of a numerical solution and they set the constant α to a very small value not to force too much $\log L$ towards $\log I$. The third term represents a Bayesian penalty, which forces reflectance gradients to be smooth. The authors declared to have introduced it to force R to be visually pleasing, without abrupt variations.

Morel, Petro and Sbert [22] analyzed Land's original Retinex model [17] without the reset mechanism. They showed that, if the Retinex paths are interpreted as symmetric random walks, then Retinex is equivalent to the following Neumann problem for a Poisson equation:

$$\begin{cases} -\Delta L(x) = F(x) & x \in \Omega \\ \frac{\partial L(x)}{\partial n} = 0 & x \in \partial\Omega, \end{cases}$$

where F is a suitable scalar field, see [22] page 2830.

Let us now consider the algorithm STRESS. We recall that the basic information needed by STRESS is given by the two envelope functions $E_{\min}$ and $E_{\max}$ which, in the original formulation, are computed through the same random spray technique of RSR [26]. To avoid the typical noise problems related to this technique, in [31], the authors proposed to compute the envelope functions via the minimization of a functional based on the total variation, instead of using the random spray technique. For this reason the corresponding algorithm is called STRETV and corresponds to the minimization of the following functional for E (in this case E denotes the envelope and not the energy functional):

$$\sum_{x \in \Omega} \left[|\nabla E(x)| + \frac{\lambda}{2} |E(x) - I(x)|^2 \right] \tag{17}$$

subjected to $E(x) \geq I(x)$ to compute $E_{\max}$ and to $E(x) \leq I(x)$ for $E_{\min}$.

The minimization of the first (total variation) term, assures the spatial smoothness of the envelope functions, the second term is a fidelity term used not to depart too much from the original image values. The authors declare that the coefficient λ must be $\ll 1$ for good results. The authors do not specify if they consider a spatial kernel to localize their computation or not.

The last variational formalization that we discuss here is that presented in [20] relative to the termite Retinex. Here an energy functional is taken into account to determine the geometry of the paths used by Retinex. Fixed a pixel $x \in \Omega$, the authors search for the path $\gamma : [0,1] \to \Omega$, $\gamma(0) = x$, the minimizes the energy functional defined by:

$$E(\gamma) = \int_0^1 \left[\frac{1}{1 + (D^2 - \|x - \gamma(s)\|^2)\|\nabla I(\gamma(s))\|^2} + \theta(\gamma(s)) \right] ds, \tag{18}$$

where D is the diagonal of Ω and 1 is introduced to avoid singularities in the case the denominator is 0. The paths that minimize $E(\gamma)$ are those which balance the fact to remain as close to x as possible and, simultaneously, to explore image areas with high values of the gradient. Both features maximize the denominator of the first term. If x lies in an area with a high density of edges, γ will not go too far from x, instead, if x lies in a rather homogeneous area, γ will be forced to explore the image points far away from x to find the important edge information. $\theta(\gamma(s))$, the so-called 'poison term', is set to zero at the beginning, and it increases each time a path has been traveled, to prevent from exploring the same image area all the time. Once a set of N path has been selected, the intensity $I(x)$ of the pixel x in each separate chromatic channel is modified with the Retinex formula 5.

6   Conclusions

In the past fifteen years, variational methods have been used to formalize color correction algorithms. This permitted to point out similarities and differences among several models that were difficult to detect just looking at their direct equations. In this paper we have described, in a self-contained way, both the direct and the variational versions of several color enhancement algorithms inspired by the seminal Retinex theory of color vision. A particular emphasis has been put in highlighting the very different variational formulations of the original Retinex of Land and McCann and those referring to Horn's interpretation, which are often misleadingly mixed in the literature.

References

1. Banić, N., Lončarić, S.: Light random sprays Retinex: exploiting the noisy illumination estimation. IEEE Signal Process. Lett. **20**, 1240–1243 (2013)
2. Banić, N., Lončarić, S.: Smart light random memory sprays Retinex: a fast Retinex implementation for high-quality brightness adjustment and color correction. JOSA A **32**(11), 2136–2147 (2015)
3. Bertalmío, M., Caselles, V., Provenzi, E.: Issues about the Retinex theory and contrast enhancement. Int. J. Comput. Vis. **83**, 101–119 (2009)
4. Bertalmío, M., Caselles, V., Provenzi, E., Rizzi, A.: Perceptual color correction through variational techniques. IEEE Trans. Image Process. **16**, 1058–1072 (2007)
5. Buchsbaum, G.: A spatial processor model for object colour perception. J. Frankl. Inst. **310**, 337–350 (1980)
6. Cooper, T.J., Baqai, F.A.: Analysis and extensions of the Frankle-McCann Retinex algorithm. J. Electron. Imaging **13**, 85–92 (2004)
7. Frankle, J., McCann, J.J.: Method and apparatus for lightness imaging. US Patent 4,348,336 (1983)
8. Funt, B., Ciurea, F., McCann, J.J.: Retinex in MATLAB. J. Electron. Imaging **13**(1), 48–57 (2004)
9. Gianini, G., Manenti, A., Rizzi, A.: QBRIX: a quantile-based approach to Retinex. JOSA A **31**(12), 2663–2673 (2014)
10. Gianini, G., Rizzi, A., Damiani, E.: A Retinex model based on absorbing Markov chains. Inf. Sci. **327**(10), 149–174 (2016)
11. Horn, B.: Determining lightness from an image. Comput. Graph. Image Process. **3**, 277–299 (1974)
12. Jobson, D., Rahman, Z., Woodell, G.: A multiscale Retinex for bridging the gap between color images and the human observation of scenes. IEEE Trans. Image Process. **6**(7), 965–976 (1997)
13. Jobson, D., Rahman, Z., Woodell, G.: Properties and performance of a center/surround Retinex. IEEE Trans. image process. **6**(3), 451–462 (1997)
14. Kimmel, R., Elad, M., Shaked, D., Keshet, R., Sobel, I.: A variational framework for Retinex. Int. J. Comput. Vis. **52**, 07–23 (2003)
15. Kolås, Ø., Farup, I., Rizzi, A.: Spatio-temporal Retinex-inspired envelope with stochastic sampling: a framework for spatial color algorithms. J. Imaging Sci. Technol. **55**(4), 40503-1 (2011)
16. von Kries, J.: Chromatic adaptation. Festschrift der Albrecht-Ludwigs-Universität, pp. 145–158 (1902)
17. Land, E.: The Retinex. Am. Sci. **52**(2), 247–264 (1964)
18. Land, E.: An alternative technique for the computation of the designator in the Retinex theory of color vision. Proc. Acad. Sci. **83**, 3078–3080 (1986)
19. Land, E., McCann, J.: Lightness and Retinex theory. J. Opt. Soc. Am. **61**(1), 1–11 (1971)
20. Lecca, M., Rizzi, A., Gianini, G.: Energy-driven path search for termite Retinex. JOSA A **33**(1), 31–39 (2016)
21. Marini, D., Rizzi, A.: A computational approach to color adaptation effects. Image Vis. Comput. **18**, 1005–1014 (2000)
22. Morel, J., Petro, A., Sbert, C.: A PDE formalization of Retinex theory. IEEE Trans. Image Process. **19**(11), 2825–2837 (2010)
23. Palma-Amestoy, R., Provenzi, E., Bertalmío, M., Caselles, V.: A perceptually inspired variational framework for color enhancement. IEEE Trans. Pattern Anal. Mach. Intell. **31**(3), 458–474 (2009)

24. Provenzi, E., Caselles, V.: A wavelet perspective on variational perceptually-inspired color enhancement. IJCV **106**, 153–171 (2014)
25. Provenzi, E., De Carli, L., Rizzi, A., Marini, D.: Mathematical definition and analysis of the Retinex algorithm. J. Opt. Soc. Am. A **22**(12), 2613–2621 (2005)
26. Provenzi, E., Fierro, M., Rizzi, A., De Carli, L., Gadia, D., Marini, D.: Random spray Retinex: a new Retinex implementation to investigate the local properties of the model. IEEE Trans. Image Process. **16**, 162–171 (2007)
27. Provenzi, E., Gatta, C., Fierro, M., Rizzi, A.: Spatially variant white patch and gray world method for color image enhancement driven by local contrast. IEEE Trans. Pattern Anal. Mach. Intell. **30**, 1757 (2008)
28. Rizzi, A., Gatta, C., Marini, D.: A new algorithm for unsupervised global and local color correction. Pattern Recogn. Lett. **24**, 1663–1677 (2003)
29. Sapiro, G., Caselles, V.: Histogram modification via differential equations. J. Differ. Equ. **135**, 238–266 (1997)
30. Simone, G., Audino, G., Farup, I., Albregtsen, F., Rizzi, A.: Termite Retinex: a new implementation based on a colony of intelligent agents. J. Electron. Imaging **23**(1), 013006 (2014)
31. Simone, G., Farup, I.: Spatio-temporal Retinex-like envelope with total variation. In: Conference on Colour in Graphics, Imaging, and Vision, vol. 2012, pp. 176–181. Society for Imaging Science and Technology (2012)

T-Rex: A Milano Retinex Implementation Based on Intensity Thresholding

Michela Lecca[1]([⊠]), Carla M. Modena[1], and Alessandro Rizzi[2]

[1] Center for Information and Communication Technology, Technologies of Vision, Fondazione Bruno Kessler, 38123 Trento, Italy
{lecca,modena}@fbk.eu
[2] Dipartimento di Informatica, Universitá degli Studi di Milano, 20135 Milano, Italy
alessandro.rizzi@unimi.it

Abstract. We present T-Rex (from the words *Threshold* and *REtineX*), a new Milano Retinex implementation, based on an intensity thresholding strategy. Like all the algorithms of the Retinex family, T-Rex takes as input a color image and processes its channels separately. For each channel, T-Rex re-scales the chromatic intensity of each pixel x by the average of a set of pixels whose intensity, weighted by a function of the distance from x, exceeds the intensity of x. The main novelty of this approach is devised by the usage of the pixel intensity as a threshold for selecting the pixels relevant to Retinex. Here we show an application of T-Rex as image enhancer, showing that, as a member of the Retinex family, it equalizes the dynamic range of any input picture and makes its details more evident.

1   Introduction

The Retinex theory [7] provides a computational model to estimate the human color sensation. It is based on the empirical evidence that, in the human vision system, the color signal is firstly processed separately by the retina photoreceptors, and then by the cortex. This latter re-works the color information taking into account the spatial arrangement of the other colors present in the observed scene. Therefore, the color sensation we derive when observing a point, depends not only on the photometric properties of that point but also on those of the surrounding regions.

According to this principle, the Retinex algorithm estimates the color sensation from a color digital picture as follows. The chromatic channels of the image are processed separately. For each channel, the chromatic intensity of each pixel x is re-scaled by a *local white reference*. This is an intensity level obtained by re-working the intensities of the pixels in a neighborhood of x, with the general prescription that the intensity of the pixels closer to x influences more the color sensation at x than the intensity of the pixels far away [2,12,19]. This procedure outputs an enhanced color image with better visible details. This image, that we refer to as *filtered*, differs from the actual color sensation in a set of pre- or

© Springer International Publishing AG 2017
S. Bianco et al. (Eds.): CCIW 2017, LNCS 10213, pp. 68–79, 2017.
DOI: 10.1007/978-3-319-56010-6_6

post- LUT calibrations, that adjust the color gamut of the device in order to estimate the actual color sensation [20].

Two key points of Retinex implementation are (*i*) the definition of the *sampling figure*, i.e. of the neighboring pixels relevant to color sensation, and (*ii*) the determination of the local white reference. Despite the importance of these issues, the original Retinex description does not provide specific details about them. This has led to many different Retinex implementations [12,13,21]. For instance, the original Retinex algorithm [7] scans the neighborhood of any pixel x by a set of paths, traveling randomly over the image and ending at x: the sampling figure at x is the union set of the pixels lying along these paths. Each chromatic intensity at x in the filtered image is obtained by computing, over each path, the product of the intensity ratios of adjacent pixels, and then by averaging these products over the number of paths (division by zero is avoided). This path-based approach has been adopted by many subsequent Retinex implementations, e.g. [5,9,14,15,22,23], which mainly impose some constraints on the path shape in order to improve the spatial exploration of the image. The methods in [1,3,6,8,16] define the neighborhood of any pixel x as a *spray*, i.e. a set of pixels distributed around x with radial density. They compute the local white reference through the equation of the so-called Milano Retinex algorithms [10,11], mathematically formalized in [15] and implemented with sprays in [16]: for each x, a set of sprays is generated and the local white reference is computed as the mean value of the maximum intensity over the sprays, averaged over the number of sprays.

In this work, we present T-Rex, a novel method belonging to the Milano Retinex family [17]. In T-Rex, for each image channel, the sampling figure of any image pixel x is the set of the image pixels whose intensity value exceeds the intensity value of x. The local white reference is obtained by averaging the intensity of the sampled pixels, weighted by their spatial distance from x. The intensity at x acts as a *threshold* for defining the pixels relevant for estimating the color sensation. The name T-Rex just comes from the keywords *Threshold* and *REtineX*, which characterize this approach.

The main novelty of T-Rex is the definition of a sampling figure specific for each pixel and based on a *self-regulating intensity threshold*. T-Rex shares with the spray based methods [1,3,4,6,8,16] the idea of defining the neighborhood of any pixel x as a 2D set of points and to compute the local white reference by reworking pixel intensities greater than the intensity at x. Nevertheless, differently from these spray based approaches, which are characterized by a radial distribution around the center, the sampling figure of T-Rex at any pixel x does not have any specific geometric structure: it may strongly vary from pixel to pixel, according to the intensity at x and to the spatial weights. Unlike the methods employing a random sampling, such as the original Retinex implementation, the path-based methods mentioned above, and many spray-based approaches, the exploration of the image performed by T-Rex is deterministic. This is an advantage because the random sampling may introduce in the filtered image chromatic noise, that is usually removed a posteriori or mitigated by repeating many times the image sampling and then averaging the results. Finally, in T-Rex, the sampled intensities do not correspond to intensity extrema over the pixel neighborhood (as in [1,3,6,8,16]), and their selection is performed in an unsupervised manner, without requiring the user to input any threshold on intensity (as is done instead in [4]).

In this work, we do not consider any pre- or post- LUT calibration, and thus we employ and evaluate T-Rex as an image enhancer, not as a model of human vision [20]. The experiments, carried out on real world color pictures, show that, as a member of the family of Milano Retinex algorithms, T-Rex improves the readability of images captured with unbalanced exposures, increasing their brightness and contrast and equalizing their dynamic range.

The rest of the paper is organized as follows: Sect. 2 describes T-Rex in details; Sect. 3 reports the experiments, and Sect. 4 outlines our conclusions and future work.

2 T-Rex

Let us introduce the notation used hereafter. We indicate a RGB image by $\overline{I}$ and any chromatic channel of $\overline{I}$ by I. For numerical reasons, we rescale the intensity values of I over $[0, 1]$. Moreover, in order to avoid division by zero, for any $x \in S$ such that $I(x) = 0$ we set $I(x) := 10^{-6}$. Then, we represent I as a function $I : S \to (0, 1]$, where S denotes the image support, i.e. the set of pixels coordinates, and $|S|$ is the size of S. We denote the filtered version of $\overline{I}$ by $\overline{L}$ and any chromatic channel of $\overline{L}$ by L.

T-Rex takes as input a RGB image $\overline{I}$. According to the Retinex theory, it processes its channels independently. For each channel I and for each pixel $x \in S$, T-Rex implements the following operations:

1. **Modeling the color spatial interaction**: T-Rex defines the function $v_x : S \to \mathbf{R}$ such that

$$v_x(y) = I(y) \exp[-\lambda d(x, y)^2] \tag{1}$$

   where $d(x, y)$ is the Euclidean spatial distance between x and y, normalized in order to range over $[0, 1]$. Precisely:

$$d(x, y) = \frac{\| x - y \|}{D} \tag{2}$$

   where D is the length of the diagonal of S. The parameter λ is a positive real number, weighting the importance of the distance term versus the intensity. As suggested by the subscript, v_x varies from pixel to pixel. It is introduced to model the spatial interaction among colors. The multiplicative term $\exp[-\lambda d(x, y)^2]$ acts as a penalty term: the intensity of the pixels close to x are weighted more than that of the pixels further from x. This is in line with the studies in [12], reporting about the influence of the distance on the color sensation.

2. **Defining the Sampling Figure**: T-Rex scans the neighborhood of x to find out the sampling figure $N(x)$ at x. We refer to x as the *center* of $N(x)$. Precisely, a pixel y of S belongs to $N(x)$ iff

(a) $v_x(y) > I(x)$

(b) $d(x, y) = \min\{d(u, x) : u \in S \text{ and } v_x(u) = v_x(y)\}$.

The sampling figure $N(x)$ is defined by thresholding the function v_x by the intensity value $I(x)$ (condition (a)). The pixels of $N(x)$ are the closest to x among the pixels satisfying the condition in (a) (condition (b)). The size and the geometry of $N(x)$ depends on the parameter λ. Differently from the sampling set of the path-based approaches, which is simply connected, the sampling figure of $N(x)$ is usually not connected. Moreover, $N(x)$ may also be empty. In this case, the local white reference is $I(x)$, as explained next.

3. **Computing the Local White Reference**: the local white reference is computed as follows:

$$w(x) = \begin{cases} \frac{1}{\sum_{y \in N(x)} \exp[-\lambda d(x,y)^2]} \sum_{y \subset N(x)} v_x(y) & \text{if } N(x) \neq \emptyset \\ I(x) & \text{otherwise} \end{cases} \quad (3)$$

and the $L(x)$ is given by

$$L(x) = \frac{I(x)}{w(x)}. \quad (4)$$

From Eq. (3), we have that the value of $w(x)$ is always greater or equal than $I(x)$. This is in line with the principles of the Milano Retinex algorithms, that select as local white reference an intensity values equal to or greater than $I(x)$.

Fig. 1. On top: the green circles indicate the pixels of the figure sampling at the pixel highlighted on a grey level image by the red circle for $\lambda = 0.5$ (left) and $\lambda = 1.5$ (right). On bottom: the corresponding T-Rex filtered images. (Color figure online)

The T-Rex algorithm requires as input an image and a value for the parameters λ. When $\lambda = 0$, no penalty is applied to the image intensities and the sampling figure of T-Rex includes all the image pixels with intensity higher than $I(x)$. When $\lambda \to +\infty$, $v_x(y)$ tends to zero, thus if $I(x) \neq 0$, the set $N(x)$ is empty, and $w(x) = I(x)$. Therefore, different values of λ produce different figure samplings and lead to different color filtering (see for instance Fig. 1).

3 Experiments

In Subsect. 3.1 we define the measures used for evaluating the T-Rex performance, while in Subsect. 3.2 we describe the dataset used in the experiments and the results, including also a comparison with two other Milano Retinex approaches.

3.1 Evaluation Measures

We evaluate the performance of T-Rex in terms of image enhancement. We observe that in the literature, there are not agreed measures for assessing the quality and/or the accuracy of image enhancement algorithms. In this framework, we consider three measures, already employed for analysing Retinex performance, e.g. [8,9]. These measures are suitable to describe numerically the variations of visual features related to the *readability* of an image: its brightness, its details and its dynamic range. These features are modified by Retinex, that usually increases the brightness and the details visibility (i.e. the contrast) and equalizes the dynamic range of the input image.

Given a color image $\overline{I}$ with support S, we compute its brightness $B_{\overline{I}}$ as the 1-channel image defined on S such that

$$B_{\overline{I}}(x) = \frac{1}{3} \sum_{i=1}^{3} I_i(x).$$

Here we do not normalize their intensity values over $[0, 1]$: the variability range of I_i ($1 \leq i \leq 3$) is thus the discrete set $\{0, \ldots, 255\}$. For each pixel x, the value $B_{\overline{I}}(x)$ is cast to an integer number between 0 and 255.

The three measures employed for evaluating the image enhancement performance of T-Rex are:

1. *Mean brightness* f_0: it is the average of the values of $B_{\overline{I}}$ over the number of pixels:

$$f_0 = \frac{1}{|S|} \sum_{x \in S} B_{\overline{I}}(x). \tag{5}$$

2. *Multi-resolution Contrast* f_1: this measure, introduced in [18], is defined by building up a pyramid of K (>0) images $B_1, \ldots, B_K$, where $B_1 = B_{\overline{I}}$, and, for each $1 < k \leq K$, B_k is computed by rescaling B_{k-1} by 0.5. The value of f_1 is then obtained by the following steps:

- Computing the mean local contrast on each pyramid image: for each $k \in \{1, \ldots, K\}$, for each x in the support S_k of B_k, we compute the local contrast

$$c_k(x) = \frac{1}{8} \sum_{u \in \mathcal{N}(x)} |B_k(u) - B_k(x)| \qquad (6)$$

where $\mathcal{N}(x)$ indicates the 3×3 window centered at x. Then, we compute the mean value

$$\bar{c}_k = \frac{1}{|S_k|} \sum_{x \in S_k} c_k(x), \qquad (7)$$

where $|S_k|$ is the cardinality of S_k;
- Computing the multi-resolution contrast on the pyramid: we average of the values $\bar{c}_k$'s over the number of images B_k's:

$$f_1 = \frac{1}{K} \sum_{k=1}^{K} \bar{c}_k. \qquad (8)$$

3. *Histogram Flatness f_2*: it measures how much the dynamic range of the image brightness has been stretched by the T-Rex filtering. Let H be the histogram of $B_{\overline{I}}$ normalized in order to range over $[0, 1]$; let U be the discrete uniform probability density function defined over the set $\{0, \ldots, 255\}$. The histogram flatness is the L^1 distance between H and U, i.e.

$$f_2 = \frac{1}{255} \sum_{b=0}^{255} |H(b) - U(b)|. \qquad (9)$$

An image enhancer "usually" increases the values of f_0 and f_1, while decreases the value of f_2. We have quoted the word *usually* because the amount of the variations of f_0, f_1, f_2 depends on the input image. In particular, we observe that the increment of f_0 and f_1 and the reduction of f_2 are more evident when the input image is dark and its details are poorly visible, than when the image is already clear.

3.2   Results

For our experiments, we consider a dataset of 20 real-world color pictures, depicting both indoor and outdoor environments. Despite its small size, this dataset is of interest because its images have been mainly captured under bad illuminant conditions, so they appear quite dark and with poorly visible details. Moreover, they display dark and bright regions with different size, proportion, and location. These cues make this image set suitable to evaluate the performance of T-Rex as image enhancer, also from a qualitative point of view. Some examples are shown in Fig. 2.

Table 1 reports the evaluation measures when no filtering is applied (NONE) and when T-Rex (with $\lambda = 1.0$) is applied. In addition, this table also reports

Fig. 2. Some images used for evaluating T-Rex performance.

Table 1. Evaluation of T-Rex performance in comparison with RSR-P and QBRIX (local and global).

Algorithm	f_0	f_1	$f_2[\times 10^{-3}]$
NONE	50.02	12.81	4.53
T-Rex	79.39	17.52	3.44
RSR-P	70.05	17.55	3.63
L-QBRIX	88.48	21.84	2.93
G-QBRIX	77.22	19.15	3.46

the performance of two other Milano Retinex algorithms (QBRIX [4] and RSR-P [3]). We have chosen to compare these approaches with T-Rex because they present some similarities with T-Rex. Precisely: (a) QBRIX and RSR-P are Milano Retinex implementations; (b) as Milano Retinex implementations, they normalize the intensity $I(x)$ of any pixel x with an intensity level greater than $I(x)$; (c) like T-Rex, they are deterministic approaches.

Both QBRIX and RSR-P derive from the algorithm Random Spray Retinex (RSR) [16], that works as follows. Given an image channel I and a pixel x, RSR re-scales the intensity $I(x)$ with the maximum intensity over a *spray*, i.e. a cloud of n pixels randomly sampled around x with radial density. In order to remove - as much as possible - the chromatic noise due to the random sampling, many sprays are generated and the final value $L(x)$ is obtained by averaging the contribution from each spray. The size n of the spray and the number N of sprays are input by the user. When n equals the number of image pixel, RSR behaves like the scale-by-max algorithm.

QBRIX proposes an approximated, probabilistic version of RSR. It is based on the observation that the colors rarely occurring in the image do not influence the color sensation, thus they can be ignored by the color filtering process. There are two implementations of QBRIX. The first one is a *global* filter (G-QBRIX): for each channel, it re-scales the chromatic intensity of each pixel by a local white reference I_Q, corresponding to a quantile Q_G of the probability density function (pdf) of the intensities of that channel. The local white reference is thus the same for each pixel, determined by the value Q_G input by the user. The second implementation is a *local* filter (L-QBRIX): in this case, the local white reference I_L depends on the pixel, and it corresponds to a quantile Q_L of the pdf of the channel intensities, weighted by a function accounting for their spatial arrangement in the image. The value Q_L is fixed by the user.

RSR-P re-writes the random sampling procedure of RSR in a deterministic, noise free, population based approach. In RSR, the local white reference is the average of the maximum intensities selected from random sprays. In RSR-P, the same local white reference is determined by re-working suitable quantities from the pdf of the chromatic intensities, without performing any random sampling. These quantities are basically related to the probability that a given pixel has the maximum intensity over a set of n samples where, as in RSR, n is an user input. Differently from the RSR approximation provided by QBRIX, RSR-P is an exact mapping of RSR into a population based approach. In particular, when $N \to +\infty$, RSR and RSR-P yield the same results.

T-Rex enhances the brightness and the contrast of the input pictures, producing higher values of f_0 and f_1, while it equalizes the brightness histogram, so that the value of f_2 decreases. The algorithms QBRIX and RSR-P exhibit a similar behaviour. In these experiments, the quantiles Q_G and Q_L are set up to 0.99, while in RSR-P n has been set up to 250.

Figure 3 shows some visual examples of color filtering produced by T-Rex, RSR-P, QBRIX (local and global).

On average, the T-Rex outputs are close to those obtained by RSR-P and G-QBRIX. The highest (lowest, resp.) values of brightness and contrast (flatness, resp.) are obtained by L-QBRIX: this is because L-QBRIX weights the contribution of the distance versus the intensity much more than the other algorithms. Precisely, in the pdf computation performed by L-QBRIX, for any pixel x, the intensity value $I(y)$ of any image pixel $y \neq x$ is weighted by the quantity

$$\left[\frac{\| x - y \|}{D} \right]^{-\alpha}$$

where D is the length of the image support diagonal, while α determines the metric adopted for modeling the spatial interaction among color, and here $\alpha = 2$.

The spatial weight introduced in L-QBRIX is similar to that expressed by the term $\exp[-\lambda d(x, y)^2]$ in the Eq. (1) of T-Rex. We observe that a high value of λ (and a low value of α in L-QBRIX) may produce a loss of the image local details, and even introduce artifacts: in particular, as already mentioned in Sect. 2, for $\lambda \to +\infty$, the local reference is the pixel intensity itself, so that the final lightness is a white image. This is illustrated in Fig. 4, showing a gray level image and its T-Rex filtered versions for increasing values of λ: for $\lambda > 1.00$, an over-enhanced region is visible on the upper left corner of the image. This effect is emphasized in the color version of this image (see first row in Fig. 5). In general, the value of λ giving a "satisfactory" output in terms of image enhancement depends on the input image. For instance, for the image shown in the second row of Fig. 5,

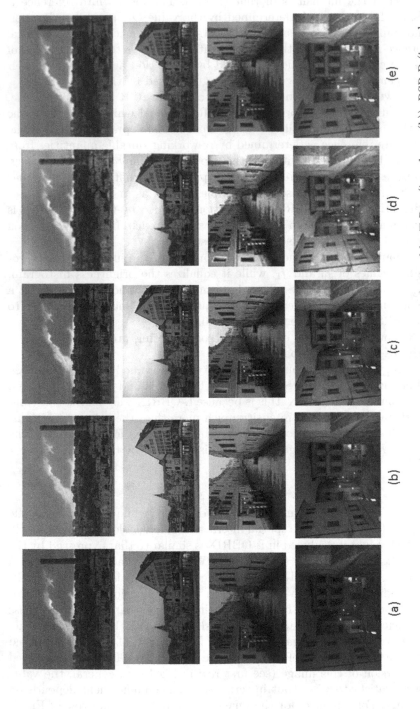

Fig. 3. Some input images (in column (a)) and their color filtered versions obtained by T-Rex (in column (b)), RSR-P (in column (c)), L-QBRIX (in column (d)), and G-QBRIX (in column (e)).

Fig. 4. In clock-wise order: an input image and its T-Rex filtered versions with $\lambda = 0.50, 0.75, 1.00, 1.25, 1.50, 2.00, 2.25, 2.50$.

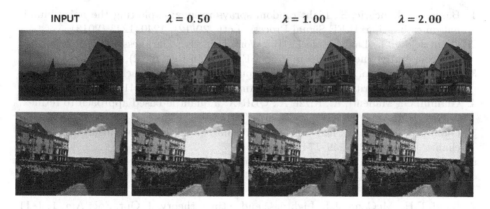

Fig. 5. Two input images and their T-Rex filtered versions for $\lambda = 0, 50, 1.00, 2.00$. For the input image in the first row, varying the λ parameter yields very different outputs. This does not happen for the input image in the second row.

all the values $\lambda = 0.5, 1.0, 2.0$ produce good results. The dependency of the parameter tuning on the image content, at a first quick analysis can appear as an unwanted characteristic, but on the contrary it is a positive one. First, it is exactly a characteristic of the HVS, that has no fixed response and thus cannot be modeled as a static filter, second, due to the image variability and complexity, a fixed thresholding usually means good results only for a subset of the input images. This characteristic is in fact common for the whole spatial color algorithms family [20].

4 Conclusions

In this paper, we have presented T-Rex, a novel, deterministic Milano Retinex implementation. It is based on the definition of a sampling figure through a self-adaptive intensity thresholding strategy. The experiments, conducted on a set of real-world color pictures, captured with unbalanced exposure, show that, in agreement with the principles of the Retinex theory, T-Rex works as image enhancer: it equalizes the dynamic range of the input image and improves the visibility of its details. The experiments also show that the final output depends on the value of λ. For instance, a very large value of λ may produce a loss of the image details. In the current implementation of T-Rex, the value of λ is input by the user. Our future work will address a more detailed analysis of the dependence of the T-Rex output on λ, and the development of a technique for an unsupervised estimation of a variability range of λ suitable for image enhancement.

References

1. Banic, N., Loncaric, S.: Light random sprays retinex: exploiting the noisy illumination estimation. IEEE Signal Process. Lett. **20**(12), 1240–1243 (2013)
2. Creutzfeldt, O., Lange-Malecki, B., Wortmann, K.: Darkness induction, retinex and cooperative mechanisms in vision. Exp. Brain Res. **67**(2), 270–283 (1987)
3. Gianini, G., Lecca, M., Rizzi, A.: A population based approach to point-sampling spatial color algorithms. J. Opt. Soc. Am. A **33**(12), 2396–2413 (2016)
4. Gianini, G., Manenti, A., Rizzi, A.: QBRIX: a quantile-based approach to retinex. J. Opt. Soc. Am. A **31**(12), 2663–2673 (2014)
5. Gianini, G., Rizzi, A., Damiani, E.: A retinex model based on absorbing markov chains. Inf. Sci. **327**, 149–174 (2016)
6. Kolås, Ø., Farup, I., Rizzi, A.: Spatio-temporal retinex-inspired envelope with stochastic sampling: a framework for spatial color algorithms. J. Imaging Sci. Technol. **55**(4), 40503-1–40503-10 (2011)
7. Land, E.H., McCann, J.J.: Lightness and retinex theory. J. Opt. Soc. Am. **1**, 1–11 (1971)
8. Lecca, M., Rizzi, A.: Tuning the locality of filtering with a spatially weighted implementation of random spray retinex. JOSA A **32**(10), 1876–1887 (2015)
9. Lecca, M., Rizzi, A., Gianini, G.: Energy-driven path search for termite retinex. JOSA A **33**(1), 31–39 (2016)
10. Marini, D., Rizzi, A.: Color constancy and optical illusions: a computer simulation with Retinex theory. In: ICIAP 1993 7th International Conference on Image Analysis and Processing, Monopoli, Italy, pp. 657–660 (1993)
11. Marini, D., Rizzi, A.: A computational approach to color adaptation effects. Image Vis. Comput. **18**(13), 1005–1014 (2000)

12. McCann, J., Rizzi, A.: The Art and Science of HDR Imaging. Wiley, New York (2011)

13. McCann, J.J., (ed.): Special session on retinex at 40. J. Electron. Imaging **13**(1), 6–145 (2004)

14. Montagna, R., Finlayson, G.D.: Constrained Pseudo-Brownian motion and its application to image enhancement. J. Opt. Soc. Am. A **28**(8), 1677–1688 (2011)

15. Provenzi, E., De Carli, E., Rizzi, A., Marini, D.: Mathematical definition and analysis of the retinex algorithm. J. Opt. Soc. Am. A Opt. Image Sci. Vis. **22**(12), 2613–2621 (2005)

16. Provenzi, E., Fierro, M., Rizzi, A., De Carli, L., Gadia, D., Marini, D.: Random spray retinex: a new retinex implementation to investigate the local properties of the model. Trans. Img. Proc. **16**(1), 162–171 (2007)

17. Rizzi, A.: Designator retinex, milano retinex and the locality issue. Electron. Imaging **2016**(6), 1–5 (2016)

18. Rizzi, A., Algeri, T., Medeghini, G., Marini, D.: A proposal for contrast measure in digital images. In: CGIV 2004 - Second European Conference on Color in Graphics, Imaging, and Vision and Sixth International Symposium on Multispectral Color Science, Aachen, pp. 187–192 (2004)

19. Rizzi, A., McCann, J.J.: Computer algorithms that mimic human vision must respond to the spatial content in images. In: SPIE Electronic Imaging & Signal Processing (2007)

20. Rizzi, A., McCann, J.J.: On the behavior of spatial models of color. In: Proceedings of SPIE - The International Society for Optical Engineering, San Jose, CA, vol. 6493 (2007)

21. Rizzi, A., McCann, J.J., Bertalmio, M., Gianini, G. (eds.): Retinex at 50. Special issue on Journal of Electronic Imaging, vol. 26(3) (2017)

22. Simone, G., Audino, G., Farup, I., Albregtsen, F., Rizzi, A.: Termite retinex: a new implementation based on a colony of intelligent agents. J. Electron. Imaging **23**(1), 013006 (2014)

23. Simone, G., Cordone, R., Lecca, M., Serapioni, R.P.: On edge-aware path-based color spatial sampling for retinex: from termite retinex to light-energy driven termite retinex. J. Electron. Imaging **26**(3), 031203 (2017). Special Issue, Retinex at 50

Color Image Quality

iFAS: Image Fidelity Assessment

B. Ortiz-Jaramillo$^{(\boxtimes)}$, L. Platisa, and W. Philips

TELIN-IPI-imec, Ghent University, Ghent, Belgium
bortiz@telin.ugent.be

Abstract. image Fidelity Assessment (iFAS) is a software tool designed to assist image quality researchers providing easy access to a range of state-of-the-art measures which can be applied on a single pair of images and/or in a full database, as well as intuitive visualizations that aid data analysis, e.g., images and histograms of pixel-wise image differences, scatter plots and correlation analysis. The software is freely available for non-commercial use.

1 Introduction

Nowadays, multiple image processing areas have shown the necessity of *fidelity assessment*, i.e., objective assessment of the perceived differences between a reference (source) and a test image sample [21,22,25]. Specifically, the objective of fidelity assessment is to quantify the visual differences between a given test sample and the corresponding reference [26,31]. The nature of the visual difference changes from application to application. For instance, *color differences* [8,15,21] are important in applications dealing with color quantization [2], color mapping [19]. In medical applications, image fidelity is often based on quantifying the visibility between a structure of interest such a vessel and its surrounding anatomical background [22,23]. In this case, the feature of interest is *image contrast* and thus the image with the highest fidelity is the one with the lowest contrast difference relative to the reference [22]. In the textile industry, the evaluation is based on the lifetime and appearance retention which is closely related to the surface appearance of the textile material. For example, appearance retention of textile floor coverings is based on measuring fine changes in *texture* between the reference (new carpet) and test sample ("used" carpet) [1]. Therefore, the task of fidelity assessment is to measure visual differences between the two images of the textile material under inspection considering texture as the feature of interest [25].

Clearly there is a need for application-specific or even application-tailored quality assessment rather than a one-size-fits-all solution. While many candidate quality measures already exist, testing them and identifying the best ones for a given use case is far from easy. The corresponding algorithms are often not publicly available and/or they are implemented for non free platforms, e.g., Matlab. Thus, it often takes a considerable amount of time and effort to even prepare the test environment for benchmarking, validation and/or developing. Consequently, many papers and reports do not present extensive comparative

© Springer International Publishing AG 2017
S. Bianco et al. (Eds.): CCIW 2017, LNCS 10213, pp. 83–94, 2017.
DOI: 10.1007/978-3-319-56010-6_7

analyses including many methods, databases and/or features. Thereby, many of the state-of-the-art algorithms are not tested and only a very limited subset of conventional fidelity indexes (which are more easily accessible) are in common use, e.g., the Peak Signal to Noise Ratio (PSNR), CIEDE2000 [14], Structural Similarity index (SSIM) [43].

To the best of our knowledge, only few related software packages are available and they have limited features/functionality and/or are not freely available. For instance, Krasula et al. proposed one Matlab based interface for testing 8 well known image quality measures [13]. However, the interface is not easy to extend for new fidelity measures and it has no mechanism of benchmarking, correlation analysis or model analysis. Murthy and Karam developed IVQUEST which is the most complete open source user interface for subjective and objective image quality evaluation as well as correlation analysis [20]. Additionally, the interface allows easy extensions by writing pieces of Matlab code. However, the benchmarking and correlation analysis are limited to global correlation analysis. Also, the interface is limited to 15 general image quality measures. Therefore, even though these platforms are very useful to test image quality measures, they are very limited in scope and available methods. Furthermore, they have been implemented in Matlab, which is a non-free platform.

With this work, we seek to alleviate such problems. We present an user friendly tool iFAS: (image Fidelity Assessment) and make it freely available for non-commercial use.[1] In the alpha version, iFAS includes eight color difference measures [21], six texture analysis algorithm [25], six contrast measures [22] and six image quality measures for objective fidelity assessment. iFAS possess a range of common mechanisms for image fidelity assessment including computation of fidelity measures on a single pair of images and/or in a full database, visualization of pixel-wise image differences and histogram of the image differences, scatter plots and correlation analysis between human scores and objective measures. This software takes away the interaction of the user with the code, reducing the time spent on the fidelity assessment phase of benchmarking of image processing algorithms. iFAS is developed using Python, GTK+3 [37] and other freely available third party tools which are easily installed (see iFAS manual for the list of used tools and installation guide). Users interested in including their own features to iFAS, can do so in the Python [28] programming language, which is very easy to use and very suitable for even for inexperienced programming. Furthermore, Python includes a wide variety of third party tools targeting specific research problems. Therefore, Python is a good alternative for developers on seek of freely available research tools compared with Matlab and more complex programming languages such as C or C++ [33].

This paper is organized as follows. In Sect. 2, we describe the key functionality of the software for data analysis. Thereafter, we show in Sect. 3 two use case scenarios of iFAS functionality. Finally, in Sect. 4, we draw conclusions and propose future work.

---

[1] iFAS and its manual will be available at http://telin.ugent.be/~bortiz/ifas after publication of this work.

2   Software Description

Figure 1 (left) shows the simplified iFAS structure. iFAS structure is based on Python and depends on GTK+3 as well ass third party libraries for the implementation of the user interface, the mathematical models and plugins. Plugins are Python modules for extending the functionality of iFAS by adding them to the configuration file. The third party libraries are Scipy 0.17.0 together with its core packages, particularly, NumPy 1.11.0, Matplotlib 1.5.1, pandas 0.17.1, nose 1.3.7, Cython 0.25.1 and Scikits 0.12.3 [41]; PIL 1.1.7 [38]; PyGObject (aka PyGI) 3.20.0 [36]; Pycairo 1.10.0 [39]; PyWavelets 0.5.0 [40].

Figure 1 (right) shows a screenshot of iFAS user interface. The interface displays seven main components: (1) the main menu, (2) the reference image, (3) the test image, (4) the pixel-wise difference image, (5) the histogram of the pixel-wise difference image, (6) the scatter plot of the MOS versus the measure values for a given reference, and (7) the results pane. iFAS includes the following types of analysis:

- Single Source - Single Sample: this type of analysis computes the selected fidelity measures between one reference image and one corresponding test image, i.e., the current images displayed on the user interface (images are selected using a file chooser).
- Single Source - Multiple Sample: this type of analysis computes the fidelity measures selected by the user between one reference image and a number of corresponding test images as specified by the user using a file chooser.
- Multiple Source - Multiple Sample: this type of analysis computes the fidelity measures selected by the user between a number of reference images and a number of test images. This is like executing a Single Source - Multiple Sample several times using different reference images and their corresponding test samples. Note that, the user has the responsibility to make sure that the test/distorted images correspond in scene to the reference/source images.

iFAS includes a detailed help document (included with iFAS files) with all the instructions for the recommended use of iFAS for maximum utility. Also, every analysis can be saved and loaded for further analysis avoiding unnecessary multiple computations of the same data. iFAS also allows visualization of scatter plots between two fidelity measures or a fidelity measure and subjective scores for a given source image. That is, it is possible to visualize the relationship between measures for a specific image content.

Additionally, iFAS computes and displays in the results pane the following correlation indexes typically used as performance indicators of fidelity measures: Pearson Coefficient of Correlation (PCC) [3], Spearman Rank Order Coefficient of Correlation (SROCC), [4], Kendall Rank Coefficient of Correlation (KRCC) [5] and Coefficient of Correlation of Distances (CCD) [32]. Note that these indexes are computed with the values currently displayed on the scatter plot component (only for Single Source - Multiple Sample and Multiple Source - Multiple Sample).

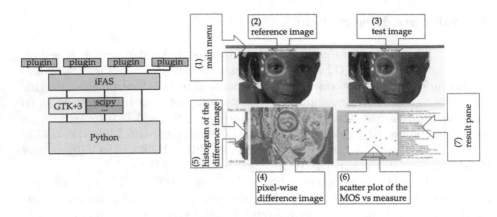

Fig. 1. (Left) Simplified iFAS structure and (right) iFAS main window screenshot.

In general, many fidelity measures pre-compute pixel-wise differences and later compute a global fidelity measure from descriptive statistics such as mean, maximum, standard deviation, among others. Therefore, iFAS also displays this intermediate result with the purpose of providing local information about the fidelity measure behavior. In the cases where the fidelity measure is based on features, iFAS computes those features on local windows and then displays the difference of the local computations (pixel-wise image difference). The pixel-wise image difference has associated a 255 bin histogram. Also, the color map of the difference image is included as scale of the histogram with its respective maximum and minimum values. This histogram can be considered to select the appropriated statistics for computing the global fidelity index during a fidelity measure design process.

3   How Do I Use iFAS?

In this section we describe and explore two use case scenarios with the purpose of showing the advanced functionality of iFAS for the analysis of objective fidelity measures. The use cases are the benchmarking of 6 texture extraction algorithms on a textile floor covering database and the evaluation of 3 color correction algorithms for multiview imaging using 2 image color difference measures. The set of methods used for the analysis in this section were selected from References [21,24,25]

3.1   Application 1: Textile Quality Assessment

Although this is not completely a fidelity task, it can be solved by assuming that the reference sample and test samples are given as pictures of the original and test carpets (original carpet after some wear degree), respectively. That is, two image of textures displaying a fine change of global texture between

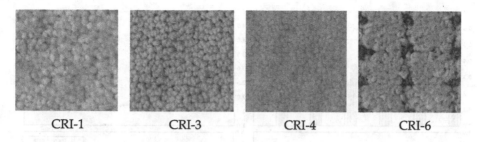

CRI-1   CRI-3   CRI-4   CRI-6

Fig. 2. Cutouts of textures evaluated from the CRI standard.

them [25]. Therefore, the fidelity task is to evaluate those fine changes of global texture between the two texture samples. iFAS can help in such a task in two ways. First in the benchmarking of possible candidate methods for measuring fine changes of global texture. The benchmarking consists of global correlation comparison, correlation analysis per reference sample. And second by finding an appropriated model using regression analysis for measuring the wear degree of future samples.

As use case, we use a set of images composed of scanned printed images from the CRI (the Carpet and Rug Institute) standard photo set [35]. The set of references (see Fig. 2) include texture types with loop (CRI-3), cut (CRI-1 and CRI-4) and tip-sheared (CRI-6) (cf. [25] for more details about carpet wear assessment). We use 32 different reference samples extracted using random cutouts (8 per CRI reference). For instance, CRI-1 has 8 cutouts representing the reference samples. Similarly, for each sample belonging to a specific wear label, we extract 2 cutouts, i.e., 16 test samples per reference. That is a total of 512 test ((16 cutout test samples per reference) × (32 reference samples)) and 32 reference samples (8 cutouts × 4 CRI samples).

Here, we benchmark 6 different texture analysis algorithms (see [25] and the related original publications for details on the algorithms and the parameter selection): power spectrum (PS) [44], Gabor filtering (GF) [18], Pseudo Wigner distribution (PWD) [7], autoregressive (AR) models [12], Local Binary Patterns (LBP) [17] and Gaussian Markov Random Fields (GMRF).

These measures are available in the alpha version of iFAS (the best performing texture analysis algorithms according to [25]). After computing the texture difference between samples using iFAS Multiple Source - Multiple Sample analysis, the global correlation is computed between the obtained data and the wear labels included with the CRI database. The global correlation analysis is very useful to identify the performance of the tested methods across different content, in this case CRI standard type, i.e., it helps to identify if only one model is necessary to perform the task.

The Fig. 3 (top left) shows the figure saved in eps format using iFAS software corresponding to the bar plot for global correlation analysis. The software also shows on the result pane the correlation values and the best performing methods according those values, e.g.,

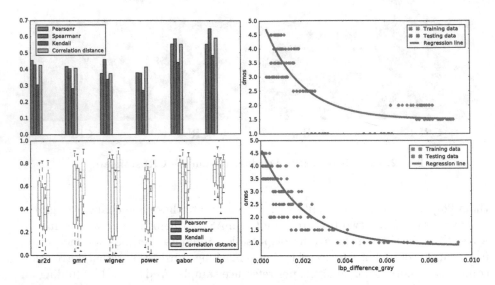

Fig. 3. Image saved in eps format using iFAS. (top left) bar plot global correlation, (bottom left) box plot of the performance per individual reference, (top right) model for CRI-3 and (bottom right) model for CRI-6

Best according to Pearsonr is gabor_features_difference: 0.55339
Best according to Spearmanr is lbp_difference_gray: 0.64797
Best according to Kendalltau is lbp_difference_gray: 0.48265
Best according to Correlation distance is lbp_difference: 0.48265

These are not very high correlations to build a model. However, since the texture patterns for the carpets are standardized on the textile industry, it is also valid to build a model per each CRI standard type [25]. Therefore, box plot analysis is very useful for identifying how well the measures perform if the content remains the same (in this case the CRI standard type). iFAS also possess this kind of analysis. Figure 3 (bottom left) shows the box plot for the considered texture features per reference sample resulting from iFAS. Additionally, the software provides on the result pane a pairwise comparison between the methods with the purpose of identifying if there are statistically significant differences in terms of the performance between the tested methods (cf. Garcia et al. [9] for details about pairwise comparisons). Also, the software presents the best performing methods according to the pairwise comparisons (here only the example for CCD):

Best method from pairwise comparison between Correlation distance
lbp and it is statistically significant better than:
ar2d p_value: 0.00000
gmrf p_value: 0.00014
power p_value: 0.00000

This indicates that LBP technique is the best performing method and it is statistically better than AR, GMRF and PS. Also, LBP performs equally or better than GF and PWD. Therefore, further analysis is performed using LBP, i.e., the modeling of each individual CRI standard type.

After selecting the best performing method, it is very useful to build a model with the current data to be used on new samples. In iFAS, we simulate that processes by building models using the current samples. The user needs to select among the samples the training and test subsets. Here we show on Fig. 3 (top-bottom right) the regression analysis for two CRI standard types, CRI-3 and CRI-6, respectively. The dots are the actual data and the line shows the fitted model using the training data. The parameters of the model are shown in the result pane together with the correlation coefficients for the model. This information comes handy for estimating the performance of the model for external use of the built models. We show as example the information displayed on the result pane for the CRI-6 type:

The optimal parameters for function	Kendalltau: 0.75341
a0 + exp(a1 * x + a2)	Correlation distance: 0.85311
a0: 0.87016	Testing values:
a1: -494.71609	Pearsonr: 0.89326
a2: 1.33914	Spearmanr: 0.90553
Training values:	Kendalltau: 0.77235
Pearsonr: 0.88335	Correlation distance: 0.88545
Spearmanr: 0.87563	

In summary, the methods presented in this section illustrate how using iFAS in a very simple fashion could support a very complicated process such as benchmarking. Additionally, the software provides enough information and an internal decision making systems to suggest the best performing methods according to each analysis, e.g., the pairwise comparisons and the global correlation analysis.

3.2 Application 2: Evaluating Color Correction in Mutliview Images

In multiview imaging, color correction is used to eliminate color inconsistencies between views. Here, the color correction algorithm modifies the color of one of the views ("color-processed" image) such that the color is visually equivalent to the other view ("reference" image). To select this algorithm, the correlation analysis does not provide the type of information we are looking for (the best color correction algorithm). Therefore, iFAS can help us instead by plotting in boxes and analyzing the color difference values between the images with the purpose of examining if there are color corrections with lower color differences. iFAS performs the analysis based on pairwise comparisons and on the assumption that "higher is better." Therefore, iFAS transforms to similarities (s) from the original differences (d) with the formula $s = 1 - d/\max_d$. Here, $\max_d$ is the maximum over the whole set of computed/available differences.

As use case, we use a database containing 144 images: 3 references × 4 distortion types × 4 distortion levels × 3 color correction algorithms. The 3 reference images were selected from SRTMI database [45]. These images are color manipulated with the purpose of simulating the multiview environment using the following types of color disparities: change of the color contrast on one of the color channels and black level shift (4 different distortion levels for each distortion type). Afterwards the following color correction algorithms are independently applied on each color processed image: color correction based on transferring statistical properties (CCstats) [30] on CIELab color appearance model [34], color correction based on point correspondences (CCpoint) [16] and color correction based on region correspondences (CCregion) [15].

The 144 images are compared in terms of color by using the following color difference measures: the CIEDE2000 formula [14] and the just noticeable CD measure [6]. These two measures and the spatial extension of the CIEDE2000 formula [46], the colorfulness difference [10], the color extension of the SSIM index [42], the chroma spread and extreme [27], the image CD measure based on image appearance models [11] and the adaptive spatio-chromatic image difference [29] presented in [21] are available in the color difference module of the alpha version of iFAS.

iFAS computes the color differences in the database and performs pairwise comparisons using the obtained differences per source content (reference sample). Figure 4 (top left-right and bottom left) show the result from such an analysis performed by iFAS. Also, iFAS provides the best performing methods according to the pairwise comparisons (we show as example the information displayed on the result pane for one of the references comparing the 3 color correction algorithms):

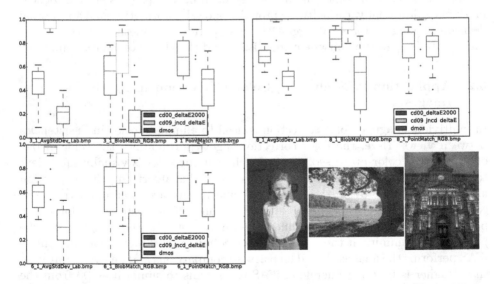

Fig. 4. Image saved in eps format using iFAS. (top left) bar plot color differences for SRTMI 3, (bottom left) bar plot color differences for SRTMI 6, (top right) bar plot color differences for SRTMI 8, and (bottom right) the three SRTMI reference samples from left to right SRTMI 3, 6 and 8, respectively.

Best method from pairwise comparison between cd00_deltaE2000
8_1_PointMatch_RGB.bmp and it's statistically better than:
Best method from pairwise comparison between cd09_jncd_deltaE
8_1_PointMatch_RGB.bmp and it is statistically better than:
8_1_BlobMatch_RGB.bmp p_value: 0.01333
Best method from pairwise comparison between dmos
8_1_PointMatch_RGB.bmp and it is statistically better than:
8_1_AvgStdDev_Lab.bmp p_value: 0.00146
8_1_BlobMatch_RGB.bmp p_value: 0.00801

That is, according to the subjective scores (in the result pane named dmos) the best performing color correction algorithm is the method CCpoint, named PointMatch_RGB on the result pane. Note that the CIEDE2000 formula does not find any statistical significant difference and the just noticeable CD measure finds only statistical differences between CCpoint and CCregion but not between CCpoint and CCstats. However, humans find differences between CCpoint and CCstats as well as between CCpoint and CCregion. Therefore, the best performing color correction algorithm is CCpoint because it produces the minimum perceived differences according to the subjective scores and the just noticeable CD measure. To finally decide, it is possible to refine the selection by looking at the reference, test and difference images displayed in the main window of iFAS.

4   Conclusions and Future Work

We presented an open source software tool designed to assist researchers, engineers and other users in the process of image fidelity assessment, named image Fidelity Assessment (iFAS). iFAS provides the following basic image fidelity assessment tools: computation of fidelity measures on a single pair of images and/or in a full database, visualization of pixel-wise image differences and histogram of the image differences, scatter plots and correlation analysis between human scores and objective measures. The correlation analysis is performed based on the most recent tools for the process of image fidelity assessment evaluation such as global correlation comparison, pairwise comparisons of correlations per reference, regression analysis and model building.

Since iFAS has been developed on Python, it can be easily modifiable. Therefore, iFAS can be extended to a wide range of applications, including benchmarking of image compression algorithms or related application, e.g., color correction, color quantization, contrast assessment, among others; model building for textile wear assessment, e.g., carpet wear assessment, wrinkles analysis, pilling, among others; image content analysis and model building based on content; and many more fidelity assessment related applications. In this paper we illustrated the use of iFAS in 2 use cases.

Since the methods are implemented with the authors' interpretation (no code was available on Python), it is necessary to perform an evaluation of the methods included with iFAS to guarantee the same output as proposed by the original authors. As future work we propose to implement one extension to perform subjective testing (using the side by side and image difference visualization capabilities offered by iFAS) and add a functionality for MOS analysis on new data sets. Furthermore, the addition of mechanism for image content analysis remains as future update. Also, as future work it will be important to keep the code uptodate by incorporating the new upcoming methods and keeping a bug free code.

Acknowledgments. This work was performed within the PANORAMA project (cofunded by grants from Belgium, Italy, France, the Netherlands, the United Kingdom, and the ENIAC Joint Undertaking).

References

1. Aibara, T., Mabuchi, T., Ohue, K.: Automatic evaluation of the appearance of seam puckers on suits. In: Proceedings of the SPIE, Machine Vision Applications in Industrial Inspection VII, vol. 3652, pp. 1–4 (1999)
2. Brun, L., Tremeau, A.: Color quantization. In: Digital Color Imaging Handbook. CRC Press (2002)
3. Chen, P., Popovich, P.: The pearson product-moment correlation. In: Correlation: Parametric and Nonparametric Measures. Sage Publications (2002)
4. Chen, P., Popovich, P.: Special cases of Pearson's R. In: Correlation: Parametric and Nonparametric Measures. Sage Publications (2002)
5. Chen, P., Popovich, P.: Other useful nonparametric correlations. In: Correlation: Parametric and Nonparametric Measures. Sage Publications (2002)
6. Chou, C., Liu, K.: A fidelity metric for assessing visual quality of color images. In: Proceedings of the International Conference on Computer Communications and Networks, pp. 1154–1159 (2007)
7. Cristóbal, G., Hormigo, J.: Texture segmentation through eigen-analysis of the pseudo-wigner distribution. Pattern Recognit. Lett. **20**, 337–345 (1999)
8. Fezza, S., Larabi, M., Faraoun, K.: Feature-based color correction of multiview video for coding and rendering enhancement. IEEE Trans. Circ. Syst. Video Technol. **24**, 1486–1498 (2014)
9. Garcia, S., Fernandez, A., Luengo, J., Herrara, F.: Advanced nonparametric tests for multiple comparisons in the design of experiments in computational intelligence and data mining: experimental analysis of power. J. Inf. Sci. **180**, 2044–2064 (2010)
10. Hasler, D., Susstrunk, S.: Measuring colourfulness in natural images. In: Proceedings of the IS & T/SPIE Electronic Imaging: Human Vision and Electronic Imaging VIII, pp. 87–95 (2003)
11. Johnson, G.: Using color appearance in image quality metrics. In: Proceedings of the International Workshop on Video Processing and Quality Metrics for Consumer Electronics, pp. 1–4 (2006)
12. Joshi, M., Bartakke, P., Sutaone, M.: Texture representation using autoregressive models. In: Proceedings of the International Conference on Advances in Computational Tools for Engineering Applications, pp. 386–390 (2009)
13. Krasula, L., Klima, M., Rogard, E., Jeanblanc, E.: Matlab-based applications for image processing and image quality assessment part i: software description. In: Proceedings of Czech and Slovak Technical Universities, pp. 1009–1015 (2011)
14. Luo, M., Cui, G., Rigg, B.: The development of the CIE 2000 colour-difference formula: CIEDE2000. Color Res. Appl. **26**, 340–350 (2001)

15. Ly, D., Beucher, S., Bilodeau, M., Persa, S., Damstra, K., Pot, R., Rooy, J.: Automatic color correction: region-based approach and performance evaluation using full reference metrics. J. Electron. Imaging **24**(061207), 1–9 (2015)

16. Ly, D., Beucher, S., Bilodeau, M.: Color correction through region matching leveraged by point correspondences. In: Proceedings of the IEEE International Conference on Image Processing, pp. 640–644 (2014)

17. Maenpaa, T.: The local binary pattern approach to texture analysis: extensions and applications. Ph.D. thesis, University of Oulu (2003)

18. Manjunath, B., Ma, W.: Texture features for browsing and retrieval of image data. IEEE Trans. Pattern Anal. Mach. Intell. **18**, 837–842 (1996)

19. Morovic, J.: Desired color reproduction properties and their evaluation. In: Color Gamut Mapping. Wiley (2008)

20. Murthy, A., Karam, L.: A matlab-based framework for image and video quality evaluation. In: Proceedings of the Conference on Quality of Multimedia Experience, pp. 242–247 (2010)

21. Ortiz-Jaramillo, B., Kumcu, A., Philips, W.: Evaluating color difference measures in images. In: Proceedings of the Conference on Quality of Multimedia Experience, pp. 1–6 (2016)

22. Ortiz-Jaramillo, B., Kumcu, A., Platisa, L., Philips, W.: Computing contrast ratio in images using local content information. In: Proceedings of the Symposium on Signal Processing, Images and Computer Vision, pp. 1–6 (2015)

23. Ortiz-Jaramillo, B., Kumcu, A., Platisa, L., Philips, W.: Computing contrast ratio in medical images using local content information. In: Proceedings of the Medical Image Perception Conference, p. 34 (2015)

24. Ortiz-Jaramillo, B., Nino-Castaneda, J., Platisa, L., Philips, W.: Content-aware objective video quality assessment. J. Electron. Imaging **25**(013011), 1–16 (2016)

25. Ortiz-Jaramillo, B., Orjuela-Vargas, S., Van-Langenhove, L., Castellanos-Dominguez, C., Philips, W.: Reviewing, selecting and evaluating features in distinguishing fine changes of global texture. Pattern Anal. Appl. **17**, 1–15 (2014)

26. Pappas, T., Safranek, R., Chen, J.: Perceptual criteria for image quality evaluation. In: Handbook of Image and Video Processing. Academic Press (2010)

27. Pinson, M., Wolf, S.: A new standardized method for objectively measuring video quality. IEEE Trans. Broadcast. **50**, 312–322 (2004)

28. Python: Python software foundation (2016). https://www.python.org/

29. Rajashekar, U., Wang, Z., Simoncelli, E.: Quantifying color image distortions based on adaptive spatio-chromatic signal decompositions. In: Proceedings of the IEEE International Conference on Image Processing, pp. 2213–2216 (2009)

30. Reinhard, E., Ashikhmin, M., Gooch, B., Shirley, P.: Color transfer between images. IEEE Comput. Graph. Appl. **21**, 34–41 (2001)

31. Silverstein, D., Farrell, J.: The relationship between image fidelity and image quality. In: Proceedings of the International Conference on Image Processing, pp. 881–884 (1996)

32. Székely, G., Rizzo, M., Bakirov, N.: Measuring and testing dependence by correlation of distances. Ann. Stat. **35**, 2769–2794 (2007)

33. C&C++: C programming and C++ programming (2016). http://www.cprogramming.com/

34. CIE: Colorimetry - part 4: CIE 1976 L*a*b* colour space (1976). https://www.iso.org/obp/ui/#iso:std:iso:11664:-4:ed-1:v1:en

35. CRI: CRI test method - 101 (2016). www.carpet-rug.org/Documents/Technical_Bulletins/0307_CRI_TM_101.aspx

36. GLib: Python Bindings for GLib/GObject/GIO/GTK+ (2016). https://wiki.gnome.org/Projects/PyGObject
37. GTK+: The GTK+ project (2016). https://www.gtk.org/
38. PIL: Python Imaging Library (PIL) (2016). http://www.pythonware.com/products/pil/
39. Pycairo: Cairo graphics library (2016). https://cairographics.org/pycairo/
40. PyWavelets: PyWavelets - Wavelet Transforms in Python (2016). https://pywavelets.readthedocs.io/en/latest/
41. SciPy (2016). https://www.scipy.org/
42. Toet, A., Lucassen, M.: A new universal colour image fidelity metric. Displays 24, 197–207 (2003)
43. Wang, Z., Bovik, A., Sheikh, H., Simoncelli, E.: Image quality assessment: from error visibility to structural similarity. IEEE Trans. Image Process. 13, 600–612 (2004)
44. Weszka, J., Dyer, C., Rosenfeld, A.: A comparative study of texture measures for terrain classification. IEEE Trans. Syst. Man Cybern. 6, 269–285 (1976)
45. Yeganeh, H., Wang, Z.: Subject-rated image database of tone-mapped images (2013). https://ece.uwaterloo.ca/~z70wang/research/tmqi/
46. Zhang, X., Wandell, B.: A spatial extension of CIELAB for digital color-image reproduction. J. Soc. Inf. Disp. 5, 61–63 (1997)

A Multidistortion Database for Image Quality

Silvia Corchs[✉] and Francesca Gasparini

Dipartimento di Informatica, Sistemistica e Comunicazione,
University of Milano-Bicocca, Viale Sarca 336, 20126 Milano, Italy
{corchs,gasparini}@disco.unimib.it

Abstract. In this paper we introduce a multidistortion database, where 10 pristine color images have been simultaneously distorted by two types of distortions: blur and JPEG and noise and JPEG. The two datasets consist of respectively 350 and 400 images, and have been subjectively evaluated within two psycho-physical experiments. We here also propose two no reference multidistortion metrics, one for each of the two datasets, as linear combinations of no reference single distortion ones. The optimized weights of the combinations are obtained using particle swarm optimization. The different combinations proposed show good performance when correlated with the subjective scores of the multidistortion database.

Keywords: Image quality assessment · Multidistortion database · No reference metrics · Blur · Noise · JPEG

1 Introduction

Image quality studies mainly focus on images corrupted by single distortions. However, consumer images suffer in general of more than one distortion simultaneously due to the different process that take place within their production flow (acquisition, compression, transmission, etc.), [1]. The vast majority of No Reference (NR) metrics have been developed to measure single distortions. In the last years, some NR metrics have also addressed multiple artifacts, most commonly blur and noise [2–5]. Also general purpose (or blind) NR metrics have been proposed that do not aim to detect specific types of distortion. These last methods approach the Image Quality Assessment (IQA) as a classification and regression problem in which the regressors/classifiers are trained using specific features obtained from natural-scene-statistics [6,7]. Following Mittal et al. [6] it is also possible to individuate two subcategories of blind models: the Opinion-Aware (OA) models, that have to be trained on a database of human rated distorted images and associated subjective opinion scores, and the Opinion-Unaware (OU) ones. An overview of the different objective and subjective IQA methods can be found in the review articles [8,9]. It is well known that any objective metric must be validated with respect to user judgments: subjective tests are at the base of objective quality metrics benchmarking and IQA databases

© Springer International Publishing AG 2017
S. Bianco et al. (Eds.): CCIW 2017, LNCS 10213, pp. 95–104, 2017.
DOI: 10.1007/978-3-319-56010-6_8

serve as ground-truth information for evaluating IQA algorithms. In general, the available databases contain images corrupted by only one of several possible distortions.

Considering multiply distorted images, Jayaraman et al. [10] have presented the LIVE-MD database. As most publicly available image quality databases, it has been created under highly controlled conditions by introducing graded simulated distortions onto high-quality images. Two scenarios are considered in LIVE-MD: images first blurred and then JPEG compressed (part 1), and images first blurred and then corrupted by white Gaussian noise (part 2). Two psycho-physical experiments have been conducted by the authors to collect the subjective data. Recently, Ghadiyaram and Bovik [11] presented the LIVE In the Wild Image Quality Challenge Database, that contains diverse authentic multi-distorted images. The images were collected without artificially introducing any distortion beyond those occurring during capture, processing, and storage by a users device. The authors conducted a very large-scale image quality assessment subjective implementing an online crowdsourcing system.

To compare objective and subjective results different performance measures are used. The Video Quality Experts Group (VQEG) [12] recommends three performance criteria for the metrics: prediction accuracy, prediction monotonicity and prediction consistency with respect to the subjective assessments. The prediction accuracy is quantified by the Pearson Correlation Coefficient (PCC) and the Root Mean Squared Error (RMSE). The Spearman Rank Order Correlation Coefficient (SROCC) measures the prediction monotonicity of a metric and the Outlier Ratio (OR) the prediction consistency. Before computing these correlation coefficients, it is customary to apply a nonlinear transformation to the predicted scores so as to bring the predictions on the same scale as the subjective scores in order to obtain a linear relationship between the predictions and the opinion scores. The VQEG suggests the use of logistic or polynomial functions. The parameters of these functions are chosen to minimize the MSE between the set of subjective values (of a particular database) and the corresponding set of transformed predicted values.

In this paper we present the Multiple Distorted IVL Database (MD-IVL). The database is composed of two parts: the MD-IVL-BJ that contains color images first blurred and then JPEG compressed, and the MD-IVL-NJ that contains color images corrupted by Gaussian noise and then JPEG compressed. Subjective studies were conducted on this database to obtain human judgments for the multiply distorted images and the corresponding psycho-visual data were collected.

We here propose to define NR-MD-metrics as linear combination of NR state-of-the-art metrics specifically designed for single distortions (blockiness, sharpness and noise). In particular we propose two different linear combinations, one for the MD-IVL-NJ dataset and the second for the MD-IVL-BJ one. The weighting coefficients of the linear combinations are obtained using a particle swarm optimization method [13]. We used half of the data to evaluate the coefficients and the remaining half to test the correlation performance of the proposed metrics for each of the two parts of the MD-IVL database. We also compare the performance of the two linear combination proposals with two competitive blind models available in the literature: an OA model, BRISQUE [6] and an OU model, NIQE [7]. Moreover we test the linear combination proposed for the MD-IVL-BJ on part 1 of the LIVE-MD, as it is composed by images suffering the same type of distortions.

2   The MD-IVL Database

The MD-IVL database originates from 10 reference color images of the SD-IVL dataset [14]. The images of 886×591 pixels (15×10 cm at 150 dpi, typical printing parameters for natural photos) are chosen to sample different contents both in terms of low level features (frequencies, colors) and higher ones (face, buildings, close-up, outdoor, landscape). The corresponding thumbnails are shown in Fig. 1.

Fig. 1. The 10 reference images of the SD-IVL database.

Starting from these images we have generated:

- A database MD-IVL-BJ of 350 blur plus JPEG distorted images. These distorted images have been generated as follows: each of the reference images has been corrupted with seven levels of Gaussian blur corresponding to standard deviations of 0.001, 0.66, 1.33, 2, 2.66, 3.33 and 4. Each of the 70 blurred images has been further corrupted with four levels of JPEG compression corresponding to Q-factor values of 100, 50, 30, 20 and 10.
- A database MD-IVL-NJ of 400 noise plus JPEG distorted images. These distorted images have been generated as follows: each of the 10 reference images has been corrupted with ten levels of Gaussian noise corresponding to 1, 2, 3, 4, 5, 6, 8, 10, 12 and 14 gray levels of standard deviation on the luminance channel. Each of the 100 noisy images has been further processed by 4 different levels of JPEG compression, corresponding to Q factor values of 100, 50, 30, and 10.

As an example, we show in Fig. 2 the most distorted blur-JPEG and noise-JPEG images.

Fig. 2. (a) A reference image from SD-IVL database and its most multiply distorted versions for blur-JPEG, and noise-JPEG.

For collecting the subjective data, we have adopted a Single Stimulus method (SS) [15], where all the images are individually shown. The observers were asked to rate the images within a continuous scale from 0 (Worst quality) to 100 (Best quality). The experiments were performed following the recommendations in ITU [15].

The subjective study was conducted in two parts: each of the databases (MD-IVL-BJ and MD-IVL-NJ) has been assessed separately. Ideally, all images in a subjective QA study should be evaluated in only one session. However, it is recommended a maximun duration of 30 min for each experimental session [15]. Therefore, to assess the entire MD-IVL database we have conducted the experiments in several sessions using different sets of images. Each session consists of approximately 100 images (chosen so as to span all the distortion range) and has been evaluated by 12 observers.

Mean subjective scores were computed for each observer as follows. The raw, subjective score r_{ij} for the i-th subject ($i = 1, \dots S$, with $S =$ number of subjects) and j-th image I_j ($j = 1, \dots N$, with $N =$ number of dataset images) was converted into its corresponding Z-score as follows:

$$z_{ij} = \frac{r_{ij} - \bar{r}_i}{\sigma_i} \tag{1}$$

where $\bar{r}_i$ and σ_i are the mean and the standard deviation of the subjective scores over all images assessed by the $i - th$ subject.

Data were cleaned using a simple outlier detection algorithm. A score for an image was considered to be an outlier if it fell outside an interval of two standard deviations width about the mean score for that image across all subjects.

The remaining Z-scores, were then averaged across subjects to yield the Mean Opinion Scores y_j for each image j:

$$y_j = \frac{1}{S} \sum_{i=1}^{S} z_{ij} \tag{2}$$

The MD-IVL database is available at: http://www.ivl.disco.unimib.it/activities/imagequality/.

3   Objective Data

The subjective scores described in Sect. 2, collected in terms of MOS can be correlated with different NR metrics, using a logistic function.

Denoting by y_i the MOS value of the $i-th$ image of the database ($i = 1, ... N$ with N the total number of distorted images) and by x_i the corresponding objective metric value, the logistic transformation reads:

$$f(x) = \frac{\alpha}{1 + exp(\beta(x - \gamma))} + \delta \tag{3}$$

where the parameters α, β, γ and δ are chosen to minimize the mean square error between the subjective scores $\{y_i\}$ and the predicted ones $\{f(x_i)\}$.

3.1   NR Metrics for Single Distortion

Among the many distortion-specific NR metrics available in the literature, we have here chosen those that highly correlate with the corresponding subjective data in the case of blur, noise and JPEG artifacts. The metrics considered in this work are:

- M1: The bluriness metric by Marziliano et al. [16]. An edge detector is applied and for pixels corresponding to an edge location, the start and end positions of the edge are defined as the local extrema locations closest to the edge. The edge width is measured and identified as the local blur measure. Global blur obtained by averaging the local blur values over all edge locations.
- M2: metric Q by Zhu and Milanfar [5]. This measure is correlated with the noise level, sharpness and intensity contrast of the structured regions of an image. Its value drops if the variance of noise rises, and/or if the image content becomes blurry.
- M3: The JPEG-blockiness metric by Wu and Yuen [17], named Generalized Block-edge Impairment. It is the most well known metric in the spatial domain. It measures the blockiness separately in horizontal and vertical direction, after which the two directions are combined into a single quality value.
- M4: The JPEG-blockiness specific metric by Wang et al. [18]. It is formulated in the frequency domain and models the blocky image as a non-blocky image interfered with a pure blocky signal.
- M5: The noise metric by Immerkaer [19]. It estimates the standard deviation of Additive White Gaussian Noise from a single image using a Laplacian mask filtering approach.

All of these metrics show high performance in terms of PCC when correlated with well known databases of single distorted images like LIVE [20], CSIQ [21] and SD-IVL [14] among others.

3.2 NR Metric for the Multiply Distorted Images: Our Proposal

We here propose a MD-NR metric as a linear combination (LC) of single distortion NR metrics:

$$LC(I_j) = \sum_{k=1}^{K} a_k \times M_k(I_j) \tag{4}$$

where I_j is the $j - th$ image of the dataset ($j = 1, \ldots N$), and M_k is the $k - th$ single distortion NR metric among the K considered ones. In this paper we propose to set the weighting coefficients $\{a_k\}$ using a population based stochastic optimization technique, called Particle Swarm Optimization (PSO) [22,23] that optimally fits the subjective scores of a proper MD database.

Recalling that one of the criteria recommended by the VQEG [12] to evaluate the performance of the regressed metrics is the PCC, we have chosen the following objective function r to be maximized within the PSO:

$$r(P) = \frac{\sum_{i=1}^{N}(f(LC_i) - \overline{f(LC)})(y_i - \bar{y})}{\sqrt{\sum_{i=1}^{N}(f(LC_i) - \overline{f(LC)})^2}\sqrt{\sum_{i=1}^{N}(y_i - \bar{y})^2}} \tag{5}$$

where the function f is the logistic transformation given by Eq. 3, $f(LC_i)$ is the logistically transformed value of the proposal LC for the $i - th$ image of the database of N images, $\overline{f(LC)}$ and $\bar{y}$ are the means of the respective data sets.

4 Results

Starting from Eq. 4 we have defined two different metrics LC_{BJ} and LC_{NJ} for images affected by blur artifacts, followed by JPEG compression, and images affected by noise followed by JPEG, respectively. To this end, we have considered separately each of the two parts of the MD-IVL database.

In the case of the MD-IVL-BJ we have defined the LC_{BJ} metric using $M1 - M4$ listed in Sect. 3.1. We have divided in half the dataset, obtaining two parts (MD-IVL-BJ1 and MD-IVL-BJ2), of 175 images each, corresponding to all the distorted versions of five original images. In this way the image contents present in each part of the dataset do not overlap. One image content is defined as all the distorted versions of a same original image.

We have performed 1000 runs of the PSO on MD-IVL-BJ1, to set the optimal parameters $\{a_k\}$ to obtain LC_{BJ}. The metrics were previously normalized in the range [0, 1], and the search space of each parameter was set in the range $[-1, 1]$. Within the 1000 runs, the average PCC (fitness function of PSO optimization, Eq. 5) is 0.9065 with standard deviation of 0.0002. These values indicate the convergence of the sequence of solutions. The optimal parameters are thus obtained averaging the 1000 solutions. The metric LC_{BJ} reads:

$$LC_{BJ} = 1.000 \times M1 + 0.006 \times M2 + 0.829 \times M3 + 0.482 \times M4 \tag{6}$$

We observe from Eq. 6 that the highest contribution to the linear combination comes from the bluriness metric $M1$ followed by the blockiness metric $M3$. The lowest contribution comes from $M2$.

We test the performance of the proposed metric on the MD-IVL-BJ2 and on the LIVE-MD part 1 datasets. We report the corresponding PCC in Table 1 compared also to BRISQUE and NIQE metrics. In Fig. 3 we plot the logistic regression curves for the MD-IVL-BJ2 dataset, comparing our LC_{BJ}, with BRISQUE and NIQE metrics.

Table 1. Performance evaluation of the LC_{BJ} in comparison to BRISQUE and NIQE, in terms of PCC for the MD-IVL-BJ2 and LIVE-MD part 1 respectively.

Dataset	LC_{BJ}	BRISQUE	NIQE
MD-IVL-BJ2	**0.8278**	0.8069	0.7372
LIVE-MD part 1	0.8761	0.8687	**0.9088**

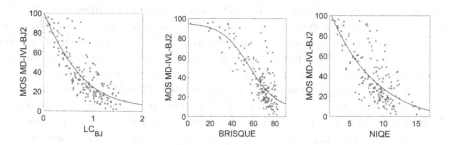

Fig. 3. Logistic regression curves for the MD-IVL-BJ dataset: LC_{BJ}, BRISQUE and NIQE.

For the new dataset MD-IVL-BJ, the performance of the proposed linear combination LC_{BJ} is the highest one. Even if for the LIVE-MD data the best performance is achieved by NIQE, our proposal shows a good performance, taking into account that it is based on simple metrics signal based.

In the case of the MD-IVL-NJ we have defined the LC_{NJ} metric using metrics $M2 - M5$ listed in Sect. 3.1. As before, we have divided in half the dataset, obtaining two parts (MD-IVL-NJ1 and MD-IVL-NJ2), of 200 images each, corresponding to all the distorted versions of five original images. We have also in this case performed 1000 runs of the PSO on MD-IVL-NJ1, to set the optimal parameters $\{a_k\}$ to obtain LC_{NJ}. Within the 1000 runs, the average PCC (fitness function of PSO optimization, Eq. 5) is 0.9272 with standard deviation of 0.0006. Again, the optimal parameters are obtained averaging the 1000 solutions. The metric LC_{NJ} reads:

$$LC_{NJ} = -0.078 \times M2 + 0.3483 \times M3 + 1.000 \times M4 + 0.6717 \times M5 \qquad (7)$$

Table 2. Performance evaluation of the LC_{NJ} in comparison to BRISQUE and NIQE, in terms of PCC for the MD-IVL-NJ2 dataset.

Dataset	LC_{NJ}	BRISQUE	NIQE
MD-IVL-NJ2	**0.8660**	0.3379	0.6960

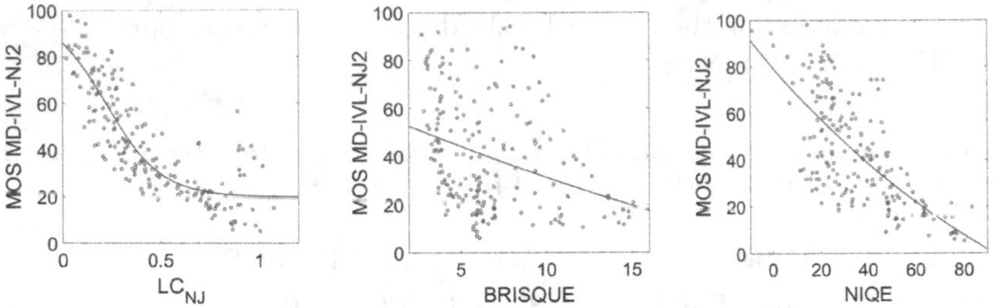

Fig. 4. Logistic regression curves for the MD-IVL-NJ dataset: LC_{NJ}, BRISQUE and NIQE.

We observe from Eq. 7 that the highest contribution to the linear combination now comes from the blockiness metric $M4$ followed by the noise metric $M5$. Also in this case the lowest contribution comes from $M2$. Considering both LC_{BJ} and LC_{NJ} we can also observe that the overall contribution of the blockiness metrics is of the same order (the sum of their weighting coefficients is similar).

We test the performance of the proposed metric on the MD-IVL-NJ2, reporting the corresponding PCC in Table 2. Also the performance of BRISQUE and NIQE are included in the table for comparison. We observe that the proposal LC_{NJ} outperforms both general purpose metrics. The low value for the BRISQUE PCC is comparable with the corresponding one for the LIVE-MD database part 2 (noise + blur) [10]. Taking into account this fact, probably the lower performance showed by BRISQUE in both cases can be attributed to the presence of noise artifacts.

In Fig. 4 the corresponding logistic regression curves for the MD-IVL-NJ2 dataset, for LC_{NJ}, BRISQUE and NIQE metrics are shown.

5   Conclusions

In this work we have focused on multiply distorted image quality assessment. We have generated a database composed of two different parts. Starting from ten original color images of the SD-IVL database we have simultaneously distorted them, considering two different combinations of distortions: blur and JPEG and noise and JPEG. Psycho-physical experiments were conducted on each of these databases. In particular we have here proposed two NR-MD metrics, one for each couple of distortions, as a linear combination of state of the art NR single distortion ones. The promising results obtained suggest possible future research. Firstly, other NR single distortions metrics can be taken into account within the linear combination. Moreover a non linear combination can be investigated using for example Genetic Programming as it was done in [24].

Acknowledgments. We gratefully acknowledge the support of NVIDIA Corporation with the donation of the Tesla K40 GPU used for this research.

References

1. Ciocca, G., Corchs, S., Gasparini, F., Schettini, R.: How to assess image quality within a workflow chain: an overview. Int. J. Digit. Libr. **15**(1), 1–25 (2014)
2. Gabarda, S., Cristóbal, G.: Blind image quality assessment through anisotropy. J. Opt. Soc. Am. A **24**(12), B42–B51 (2007)
3. Choi, M., Jung, J., Jeon, J.: No reference image quality assessment using blur and noise. Int. J. Comput. Sci. Eng. **2**(3), 76–80 (2009)
4. Cohen, E., Yitzhaky, Y.: No-reference assessment of blur and noise impacts on image quality. Signal Image Video Process. **4**, 289–302 (2010)
5. Zhu, X., Milanfar, P.: Automatic parameter selection for denoising algorithms using a no-reference measure of image content. IEEE Trans. Image Process. **19**(12), 3116–3132 (2010)
6. Mittal, A., Moorthy, A., Bovik, A.: No-reference image quality assessment in the spatial domain. IEEE Trans. Image Process. **21**(2), 4695–4708 (2012)
7. Mittal, A., Soundararajan, R., Bovik, A.C.: Making a completely blind image quality analyzer. IEEE Signal Process. Lett. **20**, 209–212 (2013)
8. Chandler, D.M.: Seven challenges in image quality assessment: past, present, and future research. ISRN Signal Processing 23 Article ID 905685, 53 p. (2013)
9. Ciocca, G., Corchs, S., Gasparini, F., Schettini, R.: Modeling image quality, pp. 569–580. IGI Global (2014)
10. Jayaraman, D., Mittal, A., Moorthy, A.K., Bovik, A.: Objective quality assessment of multiply distorted images. In: Proceedings of the Asilomar Conference on Signals, Systems and Computers (2012)
11. Ghadiyaram, D., Bovik, A.C.: Massive online crowdsourced study of subjective and objective picture quality. IEEE Trans. Image Process. **25**(1), 372–387 (2016)
12. VQEG: Vqeg final report of fr-tv phase ii validation test. Technical report, Video Quality Experts Group (VQEG) (2003)
13. Corchs, S., Ciocca, G., Bricolo, E., Gasparini, F.: Predicting complexity perception of real world images. PLoS ONE **11**(6), e0157986 (2016)
14. Corchs, S., Gasparini, F., Schettini, R.: No reference image quality classification for JPEG-distorted images. Digital Signal Process. **30**, 86–100 (2014)
15. ITU: Methodology for the subjective assessment of the quality for television pictures. Technical report, ITU-R Rec. BT. 500–511 (2002)
16. Marziliano, P., Dufaux, F., Winkler, S., Ebrahimi, T.: Perceptual blur and ringing metrics: application to JPEG2000. Signal Process. Image Commun. **19**(2), 163–172 (2004)
17. Wu, H., Yuen, M.: A generalized block-edge impairment metric for video coding. IEEE Signal Process. Lett. **4**, 317–320 (1997)
18. Wang, Z., Bovik, A.C., Evans, B.L.: Blind measurement of blocking artifacts in images. In: Proceedings of International Conference on Image Processing, vol. 3, 981–984. IEEE (2000)

19. Immerkaer, J.: Fast noise variance estimation. Comput. Vis. Image Underst. **64**(2), 300–302 (1996)
20. Sheikh, H.R., Sabir, M.F., Bovik, A.C.: A statistical evaluation of recent full reference image quality assessment algorithms. IEEE Trans. Image Process. **15**(11), 3440–3451 (2006)
21. Larson, E., Chandler, D.: Most apparrent distortion: full reference image quality assessmente and the role of strategy. J. Electron. Imaging **19**(011006), 1–21 (2010)
22. Kennedy, J., Eberhart, R.C.: Particle swarm optimization. In: Proceedings of IEEE International Conference on Neural Networks, vol. 4, pp. 1942–1948 (1995)
23. Bianco, S., Schettini, R.: Two new von kries based chromatic adaptation transforms found by numerical optimization. Color Res. Appl. **35**(3), 184–192 (2010)
24. Corchs, S., Ciocca, G., Francesca, G.: A genetic programming approach to evaluate complexity of texture images. J. Electron. Imaging **25**(6), 061408 (2016)

A Complexity-Based Image Analysis to Investigate Interference Between Distortions and Image Contents in Image Quality Assessment

Gianluigi Ciocca[1,2], Silvia Corchs[1,2], and Francesca Gasparini[1,2](✉)

[1] Dipartimento di Informatica, Sistemistica e Comunicazione,
University of Milano-Bicocca, Viale Sarca 336, 20126 Milan, Italy
{ciocca,corchs,gasparini}@disco.unimib.it
[2] NeuroMi - Milan Center for Neuroscience, Milan, Italy

Abstract. In this paper we investigate how distortion and image content interfere within image quality assessment. To this end we analyze how full reference metrics behave within three different groups of images. Given a dataset of images, these are first classified as high, medium or low complexity and the FR methods are applied within each group separately. We consider images from LIVE, CSIQ and LIVE multi-distorted databases. We evaluate 17 full reference quality metrics available in the literature on each of these the high, medium and low complexity groups. We observe that within these groups the metrics better correlate subjective data. In particular, the signal based metrics are the ones that show the highest improvements. Moreover for the LIVE multi-distorted database the gain in performance is evident for all the metrics considered.

Keywords: Image complexity · Image Quality Assessment · Full Reference metrics

1 Introduction

Image Quality Assessment (IQA) is a very active topic of research and even if today's IQA algorithms predict quality for a variety of images and distortion types remarkably well, there is still a lack of understanding about the way humans perceive artifacts in images [1]. In particular, one of the unsolved question regards the interactions between the distortions and the image contents. Humans rate the quality of images highly or slightly distorted more easily than for the intermediate range of distortion. In the latter case, the task becomes more difficult as the interactions between distortions and image contents are more severe.

Larson and Chandler [2] claim that our visual system uses different strategies to evaluate image quality depending on the signal-distortion ratio. In the high quality regime, the visual system attempts to look for distortions in the

© Springer International Publishing AG 2017
S. Bianco et al. (Eds.): CCIW 2017, LNCS 10213, pp. 105–121, 2017.
DOI: 10.1007/978-3-319-56010-6_9

presence of the image content, whereas in the low quality regime, the visual system attempts to look for image content in the presence of the distortions. Based on this hypothesis, the authors propose a Full Reference (FR) method which attempts to explicitly model these two separate strategies.

Objective image quality assessment is mainly related to measuring the presence of distortions. Humans, while scoring the quality of images, are not always able to disregard all the factors related not only to the distortion presence but also to other aspects like aesthetic or image semantic [3]. When these different aspects concur to generate final subjective rates, the objective metrics, that measure only distortions, may not properly predict human judgments.

The effect of content dependency on objective image quality metrics has been previously considered in the literature. For example, the authors in [4] addressed the problem of scene dependency and scene susceptibility in image quality assessments. They proposed image analysis as a means to group test scenes according to basic inherent scene properties that human observers refer to when they judge the quality of images. Experimental work was carried out for JPEG and JPEG2000 distortions. Oh et al. [5] analyzed the degree of correlation between scene descriptors (first and second order statistical measurements) and scene susceptibility parameters for noisiness and sharpness. Recently, Bondzulic et al. [6] analyzed the performance of the Peak Signal to Noise Ratio (PSNR) metric for video quality assessment as a function of the video content. They have shown that within a fixed content, the variation of the PSNR is a reliable indicator for predicting subjective quality of video streaming.

Attempts to improve the reliability of objective metrics involve also taking into account visual attention of the human visual system [7]. For example, Liu et al. [8] observed that adding Natural Scene Saliency (NSS) obtained from eye-tracking data can improve the performance of objective metrics and investigated the dependency of this improvement with respect to the image content. The authors demonstrated that the variation in NSS between participants largely depends on the visual content.

In this paper we investigate the interferences between distortion and image content in human quality perception. Image content here refers to image complexity described in terms of low level features. Our working hypothesis is that the correlation between subjective and predicted scores can be improved if performed within a group of images that present similar complexity. In a preliminary study [9], we presented how the correlation between No Reference (NR) metrics for JPEG distortion and subjective scores improves, considering image complexity and frequency analysis. Here we examine in depth this topic considering FR metrics and different types of distortions.

In this work we also take into account multiply distorted images. To this end the LIVE multi-distortion (LIVE-MD) database [10] is considered, together with two well known database of single distortions: the LIVE [11] and the CSIQ [12] databases. We here present an extensive analysis of this topic with respect to 17 state-of-the-art FR metrics.

In Sect. 2 we present the proposed complexity grouping strategy which is based on a fuzzy clustering algorithm, while in Sect. 3 we present and comment the results of our analysis of the FR metrics' performance on the three datasets.

2 Grouping Images by Image Complexity

Our proposal is to first categorize the images within one of the following complexity groups: low, medium or high complexity, and then to perform the regression taking into account this grouping strategy.

There exists no unique definition of the complexity of an image. Researchers from various fields have proposed different measures to estimate image complexity. Visual or image complexity can be analyzed by using mathematical treatments, based on algorithmic information theory or Kolmogorov complexity theory. Image complexity is also related to aesthetics [13]. From the experiments of Oliva et al. [14] a multi-dimensional representation of visual complexity (quantity of objects, clutter, openness, symmetry, organization, variety of colors) was proposed. Fuzzy approaches [15], information-theoretical based techniques [16], and independent component analysis [17] have been proposed in the literature to determine the complexity of an image. Rosenholtz et al. [18] presented two measures of visual clutter, based on feature congestion and subband entropy, relating them to visual complexity. Edge density has been used by Mack and Oliva [19] to predict subjective judgments of image complexity. Recently, new measures of image complexity have been proposed as combination of single image features [20, 21]. In the context of image quality, Allen et al. [22] have observed that the perception of distortions is influenced by the amount of details in the images. Following the above mentioned results, in the present work we adopt the edge density as low level feature representative of visual complexity.

2.1 A Fuzzy Approach to Group Images by Complexity

Our complexity-based grouping strategy is based on fuzzy clustering and starts from the work of Chacon et al. [23]. It is a two steps method.

First Step. The aim is to decompose the edges in the images into five levels based on their "edgeness". To this end, we have collected 23 images of about 0.5 Megapixel each. These images belong to a personal database and were chosen to represent different contents (close-ups, landscape, portraits, etc.). For each image I_k ($k = 1 \ldots 23$), we extract the norm of the gradient of the intensity channel Y_k. Edge pixels are selected by thresholding the natural logarithmic of the gradient module. The values above a threshold T are then collected in an edge vector $\mathbf{E}$:

$$\mathbf{E} = \{\{\ln \|\nabla Y_k\|_2 \, ; \quad \|\nabla Y_k\|_2 > T\} \quad k = 1 \ldots 23\} \tag{1}$$

To identify the five edge levels, we have applied the Fuzzy C-Means (FCM) algorithm [24] on the elements of $\mathbf{E}$. Fuzzy clustering methods allow objects to belong to several clusters simultaneously, with different degrees of membership. The FCM algorithm minimizes the functional:

$$J_{FCM} = \sum_{i=1}^{C} \sum_{j=1}^{N} \mu_{ij}^{p} d_{ij}^{2} \qquad (2)$$

where C is the number of cluster, N is the number of objects, $p \in [1 \; \infty)$ is a parameter which determines the fuzziness of the resulting clusters, μ_{ij} is the membership function that satisfies the following constraint, for $j = 1, 2, ..., N$:

$$\sum_{i=1}^{C} \mu_{ij} = 1 \qquad (3)$$

In Eq. 2, d_{ij} is the Euclidean norm between the j-th object defined through its feature vector $\mathbf{v}_j$ and the center $\mathbf{c}_i$ of the i-th fuzzy cluster:

$$d_{ij} = \|\mathbf{v}_j - \mathbf{c}_i\|_2 \qquad (4)$$

In our case, the objects correspond to the elements in $\mathbf{E}$. The feature space is mono dimensional, and $\mathbf{v}_j$ corresponds to the j-th element of the vector $\mathbf{E}$. N is the size of the vector and is about 2×10^6. The number of clusters C corresponds to the number of edge levels and is 5. Finally, the fuzziness parameter has been set to $p = 2$.

The minimization of the C-Means functional in Eq. 2, represents a nonlinear optimization problem that can be solved by using a variety of methods. In our work we have used Picard iteration as implemented in the Fuzzy Clustering and Data Analysis Toolbox available on line and developed by Alasko et al. [25].

Second Step. The aim is to categorize images into three complexity groups based on the edge decomposition. For this purpose, 370 images are used: 300 of them belong to the BSDS300 database [26], the remaining 70 belong to a personal database and are different from those used in the first step of clustering. We use the Fuzzy Gath-Geva (FGG) clustering method on the edge decomposition of the images to find three clusters corresponding to high, medium and low complexity. For each image I_k $(k = 1 \ldots 370)$ we compute a four dimensional feature vector $\mathbf{w}_k$. The first three elements correspond to the densities of the first three edge levels; the fourth element is the sum of these values.

We adopt here FGG as it is able to detect clusters of varying shapes, sizes and densities. FCM instead permits to only detect clusters with the same shape and orientation. In particular the Euclidean norm induces hyper-spherical clusters. This is not a problem for the edge level decomposition step where we are interested in creating more uniform clusters. The distance norm adopted by FGG is based on the fuzzy maximum likelihood estimates, proposed by [27]:

$$d_{ik} = \frac{(det\mathbf{F}_i)^{\frac{1}{2}}}{\left(\frac{1}{N} \sum_{k=1}^{N} \mu_{ik}\right)} exp \left(\frac{1}{2} \left(\mathbf{w}_k - \mathbf{c}_i\right)^T \mathbf{F}_i^{-1} \left(\mathbf{w}_k - \mathbf{c}_i\right)\right) \qquad (5)$$

where $\mathbf{F}_i$ is the fuzzy covariance matrix of the $i\text{-}th$ cluster, given by:

$$\mathbf{F}_i = \frac{\sum_{k=1}^{N} (\mu_{ik})^p (\mathbf{w}_k - \mathbf{c}_i)(\mathbf{w}_k - \mathbf{c}_i)^T}{\sum_{k=1}^{N} (\mu_{ik})^p} \tag{6}$$

In our case the fuzziness parameter is $p = 2$, and $N = 370$. Note that FGG needs a good initialization, due to the exponential distance norm. To this end we use the output of a FCM to initialize the algorithm.

The above described method basically performs an unsupervised classification of an image in one of the three complexity categories. Formally, denoting with $\mathcal{F}$ the function performing the category labelling, and given an image I_k, we have that:

$$\mathcal{F}(I_k) = z_k \text{ with } z_k \in \{l, m, h\} \tag{7}$$

where l, m, and h are the labels for the low, medium and high complexity category respectively.

3   Experimental Results

Different databases are available to test the algorithms' performance with respect to the human subjective judgments [28]. Among them, we have chosen the following three reference IQ databases: the **LIVE** database [11,29] containing 29 reference images and 779 distorted images with JPEG and JPEG2000 compression, Gaussian Blur (BLUR), Additive Gaussian White Noise (WHITE NOISE), and FAST FADING; the **CSIQ** database [2,12] containing 30 reference images and 866 distorted images with JPEG and JPEG2000 compression, Gaussian Blur (BLUR), Additive White Gaussian Noise (AWGN), Additive Pink Gaussian Noise (FNOISE), and Global Contrast (CONTRAST); the **LIVE-MD** database [10] containing 15 reference images and 405 multiply distorted images (BLUR+JPEG, and BLUR+NOISE).

We first apply the fuzzy approach described by Eq. 7 on each of the three database. The complexity categories obtained are depicted in Fig. 1.

As full reference metrics, we focus here on 17 metrics available in the literature. We consider different kinds of approaches: from the simplest ones like MSE or peak signal-to-noise ratio (PSNR) to other, more sophisticated, metrics. These metrics estimate quality based on image structure, use statistical and information-theoretic approaches, or are based on models of the Human Visual System (HVS).

The full list of the 17 FR metrics evaluated is: Mean-Squared-Error (**MSE**), Signal Noise Ratio (**SNR**), Peak Signal-to-Noise-Ratio (**PSNR**), Universal Quality Index (**UQI**) [30], Structural Similarity Index (**SSIM**) [31], Multi-Scale SSIM index (**MS-SSIM**) [32], Visual Signal-to-Noise Ratio (**VSNR**) [33], Information Fidelity Criterion (**IFC**) [34], Visual Information Fidelity (**VIF**) [35], Most Apparent Distortion (**MAD**) [2], **PSNR-HVS** [36], **PSNR-HVSM** [37], Information content Weighted-SSIM (**IW-SSIM**) [38], Information content

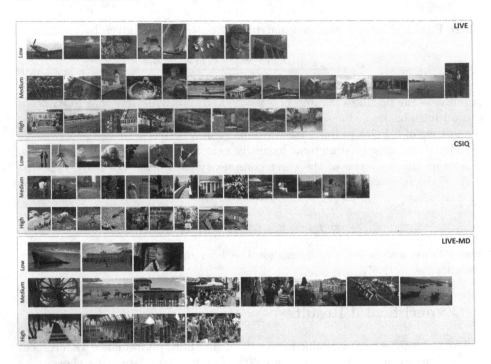

Fig. 1. Original images from LIVE, CSIQ and LIVE-MD databases grouped in the three categories: low, medium and high complexity.

Weighted-PSNR (**IW-PSNR**) [38], Feature Similarity Index (**FSIM**) [39], Gradient magnitude Similarity Deviation (**GMSD**) [40], and Divisive Normalization Metric (**DN**) [41].

If we consider a single metric and the corresponding subjective scores for a given database, a logistic regression curve can be computed. The correlation performance is evaluated using the Pearson Correlation Coefficient (PCC), that is the linear correlation coefficient between the quality predicted by the metric and the subjective scores. We refer to the regression using all the data within each database as R_{all}, while the regressions within each of the Low, Medium and High complexity groups are referred as R_L, R_M and R_H respectively.

We present the performance of the 17 FR metrics when applied to all the dataset (LIVE, CSIQ, and LIVE-MD) and on each of the corresponding complexity groups separately. To better visualize the results, for each metric and each regression, we consider the relative improvements Δ of the PCC on the three groups w.r.t. the PCC on the whole dataset:

$$\Delta = \frac{PCC(X) - PCC(R_{all})}{PCC(R_{all})} \times 100 \tag{8}$$

where X is either R_L, R_M, or R_H.

Table 1. Distortion independent analysis results. Relative increase of PCC for LIVE, CSIQ and LIVE-MD data. Positive increases are shown in bold.

FR metric	LIVE 779 images				CSIQ 886 images				LIVE-MD 450 images			
	PCC	Δ (%)			PCC	Δ (%)			PCC	Δ (%)		
	R_{all}	R_L	R_M	R_H	R_{all}	R_L	R_M	R_H	R_{all}	R_L	R_M	R_H
MSE	0.858	**5.13**	**4.66**	**3.77**	0.803	**3.11**	**3.33**	**6.13**	0.735	**13.92**	**22.05**	**29.98**
SNR	0.859	**4.39**	**1.49**	**3.93**	0.782	**3.26**	**2.75**	**7.06**	0.722	**12.61**	**17.96**	**25.87**
PSNR	0.870	**4.92**	**4.42**	**2.70**	0.800	**3.03**	**3.26**	**6.06**	0.745	**11.43**	**20.47**	**28.07**
SSIM	0.901	**1.55**	**2.49**	**4.29**	0.815	**2.06**	**3.94**	**7.67**	0.750	**20.41**	**9.15**	**18.80**
MS-SSIM	0.934	−0.69	**1.18**	**1.52**	0.897	**0.53**	**0.41**	**2.25**	0.881	−1.31	−0.46	**4.14**
UQI	0.898	**1.14**	**3.82**	**4.26**	0.829	**0.44**	**5.02**	**4.14**	0.862	−4.14	**0.01**	**5.34**
VSNR	0.923	−0.60	**0.88**	−0.34	0.800	**1.35**	**1.48**	**5.28**	0.809	**1.22**	**4.76**	**12.98**
IFC	0.924	**1.02**	**2.45**	**3.84**	0.838	**3.22**	**4.04**	**1.24**	0.903	−3.64	−0.12	**3.06**
VIF	0.959	−2.72	**0.27**	−0.10	0.922	−0.40	**1.75**	−1.12	0.897	**0.76**	**1.87**	**3.09**
MAD	0.969	−0.97	**0.60**	−0.55	0.952	**0.63**	**0.32**	−0.79	0.893	0.00	**2.78**	**7.47**
PSNR-HVSM	0.925	**1.13**	**1.72**	−1.37	0.816	**0.99**	−0.10	**4.18**	0.819	**15.57**	**10.03**	**13.85**
PSNR-HVS	0.913	**2.04**	**2.55**	**0.16**	0.790	**3.92**	**5.11**	**9.41**	0.796	**18.04**	**12.83**	**16.94**
IW-SSIM	0.943	**1.44**	**0.52**	−0.65	0.903	**3.46**	**2.04**	**1.71**	0.911	**2.40**	**2.20**	**2.16**
IW-PSNR	0.932	**0.27**	**1.24**	−1.15	0.822	**1.11**	−0.90	**1.35**	0.827	**11.70**	**7.16**	**15.00**
FSIM	0.954	**0.71**	**0.73**	−0.93	0.910	**1.89**	**0.99**	**0.81**	0.817	**16.08**	**12.62**	**11.55**
GMSD	0.960	**0.25**	**0.74**	−1.22	0.954	−1.42	**0.69**	**0.81**	0.881	**6.82**	**4.52**	**2.69**
DN	0.933	**2.10**	**0.44**	−0.37	0.876	**2.09**	**3.00**	**1.93**	0.852	**0.55**	**6.09**	**10.98**

3.1 Distortion Independent Analysis

In Table 1 we report the performance in terms of PCC using a Logistic Regression (R_{all}) for each of the 17 FR metrics on the three databases considering all the distortions together. These performance are compared with the corresponding ones obtained considering each of the complexity groups separately (R_H, R_M and R_L), and results are reported in terms of Eq. 8. We show in boldface the coefficients that have positive improvement within the complexity groups. Observing these results we note that:

- the correlation coefficients obtained for R_{all} are in agreement with the values reported in the literature [40, 42];
- MAD and GMSD are the most competitive metrics for both LIVE and CSIQ data;
- for LIVE-MD data, the performance of nearly all the metrics are lower than the corresponding ones in case of LIVE and CSIQ;
- nearly all the metrics improve the performance when evaluated on a subset of images of equivalent complexity. In particular the signal-based metrics: MSE, SNR, PSNR, as well as SSIM, PSNR-HVSM, and PSNR-HVS metrics exhibit the highest improvements;
- the metric less affected by the complexity grouping across the three datasets is the MS-SSIM;

- the most relevant results are in the LIVE-MD data where we can find several metrics that exhibit two digits improvements when the three complexity groups are considered;
- on the overall, the R_H group exhibits the most relevant improvement with respect to R_{all}.

3.2 Distortion Dependent Analysis

In Tables 2, 3, and 4 we report the detailed results, in terms of PCC and relative improvement, for each distortion present in each dataset. For LIVE and CSIQ we observe that:

- the performance of nearly all the metrics is improved when evaluated on each single complexity group;
- for both LIVE and CSIQ the signal-based metrics are the ones with greatest Δ for JPEG, JPEG2000, BLUR and FAST FADING distortions;
- for both LIVE and CSIQ metrics, UQI and IFC are the ones with highest Δ for noise distortions WHITE NOISE, AWGN, and FNOISE;
- for CONTRAST distortion, a noticeable increase of around 50% is observed for the metric IFC.

For the LIVE-MD we observe that:

- the Δ improvements result greater than in the case of single-distortion datasets;
- we notice high increases for signal-based metrics, PSNR-HVSM, and PSNR-HVS;
- we can also notice that in general for these metrics, the improvements for blur followed by JPEG are greater than the corresponding ones for blur followed by noise. These results are in accordance with the performance of the considered metrics in the case of single distortions.

Finally, we have performed the same analysis on the three datasets but now randomly grouped. We have thus verified that the improvements obtained are not due to the fact that the cardinality of the groups is lower than the whole dataset. In fact, the improvements are actually related to the fact that within each group the images have similar content (in terms of complexity). These results will be available at our website.

Table 2. Relative increase of PCC for LIVE data on the 17 metrics. Positive increase is shown in bold.

FR metric	JPEG PCC R_{all}	R_L	Δ(%) R_M	R_H	JPEG2000 PCC R_{all}	R_L	Δ(%) R_M	R_H	BLUR PCC R_{all}	R_L	Δ(%) R_M	R_H	WHITE NOISE PCC R_{all}	R_L	Δ(%) R_M	R_H	FAST FADING PCC R_{all}	R_L	Δ(%) R_M	R_H
MSE	0.889	10.66	8.63	3.66	0.900	6.01	6.60	3.83	0.789	14.38	15.48	8.93	0.983	0.31	-5.79	0.52	0.880	7.49	2.07	6.72
SNR	0.877	8.89	3.79	3.84	0.871	4.75	1.94	6.88	0.762	15.59	6.40	12.08	0.971	1.65	-0.75	0.61	0.894	3.80	4.58	6.13
PSNR	0.888	10.72	8.60	3.71	0.900	5.93	6.68	3.69	0.784	15.45	16.43	9.25	0.986	0.31	0.41	0.41	0.890	6.16	6.32	5.93
SSIM	0.950	3.44	2.48	1.21	0.941	0.96	1.89	2.59	0.874	4.55	8.68	6.56	0.970	1.10	0.75	0.60	0.942	0.84	3.00	3.10
MS-SSIM	0.981	0.94	0.16	-0.75	0.970	-0.17	0.09	0.32	0.953	1.30	1.48	-0.75	0.985	-0.35	-0.84	-1.20	0.920	0.25	0.11	1.80
UQI	0.907	6.37	6.33	6.71	0.867	-1.70	7.78	12.99	0.951	1.53	1.52	0.70	0.937	3.66	3.93	3.71	0.948	-2.24	1.01	1.45
VSNR	0.972	0.28	0.51	-0.18	0.963	-1.86	1.12	0.77	0.933	-3.54	2.34	3.10	0.978	0.67	-0.38	0.20	0.902	-1.59	1.58	3.62
IFC	0.945	4.53	2.94	4.21	0.919	6.18	5.71	6.51	0.967	0.66	0.98	0.62	0.957	2.57	2.14	2.38	0.963	-0.42	-0.06	1.40
VIF	0.986	0.94	-0.18	-0.59	0.976	0.57	0.14	0.29	0.974	0.16	0.67	-1.23	0.963	2.68	1.94	2.11	0.961	0.02	0.41	0.69
MAD	0.981	0.39	0.88	0.17	0.975	-1.56	0.65	-0.64	0.957	-2.36	1.67	-0.60	0.988	0.14	0.19	0.10	0.958	-0.60	-1.28	-0.18
PSNR-HVSM	0.975	1.54	0.47	0.26	0.960	0.86	1.56	0.76	0.920	-0.31	4.87	-0.07	0.987	-0.37	0.30	0.33	0.910	2.86	3.15	2.70
PSNR-HVS	0.958	3.15	1.84	1.08	0.937	2.79	3.42	1.98	0.878	3.18	8.07	2.29	0.985	0.10	0.49	0.50	0.906	3.63	4.16	3.59
IW-SSIM	0.981	1.11	0.34	-0.20	0.971	0.52	0.41	-13.28	0.963	0.15	0.90	-1.43	0.969	1.29	0.63	0.24	0.930	-0.18	-0.39	1.23
IW-PSNR	0.983	0.79	0.32	-0.73	0.966	-0.11	1.48	-0.08	0.942	-3.02	2.60	-0.25	0.982	0.08	0.54	0.74	0.848	2.31	2.03	3.90
FSIM	0.982	0.72	0.28	-0.60	0.979	-0.68	0.40	0.11	0.968	0.42	1.60	-1.51	0.965	1.05	1.02	0.48	0.939	-0.71	0.24	1.40
GMSD	0.985	0.89	0.09	-0.69	0.977	-0.10	0.52	0.24	0.962	-0.86	1.82	-0.91	0.966	0.25	0.38	1.07	0.941	1.85	1.71	0.78
DN	0.967	1.03	0.62	0.35	0.961	-0.70	0.35	0.74	0.950	1.88	1.35	0.25	0.968	0.86	0.35	0.92	0.936	2.11	-1.07	0.87

Table 3. Relative increase of PCC for CSIQ data for the 17 metrics. Positive increase is shown in bold.

FR metric	AWGN				JPEG				JPEG2000				FNOISE				BLUR				CONTRAST			
	PCC R_{all}	Δ(%) R_L	R_M	R_H	PCC R_{all}	Δ(%) R_L	R_M	R_H	PCC R_{all}	Δ(%) R_L	R_M	R_H	PCC R_{all}	Δ(%) R_L	R_M	R_H	PCC R_{all}	Δ(%) R_L	R_M	R_H	PCC R_{all}	Δ(%) R_L	R_M	R_H
MSE	0.901	-0.40	7.12	4.05	0.891	6.40	6.82	6.64	0.890	1.02	10.46	8.70	0.952	0.53	0.32	-0.76	0.886	9.12	13.27	6.68	0.861	1.16	3.20	4.94
SNR	0.933	2.12	-0.49	0.60	0.873	7.49	9.79	5.94	0.927	5.35	3.84	3.98	0.929	1.65	-1.08	3.40	0.899	2.59	6.36	2.42	0.852	-6.21	0.06	9.26
PSNR	0.953	2.21	1.54	-1.48	0.891	8.58	9.89	4.54	0.947	4.13	4.02	3.73	0.953	0.09	1.05	0.40	0.925	4.87	5.57	2.51	0.899	-3.27	-1.16	5.33
SSIM	0.894	8.44	6.09	6.10	0.940	0.04	3.16	4.85	0.923	-0.50	5.78	5.81	0.895	4.84	-1.53	7.28	0.900	-2.72	7.44	6.99	0.742	3.17	-0.43	27.37
MS-SSIM	0.947	2.73	3.57	0.61	0.981	0.02	-0.08	0.71	0.977	0.52	0.51	0.08	0.941	-0.63	2.44	2.78	0.959	1.18	1.13	-0.72	0.944	1.98	1.18	2.08
UQI	0.766	13.57	16.87	19.73	0.914	3.64	5.62	3.58	0.903	1.64	6.58	4.19	0.725	14.18	6.81	26.68	0.948	-0.56	2.61	1.58	0.851	0.53	0.42	12.90
VSNR	0.926	0.01	3.43	0.90	0.951	1.30	2.01	2.62	0.960	-0.53	2.07	0.30	0.920	1.99	4.80	2.47	0.934	1.82	2.04	0.78	0.873	-5.46	4.76	8.90
IFC	0.846	7.11	11.42	11.23	0.955	1.18	-0.05	3.28	0.938	3.94	5.26	4.35	0.838	4.23	10.61	12.69	0.964	-0.12	2.21	0.85	0.572	49.13	55.84	53.89
VIF	0.961	1.74	1.02	-1.63	0.988	-0.12	0.28	-0.44	0.978	0.17	1.51	0.24	0.957	-0.10	0.37	0.33	0.963	1.12	2.40	1.19	0.943	0.07	2.29	3.15
MAD	0.956	0.54	2.00	1.20	0.983	-0.81	0.61	0.07	0.982	0.12	0.69	0.13	0.955	-1.48	1.17	2.28	0.976	-0.40	0.77	-0.14	0.924	1.99	-0.97	2.37
PSNR-HVSM	0.941	3.81	1.42	1.15	0.973	-0.25	1.04	1.30	0.977	1.04	0.80	0.50	0.957	-0.18	0.79	0.13	0.968	0.77	1.27	0.46	0.903	-2.50	-1.21	5.18
PSNR-HVS	0.952	2.34	0.98	-1.21	0.906	4.65	8.61	8.70	0.968	1.49	1.69	1.18	0.953	0.08	0.99	0.41	0.962	1.51	2.41	1.56	0.950	-2.38	-1.16	4.63
IW-SSIM	0.938	3.49	4.12	1.41	0.983	0.63	0.39	0.68	0.976	1.16	0.75	0.30	0.914	0.93	5.10	5.53	0.975	1.33	0.67	-0.87	0.926	1.38	1.15	2.11
IW-PSNR	0.937	2.79	-0.85	0.36	0.983	0.09	0.28	0.16	0.986	0.37	-0.10	0.03	0.955	0.61	0.76	0.53	0.960	0.87	0.37	-0.46	0.937	2.21	-1.43	2.49
FSIM	0.929	4.27	1.44	2.51	0.983	-7.99	0.11	0.49	0.981	0.37	0.77	0.16	0.928	1.68	1.77	3.80	0.960	0.27	0.86	0.04	0.937	-0.54	2.57	3.15
GMSD	0.968	0.99	0.91	-0.93	0.984	-0.29	0.03	0.69	0.979	0.35	0.76	0.47	0.958	-0.59	0.05	1.07	0.966	-0.34	1.93	0.03	0.923	-2.65	2.45	3.77
DN	0.912	5.51	6.16	2.03	0.970	0.31	1.19	0.99	0.947	1.94	2.36	2.10	0.867	5.32	8.41	9.57	0.962	0.79	1.05	1.48	0.919	0.40	3.81	5.20

Table 4. Relative increase of PCC for LIVE-MD data. Results for the different types of distortion are shown for the 17 FR metrics. Positive increases are shown in bold.

FR metric	BLUR+JPEG				BLUR+NOISE			
	PCC	Δ (%)			PCC	Δ (%)		
	R_{all}	R_L	R_M	R_H	R_{all}	R_L	R_M	R_H
MSE	0.731	**23.13**	**24.56**	**30.89**	0.760	**10.52**	**19.03**	**27.03**
SNR	0.731	**28.05**	**7.80**	**23.93**	0.725	**9.64**	**0.47**	**26.61**
PSNR	0.722	**24.90**	**26.31**	**32.07**	0.774	**8.54**	**16.85**	**24.16**
SSIM	0.761	**12.03**	**22.40**	**17.63**	0.747	**20.91**	**7.31**	**21.86**
MS-SSIM	0.883	**3.98**	**6.27**	−5.07	0.841	**4.66**	**8.94**	**11.27**
UQI	0.884	**4.22**	**0.32**	**1.06**	0.857	−6.44	−0.39	**8.58**
VSNR	0.834	**3.84**	**5.71**	**13.63**	0.792	**3.27**	**4.42**	**16.11**
IFC	0.918	−4.01	**0.79**	**1.95**	0.895	−2.66	−0.68	**6.70**
VIF	0.919	**0.74**	**2.52**	**1.79**	0.880	**2.31**	**3.63**	**8.15**
MAD	0.919	**1.60**	**2.36**	**5.86**	0.868	−2.31	**3.12**	**10.40**
PSNR-HVSM	0.835	**12.93**	**10.51**	**13.09**	0.802	**18.70**	**9.57**	**13.99**
PSNR-HVS	0.800	**17.61**	**14.65**	**18.31**	0.789	**20.26**	**11.83**	**16.88**
IW-SSIM	0.916	**2.81**	**3.64**	**1.58**	0.911	**3.69**	**1.84**	**3.30**
IW-PSNR	0.850	**9.82**	**7.27**	**14.49**	0.808	**13.89**	**6.86**	**17.33**
FSIM	0.906	**4.15**	**3.56**	**2.01**	0.818	**16.67**	**10.95**	**10.95**
GMSD	0.894	**5.44**	**5.26**	**2.38**	0.867	**9.16**	**4.00**	**4.68**
DN	0.867	**1.63**	**7.85**	**10.25**	0.851	−1.16	**4.63**	**10.73**

4   Conclusions

In this paper we have studied the interaction between distortions and image contents when assessing image quality. We have presented an extensive analysis of the performance of state-of-the-art FR metrics when evaluated within groups of images of similar complexity. We have proposed a fuzzy clustering technique to categorize images within three groups (low, medium and high) according to their complexity in terms of low level features. Our experiments show that in general a significant gain in performance of all the FR metrics considered is achieved when quality is separately evaluated on the three complexity groups. These results are consistent across quality metrics, distortion type and image datasets. In particular signal based metrics are the ones exhibiting the highest improvements. For the multi-distorted data we also observed a significant improvement for all the metrics. This result is encouraging as image quality of multi-distorted data is a challenging task and it is currently an open issue.

Additional Material

Here we evaluate if the relative improvements are due to the lower cardinalities of the images in each group instead of the images' content. To this end, we performed the same analysis as in the paper but with randomly created groups. Specifically, we randomly assigned images in each group while retaining the original group's cardinality. We performed different random extractions and averaged the results. Tables 5, 6, 7, and 8. As in the paper, positive increments are shown in bold.

Table 5. Distortion independent analysis results. Relative increase of PCC for LIVE, CSIQ and LIVE-MD data for random grouping. Positive increases are shown in bold.

FR metric	LIVE 779 images				CSIQ 886 images				LIVE-MD 450 images			
	PCC	Δ (%)			PCC	Δ (%)			PCC	Δ (%)		
	R_{all}	R_L	R_M	R_H	R_{all}	R_L	R_M	R_H	R_{all}	R_L	R_M	R_H
MSE	0.858	−2.81	−0.70	**1.14**	0.803	−0.08	−22.61	**1.50**	0.760	−3.36	−5.40	−9.96
SNR	0.859	−2.82	−1.18	−1.77	0.782	−2.15	−4.17	−6.76	0.725	−0.01	−5.21	**5.83**
PSNR	0.870	−0.99	−0.16	−2.84	0.800	−7.17	−2.04	−8.34	0.774	−8.46	−5.83	−2.14
SSIM	0.901	−1.30	−8.04	−10.99	0.815	−11.34	−7.98	−0.98	0.747	−5.48	−11.33	**6.10**
MS-SSIM	0.934	−16.91	−19.31	−0.89	0.897	−18.86	−16.60	**0.78**	0.841	−2.87	**4.74**	−1.01
UQI	0.898	−0.72	−1.06	**1.74**	0.829	**0.62**	−2.41	−0.24	0.857	−1.96	**1.52**	**0.53**
VSNR	0.923	−0.86	**0.53**	−1.71	0.800	−16.01	−1.59	−5.49	0.792	**6.17**	**1.46**	−3.11
IFC	0.924	−0.53	−10.09	**2.31**	0.838	−36.10	−32.92	−22.26	0.895	−0.34	**2.47**	−3.75
VIF	0.959	**0.61**	−0.53	**0.55**	0.922	−0.27	**0.11**	**1.19**	0.880	−0.59	**2.74**	**1.50**
MAD	0.969	−1.65	−0.71	−0.11	0.952	−1.11	**0.37**	−1.25	0.868	**0.67**	**3.76**	**1.92**
PSNR-HVSM	0.925	**0.50**	**0.04**	−1.34	0.816	−3.35	−2.30	−7.41	0.802	−3.52	**0.20**	−1.27
PSNR-HVS	0.913	−0.96	**0.48**	−1.06	0.790	**0.24**	**0.90**	−1.79	0.789	−0.05	**1.61**	−0.13
IW-SSIM	0.943	−0.52	**0.38**	−14.68	0.903	−1.75	**0.39**	−0.53	0.911	−0.26	−0.60	−1.96
IW-PSNR	0.932	−0.48	**0.02**	−13.84	0.822	−0.38	−1.08	−7.62	0.808	−6.79	**2.75**	**7.10**
FSIM	0.954	−0.40	−11.26	−1.21	0.910	−1.50	−15.06	**2.14**	0.818	−3.12	**10.94**	**7.46**
GMSD	0.960	−0.23	−0.14	−0.15	0.954	−0.48	**0.37**	−0.22	0.867	−1.71	**2.18**	−8.58
DN	0.933	**0.26**	−0.49	**0.37**	0.876	−1.96	−0.25	**1.23**	0.851	−1.60	**1.27**	**1.20**

Table 6. Relative increase of PCC on the LIVE data for the 17 metrics and random grouping. Positive increase is shown in bold.

FR metric	JPEG				JPEG200				BLUR				WHITE NOISE				FAST FADING			
	PCC R_{all}	R_L	Δ(%) R_M	R_H	PCC R_{all}	R_L	Δ(%) R_M	R_H	PCC R_{all}	R_L	Δ(%) R_M	R_H	PCC R_{all}	R_L	Δ(%) R_M	R_H	PCC R_{all}	R_L	Δ(%) R_M	R_H
MSE	0.889	-15.90	-2.53	-18.96	0.900	-4.42	-17.80	-21.84	0.789	**1.83**	-10.39	-14.44	0.983	-16.80	-11.82	-18.18	0.880	-6.74	**0.24**	-8.66
SNR	0.877	**3.14**	-4.36	-2.59	0.871	-0.12	-0.19	-4.33	0.762	**6.62**	-10.49	**2.48**	0.971	-0.11	-0.01	-0.14	0.894	**1.01**	-2.07	**2.72**
PSNR	0.888	**0.70**	-3.07	-2.71	0.900	-0.45	-0.75	-1.52	0.784	-12.13	**0.40**	-4.35	0.986	**0.13**	-0.69	**0.08**	0.890	-0.80	-3.37	**5.69**
SSIM	0.950	-0.89	-3.29	**0.37**	0.941	-5.06	-0.05	**0.69**	0.874	-0.06	-10.01	**1.58**	0.970	-0.97	-0.11	-0.47	0.942	-0.89	**0.78**	-3.13
MS-SSIM	0.981	-0.20	-0.34	**0.20**	0.970	-11.62	-10.69	-0.02	0.953	-10.04	-9.09	**0.98**	0.985	-0.92	-1.30	-1.24	0.920	-2.54	-12.82	-10.40
UQI	0.907	-2.77	-0.16	-0.35	0.867	-1.95	-2.67	**5.59**	0.951	-7.77	-10.13	-3.70	0.937	-0.31	-1.66	**2.43**	0.948	-2.81	-0.97	-0.13
VSNR	0.972	-0.17	-0.72	-0.22	0.963	-3.04	-1.28	-1.58	0.933	-2.24	-1.95	-2.92	0.978	-0.37	**0.37**	-0.57	0.902	**2.21**	-5.43	**0.55**
IFC	0.945	**0.44**	-1.11	**1.76**	0.919	-1.29	-1.17	-1.99	0.967	-4.13	-6.01	-8.50	0.957	-0.48	**0.46**	**0.56**	0.963	-0.24	-0.86	-0.34
VIF	0.986	-0.37	-0.02	**0.07**	0.976	-3.73	-2.57	-0.75	0.974	-3.53	-2.37	-0.54	0.963	**0.51**	**0.46**	**0.54**	0.961	-0.31	**0.16**	**1.00**
MAD	0.981	-0.43	-0.33	-0.92	0.975	-0.13	-0.86	**0.48**	0.957	-0.12	-2.76	-0.12	0.988	-0.20	**0.10**	-0.48	0.958	-2.16	-1.40	**0.14**
PSNR-HVSM	0.975	**0.23**	-0.09	-0.77	0.960	-1.17	-0.21	-2.02	0.920	-0.22	-9.18	-2.58	0.987	**0.05**	-0.02	-0.08	0.910	-4.08	-2.06	**4.34**
PSNR-HVS	0.958	**0.16**	-0.32	-4.65	0.937	-1.72	-0.41	-4.61	0.878	-2.31	**0.93**	**0.64**	0.985	-0.33	-0.11	**0.36**	0.906	**1.09**	-0.21	-0.94
IW-SSIM	0.981	-0.07	-0.01	-8.72	0.971	**0.47**	-0.15	-8.88	0.963	-7.21	-0.87	-9.39	0.969	**0.82**	**0.13**	**1.54**	0.930	**0.59**	**1.17**	-3.65
IW-PSNR	0.983	**0.08**	**0.04**	-0.58	0.966	-4.38	-0.12	-0.20	0.942	-1.87	-2.03	-1.11	0.982	**0.46**	-0.52	**0.50**	0.848	-6.18	-1.79	-2.59
FSIM	0.982	-0.16	**0.56**	**0.47**	0.979	-0.69	-0.46	-7.23	0.968	-1.51	-1.24	-0.37	0.965	-0.37	-0.58	-7.19	0.939	-0.55	**1.31**	-0.87
GMSD	0.985	-0.55	-0.41	**0.07**	0.977	-0.32	**0.07**	**0.07**	0.962	**0.13**	-0.02	**0.20**	0.966	**1.56**	**0.04**	-0.73	0.941	-5.10	-1.49	-0.14
DN	0.967	**0.38**	-0.41	**0.40**	0.961	-1.15	**0.32**	-2.93	0.950	**0.08**	-1.84	-1.82	0.968	-0.32	**0.18**	**0.22**	0.936	-0.59	-0.89	-0.46

Table 7. Relative increase of PCC on the CSIQ data for the 17 metrics and random grouping. Positive increase is shown in bold.

FR metric	AWGN PCC R_{all}	R_L	Δ(%) R_M	R_H	JPEG PCC R_{all}	R_L	Δ(%) R_M	R_H	JPEG2000 PCC R_{all}	R_L	Δ(%) R_M	R_H	FNOISE PCC R_{all}	R_L	Δ(%) R_M	R_H	BLUR PCC R_{all}	R_L	Δ(%) R_M	R_H	CONTRAST PCC R_{all}	R_L	Δ(%) R_M	R_H
MSE	0.901	-2.71	-1.21	-7.25	0.891	-6.12	-12.90	-14.32	0.890	-3.10	-0.79	-0.93	0.952	-6.43	-10.54	-6.77	0.886	**0.67**	-3.57	-3.14	0.861	**3.72**	-2.57	**0.37**
SNR	0.933	-0.88	-1.39	-1.17	0.873	-5.83	-5.42	-14.28	0.927	**0.30**	-1.18	-0.92	0.929	-0.15	-1.99	-0.21	0.899	-7.74	-2.54	-4.91	0.852	-5.06	**0.82**	**0.07**
PSNR	0.953	-1.74	-0.64	-0.32	0.891	-4.60	-9.62	-14.16	0.947	-1.74	**1.04**	-1.14	0.953	-0.94	-0.49	-0.73	0.925	-1.31	-2.66	**1.26**	0.899	**1.23**	-1.23	-0.25
SSIM	0.894	-1.06	-5.24	**1.58**	0.940	-9.54	**0.71**	-5.06	0.923	-6.82	-2.50	-5.19	0.895	-2.13	-1.35	-3.31	0.900	-5.38	**1.78**	-7.52	0.742	**4.04**	**0.93**	-5.28
MS-SSIM	0.947	-11.73	-10.20	-21.94	0.981	-0.60	-0.15	-8.14	0.977	-14.23	-0.51	**0.08**	0.941	-26.00	**1.09**	-21.51	0.959	-0.79	-0.38	-0.21	0.944	**0.32**	**0.33**	**0.47**
UQI	0.766	-1.13	-1.18	-5.63	0.914	**0.02**	-0.67	-3.99	0.903	**4.52**	-0.97	-0.03	0.725	-10.07	-1.74	-7.14	0.948	**0.52**	**0.61**	-0.20	0.851	**1.60**	-1.14	-4.15
VSNR	0.926	-15.75	-1.10	-2.06	0.951	-6.76	-29.62	-8.47	0.960	-0.63	-0.15	-0.57	0.920	-0.01	-0.44	-4.79	0.934	-0.95	-1.36	-0.33	0.873	-2.36	-0.82	-2.68
IFC	0.846	-2.87	-0.61	-1.02	0.955	-18.83	-13.11	-14.67	0.938	-15.86	-1.45	-11.37	0.838	-10.91	**3.85**	**0.24**	0.964	-0.71	**1.01**	-0.92	0.572	**24.47**	**13.29**	**28.78**
VIF	0.961	-0.08	**0.98**	-0.26	0.988	-1.43	-5.20	**0.67**	0.978	-0.45	**0.49**	**0.02**	0.957	**1.13**	**0.15**	-2.52	0.963	**1.13**	**1.73**	**0.48**	0.943	-0.47	**0.66**	-0.04
MAD	0.956	-1.75	**1.06**	-1.58	0.983	-0.60	**0.21**	-1.93	0.982	**0.13**	-0.34	-0.51	0.955	**1.70**	**1.02**	**0.21**	0.976	**0.10**	-0.52	-0.32	0.924	-3.00	**1.22**	-1.72
PSNR-HVSM	0.941	**1.52**	**1.53**	**0.09**	0.973	-1.07	**0.66**	-5.69	0.977	-1.05	-2.35	-0.86	0.957	-1.97	**0.21**	-0.82	0.968	**0.73**	**1.06**	-1.21	0.903	**6.01**	-0.14	-8.47
PSNR-HVS	0.952	**1.25**	**0.12**	**0.12**	0.906	-0.20	-0.55	**1.59**	0.968	**1.07**	-0.49	-3.52	0.953	-7.34	-9.98	-0.88	0.956	**0.10**	**1.42**	-2.08	0.900	**0.31**	**0.81**	**0.95**
IW-SSIM	0.938	-12.05	-12.02	-19.82	0.983	**0.41**	-0.49	-7.89	0.976	-10.02	-0.91	-0.22	0.914	**4.54**	-22.95	-18.37	0.962	-9.43	-0.37	-14.77	0.926	-7.64	**1.45**	**2.55**
IW-PSNR	0.937	-1.40	-1.13	**1.47**	0.983	-4.37	**0.32**	**0.08**	0.986	-0.17	-0.44	-0.33	0.955	**0.48**	-0.54	**0.39**	0.975	-0.36	-12.75	-0.06	0.937	-1.54	**1.45**	**0.27**
FSIM	0.929	**0.51**	-15.10	-2.10	0.984	-0.72	-9.55	-0.38	0.981	**0.03**	**0.25**	-0.21	0.928	-13.28	-15.88	-16.87	0.960	**0.41**	-0.74	-0.46	0.937	-7.91	**3.00**	-2.57
GMSD	0.968	-0.34	**1.20**	-2.52	0.984	**0.50**	**0.01**	-0.27	0.979	-0.74	-0.09	**0.66**	0.958	-0.16	**0.09**	-0.60	0.966	**1.07**	-0.35	-0.35	0.923	**1.49**	-0.03	-0.89
DN	0.912	-1.42	**0.63**	-3.48	0.970	**0.46**	-0.13	-1.65	0.947	-4.34	**0.27**	**0.41**	0.867	-4.70	**0.01**	**0.31**	0.962	**0.41**	**0.27**	-0.84	0.919	-3.37	**0.95**	**1.10**

Table 8. Relative increase of PCC on the LIVE-MD data for the 17 FR metrics and random grouping. Positive increases are shown in bold.

FR metric	BLUR+JPEG				BLUR+NOISE			
	PCC	Δ (%)			PCC	Δ (%)		
	R_{all}	R_L	R_M	R_H	R_{all}	R_L	R_M	R_H
MSE	0.731	**5.09**	−4.73	−1.99	0.760	**2.90**	−15.75	−3.40
SNR	0.731	**6.75**	−4.24	−2.87	0.725	**6.17**	**0.55**	−1.52
PSNR	0.722	−0.12	−11.36	**5.38**	0.774	−5.92	−1.89	**0.34**
SSIM	0.761	**1.11**	−1.15	**5.93**	0.747	−9.91	**3.39**	−7.09
MS-SSIM	0.883	−10.72	−3.81	−3.81	0.841	**4.21**	**4.96**	**0.02**
UQI	0.884	**2.84**	−3.35	−1.63	0.857	−1.08	**0.79**	−0.46
VSNR	0.834	−5.03	−0.78	**2.45**	0.792	**2.22**	**0.61**	**1.46**
IFC	0.918	**1.20**	−0.71	−4.90	0.895	−2.61	−0.36	−0.38
VIF	0.919	−0.02	−1.12	**0.62**	0.880	−0.50	**0.29**	**1.32**
MAD	0.919	−5.52	**0.15**	−0.08	0.868	−3.56	−0.74	−2.20
PSNR-HVSM	0.835	−21.51	**1.31**	**0.21**	0.802	−9.00	−0.15	**3.09**
PSNR-HVS	0.800	−4.98	−2.91	−2.22	0.789	**4.97**	−9.49	**3.34**
IW-SSIM	0.916	−9.06	−0.90	−0.56	0.911	**1.02**	**0.80**	−3.07
IW-PSNR	0.850	**4.04**	−1.47	−5.16	0.808	−1.03	**0.41**	**7.69**
FSIM	0.906	−2.55	−8.85	−2.09	0.818	**5.64**	**8.13**	**9.51**
GMSD	0.894	−1.57	−2.02	**0.47**	0.867	−2.72	−6.52	**0.84**
DN	0.867	−1.37	−1.30	−3.92	0.851	**0.68**	−1.02	−1.79

References

1. Chandler, D.M., Alam, M.M., Phan, T.D.: Seven challenges for image quality research. In: Proceedings of IS&T/SPIE Electronic Imaging, p. 901402. International Society for Optics and Photonics (2014)
2. Larson, E.C., Chandler, D.M.: Most apparent distortion: full-reference image quality assessment and the role of strategy. J. Electron. Imaging **19**(1), 011006 (2010)
3. Moorthy, A.K., Bovik, A.C.: Visual quality assessment algorithms: what does the future hold? Multimedia Tools Appl. **51**(2), 675–696 (2011)
4. Triantaphillidou, S., Allen, E., Jacobson, R.E.: Image quality of JPEG vs JPEG2000: part 2: scene dependency, scene analysis and classification. J. Imaging Sci. Technol. **51**, 259–270 (2007)
5. Oh, K.H., Triantaphillidou, S., Jacobson, R.E.: Scene classification with respect to image quality measurements. In: Proceedings of IS&T/SPIE Electronic Imaging, p. 752908. International Society for Optics and Photonics (2010)
6. Bondzulic, B., Pavlovic, B., Petrovic, V., Andric, M.: Performance of peak signal-to-noise ratio quality assessment in video streaming with packet losses. Electron. Lett. **52**(6), 454–456 (2016)

7. Bianco, S., Ciocca, G., Marini, F., Schettini, R.: Image quality assessment by preprocessing and full reference model combination. In: Proceedings of IS&T/SPIE Electronic Imaging, p. 72420O. International Society for Optics and Photonics (2009)

8. Liu, H., Engelke, U., Wang, J., Le Callet, P., Heynderickx, I.: How does image content affect the added value of visual attention in objective image quality assessment? IEEE Signal Process. Lett. **20**, 355–358 (2013)

9. Corchs, S., Gasparini, F., Schettini, R.: Grouping strategies to improve the correlation between subjective and objective image quality data. In: Proceddings of IS&T/SPIE Electronic Imaging, p. 86530D. International Society for Optics and Photonics (2013)

10. Jayaraman, D., Mittal, A., Moorthy, A.M., Bovik, A.: Objective quality assessment of multiply distorted images. In: Proceedings of the Asilomar Conference on Signals, Systems and Computers (2012)

11. Sheik, H., Wang, Z., Cormakc, L., Bovik, A.: LIVE image quality assessment database release 2. http://live.ece.utexas.edu/research/quality

12. Larson, E., Chandler, D.: CSIQ: categorical subjective image quality CSIQ database (2009). http://vision.okstate.edu/csiq

13. Birkhoff, G.D.: Collected Mathematical Papers. Dover, New York (1950)

14. Oliva, A., Mack, M.L., Shrestha, M.: Identifying the perceptual dimensions of visual complexity of scenes. In: Proceedings of the 26th Annual Meeting of the Cognitive Science Society (2004)

15. Mario, I., Chacon, M., Alma, D., Corral, S.: Image complexity measure: a human criterion free approach. In: Annual Meeting of the North American Fuzzy Information Processing Society, 2005. NAFIPS 2005, pp. 241–246. IEEE (2005)

16. Rigau, J., Feixas, M., Sbert, M.: An information-theoretic framework for image complexity. In: Proceedings of the First Eurographics Conference on Computational Aesthetics in Graphics, Visualization and Imaging, pp. 177–184. Eurographics Association (2005)

17. Perkiö, J., Hyvärinen, A.: Modelling image complexity by independent component analysis, with application to content-based image retrieval. In: Alippi, C., Polycarpou, M., Panayiotou, C., Ellinas, G. (eds.) ICANN 2009. LNCS, vol. 5769, pp. 704–714. Springer, Heidelberg (2009). doi:10.1007/978-3-642-04277-5_71

18. Rosenholtz, R., Li, Y., Nakano, L.: Measuring visual clutter. J. Vis. **7**(2), 17 (2007)

19. Mack, M., Oliva, A.: Computational estimation of visual complexity. In: The 12th Annual Object, Perception, Attention, and Memory Conference (2004)

20. Corchs, S.E., Ciocca, G., Bricolo, E., Gasparini, F.: Predicting complexity perception of real world images. PloS One **11**(6), e0157986 (2016)

21. Ciocca, G., Corchs, S., Gasparini, F.: Genetic programming approach to evaluate complexity of texture images. J. Electron. Imaging **25**(6), 061408 (2016)

22. Allen, E., Triantaphillidou, S., Jacobson, R.: Image quality comparison between JPEG and JPEG2000. I: psychophysical investigation. J. Imaging Sci. Technol. **51**, 248–258 (2007)

23. Chacón, M., Aguilar, L.: A fuzzy approach to edge level detection. In: The 10th IEEE International Conference on Fuzzy Systems, 2001, vol. 2, pp. 809–812. IEEE (2001)

24. Bezdek, J.C.: Pattern Recognition with Fuzzy Objective Function Algorithms. Kluwer Academic Publishers, London (1981)

25. Balasko, B., Abonyi, J., Feil, B.: Fuzzy clustering and data analysis toolbox. Department of Process Engineering, University of Veszprem, Veszprem (2005)

26. Martin, D., Fowlkes, C., Tal, D., Malik, J.: A database of human segmented natural images and its application to evaluating segmentation algorithms and measuring ecological statistics. In: Procedings of the 8th International Conference on Computer Vision, vol. 2, pp. 416–423, July 2001

27. Bezdek, J.C., Dunn, J.C.: Optimal fuzzy partitions: a heuristic for estimating the parameters in a mixture of normal distributions. IEEE Trans. Comput. **100**(8), 835–838 (1975)

28. Winkler, S.: Analysis of public image and video databases for quality assessment. IEEE J. Sel. Top. Sig. Proces. **6**, 616–625 (2012)

29. Sheikh, H., Sabir, M., Bovik, A.: A statistical evaluation of recent full reference image quality assessment algorithms. IEEE Trans. Image Process. **15**, 3440–3451 (2006)

30. Wang, Z., Bovik, A.: A universal image quality index. IEEE Signal Process. Lett. **9**, 81–84 (2002)

31. Wang, Z., Bovik, A., Sheikh, H., Simoncelli, E.: Image quality assessment: from error visibility to structural similarity. IEEE Trans. Image Process. **13**, 600–612 (2004)

32. Wang, Z., Simoncelli, E., Bovik, A.: Multi-scale structural similarity for image quality assessment. In: 37th IEEE Asilomar Conference on Signals, Systems and Computers (2003)

33. Chandler, D., Hemami, S.: VSNR: a wavelet-based visual signal-to-noise ratio for natural images. IEEE Trans. Image Process. **16**, 2284–2298 (2007)

34. Sheikh, H., Bovik, A., de Veciana, G.: An information fidelity criterion for image quality assessment using natural scene statistics. IEEE Trans. Image Process. **14**, 2117–2128 (2005)

35. Sheikh, H., Bovik, A.: Image information and visual quality. IEEE Trans. Image Process. **15**, 430–444 (2006)

36. Egiazarian, K., Astola, J., Ponomarenko, N., Lukin, V., Battisti, F., Carli, M.: New full-reference quality metrics based on hvs. In: CD-ROM proceedings of the Second International Workshop on Video Processing and Quality Metrics, Scottsdale, USA (2006)

37. Ponomarenko, N., Silvestri, F., Egiazarian, K., Carli, M., Astola, J., Lukin, V.: On between-coefficient contrast masking of dct basis functions. In: Proceedings of the Third International Workshop on Video Processing and Quality Metrics, vol. 4 (2007)

38. Wang, Z., Li, Q.: Information content weighting for perceptual image quality assessment. IEEE Trans. Image Process. **20**(5), 1185–1198 (2011)

39. Zhang, L., Zhang, D., Mou, X., Zhang, D.: FSIM: a feature similarity index for image quality assessment. IEEE Trans. Image Process. **20**(8), 2378–2386 (2011)

40. Xue, W., Zhang, L., Mou, X., Bovik, A.: Gradient magnitude similarity deviation: a highly efficient perceptual image quality index. IEEE Trans. Image Process. **23**(2), 684–695 (2014)

41. Laparra, V., Muñoz-Marí, J., Malo, J.: Divisive normalization image quality metric revisited. JOSA A **27**(4), 852–864 (2010)

42. Jayaraman, D., Mittal, A., Moorthy, A.K., Bovik, A.C.: Objective image quality assessment of multiply distorted images. In: Proceedings of Asilomar Conference on Signals, Systems and Computers (2012)

Color In Digital Cultural Heritage

Visualization of Subsurface Features in Oil Paintings Using High-Resolution Visible and Near Infrared Scanned Images

Jay Arre Toque[1,3(✉)], Koji Okumura[1], Yashuhide Shimbata[2], and Ari Ide-Ektessabi[3]

[1] Kyoto Technology Science Center, Sabia Inc., Kyoto, Japan
{j.toque,okumura}@sabia.co.jp
[2] Ishibashi Foundation, Bridgestone Museum of Art, Tokyo, Japan
shimbata@bridgestone-museum.gr.jp
[3] Graduate School of Engineering, Kyoto University, Katsura Campus, Kyoto, Japan
ide.ari.4n@kyoto-u.ac.jp

Abstract. High-resolution imaging is on the rise in the field of digital archiving of cultural heritage. Conventionally, this is accomplished by capturing images in the visible region. However, the visible region has a very narrow spectrum. In this study, around 100 oil paintings belonging to the Bridgestone Museum of Art in Tokyo, Japan have been digitized at both visible and near infrared region (i.e. ~400–700 nm and ~850 nm respectively) at 1000 dpi scanning resolution. Since materials behave differently when irradiated by a source with different wavelengths, the resulting images from visible and near infrared scans could reveal some under-drawings which are not visible from the naked eye. By applying false color image composition, it was possible to visualize subsurface features more easily. Different false color images were investigated by substituting the individual RGB channels of the visible images with NIR image to increase the optical contrast. *Promenade* (1926) by George Grosz was selected as a test case.

Keywords: Analytical imaging · Subsurface feature detection · VIS/NIR imaging · Oil paintings · High-resolution scanning

1 Introduction

Cultural heritage investigation is undergoing fast advancements largely because of technological developments in optical devices, image processing and digital computing [1–6]. These objects are under constant threat of destruction due to calamities both natural and man-made. This makes studying these objects and documenting them using state-of-the-art techniques an imperative. Unlike ordinary objects, cultural heritage analysis requires it to be non-destructive but preferably noninvasive. There are many techniques used by scientist to accomplish this purpose such as microscopy, chromatography, spectroscopy and many more others [7–10]. In recent years, analytical imaging which can be a combination of microscopy and spectroscopy has been gaining popularity [3, 6]. This technique makes it

© Springer International Publishing AG 2017
S. Bianco et al. (Eds.): CCIW 2017, LNCS 10213, pp. 125–134, 2017.
DOI: 10.1007/978-3-319-56010-6_10

possible to extract quantitative and qualitative information using images through image processing, data mining and pattern recognition.

Visible light and near infrared imaging spectroscopy are two of the most widely used techniques for analytical imaging [11–19]. These techniques can be used to map and identify pigments from paintings, detect cracks and other surface defects and reveal underdrawings [3, 4]. In this study, visible light and near infrared images were used to visualize subsurface features from an oil painting by George Grosz (*Promenade, 1926*). Using false color composition, near infrared image was used to replace the chromatic channels of the visible light image. This was used to enhance the optical contrast between the top painting surface and the underpainting surface. Based on the result, replacing the green channel with NIR image yielded the best result. Through this method, some subsurface features from the painting were revealed which could provide an insight on the technique and style of the artist.

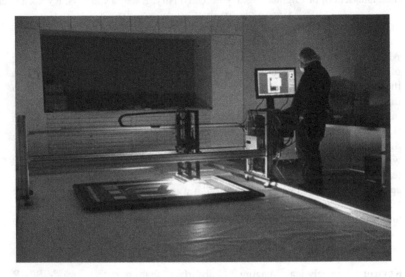

Fig. 1. High-resolution scanning set-up at Bridgestone Museum of Art in Tokyo

2   Methods and Experiments

2.1   High-Resolution Visible and Near Infrared Scanning

High-resolution images were taken using scanners manufactured by Sabia Inc., developed at the Advanced Imaging Technology Laboratory of Kyoto University. The scanner features a dual line camera head which can take simultaneous visible and near infrared images. This unique feature offers greatly reduced the acquisition time unlike conventional imaging techniques where these two type of images must be acquired separately. The light sources used were a visible LED by Nichia and near infrared LED by CCS (~850 nm spectral peak). The spectral characteristics of the light sources are shown in Figs. 2 and 3. The cameras were two Takenaka's TLC-7500CLD line camera. The spectral sensitivity of the camera is shown in

Fig. 4. One camera was filtered using a UV/IR cut filter while the other camera was filtered with an IR filter. The scanning resolution was 1000 dpi (~39 pixel/mm).

There were around 100 oil paintings digitized belonging to the collection of Bridgestone Museum of Art in Tokyo. These paintings represent the best of the best in their collection. The paintings vary in sizes the largest of which is around 2 × 2 m. Figure 1 shows the scanner set-up used in this study. The project took around 10 days to complete.

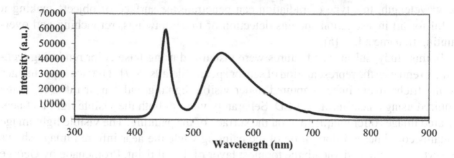

Fig. 2. Spectral characteristics of the visible LED source

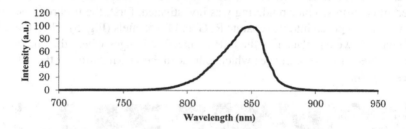

Fig. 3. Spectral characteristics of the near infrared LED source

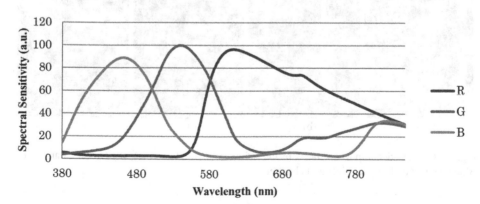

Fig. 4. Spectral sensitivities of the line camera (TLC-7500CLD)

2.2 Subsurface Feature Visualization

Visible light imaging is conventionally used to record color and spatial information of artworks. This mimics the sensitivity of human vision which is confined to a narrow spectral band of 400–700 nm. This limits the information to what the human eyes can see. For some artworks, it is important to look beyond the surface and see what lies underneath. This could be accomplished by infrared imaging [2, 7–9]. Depending on the wavelength, this type of radiation can penetrate the surface of objects making it useful for art investigation such as detection of underdrawings, retouching and over-painting to name a few [5].

In this study, subsurface features were visualized using false color rendering technique to enhance the representation of sensor specific details [5, 7]. The two input images are the trichromatic image captured under visible lighting and a near infrared image acquired using a near infrared LED. Separately viewed, both the visible light and near infrared images offer unique look on the surface of the painting. The visible light image contains colorimetric information of the painting while the near infrared image shows subsurface feature underneath the topmost layer of the oil paint. Promenade by George Grosz was chosen as a test case because it reveals some interesting subsurface feature seen from the near infrared image. In order to enhance the visualization of the underlying feature, different false color rendering was investigated. First, the trichromatic visible image was decomposed into its separate R, G and B channels (Fig. 5). Then these individual channels were replaced by the NIR image. The images where then recomposed producing three false color images which enhanced the visualization of the subsurface features (Fig. 6).

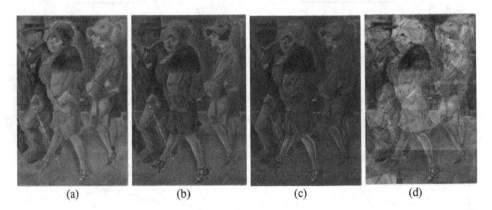

(a)   (b)   (c)   (d)

Fig. 5. Channel-decomposed images of the painting: (a) Red channel; (b) Green Channel; (c) Blue channel; and (d) Near infrared channel

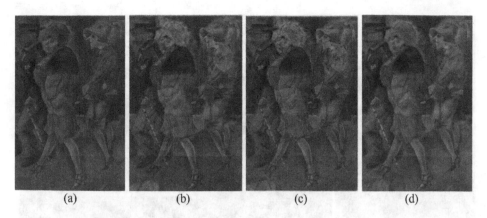

Fig. 6. Different images utilizing false color rendering to enhance the visualization of subsurface features: (a) trichromatic (RGB) visible image; (b) the R-channel was replaced with the NIR image; (c) the G-channel was replaced with the NIR image; and (d) the B-channel was replaced with the NIR image

3   Results and Discussion

Imaging is a non-destructive and non-invasive technique for investigating cultural heritage artworks. These type of objects require extra care during analysis because of its delicate nature. In the past, imaging was conventionally used to record and digitally archive color and spatial information of the art object. With the development of new sensors and light sources, images can now be used for analysis through analytical imaging. Analytical imaging refers to the technique of using images to extract information such as spectral, colorimetric, spatial and others from an object through image processing, data mining and pattern recognition [3, 4]. This is made possible by the unique response a particular material has when subjected to various type of electromagnetic radiation. In this study, the visible and near infrared region were of particular interest. Images taken from these spectral regions were used to visualize subsurface feature of an oil painting by Grosz (*Promenade*, 1926). This was accomplished by substituting a color channel from the visible image with the near infrared image. Two regions of interest (ROI), revealing some subsurface features were further investigated (Fig. 7).

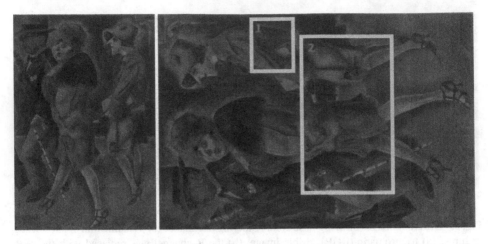

Fig. 7. ROI selection depicting subsurface feature from the oil painting.

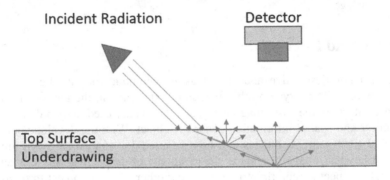

Fig. 8. Interaction model on how subsurface feature are detected when the painting was observed under near infrared radiation. Note: the incident radiation is the LED NIR source while the detector is the IR filtered line CCD camera.

A material subjected to electromagnetic radiation behaves in a predictable manner. Depending on the wavelength and amount of energy, the incident radiation could either be reflected, absorbed or transmitted. This interaction can be observed and quantified by using a sensor detector. For example, when visible light is shone on an object, the reflected light could be observed using a camera as a detector. The amount of absorption or reflection observed is how colors are formed. Materials reflecting radiation with wavelength between 490–570 nm would appear green. Similarly, a material's near infrared absorption and reflection can be observed using a sensor sensitive in this spectral region. The depth in which visible and near infrared radiation could penetrate the surface are different. Visible light mostly stays in the surface while NIR could penetrate the surface a little deeper. If there are different layers of materials overlapping within the field of view of the sensor, the optical contrast of these materials is how a subsurface feature can be detected especially in the NIR region. Figure 8 shows a simple model on how a subsurface feature such as underdrawings is observed.

The observed diffused reflection of both the top surface and subsurface pigments can be numerically using the Kubelka-Munk equation as shown below [13].

$$R = \frac{1 - R_b(a - b \cdot coth(bSt)}{a - R_b + b \cdot coth(bSt)} \tag{1}$$

Where; $a = (S + K)/S$; $b = \sqrt{a^2 - 1}$; t is the thickness of the pigment layer; S is the scattering coefficient of the pigment layer; K is the absorption coefficient of the pigment layer; and R_b is the reflectance of the background.

Using Eq. 1, it can be inferred that the optical contrast between the top pigment layer and the underdrawing will increase if the thickness of the pigment layer decreases as well as the scattering and absorption coefficient. On the other hand, as the difference in the reflectance of the top layer and the underlayer increases so will the optical contrast [5]. In this study, the optical contrast between the top painting layer and the subsurface features were enhance by applying false color redering. By replacing the color channels of the visible light images, three sets of images with varying reflectance characteristics were produced. Based on the false color rendering, replacing the green channel with the NIR image yielded the best optical contrast to reveal the underdrawing. This implies that the blue and red channels have similar reflectance characteristics as the NIR image. At the moment, the decision to pick the green channel over the other two channels is accomplished by comparing the images side by side. In the future experiments planned as continuation of this study, a more objective and numerical approach would be employed by calculating the contrast ratio when substituting each channels. This could improve the robustness of the method. Figure 9 shows examples of false color images where the green channel is replaced. In the case of ROI 1, a subsurface feature of a man with a big nose appears. This is an underdrawing because this is not observed in the visible light image. On the other hand, ROI 2 shows a figure of a woman hiding underneath the top paint layer. What is interesting in these subsurface features is that it appears that there is another set of painting underneath the top painting layer. These subsurface features were oriented 90° clockwise with respect to the actual orientation of the features on the top painting. It possible that the artist reused the canvas and painted over the underpaintings observed. Some artists are known to reuse their canvas so it is not entirely out of the realm of possibility. What is good about the technique applied in this study is that all of this investigation is done digitally. This means that it is completely noninvasive which makes it highly attractive to the cultural heritage community. However, it is important to note that not all paintings are hiding subsurface features beneath the surface. In addition, the optimum channel to use when trying to observer subsurface feature is entirely dependent on the material of the underlayer. It is possible that in some cases, the blue or red channel replacement would provide the better optical contrast. In this case, it can be inferred that using multispectral images instead of just an RGB image could provide better sampling when visualizing subsurface features using false color rendering. This has been explored in other studies but this technique could be time consuming depending on the number of spectral bands being acquired [3–6].

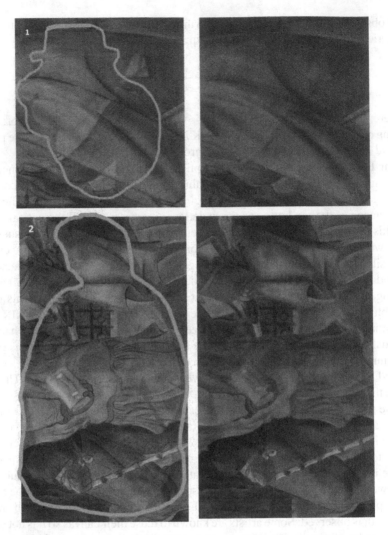

Fig. 9. False color image composition of ROI 1 and 2 where the green channel is replaced with the NIR image. (1) shows a subsurface feature of a man with a big nose while (2) reveals a figure of a woman hiding behind the top paint layer.

4   Conclusion

Digitally archived images are useful for non-destructive and noninvasive investigation of cultural heritage objects. The advances in computing technology makes it possible to extract information from a picture through image processing, data mining and pattern recognition. Images can be produced using different sensors as detectors. In this study, visible light and near infrared images were acquired. These images were used to visualize subsurface features of an oil painting belonging to the collection of the Bridgestone

Museum of Art in Tokyo. The optical contrast of the subsurface features increased when the green channel of the visible light image is replaced with the NIR image. This allows for the easier observation of underlayer hiding beneath the surface. Although the green channel replacement yielded the best result in the test case, it is important to note that the optimum false color composition is dependent on the spectral characteristics of the subsurface feature. The optical contrast of the underpainting is dependent on the thickness of the pigment layer, the scattering and absorption coefficient of the material and the difference in the reflectance characteristics of the top paint layer and underlayer. The higher the optical contrast, the easier it is to observe subsurface features.

References

1. Teke, M., Başeski, E., Ok, A.Ö., Yüksel, B., Şenaras, Ç.: Multi-spectral false color shadow detection. In: Stilla, U., Rottensteiner, F., Mayer, H., Jutzi, B., Butenuth, M. (eds.) PIA 2011. LNCS, vol. 6952, pp. 109–119. Springer, Heidelberg (2011). doi:10.1007/978-3-642-24393-6_10
2. Balas, C., Papadakis, V., Papadakis, N., Papadakis, A., Vazgiouraki, E., Themelis, G.: A novel hyper-spectral imaging apparatus for the non-destructive analysis of objects of artistic and historic values. J. Cult. Herit. **4**, 330–337 (2003)
3. Toque, J.A., Sakatoku, Y., Anders, J., Murayama, Y., Ide-Ektessabi, A.: Analytical imaging of cultural heritage by synchrotron radiation and visible light-near infrared spectroscopy. In: Proceedings of the International Joint Conference on Computer Vision, Imaging and Computer Graphic (2009)
4. Toque, J.A., Komori, M., Murayama, Y., Ide-Ektessabi, A.: Analytical imaging of traditional Japanese paintings using multispectral images. In: Ranchordas, A., Pereira, J.M., Araújo, H.J., Tavares, J.M.R.S. (eds.) VISIGRAPP 2009. CCIS, vol. 68, pp. 119–132. Springer, Heidelberg (2010). doi:10.1007/978-3-642-11840-1_9
5. Hain, M., Bartl, J., Jacko, V.: Multispectral analysis of cultural heritage artefacts. Measur. Sci. Rev. **3**, 9–12 (2003)
6. El-Rifai, I., Mahgoub, H., Ide-Ektessabi, A.: Multi-spectral imaging system (IWN) for the digitization and investigation of cultural heritage. In: Ioannides, M., Fink, E., Moropoulou, A., Hagedorn-Saupe, M., Fresa, A., Liestøl, G., Rajcic, V., Grussenmeyer, P. (eds.) EuroMed 2016. LNCS, vol. 10058, pp. 232–240. Springer, Heidelberg (2016). doi:10.1007/978-3-319-48496-9_19
7. Delaney, J.K., Zeibel, J.G., Thoury, M., Littleton, R., Palmer, M., Morales, K.M., De La Rie, E.R., Hoenigswald, A.: Visible and infrared imaging spectroscopy of picasso's harlequinn musician: mapping and identification of artist materials in situ. Appl. Spectr. **64**(6), 584–594 (2010)
8. Mansfield, J.R., Attas, M., Majzels, C., Cloutis, E., Collins, C., Mantsch, H.H.: Near infrared spectroscopic reflectance imaging: a new tool in art conservation. Vib. Spectrosc. **28**, 59–66 (2002)
9. Mosca, S., Alberti, R., Frizzi, T., Nevin, A., Valentini, G., Comelli, D.: A whole spectroscopic mapping approach for studying the spatial distribution of pigments in paintings. Appl. Phys. A **122**, 815 (2016)
10. Kockelmann, W.: Radiation in Art and Archeometry. Elsevier Science B.V. (2000)
11. Chene, G., Garnir, H.P., Marchal, A., Mathis, F., Strivay, D.: Improved energy resolution of a cyclotron beam RBS measurements. Nucl. Instr. Meth. B **266**, 2110–2112 (2008)

12. Anglos, D., Georgiou, S., Fotakis, C.: Lasers in the analysis of cultural heritage materials. J. Nano Res. **8**, 27–60 (2009)
13. Gunde, M.K., Logar, J.K., Orel, Z.C., Orel, B.: Application of the Kubelka-Munk theory to thickness-dependent diffuse reflectance of black. Appl. Spectrosc. **49**, 623–629 (1995)
14. Toque, J.A., Ide-Ektessabi, A.: Investigation of degradation mechanism and discoloration of traditional Japanese pigments by multispectral imaging. In: Proceedings of SPIE, p. 7869:78690E (2011)
15. Murakami, Y., Obi, T., Yamaguchi, M., Ohyama, N., Komiya, Y.: Spectral reflectance estimation from multi-band image using color chart. Opt. Commun. **188**, 47–54 (2001)
16. Shen, H.L., Xin, J.H., Shao, S.J.: Opt. Express **15**, 5531–5536 (2007)
17. López-Álvarez, M.A., Hernández-Andrés, J., Valero, E.M., Romero, J.: J. Opt. Soc. Am. A **24**, 942–956 (2007)
18. Shimano, N.: Opt. Eng. **45**, 013201 (2006)
19. Ntziachistos, V.: Going deeper than microscopy: the optical imaging frontier in biology. Nat. Methods **7**, 603–614 (2010)

A Simple Scanner for High Resolution Imaging of Wall Paintings

Kyohei Yoshida[1], Peng Wang[1], Jay Arre Toque[2], Masahiro Toiya[2], and Ari Ide-Ektessabi[1](✉)

[1] Advanced Imaging Technology Laboratory, Graduate School of Engineering, Kyoto University, Kyoto, Japan
yoshida.kyohei.56r@st.kyoto-u.ac.jp, ide.ari.4n@kyoto-u.ac.jp
[2] SABIA Inc., Kyoto, Japan

Abstract. The increasing demand for high-resolution digital color imaging of cultural heritage assets such as mural paintings makes it necessary to build image acquisition systems that are easy to use in different conditions and sometimes in environments without sources of electric power. Here, we propose a simple structure of a scanning system in which the motion of the scanning head utilizes gravity as its motion mechanism instead of electricity. This system enables an area image sensor camera to move along the rail at constant speed without an electrical motor, but uses gravity instead. The camera mounted on the camera stage moves slowly at constant speed with continuous shooting mode. Using this method, it is possible to acquire many images and stitch them together to obtain a panoramic image of a big object at high resolution. This paper discusses the structure and application of this system that can acquire high-resolution images.

Keywords: High resolution color image scanning · A simple color scanning device · Cultural heritage · Big color paintings scanning · Wall paintings

1 Introduction

The current global trend toward high resolution color imaging calls for a versatile, compact, user-friendly, and robust scanning system that can be operated in different outdoor and indoor environments even without electricity, such as remote mural painting sites, yet capable of acquiring images with enough details to allow the viewer to fully appreciate the imaged subjects.

Digital imaging is generally performed by either an area image sensor or a linear image sensor. The area image sensors are composed of two-dimensional array of imaging sensor elements, and the linear sensors are composed of one-dimensional array of imaging sensor elements. Area image sensors are better known because they are widely used in commercial DSLR (digital single-lens reflex) cameras. However, they can only acquire limited small to medium-sized images. On the other hand, linear sensors, in theory, have no size limit since there are no inherent limitations on the length of their travel along the scanning direction. Therefore, the linear sensors can capture very high-resolution images. But it is difficult to apply them to some environments,

© Springer International Publishing AG 2017
S. Bianco et al. (Eds.): CCIW 2017, LNCS 10213, pp. 135–143, 2017.
DOI: 10.1007/978-3-319-56010-6_11

because they have many practical limitations, for example, the issue of vibrations accompanied by motion [2–4].

A simple scanning system should be composed of a readily available area image sensor camera yet capable of capturing very high-resolution images. Here, the authors propose a scanning system stitching images acquired by area imaging sensor. It was not easy to stitch these images (in this paper, stitching means to combine multiple image tile into one panoramic image), because deformation happens after stitching, we calculated the value of deformation and introduced the scanning condition at which the deformation does not happen.

2   Modeling

In order to introduce the scanning condition at which the deformation does not happen, we introduce the camera coordinate system as shown in Fig. 1 and considered perspective projection. The relationship of the real space coordinate and image space coordinate is depicted as

$$x = f\frac{X}{Z},$$
$$y = f\frac{Y}{Z}.$$

(1)

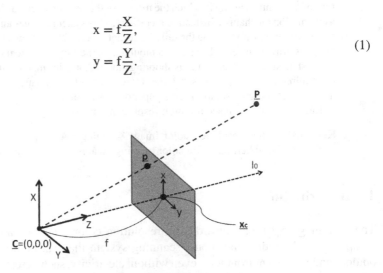

Fig. 1. *The camera coordinate system:* A point P on an object with coordinates (X, Y, Z) will be imaged at some point p = (x, y) in the image plane. A point C is called optical center and the origin of the real space coordinates. The length of the image plane and optical center f is called the focal length [1].

When a camera is moved by the distance C on X axis, Eq. 1 is depicted as

$$x - fC = f\frac{X - C}{Z},$$
$$y = f\frac{Y}{Z}.$$

(2)

The deformation is caused by the difference of the distance on X axis of any two points calculated by Eqs. 1 and 2. Each distances Δx_1 and Δx_2 are depicted as

$$\Delta x_1 = f\frac{X_2}{Z_2} - f\frac{X_1}{Z_1},$$

$$\Delta x_2 = f\frac{X_2 - C}{Z_2} - f\frac{X_1 - C}{Z_1},$$

(3)

and the difference e_x is depicted as

$$e_x = |\Delta x_1 - \Delta x_2|,$$

$$= f\frac{C|Z_1 - Z_2|}{Z_1 Z_2}$$

(4)

When two points (P_1 and P_2) is on an object, Z_1 and Z_2 are described as

$$Z_1 = Z_0 + \delta_1,$$

$$Z_2 = Z_0 + \delta_2,$$

(5)

where Z_0 is the position of a center of an object and δ_1 and δ_2 are the distance of each points and Z_0. If Z_0 is much bigger than δ_1 and δ_2, $\delta_1\delta_2$ can be neglected, Eq. 4 is depicted as

$$e_x = f\frac{C|\delta_1 - \delta_2|}{Z_0^2 + Z_0(\delta_1 + \delta_2)}.$$

(6)

When e_x is maximum, Eq. 6 is depicted as

$$e_M = f\frac{CL}{Z_0^2},$$

(7)

where L is the depth of an object.

Since the resolution (Dpi) is in direct proportion to f/Z_0, Eq. 7 is depicted as

$$e_M = \alpha\frac{CL}{Z_0}(DPI),$$

(8)

where (DPI) is the resolution of an image and α is a constant depending on an area sensor's structure.

Equation 8 indicates this system is useful for imaging objects which have very small L, for example wall paintings, because when $L \cong 0$, e_M is very small.

When $L \neq 0$, the deformations occur. Difference e_M is in direct proportion to (a) the movement distance of the camera "C", (b) the depth of the object "L", and (c) the resolution of an image "(DPI)", and inversely proportion to the distance between optical center and the object "Z_0".

3   A Scanning Device

Equation 8 shows that difference e_x is in direct proportion to the movement distance of the camera C and the depth of the object "L". We should construct a scanning device to reduce these parameters.

When an area image sensor camera moves slowly at constant speed (condition (a)) with programmed constant and continuous shooting function, the moving distance of the camera C decreases and the deformation is reduced. The slower the speed of the camera, the less image blurring occurs.

Moreover, when this system is applied for paintings, the camera direction should be as parallel to object as possible (condition (b)).

3.1   Components of the Device

The scanning system based on the proposed method is shown as Fig. 2. The conditions required mentioned above could be satisfied by this system. The constructed scanning device is composed of only four parts: (1) the area image sensor camera, (2) the camera stage, (3) two friction dampers, and (4) the rack and rail guide module. These four parts can be used together to built a high-resolution scanning system without the need for electricity supply and a PC. The brief introductions for each part are as follow:

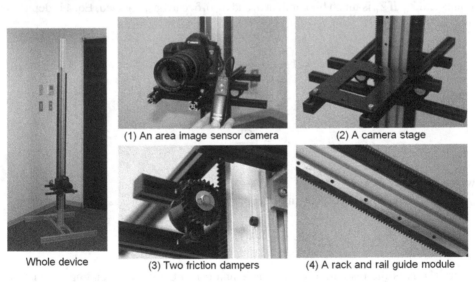

Fig. 2. *Scanning device:* This device is a simple scanning system depending on gravity force instead of electricity. This device does not need a PC and a motor to control the position of the camera. This is composed of only four parts: (1) an area image sensor camera, (2) a camera stage, (3) two friction dampers, and (4) a rack and rail guide module. Friction dampers keep the drop speed of the camera constant and slow.

Area image sensor camera: The area image sensor camera should be able to take consecutive pictures and be set at high ISO speed. The system proposed use a canon EOS 5D Mark III camera. We use a remote switch to operate the camera.

Camera Stage: The camera stage is composed of some aluminum frames, two linear guides, and a plate. It can be designed for a camera based on its size and shape, as well as its application environment and so on.

Friction Dampers: Condition (a) is satisfied through the use of friction dampers shown in the photograph. It contains several gear with special feature that the faster rotating speed, the more torque is produced. The magnitude of torque can be controlled. The drop speed can be controlled by changing the magnitude of torque. The dampers enable to control the position of the camera without electricity supply and a PC.

Rack and Rail Guide Module: Condition (b) is satisfied trough the use of the rack and rail module. A rack and rail guide module is composed of some aluminum frames, a stopper, two racks, and a rail guide. It also can be designed for specific application environments, the size of an object, and so on.

4   Experiments

This system is useful for imaging wall paintings, because they have very small depth. In order to show how this system can be used for wall paintings, an oil painting on the wall was taken as scanning object. Figure 3 shows scanning work. This system reacquires only pulling a stage up by hand and releasing it then gravity takes over.

(1) Pulling up the camera module by hand

(2) Releasing the camera module

Fig. 3. *Scanning procedure:* This system reacquires only repeating pulling the stage up on the rail and releasing it while the camera is in a continuous shooting mode.

Figure 4 shows an image acquired by this system and Table 1 shows the experiment condition including the parameter setting of the area sensor camera, dimension information of the wall painting and other detailed information. A high-resolution image is composed of several pictures taken by an area image sensor camera. The stitched image is composed about 1650 pictures (Approximately, 50 pictures in vertical direction × 33 pictures in horizontal direction). Although the painting was relatively large, this system can acquire high-resolution images without PC and electricity supply. (In this experiment, we used electricity for light source. If this system is used in an environment without electricity, a battery can be used to power the light source.) The image which is acquired without electricity supply is about 700 dpi and has very small deformation. This experiment proved that this system is useful for wall paintings.

Fig. 4. *The image acquired by the system:* Even if an object is very large, this system can acquire a high-resolution image. This image is about 700 dpi and 12.5 GB. Moreover, it was acquired without PCs and electricity supply. (Note: In this experiment, we used electricity for light source but this could also be supplied by a battery) The details of the image could be observed after zooming in.

Table 1. The condition of wall painting experiments

Camera condition								
C [cm]	L [cm]	Z0 [cm]	resolution [dpi]	the number of pictures N	f [mm]	iso speed	Aperture	Shutter Speed [s]
2.8	0	86	700	50*33=1650	200	256000	f/5.6	1/1000

Object condition		The others		
H[cm]	W[cm]	preparation time [min]	scanning time [min]	image size [Gbyte]
120	160	40	70	12.5

C : the movement distance of the camera.
L : the depth of the object.
Z0 : the sum of the focal length and the distance between the camera and the picture instead of the distance between the optical center and the object.
N : the number of images used for the high-resolution image.
f : the focal length of the area sensor camera.
H and W : the height and the width of the object.
Preparation time and scanning time indicate the actual time assuming that only one person does this experiment.

5 Application

The simplicity of the system enables many applications. One of applications is 3D reconstruction. It becomes more difficult when this system is applied to imaging objects which have three-dimensional contours, because the depth of the object "L" causes deformations. The images cannot be stitched correctly unless it is further improved for 3D scanning. As shown in Fig. 5, we developed the device that is composed of two or more cameras. This device can acquire many high resolution images for stereo vision. Moreover, arranging several cameras in a line at same time enables to acquire wide range of an object at once and reduce scanning time. This system can be applied to various situations.

6 Discussion

In the oil painting experiment mentioned in the previous section, it was demonstrated that our system is very simple and works without PC and electricity supply. It can acquire a high-resolution image with small deformation anywhere. We assumed that the blurring was caused by the movement of camera stage module, but there was negligible blurring on some part of the image being caused by the movement of camera stage module. This experiment demonstrated that we can scan big wall paintings without PC and electricity supply. When scanning in remote locations without electricity, this will be a serious problem. We used 12 V power supply for light source. A 12 V mobile battery should be applied for the light source of this system. Moreover the small deformations can be recognized on the image. They are caused by vibration in the normal direction of picture and stitching program *Photomerge*. We should improve the device and develop novel

Fig. 5. *Application for stereo vision:* This system can be applied to many kinds of demand. For example, this system can be applied to stereo vision. This system cannot digitize objects which have three-dimensional contours, but it can acquire images which can be used for 3D reconstruct.

stitching algorithms. For 3D objects, images acquired by this system have deformations. For scanning of 3D objects, the hardware and software of this system still need to be improved. Although some challenges remain, we developed scanning system which can acquire high-resolution image wherever you want to scan.

7   Conclusion

We have constructed a simple and robust scanning system that takes advantage of gravity and does not depend on electricity for its scanning motion. This device is composed of very few parts without PC and motors, yet it is capable of acquiring high-resolution images regardless of the size of the subject, making it suitable for scanning of large painting in an electric-free environment.

In order to demonstrate that this system is very useful for wall paintings, we scanned the paint on the wall. Although the paint was large, this system acquired high resolution image (700 dpi) without PC and motor. We demonstrated that this system can acquire high resolution image in spite of object's size and would be able to scan very large wall paintings.

On the other hand, when imaged objects have three-dimensional contours, we cannot develop definite way. To digitize objects which have three-dimensional contours, we should develop a 3D reconstruction method which suits for the system.

Although deformation are still a challenge, we have built an image acquisition system that is easy to use, can be applied to various environment, takes advantage of gravity instead of electric power for its scanning motion, yet capable of acquiring very high-resolution images of paintings.

This system can be used easily in remote locations without electricity or narrow-space environment. In order to scan, the user would only need to pull up the camera module along the rail, and release it while the camera is in a continuous shooting mode. This proposed system could help many researchers around world digitize the cultural heritage easily and utilize the acquired data for their field of discipline.

Acknowledgements. We would like to thank Mr. Daichi Tsunemichi for the experiments, Mr. Yusuke Isobe for discussing about the theory, Ms. Terumi Akasaka and Ms. Mie Kado for variable contribution, and people in Ide-laboratory for helping us to do the experiments.

References

1. Satou, J.: Computer Vision: Visual geometry. Korona Sha, Tokyo (1999). (in Japanese)
2. Zhang, P.: Study on high-resolution 3D reconstruction using linear CCD images. Kyoto University, doctor thesis. (2016). (in Japanese)
3. Ochi, K.: A system for simultaneous measurement of surface geometric and reflective optical properties using line sensors. Kyoto University, master thesis. (2016)
4. Yamaguchi, T.: Analysis of color and shape of object surface using high-resolution images, Kyoto University, master thesis (2015). (in Japanese)
5. Kawakatsu, S.: Developing and evaluating high-resolution 360° Panorama scanning system, Kyoto University, master thesis (2014). (in Japanese)
6. Takeda, T.: Developing whole 3D measuring system which reconstructs high-resolution surface architecture and color, Kyoto University, master thesis (2014). (in Japanese)
7. Onodera, Y.: High-resolution imaging system for scientific recording and digital archiving: applications to on-the-site scanning of large-sized two-dimensional cultural heritage objects. Kyoto University, master thesis (2013)
8. Kaneko, J.: Material analysis of metallic foils using spectral reflection characteristic. Kyoto University, master thesis (2012)
9. Ogiso, Y.: A research for material analysis of paper with high-resolution scanning, Kyoto University, master thesis (2011). (in Japanese)
10. Toque, J.A., Sakatoku, Y., Ide-Ektessabi, A.: Analytical imaging of cultural heritage paintings using digitally archived images. In: Proceedings of SPIE, Vol. 7531, p. 75310N (2010)
11. Toque, J.A., Murayama, Y., Ide-Ektessabi, A.: Pigment identification based on spectral reflectance reconstructed from RGB images for cultural heritage investigations. In: Proceedings of SPIE, Vol. 7531, p. 75310K (2010)

Visualizing Lost Designs in Degraded Early Modern Tapestry Using Infra-red Image

Masaru Tsuchida[1(✉)], Keiji Yano[2], Kaoru Hiramatsu[1], and Kunio Kashino[1]

[1] NTT Communication Science Laboratories, Kanagawa, Japan
{tsuchida.masaru,hiramatsu.kaoru,kashino.kunio}@lab.ntt.co.jp
[2] Ritsumeikan University, Kyoto, Japan
yano@lt.ritsumei.ac.jp

Abstract. This paper shows how to experimentally visualize lost designs in damaged early modern tapestries used in the Kyoto Gion festival. Unlike cloth weaving, tapestry is weft-faced weaving. As the surface welt threads become worn or turn over time, the design in a tapestry is gradually lost. On the other hand, weft threads hidden by warp threads still remain. In the tapestries of the Kyoto Gion festival, gold and silver threads were often used as weft, and they reflect infrared radiation. In experiments, a tapestry woven in the seventeenth century was used. Six-band images were taken for accurate color reproduction and infrared images were taken for visualizing the lost design. The viewing angle and image resolution of both types of images were the same. Superimposing the infrared image on color image after correcting registration errors revealed the original design of the tapestry.

Keywords: Tapestry · Visualization of degraded design · Infrared image · Multiband image · Giga-pixel image · Color reproduction

1 Introduction

1.1 Background

The float procession of the Kyoto Gion festival started in the fourteenth century. It was registered in the Representative List of the Intangible Cultural Heritage of Humanity by UNESCO in 2009. The floats, called "Yamaboko", are known as "moving museums" for their elaborate decorations with tapestries and wooden and metal ornaments. Although civil wars in the fifteenth century destroyed several Yamaboko, many of the surviving tapestries and ornaments are still in use as are many imported from Europe and China or made by Japanese craftsmen from the seventeenth to nineteenth centuries.

Some tapestries have been damaged through long-term use and their original colors and designs have been lost. There are few records of their weaving method and original designs, which makes it difficult to restore them to their original state. Recording and analyzing existent original tapestries are quite important to gain a better understanding of traditional craftsmanship and the cultural background of that time.

High-resolution image capturing is one of the effective approaches for recording and analyzing the woven structures of tapestry. Today's craftsmen have said that resolution

© Springer International Publishing AG 2017
S. Bianco et al. (Eds.): CCIW 2017, LNCS 10213, pp. 144–149, 2017.
DOI: 10.1007/978-3-319-56010-6_12

from 0.05 to 0.01 mm/pixel (> 500 dpi) is required for this purpose. Using the digital cameras with 50 M-pixel image sensors available on the market, we can take high-resolution images of a part of a tapestry. However, special equipment and techniques for obtaining an image of whole tapestry with sufficient resolution are still under development and have been not generalized yet.

Accurate color reproduction is also important for analyzing the weaving method. The spectral reflectance of an object can be measured by using multiband and hyperspectral imaging technology [1–5], although this requires special and expensive equipment.

To meet the above spatial and spectral resolution requirements, a two-shot type six-band camera system has been developed [6, 7]. The system consists of an RGB image sensor (i.e. a digital camera), a large format camera and a custom interference filter. An object is divided into several parts and an image of each part is captured. The obtained images are synthesized into a large pixel-number image. To take divided images, the image sensor is shifted horizontally and verticality by using a function of the large-format camera. An advantage of this method is that the effects of lens aberration can be ignored when images are synthesized. This camera system can also take infrared (IR) images when IR cut filter on the image sensor is removed.

1.2 Motivation and Overview

Our final goal is to achieve the visualization and virtual restoration of the lost original designs of the tapestries featured in the Kyoto Gion festival. In this work, we focuses on the visualization of the lost designs of damaged tapestry using IR images.

In Sect. 2, we describe the principle of the visualization of the lost designs. In Sect. 3, we introduce the camera system used in experiments and show experimental results. Visible six-band images and IR images of a tapestry were captured. Finally, we summarize the paper in Sect. 4.

2 Principle of Visualization of Lost Design of Tapestry with Gold and Silver Threads

Tapestry is a form of textile art woven on a vertical loom. It is weft-faced weaving, where weft threads of different colours work over portions of the warp threads to form the design. Figures 1 shows a tapestry of the float "Hachiman-yama", woven in the seventeenth century and used for experiments in this work. Although the back of the tapestry is covered by cloth, we can see the woven structure from the front. The warp threads are dark navyblue, and gold and silver threads are used as weft to form the design, such as the chinese characters in the top and bottom areas of the tapestry. Around the center of the tapestry, we can find animal and human figures. Some of them are blurred or lost because the weft threads in these erea have worn to rags. Detecting the weft threads remaining behind the warp ones is an approach for visualizing lost designs.

The spectral reflectance characaristics of gold and silver threads are such that they strongly reflect IR radiation, unlike ordinary cotton or wool threads. IR light penetrates the surface of tapestry (e.g., warp threads) and is reflected from gold or silver ones, and

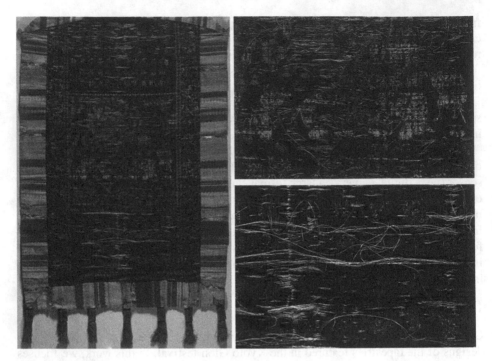

Fig. 1. Tapestry of the float "Hachiman-yama", woven in the seventeenth century (called "keiju-gire no maekake").

an IR camera can capture their distribution. IR image capturing is often used for visualizing sketches under paintings. We adopted this technique for tapestry in this work.

3   Experiments

3.1   Image Capturing Setup

Figure 2 shows the whole experimental setup and the geometrical setup for image capturing. The tapestry was put on the floor to avoid movements caused by air vibration and prevent the possibility of damage caused by its own weight had it been hung. Images were taken from overhead using the seven-band camera system (six-channels for visible and one for IR) mounted on the end of the arm of the camera stand. The tapestry was divided into several parts to enlarge image resolution. The arm was extended one dimensionally, and the tapestry was moved in the orthogonal direction. Then images of each part were captured. Finally, the obtained images were synthesized into a large pixel-number image.

The camera system consisted of a large format camera (TOYO-VIEW 45GII), a digital camera back (Hasselblad H4D-50MS) whose IR-cut filter was removed, a digital-controlled shutter system (Horseman ISS-G3), and a camera lens (Rodenstock Apo-macro-sironar 180 mm F5.6). A custom interference filter, an IR-cut filter and an IR filter (cut-off wavelength was 960 nm) were mounted infront of the camera lens. The custom interference filter cuts off the left sides (i.e., the short-wavelength domain) of

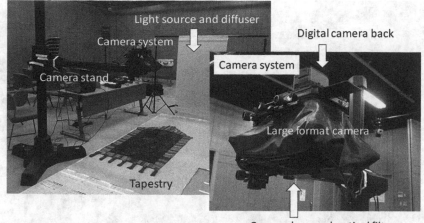

Light source and diffuser

Camera system

Camera stand

Digital camera back

Camera system

Large format camera

Tapestry

Camera lens and optical filter

Fig. 2. Overview of whole experimental setup and geometrical setup for image capturing.

the peaks of both the blue and red in original spectral sensitivity of camera. It also cuts off the green's right side (i.e., the long wavelength domain) [4, 6]. An artificial solar lighting systems (XELIOS XG-500 series, SERIC Ltd.) were used for illumination. Figure 3 shows the spectral sensitivity of the camera system and Fig. 4 shows the spectral power distribution of illumination. The solid line represents the spectral sensitivity when IR-cut filter was used, while dashed line represents the spectral sensitivity when the interference and IR filters was used. Three images were taken from each viewing position; the first one with the IR-cut filter, the secound one with the IR-cut filter and the interference filter, and the third with IR filter.

The tapestry is 110 cm wide and 65 cm high. The distance between the camera lens and the tapestry was 95 cm and viewing area of the camera was 26 × 19 cm. The image size of the digital camera back was 8,000 × 6,000 pixels and size of synthesized image was 28,000 × 43,000 pixels. Resolution was 0.03 mm/pixel (800 dpi). Bit depth of each pixel value of each color channel was 16.

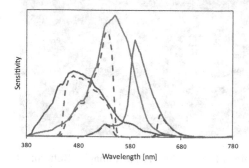

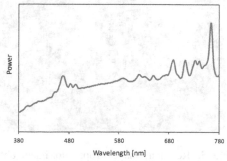

Fig. 3. Spectral sensitivity of camera system. (Color figure online)

Fig. 4. Spectral power distribution of illumination. (Color figure online)

Fig. 5. Resultant images. Top: color image obtained from visible six-band images. Bottom: IR image.

3.2   Results

Figure 5 shows resultant images. The top one is a color image reproduced from the visible six-band images and the bottom one is the IR image. These are images of the center region of the tapestry. When we compare these two images, we can see totally two human figures on the left and right sides of the color image, but it is difficult to find animal and other human figures. On the other hand, at least two animals (perhaps deers) can be seen in the IR image at the center of the tapestry. Human figures in the IR image also look much clearer than those in the color image. In addition, we can see the woven structure from the IR image. These results show that IR light penetrated the surface of the tapestry and was reflected from the gold and silver threads behind the warp.

4   Conclusion

In this paper, we discussed the ability of IR imaging for digital archiving of tapestry. Experimental results show that lost designs caused by damage to weft threads on the surface can be visualized using IR images. IR image capturing is effective not only for visualizing sketches under paintings but also for analyzing tapestry weaving.

Acknowledgement.   We thank the Gion-Matsuri Hachiman-yama Preservation Society, as a generous collaborator in this project. We are grateful to Mr. Sato Hirotaka, a Ph.D. student of Ritsumaikan University, for his assistance in this work.

References

1. Yamaguchi, M., Murakami, Y., Uchiyama, T., Ohsawa, K., Ohyama, N.: Natural vision: visual telecommunication based on multispectral technology, In: Proceeding of IDW 2000, pp. 1115–1118 (2000)
2. Tominaga, S., Okajima, R.: Object recognition by multi-spectral imaging with a liquid crystal filter. In: Proceeding of the International Conference on Pattern Recognition, pp. 708–711 (2000)
3. Helling, S., Deidel, E., Biehig, W.: Algorithms for spectral color stimulus reconstruction with a seven-channel multispectral camera. In: Proceeding CGIV, pp. 254–258 (2004)
4. Ohsawa, K., et al.: Six-band HDTV camera system for spectrum based color reproduction. J. Imag. Sci. and Tech. **48**(2), 85–92 (2004)
5. Pratt, W.K., Mancill, C.E.: Spectral estimation techniques for the spectral calibration of a color image scanner. Appl. Optics, OSA **15**, 73–75 (1976)
6. Hashimoto, M., Kishioto, J.: Two-shot type 6-band still image capturing system using Commercial Digital Camera and Custom Color Filter. In: Proceeding CGIV, pp. 538– 541 (2008)
7. Tsuchida, M., Yano, K., Tanaka, H.: Development of a high-definition and multispectral image capturing system for digital archiving of early modern tapestries of Kyoto Gion Festival. In: Proceeding ICPR2010, pp. 2828–2831 (2010)

A Novel Scanning Technique for Imaging of Gold and Silver Foils Used in Art Works

Ryo Kanai[1(✉)], Yoshiharu Kowada[1], Peng Wang[1], Masahiro Toiya[2],
Jay Arre Toque[2], and Ari Ide-Ektessabi[1]

[1] Advanced Imaging Technology Laboratory, Graduate School of Engineering,
Kyoto University, Kyoto, Japan
`kani.ryo.76m@st.kyoto-u.ac.jp`
[2] SABIA Inc., Kyoto, Japan

Abstract. Digital archiving has seen rapid growth in the recent years, accompanied by ever-increasing demands for high resolution and high-color definition color images. Despite the advances in imaging techniques, gold leaves and golden objects remain as some of the most difficult-to-image materials due to their highly reflective surfaces. Oversaturation commonly occurs when direct reflection is captured by an imaging element.

To solve this problem, we have developed a new scanner-type image acquisition method which can acquire high-resolution digital image and high-definition color information. In this paper, we outline the strategy employed in the new system to image gold, i.e., adjustment of light sources with respect to the sensor and use of polarizing filters to separate specular and diffuse reflection components.

Keywords: Gold leaf · High-color definition · Saturation · Line sensor camera · Japanese-painting · Polarization · Shading · Light source · Imaging gold · Digital museum · Digital archiving

1 Introduction

Cultural assets that are known all over the world are being appreciated by many people by means of traveling exhibitions organized by art museums around the world. Due to the increasing demand for protection of art and cultural assets, more museums now choose to provide digital images of their collections on the internet, rather than subjecting the fragile objects to potentially damaging and risky journeys to other locations [1]. However, subjects having glossy surfaces such as gold leaf on Japanese paintings are notoriously challenging to image by conventional photography. A glossy subject causes specular reflection (direct reflection of source light incident upon the subject's surface), creating saturated portions in the image (white stray) which contain no meaningful data. These glossy subjects are very sensitive to the angle of the incident light. Simply changing the image grabbing conditions such as closing the lens aperture or reducing the exposure time may eliminate saturation, however, the rest of the image becomes too dark and correct color information cannot be recorded [2].

© Springer International Publishing AG 2017
S. Bianco et al. (Eds.): CCIW 2017, LNCS 10213, pp. 150–162, 2017.
DOI: 10.1007/978-3-319-56010-6_13

In order to acquire a high-definition and high-quality image of this glossy subject, a new scanning system was devised where adjustable light source [3–5]. And a variable polarizing filter are used to capture specular reflection and diffuse reflection from the subject on separate images to represent fuller metallic luster information [6, 7]. The images are processed later to form a final image having more realistic visual appearance of the subject, making it suitable for uses in digital museums or reproductions.

Conventionally, two types of cameras i.e., line sensor type and area sensor type, are used for imaging. We used a line sensor camera to acquire high quality images in this research. There are two reasons for choosing a system featuring a scanning head with a line sensor camera. First, there is no inherent limit to the length of travel of the scanning head along the sub-scanning direction, provided that an appropriate gantry system and cabling are available. Second, generally speaking, line sensor cameras are capable of acquiring higher quality images more easily than area sensor cameras.

In this paper, we present a new scanning system for acquisition of high-resolution and high-definition digital color information on Japanese paintings decorated with gold foil by a line sensor camera, and demonstrate that we can obtain images containing only specular reflected light and images containing only diffuse reflected light by use of a polarizing filter oriented various angles.

2   Methods

2.1   Line Sensor Camera

In this section, we describe the design of a two-dimensional scanner to acquire an image of a large object with high-resolution and high-color definition. First of all, we write about the line sensor camera we used. The arrangement of the elements of the line sensor camera and the area sensor camera are shown in Fig. 1. In general, elements in an area sensor are arranged two-dimensionally, whereas the elements of the line sensor are one-dimensionally arranged in a single row. Therefore, to obtain a two-dimensional image using a line sensor camera, the line sensor camera itself needs to be moved perpendicular to the arrangement of the sensor element.

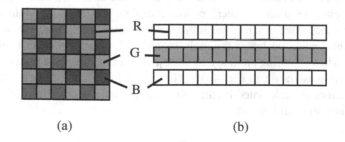

(a)   (b)

Fig. 1. Arrangement of RGB sensor: (a) area sensor camera, (b) line sensor camera

2.2 Scanner

In this section, we explain the line scanner for acquiring images of Japanese paintings decorated with gold leaf. The appearance of the scanner is shown in Fig. 2. Schematic diagrams of a scanner using a polarizing filter and a light source with a second polarizing filter are shown in Fig. 3. The camera was a line sensor camera TLC-7500CLD manu-factured by Takenaka Co., Ltd. The lens system was composed of an Apo-Rodagon-N 105 mm F 2.8 and an 88 cm of extra tube. The resolution was set to 1100 DPI.

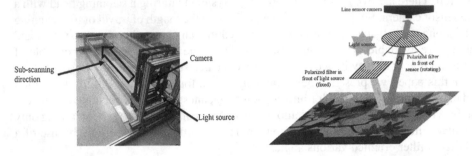

Fig. 2. Scanner

Fig. 3. Conceptual diagram of the scanning system

2.3 Shading

In line sensor cameras, dedicated light sources are used to improve color reproducibility, and color conversion is performed in consideration of spectral characteristics of the light sources and sensitivity characteristics peculiar to the camera to acquire accurate color information. One of the color transformations is shading correction. The shading correc-tion is performed to reduce the influence of illuminance unevenness along the main scanning direction, sensitivity unevenness of the CCD pixel, peripheral light reduction of the lens.

A shading correction is performed in the following manner when an image of a two-dimensional plane is acquired by a line scanner. When acquiring an image of a two-dimensional plane by a line scanner, recording of data is performed while the camera and the light source sweep across the subject at the same time. Therefore, as shown in Fig. 4 (a), unevenness occurs in the main scanning direction. In order to reduce this unevenness, when capturing an image of a subject, a white reference image is captured at the same time as shown in Fig. 4 (b). Then, based on this reference white image, correction factors are calculated by the following formula so that the white reference image becomes uniformly white.

$$d^i_{cal} = \frac{d^i_{in} - d^i_{bk}}{d^i_{wh} - d^i_{bk}} \tag{1}$$

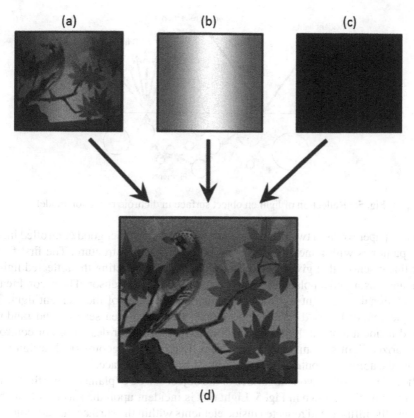

Fig. 4. (a) Before shading (b) white standard (c) black standard, (d) after shading

For the i th pixel in the main scanning direction, d^i_{cal} is the corrected value, d^i_{in} sensor response value of the image to be corrected, d^i_{wh} is the sensor response value of the castle reference image, d^i_{bk} is the sensor response value of the black reference image. Figure 4 (d) shows the results of correction using this equation. In a two-dimensional image, by using the above-described method, it is possible to obtain a color with uniform light intensity on the surface of the imaging object before color conversion.

2.4   Principle of Reflection Polarized Light Scanning

The imaging of a reflective metallic surfaces, such as the golden and the other metallic materials in a painting, has a challenge of how we can control the interactions of light and surfaces. The main parameters dominating these interactions are:

(1)   Surface structure (unevenness, roughness),
(2)   Incident direction (angle) of the light, and,
(3)   Polarization degree of the incident light.

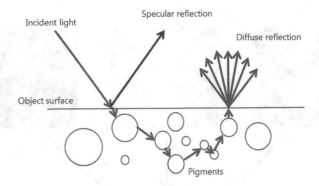

Fig. 5. Reflection of light on object surface in dichroic reflection model

In this paper we used two design features to successfully get good controlled images of big paintings with a metallic randomly oriented surface structure. The first feature was a linear sensor that gives us the controllability on collecting the reflected light on the image sensor and a polarization filter close to the linear sensor. The second feature was directional LED light as well as the polarization angle of the incident light. This technique cannot be used in imaging systems that have area sensors and randomly diffused incident ambient light sources. The basic criteria for design of our controlled and polarized light system was the near field light, and the geometrical design which gives us the ability to control the interaction of light and surface.

The reflection of light on the surface of the object can be explained using the dichroic reflection model as shown in Fig. 5. Light that is incident upon the surface of an object is repeatedly diffused and reflected inside elements within the surface. In addition to this diffuse reflected light appearing on the object surface, specular reflected light directly reflected by the object surface are also present, more noticeably on glossy surfaces. This diffuse reflected light is the original color of the object unaffected by the external environment, and the specular reflected light largely changes due to the influence of the external environment of the light source. Supposing that the intensity of specular reflection light is $I_{supecular}$ and the intensity of diffuse reflection light is $I_{diffuse}$, then the intensity I of the observed reflected light can be expressed as Eq. 2.

$$I = I_{specular} + I_{diffuse} \tag{2}$$

A polarizer is an optical element that allows components of light whose polarization is along that of the polarizer to pass through. In this study, a polarizing filter in the form of a film was used. Only light that oscillates in a specific direction is transmitted through the filter, and other components are absorbed. Therefore, when linearly polarized light of amplitude E_0 is incident on the polarizing axis of the polarizer at an angle θ, the amplitude E after transmission is expressed by Eq. (3). Since the square of the amplitude of the light is the intensity of the light, the intensity I after passing through the polarizer is given by I_0 as the intensity before transmission, it is expressed by Eq. (4).

$$E = E_0 \cos \theta \tag{3}$$

$$I = I_0 \cos^2 \theta \tag{4}$$

Also, non-polarized light is light mixed with various linearly polarized lights, so it can be handled in the same way as circularly polarized light by taking a time average. Since circularly polarized light can be regarded as combined light of two orthogonal linearly polarized lights of the same intensity, if the intensity of the circularly polarized light before passing through the polarizer is I_{r0}, I is expressed by Eq. (5).

$$I = \frac{1}{2}I_{r0} \cos^2 \theta + \frac{1}{2}I_{r0} \cos^2 \left(\frac{\pi}{2} - \theta \right) = \frac{1}{2}I_{r0} \tag{5}$$

From the above, the intensity of linearly polarized light and the intensity of non-polarized light were derived. In the dichroic reflection model, the component of the reflected light consists of two components, specular reflection and diffuse reflection as described in Eq. (2). Since the specular reflection is a reflection occurring at the boundary between the medium and the other medium, it can be described by the Fresnel equation below. Here, θ_i, θ_r represent the incident angle and refraction angle to the boundary, A_p, A_s are electric field vectors of incident light, R_p, R_s are parallel (p) and vertical (s). When $\theta_i = \theta_r = 0$ [deg], the reflection coefficient is expressed by (8).

$$R_p = -\frac{\tan(\theta_i - \theta_r)}{\tan(\theta_i + \theta_r)}A_p = \frac{n_2 \cos \theta_i - n_1 \cos \theta_r}{n_2 \cos \theta_i + n_1 \cos \theta_r}A_p \tag{6}$$

$$R_s = -\frac{\sin(\theta_i - \theta_r)}{\sin(\theta_i + \theta_r)}A_s = \frac{n_1 \cos \theta_i - n_2 \cos \theta_r}{n_1 \cos \theta_i + n_2 \cos \theta_r}A_s \tag{7}$$

$$\frac{R_p}{A_p} = \frac{R_s}{A_s} = -\frac{n_2 - n_1}{n_2 + n_1} \tag{8}$$

In this paper, since $n_2 > n_1$, the reflection coefficient becomes negative, only the phase shifts by 180 [deg] at the boundary, and the intensity ratio of the parallel and the vertical components do not change. In other words, when linearly polarized light comes from above, the reflected polarized light oscillating in the same direction is the dominated component. Since the optical system used in this chapter is irradiated almost directly perpendicular to the imaging surface, the effect of angle of the polarizing filter attached to the light source can be neglected. When linearly polarized light is incident on the object from the light source side, the specular component of the light is reflected in the same direction as the polarization direction of the incident light. When observing this reflected light through the polarizer on the sensor side, the observed light intensity $I_{observe}$ is the specular reflection component of light $I_{specular}$, the diffuse component $I_{diffuse}$, the angle between the axes of the two polarizing directions is defined as θ. Equation (9) shows the relation between the main components of the light using Eqs. (4) and (5).

$$I_{\text{observe}} = I_{\text{specular}} \cos^2 \theta + \frac{1}{2} I_{\text{diffuse}} \tag{9}$$

This equation can be regarded as a linear model of intercept $\frac{1}{2} I_{\text{diffuse}}$, gradient I_{specular}, and independent variable $\cos^2 \theta$. Acquire two or more images with different values of $\cos^2 \theta$ (different angle θ) and acquire the specular component and diffuse component by obtaining the intercept and the gradient. In this paper, by changing the angle of the polarizing filter by 90° at a time, a total of four images were acquired and a component separated image was acquired.

2.5 Gold Leaf Chart

In this paper, we used a gold leaf chart to scan gold leaf without color skipping. A gold leaf chart is a piece of gold leaf which is cut into small pieces and affixed on one piece of paper as shown in Fig. 6. We studied metallic foil materials which are used as art objects in the state of foil. For the gold foil, 6 types of gold foils with different gold purity and thickness were used, and for other metals, brass that is an alloy of copper and zinc and platinum foil were used [8–10]. The gold leaf chart was irradiated with light from a light source. Then, with any gold leaf, the amount of light that can be photographed was adjusted without color fading while leaving the metallic luster.

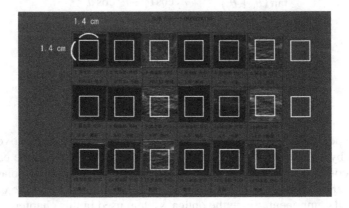

Fig. 6. Gold leaf chart

2.6 Light Source

In this paper, to obtain images expressing various metallic luster, a total of 3 patterns of light sources were created. A schematic diagram of the created light source is shown in Figs. 7 and 8. The CCT value of this LED light was 4000–4500 K. The distance between the subject and the light source was 185 mm. Figure 9 Shows the light source when polarizing filter is used. Only the upper light was used. The reason for this is to irradiate the subject with light directly from above. The distance from the subject was 60 mm.

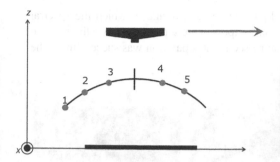

Fig. 7. The number shows the position of the LED column with respect to the scanning direction.

Fig. 8. LED columns

Fig. 9. Light source with polarized filter

3 Results and Discussion

Figures 10, 11 and 12 shows images scanned with different light source configurations, respectively. As can be seen from the image, it was possible to obtain images expressing

Fig. 10. Japanese painting 1 (Left, 1 to 3 LED columns, Center 1 to 4 LED columns, Right 1 to 5 LED columns), 1100 DPI. The numbers show the LED light columns corresponding to Fig. 7.

various metallic luster by using different light sources. An image in which the spectral reflection component and the diffuse reflection component are separated using a light source filter is shown in Figs. 13, 14 and 15. It can be seen that separation was successful by the method proposed in this paper.

Fig. 11. Japanese painting 2 (Left, 1 to 3 LED columns, Center 1 to 4 LED columns, Right 1 to 5 LED columns), 1100 DPI. The numbers show the LED light columns corresponding to Fig. 7.

Fig. 12. Japanese painting 3 (Left, 1 to 3 LED columns, Center 1 to 4 LED columns, Right 1 to 5 LED columns), 1100 DPI. The numbers show the LED light columns corresponding to Fig. 7.

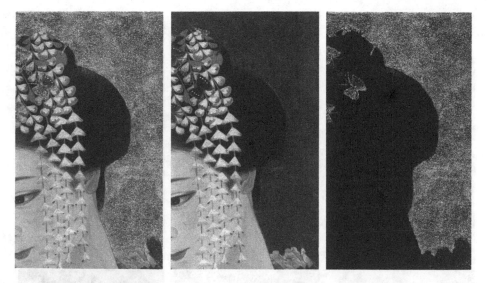

Fig. 13. Polarized light showing separation of diffused and specular reflection (painting 1). The image on left is the total reflection image, center is the diffuse light, and right is the specular image.

Fig. 14. Polarized light showing separation of diffused and specular reflection (painting 2). The image on left is the total reflection image, center is the diffuse light, and right is the specular image.

Fig. 15. Polarized light showing separation of diffused and specular reflection (painting 3). The image on left is the total reflection image, center is the diffuse light, and right is the specular image.

4   Conclusion

The imaging of a reflective surface, such as the golden and other metallic materials in a painting is a question of how we can control the interactions of light and surface. The parameters governing these interactions are the surface structure (unevenness, roughness) and incident direction (angle) of the light and polarization degree of the incident light. In this paper we used two advantageous points to successfully get good controlled images of big paintings with a metallic randomly oriented surface structure. The first point is a linear sensor that gives us the controllability on collecting the reflected light on the image sensor and a polarization filter close to the linear sensor. The second point was a directional LED light as well as the polarization angle of the incident light. Obviously this technique cannot be used in imaging systems that have area sensors and randomly diffused incident light sources. The basic criteria for design of our controlled and polarized light system was the near field light, and the geometrical design which gives us the ability to control the interaction of light and surface.

In an experimental approach a new scanning system was designed and constructed and used in practice to accurately capture highly reflective surfaces such as gold leaves commonly found in Japanese paintings, and its capabilities were demonstrated. The scanner utilized light sources that are adjustable in flux, intensity and direction of the light as well as a rotatable polarizing filter. By controlling the relative direction of the polarized filters we can separate the specular reflection and diffuse reflection which differ in terms of intensity by orders of magnitude. In this paper, specular reflection and diffuse reflection were captured under various polarization degree and different images were grabbed. Then these images under various polarization degree were superimposed to obtain images which show the metallic parts with various intensity. However, some important problems remain in the image processing stage. It is practically difficult to determine the optimal polarization angle for each grabbed image, hence it was determined manually. The second problem is related to the positional accuracy of the scanner that causes mis-alignment in each scanned image.

Acknowledgements.   The paintings in this paper are art works of Ms. Masako Kurokawa, the models are Mameryu (painting 1), Manayo (painting 2), Aoitayuu (painting 3). We are very indebted to the artist and the models who gave us permission to use these invaluable images. We would like to thank Mr. Yusuke Isobe and Mr. Daichi Tsunemichi for discussion about the theory and the experiments, Ms. Mie Kado and Ms. Terumi Akasaka for valuable contribution and the staff in Ide-laboratory, Kyoto University for helping us to do the experiments.

References

1. Yastikli, N.: Documentation of cultural heritage using digital photogrammetry and laser scanning. J. Cult. Heritage **8**(4), 423–427 (2007)
2. Kaneko, J., Toque, J.A., Murayama, Y., Ide-Ektessabi, A.: Non-destructive Analytical Imaging of Metallic Surfaces Using Spectral Measurements and Ultrahigh-resolution Scanning for Cultural Heritage Investigation (2011)
3. Toque, J.A., Murayama, Y., Ide-Ektessabi, A.: Polarized light scanning for cultural heritage investigation. In: *Proceedings of SPIE*, vol. 7869, 78690N (2011)
4. Murayama, Y.: Development of acquisition system of specular reflection component separated image using polarizer. Bachelor thesis, Kyoto University (2008). (in Japanese), (Henkousi wo motiita kyoumenhansyaseibun-bunrigazou no syutoku sisutemu no kaihatsu)
5. Ogino, R.: A high speed dynamic system for scanning reflective surface with rotating polarized filters. Master thesis, Kyoto University (2015). (in Japanese), (Rainsensakamera wo motiita dainamikku-firuta-sukyaningu-sisutemu no kaihatsu)
6. Ozawa, S.: Acquisition of three-dimensional shape and color information of golden large cultural property. Master thesis, Kyoto University (2016). (in Japanese), (Ougon-oogata-bunkazai no sanzigen-keizyou oyobi sikisaizyouhou no syotoku)
7. Ochi, K.: A system for simultaneous measurement of surface geometric and reflective optical properties using line sensors. Master thesis, Kyoto University (2016)

8. Shafer, S.: Using color to separate reflection components. Color Res. Appl. **10**(4), 210–218 (1985)
9. Kitada, M., Kirino, H.: Kinnzoku ni Irodori wo Soeru Dentou Kougei Tyakusyuhou Hyoumenkagaku, **26**(4), 226–230 (2005)
10. Ago, S., Tanaka, T., Yokote, T., Onodera, R.: Mechanics on Fabrication of Thin Metal Foils by Forging. In: The Japan Society of Mechanical Engineers, 7–8 (2002)

A Transmission Type Scanning System for Ultra High Resolution Scanning

Tatsuya Komiyama(✉), Daichi Tsunemichi, Peng Wang,
Yusuke Isobe, and Ari Ide-Ektessabi

Advanced Imaging Technology Laboratory,
Graduate School of Engineering, Kyoto University, Kyoto, Japan
komiyama.tatsuya.52w@st.kyoto-u.ac.jp,
ide.ari.4n@kyoto-u.ac.jp

Abstract. In an exceptional photography project, wall paintings of golden hall in Horyu-ji Temple were photographed on a one-to-one scale on glass dry plates 80 years ago. Unfortunately the temple burned in a fire and major parts of the wall paintings were destroyed. Because of the size of the glass plates, it is difficult to find a proper image grabbing systems to scan them with high resolution. Moreover, there were no color reference charts when the wall paintings were photographed, so it is not possible to create a reference data using a color chart. The method of creating the reference data without using color chart has not been systematized. Therefore, this paper gives a brief record of our project to develop a scanning system that is capable of digitizing these large glass plates with ultra high resolution and a method to reproduce the colours with high color definition from available information.

Keywords: High-resolution · Scanning · Color · Reproduction · Color correction · Image alignment · Dry glass plate · Pigment · Image processing

1 Introduction

Important historical and cultural assets are under threat of destruction for degradation and destruction due to aging, natural disasters such as fire and earthquakes, wars and social conflicts. Nowadays it is a common understanding that high quality documentation of these important assets using the state-of-the-art digital technology is an urgent social need [1, 2]. During the past decades, especially during the world war two which destroyed enormous amount of cultural assets in Europe and in Asia, local wars and invasions such as the events in Afghanistan, Iraq, and Syria destroyed some extremely important human cultural assets. In this paper we focus on developing an ultra high resolution digital imaging system with high definition color (including monochromatic tone) reproduction of large objects, glass plates as the main items. In an exceptional documentation (photography) project, wall paintings of golden hall in Horyu-ji Temple were photographed on a one-to-one scale on glass dry plates with multi-band filter 80 years ago. The glass plates were 45 by 60 cm and were photographed by using a special made camera, on 362 pieces of glass plates, using 4 colors and IR (5 spectral bands).

S. Bianco et al. (Eds.): CCIW 2017, LNCS 10213, pp. 163–174, 2017.
DOI: 10.1007/978-3-319-56010-6_14

Because of the importance of these wall paintings of about seven century, almost 1300 years old, and the invaluable cultural importance of this temple, the project was financed and supervised by Japanese Ministry of Culture (of that period) and a team of experts from Benrido Inc., a printing company in Kyoto, was assigned to implement the project. This amazing project was successfully carried out and the result, 431 large glass plates, was produced, 70 of them in 5 band spectral images [3]. A few years after the photography, the temple was on fire and the major part of the temple's wall paintings were heavily burnt (1949). In 1993, Horyu-ji together with Hokki-ji was designated as a UNESCO World Heritage Site under the name Buddhist Monuments in the Horyu-ji Area. What exist now after the fire are some burnt wall paintings, part of the building, many mosha (replica reproduction of the wall images before fire) and a collection of photographic 5-band spectral images on large glass plates. Because of the importance of these historical remains, the glass plates are designated as Japanese National Heritage in recent years.

On the other hand, glass dry plates deteriorate over time and also affected by preservation condition. Therefore, there is a need to preserve them in digital format. Because of the size of the glass plates, it is difficult to find a proper image grabbing systems to scan them with high resolution. There were no color reference charts when the wall paintings of Horyu-ji Temple were photographed. Although the team carried out a tremendous technical job, the level of the technology of those days were very low. Creating the original data without having standard reference data is a very difficult job. Using a color chart has not been systematized. Therefore, this paper gives a brief record of our project to develop a scanning system that is capable of digitizing these large glass plates with ultra high resolution (2500–5000 dpi) and a method to reproduce the colours with high color definition from available information. The imaging mechanism of traditional scanning systems is that the light reflected from an object was detected by the camera sensor then collected light would be changed into electrical signal [4]. And usually the traditional scanner has limited size requirement for an object and the glass dry plate of Horyu-ji Temple is large. Therefore, in a scanning of the glass dry plate, they cannot be used. In this study, we develop a scanning system that can be used for large permeable objects with practically no limit in size. This study can make it possible to increase the number of objects for high-resolution digital archiving and to enable everyone to access the wall painting of Horyu-ji Temple by preserving it in digital format.

2 Image Acquisition Experiment

2.1 Mechanism of Scanning System

Line sensor camera and area sensor camera are widely used to acquire images. Line sensor camera can get higher resolution images compared with area sensor camera [5]. Therefore, line sensor camera is more suitable for this study. In this paper, main scanning direction means the direction in which sensors are lined up and sub scanning direction means vertical direction to the main scanning direction.

There are several points need to be noticed. The glass dry plate is a transparent object, and it is difficult to finish it in one scan. In addition, this significant cultural heritage would be digitized as monochromatic image in this experiment. Therefore, there is a need to construct a non-contact-type scanner that can scan transparent object in monochromatic image without size limitation.

Imaging system is roughly divided into a camera unit, a subject base unit, and a light source unit, and arranged in this order so that light from the light source passes through the subject and enters the camera. The scanner that has this structure is named as transmission type scanner. Figure 1 shows the mechanism of my system. One object is acquired by moving the subject base portion in the sub scanning direction in a state where the camera and the light source are fixed. Also, since the subject in this study is a cultural property, it is not permissible for the subject to be damaged. Light and heat are known to degrade color, and ultraviolet rays and heat are factors that deteriorate cultural properties, so they cannot be used. For this reason, we use a LED light source with less heat and ultraviolet emission compared with halogen lamps and HMI (Hydrargyrum Medium-arc Iodide). Since the whole image cannot be acquired with the line sensor camera at high-resolution, it is necessary to move the subject in the sub scanning direction with a fixed width, and the subject is moved in the main scanning direction, and by repeating this, several images are acquired. High-transmission glass is used for the subject base part in order to image an object that transmits light.

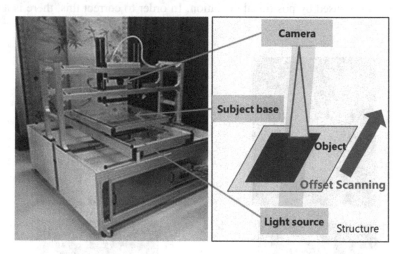

Fig. 1. The mechanism of the transmission type scanner.

2.2   Device Details and Imaging Conditions

In the transmission type line scanner developed in this research, it is possible to freely set the resolution of the image and the size of the object. For each part of the scanner, we used monochrome line sensor camera, lens, IR-UV cut filter for camera part, LED light for light source, and high-transparency glass for object base part.

The imaging resolution is set to 2400 dpi. In this setting, it is possible to acquire a monochrome image of 8000 pixels in the main scanning direction, and imaging with a width of 8.5 cm can be performed in one scan. It is known that the image acquired by the line sensor camera is uneven in the main scanning direction due to unevenness of the light source or the sensitivity of the sensor, and the edge of the image tends to be dark. Since the width of the subject is 45 cm, one glass dry plate is scanned in nine times of imaging with an offset interval of 5 cm and joined by image processing.

2.3   Imaging Result and Image Alignment with Affine Transformation

Figure 2 shows acquired images of four color decomposed glass dry plate of wall painting of golden hall of Horyu-ji Temple. The four glass plates were taken through filters with different extraction wavelength ranges, respectively. In this study, glass plates were captured by filters of cyan, magenta, yellow and black are defined as C, M, Y and K, respectively. We must superimpose the images with a perfect pixel to pixel registration. However this can only be done if the acquisition system is with high resolution and high special accuracy. Therefore positional deviation can be seen. Since luminance values are used for color correction, it is necessary to correct positional deviation. Figure 3 shows a diagram in which four images are superimposed on the same portion as a reference only with parallel shift. As shown in Fig. 3, the color blurring phenomenon is caused by positional deviation. In order to correct this, there is a need

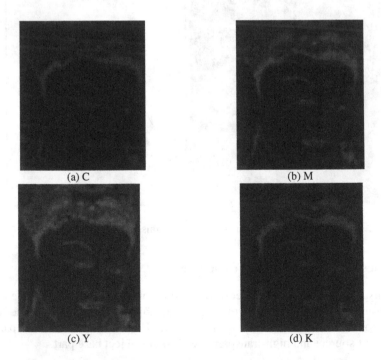

(a) C

(b) M

(c) Y

(d) K

Fig. 2. Photographed images of four color decomposed glass plate.

to perform image alignment with more linear transformations such as rotation and scaling. For this reason, we used affine transformation for image alignment.

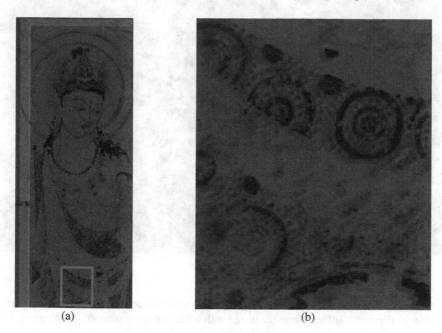

(a)   (b)

Fig. 3. The whole image aligned by affine transformation and enlarged image of blue frame. (a) represents the whole image. (b) represents the enlarged image of the blue frame in (a). (Color figure online)

Affine transformation is a combination of some linear transformations (rotation, scaling, shearing). Since a combination of several transformations is obtained as one linear transformation, if X and Y are affine spaces, then every affine transformation $f: X \rightarrow Y$ is the form $x \mapsto Ax + b$, where A is a linear transformation on X and b is a vector in Y. Affine transformation is generally described as follows:

$$\begin{pmatrix} y \\ 1 \end{pmatrix} = \begin{pmatrix} A & b \\ 0, \cdots, 0 & 1 \end{pmatrix} \begin{pmatrix} x \\ 1 \end{pmatrix} \tag{1}$$

This is equivalent to $y = Ax + b$.

Figure 4 shows the result comparison of the alignment manually and using affine transformation. According to Fig. 4, the color blur with manual alignment has disappeared. Then, the detail of color correction would be discussed in next part.

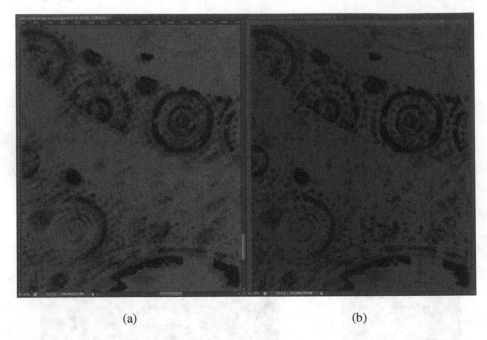

(a)　　　　　　　　　　　　　　　　　　　(b)

Fig. 4. Enlarged images aligned by hand and by affine transformation. (a) represents the image with manual alignment. (b) represents the image with affine transformation. (Color figure online)

3　Color Correction Based on Pigment Information

3.1　Method for Color Correction

In general, for color correction, it is necessary to convert RGB values, that is a luminance obtained from imaging, into XYZ values and then L*a*b* values [6]. In conversion from RGB values into XYZ values, linear multiple regression analysis is often used. Setting the matrix F as a transformation matrix from RGB values to XYZ values and using the image luminance value matrix S obtained from the raw data and the matrix X' of XYZ values of the reference data, the linear multiple regression analysis can be represented as $X' = FS$. By defining S and X', the coefficient matrix F of the multiple regression analysis model is determined by following equation using Moore–Penrose generalization inverse matrix: $F = X'S^{\mathrm{T}}(SS^{\mathrm{T}})^{-1}$. Here, symbol ^{T} expresses transposition of a matrix. By applying the coefficient matrix F to each pixel value of the target image, the color information of the image can be converted into XYZ space. Then, the pixel values are converted into L*a*b* values based on the definition by CIE. Calculation formulas are shown below:

When $Y/Y_{\mathrm{n}} > 0.008856$,

$$L^{*} = 116(Y/Y_{n})^{1/3} - 16 \tag{2}$$

or when $Y/Y_n \leq 0.008856$,

$$L^* = 903.29(Y/Y_n) \tag{3}$$

where Y_n is the value of Y due to the standard illuminant of the fully diffused reflector and the auxiliary standard illuminant.

$$a^* = 500[(X/0.9505)^{1/3} - Y^{1/3}] \tag{4}$$

$$b^* = 200[Y^{1/3} - (Z/1.089)^{1/3}] \tag{5}$$

Then, minimize the color difference in the L*a*b* space to make it look more faithful to the real image when viewing the image with human eyes. Setting the matrix G as a transformation matrix from L*a*b* values to L*a*b* values and using the matrix L obtained from Eqs. (3, 4, 5) and the matrix L' of L*a*b* values of the reference data, the linear multiple regression analysis is described as $L' = GL$. As with the matrix F, by determining L and L', G is obtained from the following equation: $G = L'L^T (LL^T)^{-1}$. By applying the coefficient matrix G to each pixel value of the target image, a color closer to the reference data can be obtained. In order to output as an image, the obtained L*a*b* values are translated into XYZ values and then into RGB values.

3.2 Color Correction Without Reference Color Chart

There was no color chart when the wall paintings of golden hall of Horyu-ji Temple were photographed, so it is not possible to create a reference data using a color chart. The method of creating the reference data without using a color chart has not been developed yet. Therefore, some existing pigment information documents or database are employed for color correction in this study. In this method, pigments are specified by reference documents, and a reference data base is prepared from them. As a result of literature survey, we found the pigments that were used in each part of the mural painting by artists visual observations and a rough classification of the pigment color [7–9], although there is no scientific analytical proof. Table 1 shows the pigment used in the mural painting of Horyu-ji Temple. However, it is the rough classification of the pigment and to make a reference data, it is necessary to specify detail classification. Therefore, we referred to our own data base, mainly after the book [10] with more than 1000 kinds of pigment such as classical natural mineral pigments and synthetic mineral pigments, etc. and detailed explanations of each color. Then, most of the pigment colors of the mural painting of Horyu-ji Temple were specified based on whether it had existed during that time or on the basis of the main component and the size of the grain. The color information of the pigment was obtained from the list which obtained XYZ values and L*a*b* values from spectral reflectance of enormous number of colors in our laboratory. For colors not listed, XYZ values and L*a*b* values were identified using the pigment estimation software developed in my laboratory [11–13]. From these results, reference data could be created.

Table 1. Pigment table of the wall painting of golden hall of Horyu-ji Temple.

Color	Pigment name	Chemical composition	Change due to fire
White clay	White clay	Aluminum silicate (siliceous earth)	Lose moisture but appearance invariant
	Chuka	Calcium carbonate	Change to calcium oxide
Red	Vermillion	Mercury sulfide	Volatile decomposition and disappearance
	Minium	Lead tetraoxide	It turns into litharge (Yellow)
	Bengara	Iron oxide	Immutable
Yellow	Loess	Hydrous silver oxide	It loses moisture and turns red
	Litharge	Lead monoxide	It melts at 880°C, it does not change color
Green	Rock patina	Basic copper carbonate	It becomes black cupric oxide
Blue	Rock ultramarine	Basic copper carbonate (different from ingredients in patina)	Same as above
Purple		Mixing vermillion and indigo (presumption)	
Ink	Carbon		It disappeared

Regarding the method of acquiring a sample data of each color, it is found that the color correction result obviously became better when the sample data was not acquired from the position too closed to each other but different positions or non-adjacent positions. Figure 5 shows the model of acquiring a sample data in the case of acquiring 81 pixels and Fig. 6 shows the result comparison of color correction by different sample

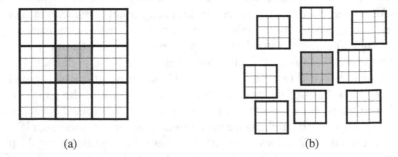

(a)   (b)

Fig. 5. Acquisition models of sample data when obtaining 81 pixels. (a) represents the case of obtaining a cluster of points from one place. (b) represents the case of obtaining a cluster of points from various places.

data acquisition methods. According to Fig. 6, it can be seen that there is color collapse in the image of (a), but the image of (b) is reproduced without color collapse. Therefore, the luminance value acquisition area is selected from as many locations as possible, and the luminance values of all the pixels in the selected area are adopted as input data.

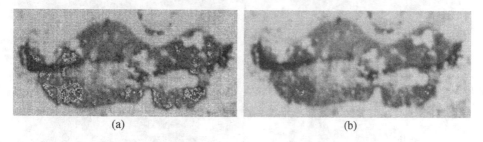

(a)   (b)

Fig. 6. Images that show difference between two cases to obtain 405 pieces of data around the lips of the figure. (a) represents the case of obtaining a cluster of points from one place. (b) represents the case of obtaining a cluster of points from various places. (Color figure online)

4   Results and Discussion

Figure 7 shows the image as a result of green-based color correction. From the image, it can be seen that color restoration is performed with high resolution. On the other hand, there are some problems with color reproduction. Figure 8 shows the result of color correction when different green-based colors are used as reference data. First, according to Fig. 8, the result varies depending on minor difference in reference data. Although the related documents about pigment and replica of wall painting are employed as reference in this study, it is still difficult to confirm the appearance of real pigments used on that wall painting. Moreover, some pigment color changed over the years. There is a need to consider pigment discoloration and fading. However, it is difficult to quantify and estimate the discoloration, so it is not included in this study. Therefore, it is a future task to study how much they can affect the final result of color reproduction. Second, color correction using color chart is performed with 228 types of color information with different hue and lightness, whereas five types of pigments ware used in this study. The color reproducibility is inferior to that of general digital archiving. In fact, the color difference of the image reproduced in this research is 9.82, 14.7, 10.9 of Fig. 8(a), (b) and (c), respectively, much higher than that of the conventional digital archiving using the color chart that is 1.6 to 3.2. However this work is a primary stage and when information on pigments used for the paintings of golden hall of Horyu-ji Temple is increased and reference data can be added, color difference can be reduced.

Fig. 7. Green type color correction result with referring to burned patina color and a replica. (a) represents the result of color correction (2400 dpi). (b) represents the replica (96 dpi). (Color figure online)

Fig. 8. Comparison of results of color correction using some green colors as reference data. (a) represents the result image of ancient patina color. (b) represents the result image of pine needle patina color. (c) represents the result image of burned patina color. (Color figure online)

Although there are many more factors to consider, a transmission type scanner has been successfully developed, and a method for color reproduction has been proposed.

And the color reproduction method can reproduce high-fidelity-color according to the reference data.

5 Conclusion

In this study, we constructed a transmission type scanning system with ultra high resolution (2500–5000 dpi) and a method to reproduce colors in high-fidelity from color information by using digital image processing. Our objects were numerous old glass plates having the images of the wall paintings of the golden hall of Horyu-ji Temple that is designated as a UNESCO World Heritage Site, and these glass plates are also designated as Japanese National Heritage in recent years. Because of the importance of these wall paintings, there is a need to construct a non-contact-type scanner that can scan transparent object in monochromatic image without size limitation. Usually traditional scanners have limited size requirement for an object and the glass dry plate of Horyu-ji Temple is large. Therefore, in a scanning of the glass dry plate, they cannot be used. In this study, we developed a scanning system that can be used for large permeable objects with practically no limit in size and succeeded in imaging monochrome dry glass plate decomposed into four colors. However, when four images are superimposed, positional deviation can be seen and the color blur phenomenon was caused by position deviation. In order to correct this, we adopted affine transformation to alignment and then the color blur with manual alignment has disappeared.

In this study, we established a color reproduction method based on pigment information and realized color reproduction at high resolution. There was no color chart when the wall paintings of Horyu-ji Temple were photographed, so it is not possible to create a reference data using a color chart. The method of creating the reference data without using color chart has not been systematized. Therefore, some existed pigment information documents or database are employed for color correction in this study. In this method, pigments are specified by reference documents, and a reference data is prepared from them.

From the result of green-based color correction, it can be seen that color correction is performed with high resolution. However, the result varies depending on delicate difference in reference data and some pigment color changed over the years. It is difficult to quantify the discoloration, so it is not considered in this study. And color correction using color chart is performed with 228 types of color information with different hue, lightness, and saturation, whereas five types of pigments can be adopted in this study. Therefore, the color difference of the image reproduced in this research is inferior to that of the conventional digital archiving using color chart. Therefore, it is a future task to study how much the discoloration can affect the final result of color reproduction and to investigate information on pigments used for the paintings of golden hall of Horyu-ji Temple and to increase reference data. Although there are some things to consider, we developed a transmission type scanner and a method for color reproduction for high-fidelity-color without color chart.

Acknowledgements. We would like to thank Benrido Inc., a printing company in Kyoto, for their cooperation of experiments, Ms. Terumi Akasaka and Ms. Mie Kado for valuable contribution, Dr. Jay Arre Toque and Dr. Masahiro Toiya for the discussion of the thesis, and other members of Ide Laboratory for helping us to do the experiments.

References

1. Denis, N.H.: Handling of collections in storage. In: Cultural Heritage Protection Handbook (2010)
2. Matsumura, T.: An International initiative for the preservation of digital information - UNESCO's Charter on the Preservation of Digital Heritage. Inf. Manage. **47**(7), 471–475 (2004). (in Japanese)
3. Nishimura, S.: Photography of cultural assets - a century of photographs by Benrido -. Jpn. Photographic Soc. J. **75**(6), 489–492 (2012). (in Japanese)
4. Nakashima, M., Ide-Ektessabi, A.: Development of transmission type ultra high definition scanner and digital color reproduction using filter coefficients. Kyoto University, Master thesis (2016). (in Japanese)
5. Ogane, Y., Ide-Ektessabi, A.: Construction of high resolution three-dimensional shape measurement system by line sensor camera. Kyoto University, Master thesis (2013). (in Japanese)
6. Murayama, Y., Ide-Ektessabi, A.: Bayesian image superresolution for hyperspectral image reconstruction. In: IS&T/SPIE Electronic Imaging, San Francisco, p. 8296-36 (2012)
7. Yamazaki, K.: Chemical Study on Pigments Used in Golden Hall of Horyu-ji Temple and Five-stories Pagoda (Horyuji-kondooyobi gojunoto ni shiyosareta ganryo no kagakutekikenkyu). Art research, Art institute, p. 145 (1947). (in japanese)
8. Yamazaki, K.: Pigments of Wall Paintings of Golden Hall of Horyu-ji Temple and Their Changes due to Fire (Horyuji-kondo-hekiga no ganryo oyobi sono kasai niyoru henka ni tsuite). Art research, Art institute, p. 167 (1953). (in Japanese)
9. Yamaguchi, A.: Wall Paintings of Golden Hall of Horyu-ji Temple - Beauty of Hakuho Revived from Glass Dry Plate - (Horyuji-kondo-hekiga – garasu-kanban kara yomigaetta hakuho no bi) -, pp. 210–213. Horyuji Temple Mural Publication, Iwanami Shoten (2011). (in Japanese)
10. Otsuki, Y.: Japanese Painting Color (Nihonga no iro). Shikosha (1989). (in Japanese)
11. Katayama, T., Ide-Ektessabi, A., Kobayashi, N., Fuji, T.: Development of large high precision scanner system. J. Jpn. Soc. Mech. Eng. **80**, 943–944 (2005)
12. Ichida, T., Ide-Ektessabi, A.: On-the-site pigment analysis using VIS-NIR multispectral imaging and Raman spectroscopy. Kyoto University, Master thesis (2013). (in Japanese)
13. Nishimura, R., Ide-Ektessabi, A.: Modeling of fading behavior and establishment of primary color estimation method. Kyoto University, Master thesis (2008). (in Japanese)

When It Is Not Only About Color: The Importance of Hyperspectral Imaging Applied to the Investigation of Paintings

Tatiana Vitorino[1,2(✉)], Andrea Casini[1], Costanza Cucci[1], Marcello Picollo[1], and Lorenzo Stefani[1]

[1] "Nello Carrara" Institute of Applied Physics of the National Research Council, 50019 Sesto Fiorentino, Florence, Italy
{a.casini,c.cucci,m.picollo,l.stefani}@ifac.cnr.it
[2] Department of Conservation and Restoration and LAQV-REQUIMTE, Faculty of Sciences and Technology, NOVA University of Lisbon, 2829-516 Caparica, Portugal
tm.vitorino@campus.fct.unl.pt

Abstract. This paper illustrates some of the developments achieved in the field of non-contact analytical tools for two-dimensional polychrome artworks. It reports significant advantages within the application of hyperspectral imaging for high-quality documentation, accurate color reproduction, study of artists' materials and techniques, and identification of past conservation treatments. In particular, Dürer's oil painting on panel, Adoration of the Magi (1504), was analyzed with a pushbroom hyperspectral imaging system in the visible-near-infrared range (Vis-NIR, 400–900 nm). The results obtained, including high-resolution color-accurate and false-color images, as well as high-resolution reflectance spectra, are reported and discussed, and the importance of hyperspectral imaging applied to the investigation of paintings is shown.

Keywords: Color-accurate image · False-color image · Hyperspectral imaging · Oil painting · Reflectance spectroscopy

1 Introduction

Since the 2000s imaging spectroscopy, also known as spectral imaging, has presented promising advances in the field of non-contact analytical tools for cultural heritage [1]. Reflectance hyperspectral imaging (HSI) systems in particular, consist of the collection of images in hundreds of contiguous narrow spectral bands (bandwidth <10 nm), offering high spatial and spectral resolution. The data set obtained, often referred to as an image-cube, includes a unique collection of spatial and spectral information of the imaged object, which can be processed and analyzed by several sophisticated tools. These tools can be used and adapted according to the specific purposes of the scan. The exploration of the image-cube, including the possibility to view, superimpose and compare high-resolution images at different wavelengths, as well as to extract a reflectance spectrum from each spatial pixel, can bring essential insight into the study and conservation of two-dimensional polychrome artworks. Some important advantages of

© Springer International Publishing AG 2017
S. Bianco et al. (Eds.): CCIW 2017, LNCS 10213, pp. 175–183, 2017.
DOI: 10.1007/978-3-319-56010-6_15

the application of HSI to these cultural heritage objects are the possibility to document them with high-quality, to accurately reproduce color, to distinguish and map artists' materials and study their techniques, and to identify non-original areas containing inpaints.

The usefulness of applying HSI to polychrome artworks is illustrated in the present paper through a case-study investigated with a HSI scanner, Albrecht Dürer's oil painting on panel, Adoration of the Magi (1504) at the Uffizi Gallery, Florence, Italy. This painting is one of the most beautiful works by the German painter, printmaker and theorist Albrecht Dürer (1471–1528), who was born in the Franconian city of Nuremberg, one of the strongest artistic and commercial centers in Europe during the fifteenth and sixteenth centuries. Dürer was particularly engaged by the artistic practices and theoretical interests of Italy, which he visited twice between 1494 and 1507. During these periods, the artist was fascinated by some of the great works of the Italian Renaissance, as well as by the classical heritage and theoretical writings of the region. Dürer's talent, ambition, and sharp, wide-ranging intellect earned him the attention and friendship of some of the most prominent figures in the German society [2]. Dürer's Adoration of the Magi is an altar-piece, which was commissioned by the king Friedrich III, who came to be known as Frederick the Wise, for the Schlosskirche at Wittenberg, Germany. The painting has an unusual setting and the fact that Joseph is missing from the scene is unconventional. The magi are richly clothed and their offerings impressive. On the right side, a servant appears to be taking more gifts from a bag. Some of Dürer's scholars consider that the magus with the green mantle possibly is the self-portrait of the painter himself.

The painting was scanned during a restoration process in 2006 at the former Restoration Laboratory of the *Soprintendenza Speciale per il Patrimonio Storico, Artistico ed Etnoantropologico e per il Polo Museale della città di Firenze* with the "Nello Carrara" Institute of Applied Physics of the National Research Council (IFAC-CNR) hyperspectral imaging camera in the visible-near-infrared range (Vis-NIR, 400–900 nm). The scan yielded high-resolution color-accurate and false-color images, as well as high-resolution reflectance spectra, which allowed to create an accurate record of the painting, get insight into the painting's colored materials, and identify areas that underwent past conservation treatments.

2   Hyperspectral Imaging System

Measurement of the Adoration of the Magi was carried out in the 400–900 nm range with the hyperspectral imaging scanner designed and assembled at IFAC-CNR, which was optimized for acquiring data on paintings with high spatial and spectral sampling (Fig. 1). The system has been thoroughly described by the authors in previous publications [1, 3–5]. It is based on a prism-grating-prism line-spectrograph, which is connected to a high sensitivity camera. Data acquisition is made following the pushbroom approach, also known as line scanning, in which a complete spectrum of each point along a line is formed on one column of the 2D detector array and the area of interest has to be scanned one line at a time. Illumination of the line-segment with a QTH lamp is made by two fiber-optic line-lights equipped with focusing lenses that are fixed to the scanner and symmetrically project their beams at 45° angles with respect to the normal direction at the imaged surface (0°/2 × 45° observation/illumination geometry). To calibrate the system and to compensate for the variation of emission of the QTH lamp, before each vertical scan the scan-head is positioned on a certified standard target of diffuse reflectance (99% Spectralon® Diffuse Reflectance Standard, Labsphere INC., North Sutton, NH, USA).

Fig. 1. IFAC-CNR HSI scanner during the measurement of the panel Adoration of the Magi (1504) by Albrecht Dürer at the former Restoration Laboratory of the *Soprintendenza Speciale per il Patrimonio Storico, Artistico ed Etnoantropologico e per il Polo Museale della città di Firenze*

3   Results and Discussion

Figure 2 shows the overall calibrated accurate RGB image of the oil painting on panel (100 cm × 114 cm) extracted from the image-cube. The RGB values are calculated following the standard IEC 61966-2-1:1999, originally proposed by Hewlett-Packard hp® and Microsoft® in 1996 for the exploitation of the gamut of computer display devices (with gamma 2.2). In summary, a linear transformation is applied to the XYZ values obtained by integration of each reflectance spectrum weighted with the CIE 1931 2° Standard Observer coordinates and the D65 illuminant curve. An exponential function is then applied to the three "RGB-linear" results to obtain the sRGB components, usually scaled as integer values between 0 to 255. If needed, other color components can be readily calculated, such as in the Adobe D50 illuminant color space or in the CIE L*a*b* (CIELAB), more suitable for accurate evaluation of colorimetric differences [6].

The high-resolution images (11.4 line/mm) obtained from the image-cube allow to view very small details, as can be seen by the magnified details of the RGB image reported in Fig. 3. Images can also be extracted from the image-cube at specific wavelengths. An image was extracted at 880 nm to complement the information obtained with the visible image and get further knowledge about the painting's materials and techniques (Fig. 4). This image revealed that some materials, which appear to be the same in the RGB image, have different behavior in the near-infrared, for example, the blue sky in the top right corner and the green mantle of one of the magi. Following this result, the infrared false-color (IRFC) image, in which infrared and visible bands are selected to create a pseudo-color image, was also reconstructed from the image-cube and evidenced the presence of non-original areas of paint (Fig. 5). This image is an average of the following wavelengths: R, 751–900 nm; G, 581–750 nm; B, 520–580 nm. For its reconstruction, the 99% Spectralon® Diffuse Reflectance Standard is used to verify and calibrate the procedure since after the IRFC process the reflectance standard has to appear as a perfect white surface. It should also be noted that the digitally reconstructed IRFC image is fully comparable to the traditional IRFC photo obtained by using IRFC Kodak films [7].

Fig. 2. RGB color image of the oil painting on panel Adoration of the Magi reconstructed from the image-cube (the dark shadow in the bottom center corresponds to the easel holding the painting during the measurement with the HSI scanner) (Color figure online)

Fig. 3. Magnified details of the RGB color image of the oil painting on panel Adoration of the Magi reconstructed from the image-cube (*left:* butterfly in the bottom left corner of the painting; *right:* castle on top of the green mountain in the background of the painting) (Color figure online)

Fig. 4. 880 nm image of the oil painting on panel Adoration of the Magi reconstructed from the image-cube

Materials with similar color, which means that they have similar absorbance spectra in the visible, but different infrared behavior, can be distinguished in the painting by their false color. In other words, since the information from the infrared region is presented in the IRFC image with color, different pigments can have a specific false-color appearance according to their reflectance in the infrared, which can be used for their identification [7]. An example of the utility of IRFC is shown by the magnified detail of the blue sky in Fig. 6. Here, the same area shows two different IRFC behaviors:

Fig. 5. Infrared false-color image of the oil painting on panel Adoration of the Magi reconstructed from the image-cube (Color figure online)

most of the sky is reported with a dark purple-bluish color while the non-original areas of paint are presented in a pale pink-reddish color, despite their similar appearance in the visible. The average CIELAB76 color values for both areas are L* = 34.7, a* = −15.2, b* = −7.5 and L* = 34.8, a* = −12.8, b* = −6.0 for the original and the inpainted areas, respectively. These values, calculated from the reflectance spectrum extracted from the respective pixels, mean that the color parameters of both areas are very close to each other. It can be concluded that the conservator was successful in creating the inpainted areas starting from the surrounding original colors even if the blue pigments used were different from the original one. In this case, by looking at the IRFC image it can be suggested that the original sky was painted with azurite while blue ultramarine, smalt, or cobalt blue might have been used in the inpainted areas.

The possibility to extract from the image-cube a high-resolution reflectance spectrum from each spatial pixel allows to go further in the suggestion of the original artist's materials and those used in the inpainted areas. In this sense, it is possible to make a more accurate suggestion of the identification of materials. Reflectance spectra with a spectral resolution of approximately 2.5 nm were extracted from averaged 2.3 mm × 2.3 mm areas (25 px × 25 px) of the original blue in the sky and the inpainted blue areas (Fig. 7). Spectra of the original blue areas confirmed the use of the pigment azurite (basic copper carbonate), with its characteristic high absorbance from 600 nm to 900 nm [8, 9]. On the other hand, the spectral shape of the inpainted blue areas, with the presence of an absorption band around 620 nm, reveals that a mixture of pigments was likely used. In particular, the presence of the modern pigment cerulean blue or phthalocyanine blue can be suggested [10, 11].

Fig. 6. Magnified details of the RGB color image (*left*) and IRFC image (*right*) of the oil painting on panel Adoration of the Magi reconstructed from the image-cube (*top row:* blue sky in the top right corner of the painting; *bottom row:* green mantle of one of the magi). The yellow circles mark the areas from where the reflectance spectra were extracted (Color figure online)

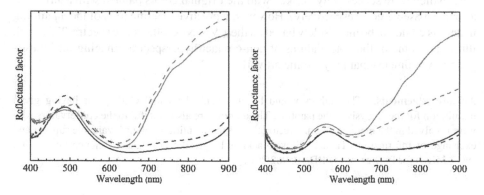

Fig. 7. Reflectance spectra of the oil painting on panel Adoration of the Magi extracted from the image-cube (*left:* blue sky; *right:* green mantle). Black lines = original areas; grey lines = inpainted areas

As previously stated, a similar situation is observed for the green color of one of the magi's mantle, which presents different IRFC behavior (the average CIELAB76 color values are $L^* = 18.1$, $a^* = -3.2$, $b^* = 13.8$ and $L^* = 20.9$, $a^* = -2.8$, $b^* = 13.3$ for the original and inpainted areas, respectively). The original green, which appears dark blue in the IRFC image (see the magnified detail in Fig. 6), is probably a copper-based green pigment, such as malachite or verdigris. The reflectance spectra extracted from these areas (Fig. 7) confirm the presence of a basic copper carbonate due to the wide absorption from 600 nm to 900 nm [9, 12]. The green color used for the inpainted areas has not been identified through its reflectance spectra. Complementary analytical techniques, commonly used for the study of artists' materials such as X-ray fluorescence, and Raman and infrared spectroscopies, would be required to make a positive identification.

Apart from the blue and green colors of the Adoration of the Magi, the reddish and pinkish colors were also investigated with HSI. This study was the subject of a previous publication by the authors [13].

4   Conclusions

This paper presents the use of an HSI scanner, which operates in the visible-near-infrared range (400–900 nm) and is based on a prism-grating-prism line-spectrograph, for the analysis of paintings. The system provides images with high spatial resolution and accurate color reproducibility. It is also able to acquire spectroscopic data with a very high resolution, making it possible to distinguish between different materials and to map them. However, despite this possibility, HSI does not provide by itself a straightforward or complete identification of the materials and complementary techniques such as X-ray fluorescence, and Raman and infrared spectroscopies were proved to be needed.

The investigation of Dürer's oil painting on panel, Adoration of the Magi, through its high-resolution color-accurate and false-color images, as well as high-resolution reflectance spectra extracted from the image-cube, revealed blue and green inpainted areas which were successfully masked with the original colors painted with azurite and a copper-based green (respectively). However, a positive identification of the inpainting materials could not be made solely based on their Vis-NIR reflectance spectra. This work illustrates some of the potentialities of non-contact hyperspectral imaging for investigating two-dimensional polychrome artworks.

Acknowledgements. The authors would like to thank the Uffizi Gallery for having given permission for the analysis of the painting. The authors are also grateful to the conservators who were involved in the maintenance and restoration of the painting for their invaluable support and exchange of information. Tatiana Vitorino acknowledges the Portuguese Science Foundation (FCT-MEC) for PhD grant PD/BD/105902/2014.

References

1. Cucci, C., et al.: Reflectance hyperspectral imaging for investigation of works of art: old master paintings and illuminated manuscripts. Acc. Chem. Res. **49**, 2070–2079 (2016)
2. Wisse, J.: Albrecht Dürer (1471–1528) - Heilbrunn Timeline of Art History, The Metropolitan Museum of Art, http://www.metmuseum.org/toah/hd/durr/hd_durr.htm

3. Vitorino, T., Casini, A., Cucci, C., Gebejesje, A., Hiltunen, J., Hauta-Kasari, M., Picollo, M., Stefani, L.: Accuracy in colour reproduction: using a ColorChecker chart to assess the usefulness and comparability of data acquired with two hyper-spectral systems. In: Trémeau, A., Schettini, R., Tominaga, S. (eds.) CCIW 2015. LNCS, vol. 9016, pp. 225–235. Springer, Heidelberg (2015). doi:10.1007/978-3-319-15979-9_21

4. Cucci, C., et al.: Open issues in hyperspectral imaging for diagnostics on paintings: when high spectral and spatial resolution turns into data redundancy. In: Salimbeni, R., Pezzati, L. (eds.) Proceedings of SPIE, vol. 8084, pp. 80848.1–80848.10 (2011)

5. Casini, A., et al.: Fiber optic reflectance spectroscopy and hyper-spectral image spectroscopy: two integrated techniques for the study of the Madonna dei Fusi. In: Salimbeni, R., Pezzati, L. (eds.) Proceedings of SPIE, vol. 5857, pp. 177–184 (2005)

6. Oleari, C.: Standard Colorimetry: Definitions, Algorithms and Software. John Wiley & Sons, UK (2016)

7. Moon, T., et al.: A note on the use of false-color infrared photography in conservation. Stud. Conserv. 37, 42–52 (1992)

8. Bacci, M.: UV-Vis-NIR FORS spectroscopies. In: Ciliberto, E., Spoto, G. (eds.) Modern Analytical Methods in Art and Archaeology. Chemical Analytical Series, vol. 155, pp. 321–361. Wiley & Sons, New York (2000)

9. Aceto, M., et al.: Characterisation of colourants on illuminated manuscripts by portable fibre optic UV-visible-NIR reflectance spectrophotometry. Anal. Methods 6, 1488–1500 (2014)

10. Bacci, M., et al.: A study of the blue colors used by telemaco signorini (1835–1901). J. Cult. Heritage 10, 275–280 (2009)

11. Rubio, M.T.: UV-VIS-NIR Spectroscopic Characterization of Two Modern Blue Pigments: Blue Phthalocyanine and Blue Indanhtrene. M.S. 1st Level Thesis in Materials and diagnostics techniques for Cultural Heritage. Pisa, Italy: Pisa University, Chemistry and Industrial Chemistry Department (2006)

12. Ricciardi, P., et al.: 'It's not easy being green': a spectroscopic study of green pigments used in illuminated manuscripts. Anal. Methods 5, 3819–3824 (2013)

13. Vitorino, T., et al.: Non-invasive identification of traditional red lake pigments in fourteenth to sixteenth centuries paintings through the use of hyperspectral imaging technique. Appl. Phys. A 121, 891–901 (2015)

Spectral Imaging

A Database of Spectral Filter Array Images that Combine Visible and NIR

Pierre-Jean Lapray[1](✉), Jean-Baptiste Thomas[2,3], and Pierre Gouton[3]

[1] MIPS Laboratory, Université de Haute Alsace, 68093 Mulhouse, France
pierre-jean.lapray@uha.fr
[2] The Norwegian Colour and Visual Computing Laboratory,
NTNU, 2816 Gjøvik, Norway
[3] Le2i, Université de Bourgogne, Franche-Comté, 21000 Dijon, France

Abstract. Spectral filter array emerges as a multispectral imaging technology, which could benefit several applications. Although several instantiations are prototyped and commercialized, there are yet only a few raw data available that could serve research and help to evaluate and design adequate related image processing and algorithms. This document presents a freely available spectral filter array database of images that combine visible and near infra-red information.

Keywords: Multispectral imaging · Spectral filter arrays · Image database

1 Introduction

Multispectral imaging (MSI) has been proven to be beneficial to a great variety of applications, but its use to general computer vision was limited due to complexity of imaging set-up, calibration and specific imaging pipelines. Spectral filter arrays (SFA) technology [9] seems to provide an adequate solution to overcome this limitation. In fact, increasing the number of spectral bands in filter arrays, along with using a high resolution sensor could lead to a small, efficient and affordable solution for single-shot MSI. In addition, SFA was developed around a very similar imaging pipeline than color filter arrays (CFA), which is rather well understood and already implemented in most solutions. In this sense, SFA provide a conceptual solution that could be exploitable in actual vision systems in a relatively straightforward manner.

We consider that the use of the SFA technology may reach a large scale of use soon. On one hand, SFA concept has been developed to a great extend using data from simulations, in particular on demosaicing [11,12,14,26,27,29], but also on other aspects [8,17,21,24,28]. On the other hand, recent practical works on optical filters [1,15,16,30] in parallel to the development of SFA camera prototypes in the visible electromagnetic range [5], in the near infra-red (NIR) [2] and in combined visible and NIR [7,25], lead to the commercialization of solutions (e.g. IMEC [3], SILIOS [23], PIXELTEQ [18]). Furthermore, several cameras include

© Springer International Publishing AG 2017
S. Bianco et al. (Eds.): CCIW 2017, LNCS 10213, pp. 187–196, 2017.
DOI: 10.1007/978-3-319-56010-6_16

custom filter arrays that are in-between CFA and SFA (e.g. Jia *et al.* [4] and Monno *et al.* [13]). Rest to validate the simulations with real data and adapt the imaging framework to state that this solution is ready to be used into practical applications. We help to address the first point by providing experimental data that can serve to the validation of simulation.

Through this article, we provide a freely accessible database of SFA images. The spectral calibration of the camera and the illuminant used during acquisition are provided along with several SFA raw images of various scenes. These data can be used as benchmarks for future works by the research community, and could lead to further development on SFA technology.

In the following sections, we first describe the camera design in term of spectral sensitivity, spatial arrangement and hardware. We then show the method to construct our SFA database, by presenting the experiment setup and the illuminant used. Finally, we draw a first benchmark to exploit the data; a visualization framework to display the multispectral data as a *sRGB* representation. To conclude, we outline the potential use of the proposed database in the research area and discuss future work.

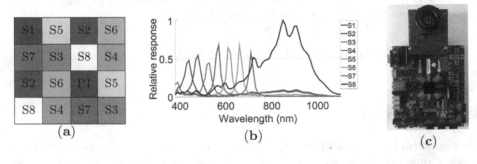

(a)   (b)   (c)

Fig. 1. (a) Joint spectral characteristics of optical filters and sensor from the camera used to recover the database images [25]. (b) Spatial distribution of filters over the sensor, following Miao *et al.* [10] method. (c) Camera designed at Le2i laboratory, composed of a FPGA board and an attached sensor board holding the detector array.

2   Camera Design

From our previous work [9,25], we designed and developed a proof-of-concept prototype SFA imaging system, that achieves multispectral snapshot capabilities. The camera setup is based on a commercial sensor coupled with a hybrid filter array for recovering visible and NIR information. The commercial sensor is from the e2v [22] manufacturer. The associated spectral filter array is manufactured by hybridization of the Silios Technologies [23]. The relative spectral sensitivities of the camera cover the electromagnetic spectrum from 380 nm to 1100 nm. Spectral characterization of the camera is fully described in the related paper [25]. The resulting characteristics of this vision system are shown in Fig. 1. From this work, we want to provide a useful set of data to go further in the practical investigation.

3   Database Description

We capture 18 scenes, composed of several categories of objects, ranging objects from: metal, biological, spatially homogeneous/heterogeneous, spectrally homogeneous/heterogeneous, showing specular reflections, translucent materials, containing industrial pigments, containing art pigments, clothes, etc. For the dataset, we fix a single exposure time, a single aperture and a single illuminant to limit multiple parameter dependence problems that could arise when analyzing multispectral images.

In practice, data is recovered from our camera through an Ethernet connection, linking the FPGA board (Zedboard, see Fig. 1(c)) and a PC. The FPGA holds a mezzanine card, which is an electronic interface towards the SFA sensor (the electronic design was initially developed by Lapray *et al.* [6]). Information concerning the hardware, like the optics, the electronics and the exposure times are given in Table 2. A simulated D65 source has been chosen to illuminate the scene (see Fig. 2). The object was small enough to be in a part where illumination was supposed to be sufficiently uniform, we will see later that illumination is yet far from flat.

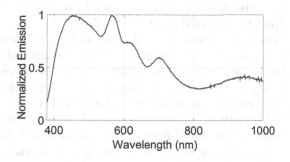

Fig. 2. Measurement of D65 simulator emission spectra used for the acquisition of the database.

A pre-processing step is necessary before any use of the produced images. This processing is composed by a dark correction and a downsampling; it is described in Thomas *et al.* [25]. All the images provided with this document are pre-processed accordingly and ready to use. The mosaiced images of the database are shown on Fig. 3. The entire database can be freely downloaded at http://chic.u-bourgogne.fr. The zip file is organised according to Table 1.

Table 1. The files can be downloaded at http://chic.u-bourgogne.fr, the link SFA_LDR point out to a zip file which contains directories, one directory for each of the scenes.

Scene name	Exposure time	File name RAW	File name demosaiced	File name sRGB
CD	4 ms	cd_4ms.tiff	cd_4ms.tiff	cd_4ms.png
Knife	4 ms	knife_4ms.tiff	knife_4ms.tiff	knife_4ms.png
Water	4 ms	water_4ms.tiff	water_4ms.tiff	water_4ms.png
Train front	16 ms	train_front_16ms.tiff	train_front_16ms.tiff	train_front_16ms.png
Pens	4 ms	pens_4ms.tiff	pens_4ms.tiff	pens_4ms.png
Kerchief	8 ms	kerchief_8ms.tiff	kerchief_8ms.tiff	kerchief_8ms.png
Kiwi	4 ms	Kiwi_4ms.tiff	Kiwi_4ms.tiff	Kiwi_4ms.png
MacBeth	4 ms	macbeth_4ms.tiff	macbeth_4ms.tiff	macbeth_4ms.png
Black swimsuit	16 ms	black_swimsuit_16ms.tiff	couteau_16ms.tiff	black_swimsuit_16ms.png
Origan	4 ms	origan_4ms.tiff	origan_4ms.tiff	origan_4ms.png
Orange object	4 ms	orange_object_4ms.tiff	orange_object_4ms.tiff	orange_object_4ms.png
Pastel	4 ms	pastel_4ms.tiff	pastel_4ms.tiff	pastel_4ms.png
Battery	4 ms	battery_4ms.tiff	battery_4ms.tiff	battery_4ms.png
Train side	16 ms	train_side_16ms.tiff	train_side_16ms.tiff	train_side_16ms.png
Raspberry	8 ms	raspberry_8ms.tiff	raspberry_8ms.tiff	raspberry_8ms.png
Ruler	4 ms	ruler_4ms.tiff	ruler_4ms.tiff	ruler_4ms.png
SD card	4 ms	sd_4ms.tiff	sd_4ms.tiff	sd_4ms.png
Painting	16 ms	painting_16ms.tiff	painting_16ms.tiff	painting_16ms.png

4   Obtention of Color Images

Prior to perform any visualization, it is necessary to reconstruct the full resolution color image from the sampled spectral mosaiced data.

Since the information acquired using SFA method is intrinsically sparse over the full image resolution, we need a mean in order to reconstruct the full spatial information on the spectral image. Here, Miao *et al.* [10] demosaicing algorithm is employed. This method is naturally chosen to be the benchmark method because the spatial arrangement of our filters (see Fig. 1(a)) has been specially selected following this method. There are 8 channels in the camera design, thus 8 independent images are produced from one mosaiced image. An example of a demosaiced image is shown on Fig. 4. These images are stored in a multiband tiff file in the database. Note that we have not implemented any devignetting correction on the data. This could be seen on some images.

The color version of these images, in Fig. 5 is obtained by fitting a linear color transform from the 8 bands to $CIEXYZ$ values, then to $sRGB$ values. The linear model is based on the reflectance measurements of the Gretag Macbeth color checker in the visible and NIR shown in Fig. 6.

The model is defined by M, that transforms color values C from the object into sensor values S, such as in Eq. 1.

$$C = M^+.S, \tag{1}$$

where M^+ is the generalized inverse of M (*i.e.* Moore-Penrose pseudo-inverse here) computed from the data obtained by integrating the Gretag Macbeth

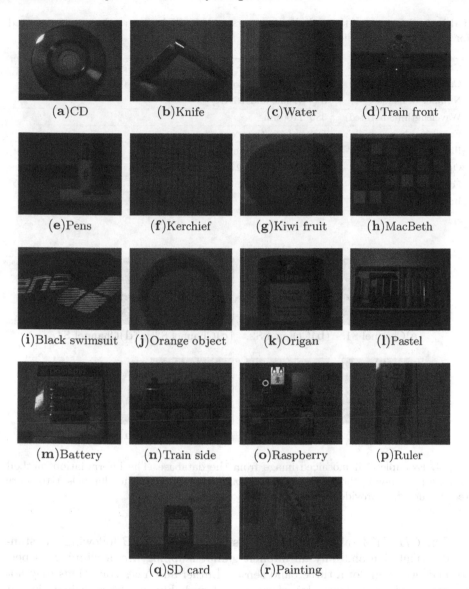

Fig. 3. Raw data after pre-processing applied described in [25]. We can clearly distinguish the SFA arrangement described in Fig. 1 when zooming in an image.

reflectance spectra and the illumination over the sensor sensitivities and over the standard 2 degrees CIE 1931 standard observer of the CIE according to the CIE recommendations. To this aim, all data are re-sampled at 10 nm by using linear interpolation, and the normalization factor k is computed according to $\bar{y}(\lambda)$ and the normalized illumination of Fig. 2. The data are provided in Table 3.

Table 2. Summary of the global parameters and the SFA camera characteristics used for the acquisition of the database.

Camera sensor	E2V EV76C661 + MSFA - Global shutter mode
Camera resolution	1280 × 1024 (sensor native) - 319 × 255 (image pre-processed)
Number of bands	8 (7 visible and 1 NIR)
Wavelength (calibrated)	380–1100 nm
Exposure time	Depends on the scene
Illuminant	D65 simulator (see Fig. 2)
Optics/Aperture	Edmund optics 12 mm 58001 - F/1.8
Focus	Fixed (20 cm)
Image format	Tiff 8 bits

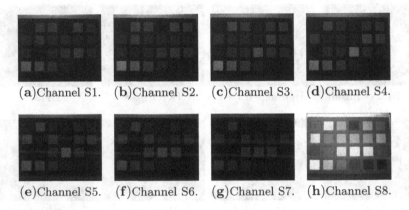

(a)Channel S1.   (b)Channel S2.   (c)Channel S3.   (d)Channel S4.

(e)Channel S5.   (f)Channel S6.   (g)Channel S7.   (h)Channel S8.

Fig. 4. Example of demosaiced image from the database. The interpolation method is done by applying the Miao binary tree algorithm [10]. So the channels 1 to 8 are reconstructed to provide the full spatial resolution of images.

The $CIEXYZ$ values are then transformed into $sRGB$ following the standard formulation and only an implicit gamut mapping, i.e. a clipping, is performed. Although for a three band sensor, Luther and Yves conditions may not be respected and a linear transform would probably not be sufficient, in our case of multispectral values, the colorimetric error is very small. Note, however, that even if we incorporated the NIR part in the color characterization, the sensitivity of the sensor in the NIR domain impacts the accuracy of the color reconstruction due to some amount of metamerism. Indeed, as it has been shown by Sadeghipoor et al. [19,20], the NIR contribution to the signal is a source of noise for the color accuracy. Our database may also help to evaluate the adequate processing that must be used to correct these data.

Fig. 5. Color image representation of reconstructed multispectral images after applying a linear interpolation algorithm that map the 8 channels to 3 color channels.

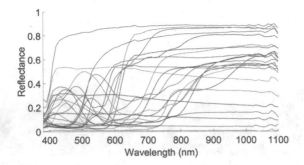

Fig. 6. Reflectance of the color checker patches used in our experiment. It is interesting to note that in the NIR, reflectance is mostly flat, but not the same for every color patch. (Thanks to Dr Yannick Benezeth and to the multispectral platform at Université de Bourgogne for measurement and facilities)

Table 3. Coefficients of the linear transform which converts the normalized camera data into colorimetric data.

	X	Y	Z
S_1	18.71202393	−68.36308577	349.4442091
S_2	43.97557926	18.67082953	258.8288447
S_3	−67.36621595	197.9637378	−95.61688044
S_4	220.0254892	250.802883	53.18126713
S_5	266.4136662	123.0658162	−22.48363478
S_6	8.903488711	−19.34440853	0.160100687
S_7	−28.61265672	−38.32399335	−65.19256704
S_8	−26.06896941	−37.46125383	−48.41522273

5   Conclusion

We acquired a database of SFA images with a prototype sensor sensitive in the visible and NIR part of the electromagnetic field. A great variety of objects have been captured and the parameters of the acquisition have been measured, such as scene illumination. In addition, the colorimetric transform that permits to generate color images is provided. A benchmark demosaicing performed with the most established demosaicing method for SFA is also given. These data may serve for evaluation of state of the art demosaicing and color reconstruction methods as well as for further development and proof of concept in this field.

References

1. Eichenholz, J.M., Dougherty, J.: Ultracompact fully integrated megapixel multispectral imager. In: SPIE OPTO: Integrated Optoelectronic Devices, p. 721814. International Society for Optics and Photonics (2009)

2. Geelen, B., Blanch, C., Gonzalez, P., Tack, N., Lambrechts, A.: A tiny VIS-NIR snapshot multispectral camera. In: SPIE OPTO, p. 937414. International Society for Optics and Photonics (2015)
3. IMEC: Hyperspectral-imaging. http://www2.imec.be
4. Jia, J., Barnard, K.J., Hirakawa, K.: Fourier spectral filter array for optimal multispectral imaging. IEEE Trans. Image Process. 25(4), 1530–1543 (2016)
5. Kiku, D., Monno, Y., Tanaka, M., Okutomi, M.: Simultaneous capturing of RGB and additional band images using hybrid color filter array. In: Proceedings of SPIE, vol. 9023, pp. 90230V–90230V-9 (2014). http://dx.doi.org/10.1117/12.2039396
6. Lapray, P.J., Heyrman, B., Ginhac, D.: Hardware-based smart camera for recovering high dynamic range video from multiple exposures. Opt. Eng. 53(10), 102110 (2014). http://dx.doi.org/10.1117/1.OE.53.10.102110
7. Lapray, P.J., Thomas, J.B., Gouton, P.: A multispectral acquisition system using MSFAs. In: Color and Imaging Conference 2014, pp. 97–102 (2014). http://www.ingentaconnect.com/content/ist/cic/2014/00002014/00002014/art00016
8. Lapray, P.J., Thomas, J.B., Gouton, P., Ruichek, Y.: Energy balance in spectral filter array camera design. J. Eur. Opt. Soc. Rapid Pub. 13(1), 1 (2017). http://dx.doi.org/10.1186/s41476-016-0031-7
9. Lapray, P.J., Wang, X., Thomas, J.B., Gouton, P.: Multispectral filter arrays: recent advances and practical implementation. Sensors 14(11), 21626 (2014). http://www.mdpi.com/1424-8220/14/11/21626
10. Miao, L., Qi, H., Ramanath, R., Snyder, W.E.: Binary tree-based generic demosaicking algorithm for multispectral filter arrays. IEEE Trans. Image Process. 15(11), 3550–3558 (2006)
11. Mihoubi, S., Losson, O., Mathon, B., Macaire, L.: Multispectral demosaicing using intensity-based spectral correlation. In: The fifth International Conference on Image Processing Theory, Tools and Applications, IPTA 2015, Orléans (2015). https://hal.archives-ouvertes.fr/hal-01196983
12. Mihoubi, S., Losson, O., Mathon, B., Macaire, L.: Multispectral demosaicing using intensity in edge-sensing and iterative difference-based methods. In: SITIS, COMI 2016, Naples, December 2016
13. Monno, Y., Kikuchi, S., Tanaka, M., Okutomi, M.: A practical one-shot multispectral imaging system using a single image sensor. IEEE Trans. Image Process. 24(10), 3048–3059 (2015)
14. Monno, Y., Tanaka, M., Okutomi, M.: N-to-sRGB mapping for single-sensor multispectral imaging. In: 2015 IEEE International Conference on Computer Vision Workshop (ICCVW), pp. 66–73, December 2015
15. Park, H., Crozier, K.B.: Multispectral imaging with vertical silicon nanowires. Sci. Rep. 3, 2460 (2013)
16. Park, H., Dan, Y., Seo, K., Yu, Y.J., Duane, P.K., Wober, M., Crozier, K.B.: Vertical silicon nanowire photodetectors: spectral sensitivity via nanowire radius. In: CLEO: Science and Innovations, p. CTh3L-5. Optical Society of America (2013)
17. Péguillet, H., Thomas, J.B., Ruicheck, Y., Gouton, P.: Energy balance in single exposure multispectral sensors. In: CVCS 2013 (2013)
18. PIXELTEQ: Micro-patterned optical filters. https://pixelteq.com/
19. Sadeghipoor, Z., Lu, Y.M., Ssstrunk, S.: Correlation-based joint acquisition and demosaicing of visible and near-infrared images. In: 2011 18th IEEE International Conference on Image Processing (ICIP), pp. 3165–3168, September 2011

20. Sadeghipoor, Z., Thomas, J.B., Süsstrunk, S.: Demultiplexing visible and near-infrared information in single-sensor multispectral imaging. In: Color and Imaging Conference 2016, (24), 1 (2016). http://www.ingentaconnect.com/content/ist/cic/2016

21. Shrestha, R., Hardeberg, J.Y., Khan, R.: Spatial arrangement of color filter array for multispectral image acquisition. In: Proceedings of SPIE, vol. 7875, pp. 787503–787503-9 (2011). http://dx.doi.org/10.1117/12.872253

22. e2v Technologies: Ev76c661 BW and colour CMOS sensor (2009). http://www.e2v.com/products-and-services/high-performance-imaging-solutions/imaging-solutions-cmos-ccd-emccd/, www.e2v.com

23. SILIOS Technologies: Micro-optics supplier. http://www.silios.com/

24. Thomas, J.: Illuminant estimation from uncalibrated multispectral images. In: Colour and Visual Computing Symposium, CVCS 2015, Gjøvik, 25–26 August 2015, pp. 1–6. IEEE (2015). http://dx.doi.org/10.1109/CVCS.2015.7274900

25. Thomas, J.B., Lapray, P.J., Gouton, P., Clerc, C.: Spectral characterization of a prototype SFA camera for joint visible and NIR acquisition. Sensors 16(7), 993 (2016). http://www.mdpi.com/1424-8220/16/7/993

26. Wang, C., Wang, X., Hardeberg, J.Y.: A linear interpolation algorithm for spectral filter array demosaicking. In: Elmoataz, A., Lezoray, O., Nouboud, F., Mammass, D. (eds.) ICISP 2014. LNCS, vol. 8509, pp. 151–160. Springer, Cham (2014). doi:10.1007/978-3-319-07998-1_18

27. Wang, X., Thomas, J.B., Hardeberg, J.Y., Gouton, P.: Discrete wavelet transform based multispectral filter array demosaicking. In: Colour and Visual Computing Symposium (CVCS 2013), pp. 1–6 (2013)

28. Wang, X., Green, P.J., Thomas, J.-B., Hardeberg, J.Y., Gouton, P.: Evaluation of the colorimetric performance of single-sensor image acquisition systems employing colour and multispectral filter array. In: Trémeau, A., Schettini, R., Tominaga, S. (eds.) CCIW 2015. LNCS, vol. 9016, pp. 181–191. Springer, Cham (2015). doi:10.1007/978-3-319-15979-9_18

29. Wang, X., Thomas, J.B., Hardeberg, J.Y., Gouton, P.: Median filtering in multispectral filter array demosaicking. In: Proceedings of SPIE (EI), vol. 8660, pp. 86600E–86600E-10 (2013). http://dx.doi.org/10.1117/12.2005256

30. Yi, D., Kong, L., Wang, J., Zhao, F.: Fabrication of multispectral imaging technology driven MEMS-based micro-arrayed multichannel optical filter mosaic. In: SPIE MOEMS-MEMS, p. 792711. International Society for Optics and Photonics (2011)

Analytical Survey of Highlight Detection in Color and Spectral Images

Haris Ahmad Khan[1,2(✉)], Jean-Baptiste Thomas[1,2], and Jon Yngve Hardeberg[1]

[1] The Norwegian Colour and Visual Computing Laboratory, NTNU - Norwegian University of Science and Technology, Gjøvik, Norway
{haris.a.khan,jean.b.thomas,jon.hardeberg}@ntnu.no
[2] Le2i, FRE CNRS 2005, Univ. Bourgogne Franche-Comté, Dijon, France

Abstract. Detection of highlights is a prominent issue in computer vision, graphics and image processing. Applications which require object properties measurement or rendering are affected by specular reflection since the models assume matte diffusing surfaces most of the time. Hence, detection, and sometimes removal, of specular reflection (highlights) in an image may be critical. Several methods are proposed for addressing this issue. In this paper, we present a review and analysis of these techniques in color and spectral images.

Keywords: Image analysis · Highlights detection · Specular reflection · Diffuse reflection · Spectral imaging

1 Introduction

The process of extracting information from an image, and its transformation into a useful representation, enables the description of intrinsic characteristics of objects in the scene. Barrow et al. [1] introduced the term "intrinsic images" and suggested that the function of the human visual system at its earlier stage is to determine the orientation of the illumination and the surface being observed. The authors describe such details of scenes in term of shading and reflectance images, which are collectively denoted as intrinsic images. There are other intrinsic properties as well, including shading, reflectance, diffuse reflection components and specular reflection components. Diffuse reflection is caused by scattering of light in all directions after hitting the surface, while specular reflection occurs when incident light is reflected in a single direction. Lee et al. [2] presented a neutral interface reflection model by examining the light reflection problem through the use of bidirectional spectral-reflectance distribution function (BSRDF) for specifying both incident and reflected beam geometry. They proposed that specular reflection is identical to scene illuminant in color while diffuse reflection contains the intrinsic properties of the surface. There can be significant variations in appearance of a surface in presence of specular reflection, and they appear as an additional surface property which is not intrinsic [3,4].

© Springer International Publishing AG 2017
S. Bianco et al. (Eds.): CCIW 2017, LNCS 10213, pp. 197–208, 2017.
DOI: 10.1007/978-3-319-56010-6_17

We are interested in the detection of specular reflection in images. Several computer vision applications such as 3D reconstruction, object detection, recognition, target tracking, and dichromatic editing use the intrinsic information and are mostly based on the assumption of the surfaces having perfect diffusion. In most of such algorithms, specular reflections and highlights are termed as outliers [5]. However, the presence of specular reflection is unavoidable in most of the real world scenes since the materials and surfaces not only possess diffuse reflection but also show specular reflections, which is explained in the Dichromatic Illumination Model (DIM) [6]. Hence, the assumption of absence of specular reflection for such algorithms introduce constraints and reduce their robustness. There is a loss of details in case of specular reflection, for example texture and color of surface being observed. Highlight removal is often considered as an inpainting problem [7–10]. This methodology is implemented after identification of highlights. In this paper, we discuss the methods for highlight detection. Discussion about removal of specular highlights is out of scope of this paper.

As an example, Fig. 1 shows an image of a printed circuit board. The information about connectivity of the circuit is totally washed out in the area which is under direct specular reflection. In addition, there are highlight spots on the metallic surfaces of diodes and resistors. Such spots follow the DIM and create ambiguity concerning the intrinsic characteristics of the object surface. It may thus be desirable to remove the effect of highlights from the image for recovery of information.

Highlight detection algorithms can be classified into various categories on the basis of data being used for input. For color images, we propose two major categories, namely the *single-image* and *multi-images* based techniques, presented

Fig. 1. Image of printed circuit board with transistors, resistors and diodes. Specular highlights can be observed in the highly saturated areas, where it washes out the information. In addition, specular spots are also observed on the metallic parts and resistors.

in Sects. 2 and 3, respectively. Furthermore, a relatively recent development in imaging technology is spectral imaging. The problem of specular highlights occurs also in spectral images, therefore we have included it in this review as another category (Sect. 4). However, this review focuses only on close range spectral imaging and does not address remote sensing images. In Sect. 5, we discuss and compare key features of the presented algorithms, before concluding.

2 Single Color Image Based Techniques

We have defined two major categories of algorithms to detect and remove specularities in a single color image. Those categories use either the color space analysis, or spatial information analysis.

The techniques based on color space analysis treat an image pixel by pixel. Klinker *et al.* [11] classified color pixels in the categories of *diffuse, highlight* and *saturated* pixels. A diffuse pixel is defined as a pixel containing only the body reflectance (although the color of body is influenced by scene illuminant), a highlight pixel contain both body and specular reflections while a saturated pixel is created when a highlight pixel exceeds the maximum measurable light intensity of camera sensor. Klinker *et al.* [11] analyzed the color histogram and observed that the specular and diffuse components from a uniform surface form a skewed T shape. To separate these components, convex polygon fitting technique is used in their work. Linking color space with DIM [6] is also proposed [12,13]. This color information is used to separate reflection components by fitting it into a dichromatic plane.

Transformation into other color spaces for detection of specularities is also a technique where the characteristics of an adequate color space are exploited. Schlüns and Teschner [14,15] transformed the image from RGB to Y'U'V' color space. Bajcsy *et al.* [16] proposed S-space for analysis of variation in color of objects. There are three orthogonal basis functions in S space named S_0, S_1 and S_2. The S_0 basis function corresponds to specular reflection in S space. A data-driven color space called SUV color space was introduced by Mallick *et al.* [17]. Yang *et al.* [18] proposed Ch-CV space. This color space is spanned by maximum chromaticity (Ch) and the coefficient of variation (CV) in RGB. Yang *et al.* [19] proposed separation of specular and diffuse components in HSI color space as further improvement in their already proposed Ch-CV space. Recently, Akashia and Okatani [20] proposed an optimization technique for sparse non-negative matrix factorization for the identification of specular reflections in an image.

In spatial information based techniques, detection of specularities is performed through the use of local information in an image. Tan *et al.* [21] introduced Maximum Chromaticity-Intensity Space to differentiate between the maximum intensity and maximum chromaticity in an image. A pseudo-diffuse component image is created, which is later utilized for separation of specular reflection from the image. The ratio of intensities and colors amongst neighbouring pixels is preserved in the pseudo-diffuse image and is called the specular free image. The specular free image is obtained by Yoon *et al.* [22] through subtracting the minimum value for each channel from the input image. Shen and Cai [23] introduced a modified specular free image by adding an offset to the subtraction method provided in [22]. This offset can either be constant for the whole image [24] or can be varying for each pixel [23]. In [4], intensity logarithmic differentiation is used on both the specular-free and the input image for determination of diffuse pixels. Using this method, performance of the technique of creation of specularity free image is improved for highly textured surfaces. However, the position of highlights should be known for applying this method. Liu *et al.* [25] proposed the preservation of surface color saturation by initially producing a specular free image and then increasing the achromatic component of diffuse chromaticity. It is important to note that in all the specularity free image creation techniques, the input image is normalized for illuminant. Hence, the illuminant should either be known or should be estimated first before applying those techniques.

Yang *et al.* [26,27] treat the specular pixels as noise and use a bilateral filter for smoothing the maximum fraction of color components. In this way, the noise caused by specular pixels is eliminated. Kim *et al.* [28] observed that a diffuse pixel has low intensity in, at least, one channel. They called it the *"dark channel"* and proposed that the dark channel of an image contains no specular reflection. Their technique uses a maximum a-posteriori formulation that helps in the recovery of specular reflection and chromaticity. An *et al.* [29] proposed the pure diffuse pixel distribution model. This model is built on the assumption that there is at-least one purely diffuse pixel for each material in the scene. Shen and Zheng [30] assumed that some area of a surface contain only the diffuse reflection. They define the range value for an image as maximum minus minimum intensity for a surface and observed that the intensity ratio between maximum value of a pixel and range value is independent of the geometry of the surface. With the assumption for certain pixels to be diffuse, specular components from remaining pixels are computed through their proposed model.

Highlight detection techniques based on a single color image are practical as they do not require any additional hardware and data. However a problem associated with such algorithms is that they rely on image statistics and are based on strong prior assumptions. Therefore, such methods are not robust for change in imaging environment but works reasonably well when the required conditions are fulfilled.

3   Multiple Images Based Techniques

The use of multiple images for separation of reflectance components from the scene is proposed in a number of studies. Since highlights are not intrinsic properties of an image, they can occur at any point and are dependant on the viewing angle. The direction of illumination also has its impact on the location of highlight spots. A surface area of an image which is affected by highlight in one image can appear as a diffuse surface if the viewing angle, or the illumination direction is changed. Based on this phenomenon, multiple images based highlight removal techniques are proposed in the literature, which require a number of images, captured using different imaging conditions.

Lee and Bajcsy [31] proposed the use of Lambertian consistency, which states that the Lambertian reflection does not vary in brightness and spectral contents with change in the viewing angle while the specular reflection changes the behaviour. They defined the spectral distance as euclidean distance between two colour points in a three-dimensional space. Minimum spectral distance is calculated to detect the inconsistency in color among two images of same scene but with different viewing angle. Sato and Ikeuchi [32] introduced temporal-color space analysis by using a moving light source. Lin and Shum [33] used different illuminations for the same scene, and then proposed linear basis functions for separating diffuse and specular components. Lin et al. [34] used stereo images for the detection of specularities. Weiss [35] acquired an image sequence with varying specularities and used maximum likelihood estimation by assuming that the change in illumination gives rise to sparse filter outputs.

Feris et al. [36] used flash images taken with same point of view but different positions of flash for recovering the diffuse component. Agrawal et al. [37] proposed a method for image enhancement by using two images of a scene. One is taken with flash and one without flash. Reflection from the flash image is removed by using a gradient projection scheme.

Chen et al. [38] reconstructed the specular field by using histograms of the same image but with different intensities. Yang et al. [39] proposed statistical methods for removal of specularities from stereo images. They assume non-overlapping highlight regions in their method. Wang et al. [40] used three cameras for taking images of transparent plastic package containing tablets. They normalized the acquired images and then generated an image consisting of average intensities of corresponding pixels. In this way, pills are retained with higher intensity while varying regions of specular reflection are removed. Generation of specularity map from video sequence is proposed by Prinet et al. [41]. Recently, Wang et al. [42] proposed the use of light field imaging technology for capturing multiple views of a scene and then used that information for detection of specularities in the scene.

Nayar et al. [43] noticed that the specular reflection is highly polarized and proposed the use of polarization filter to separate the diffuse and specular reflections. They used a polarization filter by placing it in front of a camera and observed that by rotating the polarization filter, the brightness of diffuse materials is not changed, while the specular reflection is changed, since it is highly polarized, and varies following a cosine function. Polarization based methods are also proposed by Wolff [44,45], Kim et al. [46], Atkinson and Hancock [47,48], Müller [49], Umeyama and Godin [50], Lamond et al. [51] and Zhang et al. [52].

Although the above mentioned specularity detection techniques are able to show good performance, the major limitation associated with them is the availability of multiple images of the same scene with varying illumination direction or viewing angle. This limitation causes those techniques to become less practical compared to the approaches which are based on a single image.

4 Spectral Image Based Techniques

Hyperspectral and multispectral imaging has been used extensively for remote sensing. Recently, with advancement in sensor technology, spectral imaging is widely available for imaging of objects at shorter distance. Such imaging comes with the problem of highlights, the same as in the case of color images. However, since spectral images contain more data compared to a color image, therefore highlight detection techniques are not exactly the same.

Bochko and Parkkinen [53] proposed probabilistic principal component analysis for detection of spectral and diffuse parts in images. Fu *et al.* [54] proposed orthogonal subspace projection (OSP) and dichromatic model for specularity-free representation of hyperspectral images. OSP results in projecting the radiance and illumination spectrum being orthogonal to each other in the subspace. In this way, the illuminant spectra is removed from mixed spectra and a spectral image without highlights is obtained. It is important to note that prior information about illuminant is required in this method. Koirala *et al.* [55] proposed spectral unmixing of end-members for separation of specular and diffuse components in spectral images. Spectral end-members consist of pure spectra corresponding to objects in a scene. Spectral unmixing method is widely used in hyperspectral remote sensing where the end-members correspond of pure spectra of land cover classes. In the method by Koirala *et al.* [55], Automated target generation program (ATGP) is employed for selection of end-members. When the scene illuminant is known, then the initial target detected by ATGP is the illuminant spectra. In case of unknown illuminant, a pixel with maximum value along the whole spectra is considered as the initial target. Using constrained energy minimization, the diffuse part of the image is identified.

5 Analysis of Various Specularity Detection Methods

In Table 1, we compare the characteristics of various specularity detection techniques. In these tables, different techniques are divided in general categories. The concept behind the technique is briefly defined along with the general assumptions being made. Use of DIM is common in the specularity detection techniques but there are some algorithms that do not use this model, so it is also given in the table. White balancing (WB) and image segmentation (Seg.) is also a constraint in such algorithms. We make analysis of various categories of highlight detection algorithms on the basis of the above expressed factors. Finally, general remarks about strength of those techniques is provided.

Table 1. Comparison of characteristics of highlight removal techniques

Category	Images	Concept	Assumptions	DIM use	WB Req.	Seg. Req.	Strength
Color histogram analysis [11–13]	Single	Skewed T-shape formation between specular and diffuse components	Lambertian body reflection, interface reflection is function with a sharp peak around the angle of perfect mirror reflection	Yes	Yes	Yes	Works well for dielectric materials but not for metals
Dichromatic illumination based Model [6]	Single	Description of reflected light from a dielectric object as linear combination of object color and highlight	Single illumination, existence of matte cluster	Yes	Yes	Yes	Works well for dielectric materials but not for metals
Color space transformation [14–19]	Single	Segmentation of specular regions for obtaining the max. diffuse chromaticity in each segmented region	Single illumination, each segmented cluster has uniform diffuse chromaticity	Yes	Yes	Yes	Iterative process can be time consuming, colors are distorted in some algorithms. Overall good result on dielectric materials with single illumination
Saturation preservation model [25]	Single	Creation of over-saturated diffuse reflectance and then putting the achromatic regions back to the diffuse reflection	Pure white illuminant	Yes	Yes	No	Color saturation of surface is preserved in this method
Sparse matrix factorization [20]	Single	Sparse non-negative matrix factorization for separation of specular components	Single illuminant, presence of diffuse component for every surface	Yes	Yes	No	No assumption about spatial priors

Table 1. (*Continued*)

Category	Images	Concept	Assumptions	DIM use	WB Req.	Seg. Req.	Strength
Pseudo diffuse image [3, 4, 21]	Single	Dark channel prior	Pure white illuminant	Yes	Yes	Yes	Color ratio among neighbouring pixels is preserved
Inpainting technique [7–10]	Single	Removal of highlight part through use of neighbouring pixels info. and inpainting	Single illuminant, presence of diffuse component for every surface	No	Yes	Yes	Preservation of color for dielectric surfaces
Multiple images acquisition [31–42]	Multiple	Highlights behave different when viewing angle or illumination is changed	Points which show specular reflection in one image can behave purely diffuse in another image when viewing condition is changed	Yes	–	–	Efficient detection of highlights when the required conditions and no. of images are available
Polarization [43–52]	Multiple	Use of polarization filter during image acquisition	Specular highlights are polarized while diffuse reflections are unpolarized	Yes	No	No	With use of additional hardware (polarization filter), highlights can be detected efficiently
Orthogonal sub-space projection [54]	Spectral	Separation of radiance and illumination spectrum through orthogonal subspace projection	SPD of illuminant is known	Yes	Yes	No	With knowledge of a particular illuminant, highlight caused by it can be removed
PCA [53]	Spectral	Use of probabilistic PCA for separation of specular and diffuse components	Colored objects already segmented, constant hue	Yes	No	Yes	Performs efficient highlight removal if segmentation is already performed
Spectral unmixing [55]	Spectral	Spectral unmixing method	End-member of highlight part is SPD of illuminant	Yes	No	No	With the use of a proper spectral segmentation method, highlights can be removed

6   Conclusion

In this paper, we provide a survey of highlight detection algorithms in color and spectral images. In most of the literature, results from detection and removal of highlights is presented qualitatively while comparing with other methods. Although qualitative analysis provide a general overview, quantitative measurement should also be used to provide a fair comparison.

Generally, strong assumptions and priors are used for highlight detection. However, the highlight detection is still able to provide much of the useful information and is therefore a critical issue in image analysis. We also review state-of-the-art on highlight detection in spectral images. There is less work done on it and much is yet to be explored. The amount of spectral information being acquired in spectral imaging can certainly provide benefit for highlight detection and is still an open area of research.

References

1. Barrow, H., Tanenbaum, J.: Recovering intrinsic scene characteristic from images. In: Computer Vision System, pp. 3–26 (1978)
2. Lee, H.C., Breneman, E.J., Schulte, C.P.: Modeling light reflection for computer color vision. IEEE Trans. Pattern Anal. Mach. Intell. **12**, 402–409 (1990)
3. Tan, P., Quan, L., Lin, S.: Separation of highlight reflections on textured surfaces. In: Proceedings of the 2006 IEEE Computer Society Conference on Computer Vision and Pattern Recognition, CVPR 2006, Washington, D.C., vol. 2, pp. 1855–1860. IEEE Computer Society (2006)
4. Tan, R.T., Ikeuchi, K.: Separating Reflection Components of Textured Surfaces Using a Single Image. Digitally Archiving Cultural Objects, pp. 353–384. Springer, Boston (2008)
5. Artusi, A., Banterle, F., Chetverikov, D.: A survey of specularity removal methods. Comput. Graph. Forum **30**(8), 2208–2230 (2011)
6. Shafer, S.A.: Using color to separate reflection components. Color Res. Appl. **10**(4), 210–218 (1985)
7. Park, J.W., Lee, K.H.: Inpainting highlights using color line projection. IEICE Trans. Inf. Syst. **E90–D**, 250–257 (2007)
8. Budianto, Lun, D.P.K.: Inpainting for fringe projection profilometry based on geometrically guided iterative regularization. IEEE Trans. Image Process. **24**, 5531–5542 (2015)
9. Ortiz, F., Torres, F.: A new inpainting method for highlights elimination by colour morphology. In: Singh, S., Singh, M., Apte, C., Perner, P. (eds.) ICAPR 2005. LNCS, vol. 3687, pp. 368–376. Springer, Heidelberg (2005). doi:10.1007/11552499_42
10. Tan, P., Lin, S., Quan, L., Shum, H.-Y.: Highlight removal by illumination-constrained inpainting. In: Proceedings of 9th IEEE International Conference on Computer Vision, vol. 1, pp. 164–169, October 2003
11. Klinker, G., Shafer, S., Kanade, T.: Using a color reflection model to separate highlights from object color. In: Proceedings of 1st International Conference on Computer Vision, pp. 145–150 (1991)

12. Klinker, G.J., Shafer, S.A., Kanade, T.: The measurement of highlights in color images. Int. J. Comput. Vis. **2**(1), 7–32 (1988)
13. Klinker, G.J., Shafer, S.A., Kanade, T.: A physical approach to color image understanding. Int. J. Comput. Vis. **4**(1), 7–38 (1990)
14. Schlüns, K., Teschner, M.: Analysis of 2D color spaces for highlight elimination in 3D shape reconstruction. In: Proceedings of the Asian Conference on Computer Vision, vol. 2, pp. 801–805 (1995)
15. Schlüns, K., Teschner, M.: Fast separation of reflection components and its application in 3D shape recovery. Color Imaging Conf. (1), 48–51 (1995)
16. Bajcsy, R., Lee, S.W., Leonardis, A.: Detection of diffuse and specular interface reflections and inter-reflections by color image segmentation. Int. J. Comput. Vis. **17**(3), 241–272 (1996)
17. Mallick, S.P., Zickler, T., Belhumeur, P.N., Kriegman, D.J.: Specularity removal in images and videos: a PDE approach. In: Leonardis, A., Bischof, H., Pinz, A. (eds.) ECCV 2006. LNCS, vol. 3951, pp. 550–563. Springer, Heidelberg (2006). doi:10. 1007/11744023_43
18. Yang, J., Cai, Z., Wen, L., Lei, Z., Guo, G., Li, S.Z.: A new projection space for separation of specular-diffuse reflection components in color images. In: Lee, K.M., Matsushita, Y., Rehg, J.M., Hu, Z. (eds.) ACCV 2012. LNCS, vol. 7727, pp. 418–429. Springer, Heidelberg (2013). doi:10.1007/978-3-642-37447-0_32
19. Yang, J., Liu, L., Li, S.Z.: Separating specular and diffuse reflection components in the HSI color space. In: IEEE International Conference on Computer Vision Workshops, pp. 891–898, December 2013
20. Akashi, Y., Okatani, T.: Separation of reflection components by sparse non-negative matrix factorization. Comput. Vis. Image Underst. **146**, 77–85 (2016)
21. Tan, R.T., Ikeuchi, K.: Separating reflection components of textured surfaces using a single image. IEEE Trans. Pattern Anal. Mach. Intell. **27**, 178–193 (2005)
22. Yoon, K.J., Choi, Y., Kweon, I.S.: Fast separation of reflection components using a specularity-invariant image representation. In: International Conference on Image Processing, pp. 973–976, October 2006
23. Shen, H.-L., Cai, Q.-Y.: Simple and efficient method for specularity removal in an image. Appl. Opt. **48**, 2711–2719 (2009)
24. Shen, H.-L., Zhang, H.-G., Shao, S.-J., Xin, J.H.: Chromaticity-based separation of reflection components in a single image. Pattern Recogn. **41**(8), 2461–2469 (2008)
25. Liu, Y., Yuan, Z., Zheng, N., Wu, Y.: Saturation-preserving specular reflection separation. In: IEEE Conference on Computer Vision and Pattern Recognition (CVPR), pp. 3725–3733, June 2015
26. Yang, Q., Wang, S., Ahuja, N.: Real-time specular highlight removal using bilateral filtering. In: Daniilidis, K., Maragos, P., Paragios, N. (eds.) ECCV 2010. LNCS, vol. 6314, pp. 87–100. Springer, Heidelberg (2010). doi:10.1007/978-3-642-15561-1_7
27. Yang, Q., Tang, J., Ahuja, N.: Efficient and robust specular highlight removal. IEEE Trans. Pattern Anal. Mach. Intell. **37**, 1304–1311 (2015)
28. Kim, H., Jin, H., Hadap, S., Kweon, I.: Specular reflection separation using dark channel prior. In: IEEE Conference on Computer Vision and Pattern Recognition, pp. 1460–1467, June 2013
29. Suo, J., An, D., Ji, X., Wang, H., Dai, Q.: Fast and high quality highlight removal from a single image. IEEE Trans. Image Process. **25**, 5441–5454 (2016)
30. Shen, H.-L., Zheng, Z.-H.: Real-time highlight removal using intensity ratio. Appl. Opt. **52**, 4483–4493 (2013)
31. Lee, S.W., Bajcsy, R.: Detection of specularity using colour and multiple views. Image Vis. Comput. **10**(10), 643–653 (1992)

32. Sato, Y., Ikeuchi, K.: Temporal-color space analysis of reflection. J. Opt. Soc. Am. A **11**, 2990–3002 (1994)
33. Lin, S., Shum, H.-Y.: Separation of diffuse and specular reflection in color images. In: Proceedings of the IEEE Computer Society Conference on Computer Vision and Pattern Recognition, vol. 1, pp. 341–346 (2001)
34. Lin, S., Li, Y., Kang, S.B., Tong, X., Shum, H.-Y.: Diffuse-specular separation and depth recovery from image sequences. In: Heyden, A., Sparr, G., Nielsen, M., Johansen, P. (eds.) ECCV 2002. LNCS, vol. 2352, pp. 210–224. Springer, Heidelberg (2002). doi:10.1007/3-540-47977-5_14
35. Weiss, Y.: Deriving intrinsic images from image sequences. In: Proceedings Eighth IEEE International Conference on Computer Vision, ICCV, vol. 2, pp. 68–75 (2001)
36. Feris, R., Raskar, R., Tan, K.-H., Turk, M.: Specular highlights detection and reduction with multi-flash photography. J. Braz. Comput. Soc. **12**(1), 35–42 (2006)
37. Agrawal, A., Raskar, R., Nayar, S.K., Li, Y.: Removing photography artifacts using gradient projection and flash-exposure sampling. ACM Trans. Graph. **24**, 828–835 (2005)
38. Chen, T., Goesele, M., Seidel, H.P.: Mesostructure from specularity. In: IEEE Computer Society Conference on Computer Vision and Pattern Recognition (CVPR), vol. 2, pp. 1825–1832 (2006)
39. Yang, Q., Wang, S., Ahuja, N., Yang, R.: A uniform framework for estimating illumination chromaticity, correspondence, and specular reflection. IEEE Trans. Image Process. **20**, 53–63 (2011)
40. Wang, C., Kamata, S.I., Ma, L.: A fast multi-view based specular removal approach for pill extraction. In: IEEE International Conference on Image Processing, pp. 4126–4130, September 2013
41. Prinet, V., Werman, M., Lischinski, D.: Specular highlight enhancement from video sequences. In: IEEE International Conference on Image Processing, pp. 558–562, September 2013
42. Wang, H., Xu, C., Wang, X., Zhang, Y., Peng, B.: Light field imaging based accurate image specular highlight removal. PLOS ONE **11**, 1–17 (2016)
43. Nayar, S.K., Fang, X.-S., Boult, T.: Separation of reflection components using color and polarization. Int. J. Comput. Vis. **21**(3), 163–186 (1997)
44. Wolff, L.B.: Classification of material surfaces using the polarization of specular highlights. In: Proceedings of SPIE - The International Society for Optical Engineering, vol. 1005, pp. 206–213, January 1988
45. Wolff, L.B.: Polarization-based material classification from specular reflection. IEEE Trans. Pattern Anal. Mach. Intell. **12**, 1059–1071 (1990)
46. Kim, D.W., Lin, S., Hong, K.-S., Shum, H.: Variational specular separation using color and polarization. In: Proceedings of the IAPR Workshop on Machine Vision Applications (2002)
47. Atkinson, G.A., Hancock, E.R.: Recovery of surface orientation from diffuse polarization. IEEE Trans. Image Process. **15**, 1653–1664 (2006)
48. Atkinson, G.A., Hancock, E.R.: Two-dimensional BRDF estimation from polarisation. Comput. Vis. Image Underst. **111**(2), 126–141 (2008)
49. Müller, V.: Polarization-based separation of diffuse and specular surface-reflection. In: Sagerer, G., Posch, S., Kummert, F. (eds.) Mustererkennung 1995: Verstehen akustischer und visueller Informationen. Informatik aktuell, pp. 202–209. Springer, Heidelberg (1995)
50. Umeyama, S., Godin, G.: Separation of diffuse and specular components of surface reflection by use of polarization and statistical analysis of images. IEEE Trans. Pattern Anal. Mach. Intell. **26**, 639–647 (2004)

51. Lamond, B., Peers, P., Debevec, P.: Fast image-based separation of diffuse and specular reflections. In: ACM SIGGRAPH Sketches, SIGGRAPH 2007. ACM, New York (2007)

52. Zhang, L., Hancock, E.R., Atkinson, G.A.: Reflection component separation using statistical analysis and polarisation. In: Vitrià, J., Sanches, J.M., Hernández, M. (eds.) IbPRIA 2011. LNCS, vol. 6669, pp. 476–483. Springer, Heidelberg (2011). doi:10.1007/978-3-642-21257-4_59

53. Bochko, V., Parkkinen, J.: Highlight analysis using a mixture model of probabilistic PCA. In: Proceedings of the 4th WSEAS International Conference on Signal Processing, Robotics and Automation, ISPRA 2005, Stevens Point, Wisconsin, pp. 15:1–15:5. World Scientific and Engineering Academy and Society (WSEAS) (2005)

54. Fu, Z., Tan, R.T., Caelli, T.: Specular free spectral imaging using orthogonal subspace projection. In: 18th International Conference on Pattern Recognition (ICPR), vol. 1, pp. 812–815 (2006)

55. Koirala, P., Pant, P., Hauta-Kasari, M., Parkkinen, J.: Highlight detection and removal from spectral image. J. Opt. Soc. Am. A **28**, 2284–2291 (2011)

Color Characterization

Characterization by Hyperspectral Imaging and Hypercolor Gamut Estimation for Structural Color Prints

Mathieu Hébert[1(✉)], Juan Martínez-García[1], Thomas Houllier[2],
Hayk Yepremian[2], Nicolas Crespo-Monteiro[1], Francis Vocanson[1],
Alain Trémeau[1], and Nathalie Destouches[1]

[1] Univ Lyon, UJM-Saint-Etienne, CNRS, Institut d Optique Graduate School,
Laboratoire Hubert Curien UMR 5516, Saint-Etienne, France
`mathieu.hebert@univ-st-etienne.fr`
[2] Institut d'Optique Graduate School, Saint-Etienne, France

Abstract. A recently developed color printing system on glass plates, based on dot-by-dot laser irradiation generating the growth of metallic nanoparticles in a special coating, produces structural colors depending strongly on the illumination and observation configuration. The difficulty for an exhaustive color characterization of the printing technology comes not only from the goniochromaticity of the samples, but also from their very high specularity, to which classical measurement instruments are not adapted. Moreover, as the light-matter interaction relies on a number of optical phenomena (surface plasmon resonance, interferences, diffraction, effects of polarization of light) for which no predictive model is available today, their characterization requires measurement of many printed samples. In this paper, we present a characterization method based on multispectral imaging and on spectral prediction for halftone colors that permitted a first gamut estimation in three specific illumination/viewing configurations.

Keywords: Structural colors · Multiview prints · Specular surface · Hyperspectral imaging · Nano-technologies

1 Introduction: Laser-Induced Color Lusters on Glass

Recent progresses in nanotechnologies enable the coloration of glass with interesting visual rendering. This is for example the case of the technology developed by the laboratoire Hubert Curien, called PICSULP [1], where a coating containing silver [2] is deposited on the glass plate, then irradiated by a laser beam in order to anneal the coating and cluster the metallic ions into metallic nanoparticles (NPs). Goniochromatic coloration of the glass plate surface is thus obtained thanks to various optical phenomena: the presence of silver NPs generates surface plasmon resonance, therefore wavelength-selective absorption as in stained glass [3]; the organization of the NPs along one plane parallel to the coating-air interface generates interferences as in thin films; the NPs can even be aligned along parallel lines, as shown in Fig. 1-a, which produces diffraction effects visible at grazing angles, and also gives to the sample a dichroic spectral behavior,

© Springer International Publishing AG 2017
S. Bianco et al. (Eds.): CCIW 2017, LNCS 10213, pp. 211–222, 2017.
DOI: 10.1007/978-3-319-56010-6_18

i.e. polarization sensitive colors [4, 5]. These optical effects are influenced by several physical parameters: the nanoparticle shape, size and spatial organization, as well as the coating thickness and refractive index that evolve during the laser treatment. Four command parameters can be varied: exposure (tuned by the laser scanning speed), power, wavelength, and focusing of the laser beam. Polarization of the laser can also be varied.

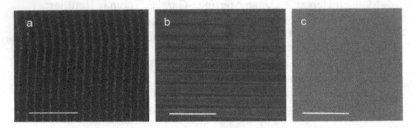

Fig. 1. Printed glass plate observed at (a) nanometric scale where we can see the NPs aligned along parallel lines (scale bar: 2 μm), (b) at microscopic scale where we can see many segments each one printed with different laser parameters (scale bar: 200 μm), and (c) at macroscopic scale in specular reflection mode (scale bar: 2 mm).

In opposition to classical printing techniques on paper or transparency films where a color patch has "one color" almost independent of the viewing conditions, a glass plate uniformly treated by the PICSLUP technology with constant laser command parameters can display many colors according to the illumination/observation configuration (IOC). Figure 2 shows this dramatic color change through the example of a four-color image observed in three IOCs. Therefore, a sample cannot be attributed one color, but should be assigned a set of colors that we propose to call "hypercolor". A second difference with conventional printing is that no model allows predicting the color viewed in a given IOC as a function of the printing command parameters. An exhaustive color characterization therefore requires a huge amount of samples produced each one with different laser command parameters, incrementally varied, to be measured in several IOCs. This represents too many measurements for a reasonable calibration process. Moreover,

Fig. 2. Color image printed with PICSLUP (1 × 1 cm), showing the dramatic color change according to the illumination/observation geometry. Left: Specular reflection mode (45°:45° geometry); Center: Off-specular reflection mode (45°:0° geometry); Right: Transmission mode (0°:0° geometry) [1].

radiances reflected or transmitted in the regular directions (given by Snell's laws) differ from the ones scattered in the rest of the hemisphere by several orders of magnitude: the sensitivity of the measurement setup must therefore be adapted to different IOCs.

In this paper, we present a color characterization method that is not exhaustive, but already representative of the color generation capacities of the PICSLUP technology. It relies on a set of primary colors printed with different laser parameters on one glass plate, and three measurement geometries: specular reflection, off-specular reflection, and normal transmission. Spectral measurements are carried out by using a self-made hyperspectral imaging system. From this set of primary colors, secondary colors can be predicted by juxtaposing lines of different primary colors, and color gamuts can be computed for each of the selected measurement geometries.

2 Selection of Samples and Geometries

In a previous study [6], an exhaustive color characterization has been performed for the 0°:0° specular reflection mode by measuring the XYZ color coordinates of the reflected radiances under a A illuminant thanks to a calibrated camera mounted on top of a microscope. This geometry was the only one allowed by the microscope. The colorimetric calibration of the camera was developed in order to suit the very high specularity of the samples by using of a specific color chart presenting as high specularity as the samples. Microscopic patches of 10656 hypercolors, similar to those displayed in Fig. 1b, were printed and analyzed in this way by excluding the edges of each patch. For the present study, we selected a subset of 330 hypercolors printed over 1 × 1 mm squares, with the following combinations of laser command parameters [1]: 2 wavelengths (488 and 647 nm), 3 powers (300, 400, and 600 mW), 11 laser scanning speeds (30000, 3200, 2000, 1400, 1200, 1000, 900, 800, 600, 500, and 300 µm/s) and 5 focus distances (0, 0.5, 0.8, 1.8, and 2 mm).

These 330 hypercolors were measured with the hyperspectral imaging setup described in the next section, in three different geometries: 15°:15° specular reflectance (illumination by collimated light at 15° from the normal of the sample, and observation in the specular direction), 45°:0° off-specular reflectance (illumination at 45° from the normal of the sample, observation along the normal), 0°:0° transmittance (illumination by collimated light at the normal of the sample, and direct observation of the transmitted collimated beam).

3 Hyperspectral Imaging System

The optical bench assembled for the hyperspectral measurements is shown in Fig. 3. The illumination module was placed on a rotating arm permitting to vary the incidence angle at both sides of the sample; it comprised an optical fiber connected to a light source (HL-2000-HP 20 W halogen lamp by Ocean Optics) placed at the focus of a lens in order to obtain a collimated light beam of 4 cm diameter. The detection module comprised a lens-free 12-bit gray-level camera, a set of 31 interferential filters of 10 nm spectral width centered every 10 nm from 400 to 700 nm, and a telecentric lens made of two lenses whose foci meet each other, the sample being placed in the other focal plane of the first lens, the detector of the camera in the one of the second lens [7]. The advantage of the telecentric lens is that it allows the simultaneous measurement of many patches, in strictly similar measurement conditions. This is a crucial point for our very specular samples since a very small angular variation may modify considerably the detected radiance (variations up to 50% can be easily observed, which is still small in comparison to the 10^{10} dynamic of the BRDF of the samples). In this context, the telecentric lens is crucial to ensure that all points of the sample are viewed under the same angle. With a conventional lens, the image of a uniform hypercolor patch would be non-uniform because of the goniochromaticity of the sample and the obliquity of the captured rays at the border of the image.

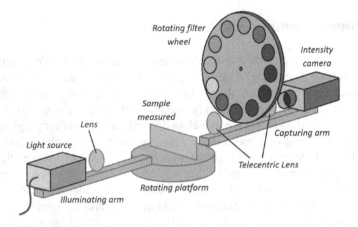

Fig. 3. Scheme of the hyperspectral imaging system for the measurement of samples, here in transmission mode.

The calibration of the spectral bench was done by using a neutral color reference sample reflecting or transmitting similar radiance as the studied samples. In specular reflection mode, the reference sample was a silicon mirror whose spectral reflectance was measured with a spectrophotometer in the 15°:15° geometry. Once placed in the hyperspectral bench, for each band-pass filter (denoted by its central wavelength λ), the aperture and exposure of the camera was adjusted in order to obtain a maximum signal without saturation of the camera. These camera parameters as well as the captured images $I_{ref}(x, y, \lambda)$ of the reference sample were stored, then the images $I(x, y, \lambda)$ of the PICLSUP print were captured by using for each band-pass filter the same camera parameters as those used for the reference sample. Lastly, we considered for each pixel (x, y) and each waveband λ, the ratio $I(x, y, \lambda)/I_{ref}(x, y, \lambda)$, which corresponds to a reflectance factor.

In off-specular reflection mode, the reference sample was a green diffusing ceramic tile, whose spectral reflectance was comparable in all wavebands to the one of the samples (these latter exhibiting a greenish hue in this IOC). Since the BRDF of our specular samples is extremely low at 45° from the illumination direction, we illuminated them with a high conical irradiance coming from an integrating sphere with a 500 lm halogen lamp in it. Similar procedure as for the specular reflection mode was then applied.

In transmittance mode, the reference sample was simply void. Once again, similar procedure as for the specular reflection mode was applied. By way of illustration, we show in Fig. 4 the images of the sample and the reference sample captured in two wavebands around 460 nm and 600 nm. Note that spatial variations of the illuminance, lens transmittances, vigneting and other aberrations introduced by the system, are systematically corrected as they are similar in both the sample and reference images.

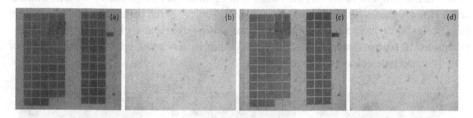

Fig. 4. (a, c) Images of a sample printed by the PICSLUP system and (b, d) images of the reference sample (void) (b, d) obtained in transmission mode at 460 nm (a, b), and 600 nm (c, d).

From the 31 pairs of images obtained in each mode, we can reconstruct the hyperspectral image with a wavelength sampling of 10 nm, which is a rather good spectral (10 nm) and spatial (1024 × 768 pixels) resolution compared to hyperspectral imaging systems with variable lighting geometry existing today [8, 9]. Before obtaining the hyperspectral image, an important step is the registration of the different images because the band-pass filters can introduce a small shift between the different images captured [10]. An image processing applet was developed to perform registration automatically.

At the end of the process, we have the spectral and spatial information of the prints. A good way to visualize their colors in a computer display is to render them by assuming an illuminant to obtain their CIE-XYZ values and then obtain sRGB colors by using standard transformations. In Fig. 5, we can see a color version of the hyperspectral images obtained in the three measurement geometries, by assuming a D65 illuminant. We can notice the dramatic change in color of the same printed areas according to the IOC used. Some patches look scratched in the specular reflectance mode: a surface

Off-specular
reflection

Specular
reflection

Transmission

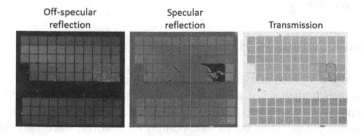

Fig. 5. sRGB color images rendered from the hyperspectral images in three different measurement geometries. The areas of the squares are: 1 mm × 1 mm.

pealing effect due to thermal and mechanical strains produced by the laser treatment in specific parameter ranges can roughen the surface, which thus reflects a much lower radiance in the specular direction.

Each hyperspectral image obtained contains one spectrum per pixel. By averaging the spectra of pixels belonging to a same patch, we could obtain the spectra of all the printed patches and calculate the corresponding CIE 1976 LAB color coordinates by assuming a D65 illuminant (Fig. 6). In **off-specular reflection mode**, the volume of colors that can be obtained have a moderate size, with a strong presence in the green hue which are lacking in the other configurations. The **specular reflection mode** produces a wider range of chromaticities in the samples. However, the variation in lightness in that geometry is rather limited, presenting L* values between 40 and 65 units. The colors in the back side of the samples in this configuration have a much smaller volume, with very reduced chromatic and lightness variations. In **transmission mode**, the color gamut is very reduced, consisting mainly of very light and pale colors of orange hue.

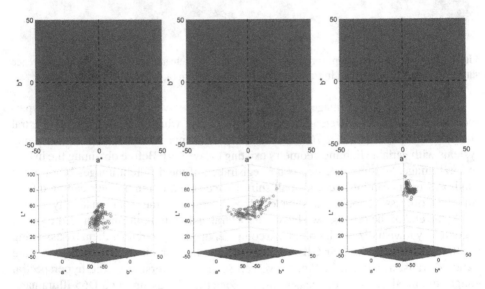

Fig. 6. Colors obtained for the 45°:0° off-specular reflection geometry (left), 15°:15° specular reflection geometry (center) and 0°:0° transmission geometry (right) of the 330 printed hypercolor patches, represented in the CIE 1976 L*a*b* color space (bottom line) and projected onto the (a*,b*)-plane (top line).

4   Gamut extension by Halftoning

In contrast with ink-based printers which need halftoning in order to reproduce many colors from their limited set of inks (four inks in quadrichromy), the PICSLUP technology can produce a wide variety of hypercolors in each point, and cover the plate with one uniform hypercolor (continuous tone printing). However, since only 330 hypercolors have been characterized, we propose to use halftoning to obtain additional, intermediate hypercolors. Since the set of printable halftones is considerable, we wanted to know whether it is possible to predict their color in the OIC instead of measuring them. We thus propose to verify the validity of a classical prediction model for halftone colors in case of low light scattering in the printing support: the Spectral Neugebauer model [11].

A set of 30 different 2 × 2 mm patches where printed on the same glass support, with different combinations of five primaries and different proportions of area coverage; line halftoning was used by juxtaposing lines of 20 μm width. An image of the squares, captured with the hyperspectral imaging system in the 15°:15° specular reflection configuration is shown in Fig. 7, as well as the composition of each of the printed patches. The leftmost column corresponds to patches wholly covered by one primary. These are used as inputs in the prediction models in order to estimate the colors obtained from the combination of several primaries. The remaining 25 patches correspond to areas printed with the combinations of two or three different primaries. The primaries used are specified by the numbers in the brackets, and the ratio of the area covered by each of them is specified below the primaries. For example, the square located in the 2nd row and 5th column is made with the primaries 1 and 5, with a ratio of 2 lines of Primary 1 for each line of Primary 5.

Full Primary 1	(1,2) 1:1	(1,3) 1:1	(1,4) 1:1	(1,5) 1:1	(2,3) 1:1
Full Primary 2	(1,2) 2:1	(1,3) 2:1	(1,4) 2:1	(1,5) 2:1	(2,3) 2:1
Full Primary 3	(1,2) 3:1	(1,3) 3:1	(1,4) 3:1	(1,5) 3:1	(2,3) 3:1
Full Primary 4	(2,4) 1:1	(2,5) 1:1	(3,4) 1:1	(3,5) 1:1	(4,5) 1:1
Full Primary 5	(1,2,3) 1:1:1	(1,2,5) 1:1:1	(1,3,5) 1:1:1	(2,1,3) 2:1:1	(2,4,5) 2:1:1

Fig. 7. Image of the squares printed for halftoning prediction testing, captured with the hyperspectral imaging bench. Specification of squares printed for halftoning evaluation. The squares on the leftmost column were printed by using only one primary, while the other 25 were printed by combining the primaries in the parenthesis in the proportions shown. (Color figure online)

The spectral properties of the samples were measured in the three IOCs presented in Sect. 3. The Spectral Neugebauer model predicts, for a given IOC, the spectrum of a halftone hypercolor, $S_{halftone}(\lambda)$, as a function of the spectra $S_i(\lambda)$ of the primaries i and their respective surface coverage a_i, as:

$$S_{halftone}(\lambda) = \sum_i a_i S_i^{1/n}(\lambda) \tag{1}$$

Figure 8 shows the measured and predicted spectra of the first halftone patch, located in the first row and second column of the sample (see Fig. 7), for each of the different measurement configurations. The prediction accuracy, assessed by the CIE94 color difference between the measured and predicted colors by assuming a D65 illuminant, is rather good, considering that the just-noticeable-difference threshold of the human visual system is approximately 1 unit. The prediction accuracy for the Neugebauer model over the set of samples that we produced is slightly poorer than the one usually achieved in color reproduction by digital printers (e.g. inkjet on photo-quality paper), e.g. the Yule-Nielsen modified Spectral Neugebauer model which is one of the more efficient [12]. In the present case, as expected since our samples are non-scattering, no improvement is achieved by using the Yule-Nielsen modified Spectral Neugebauer model. The PICSLUP printing system is probably less reproducible than commercial digital printers, especially due to small artifacts which may have small but noticeable impact on the

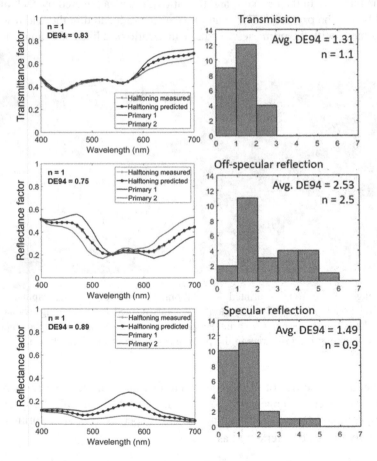

Fig. 8. Left: Measured and predicted spectra of one halftone patch and measured spectra of its composing primaries in the three measurement modes: transmission (top row), specular reflection (middle row), off-specular reflection (bottom row). Right: histograms of the DE94 color distances between the measured and predicted spectra for the 20 halftone samples tested.

spectral properties of the prints. Moreover, the measurement process is also subject to some imprecision and noise. Being given these constraints, we can be satisfied with the prediction accuracy that is achieved.

By using the Spectral Neugebauer model, we can predict the colors that can be produced in each geometrical configuration by the combination of the numerous primaries produced by the PICSLUP system, shown in Fig. 6. To obtain the complete set of colors that can be produced with the PICSLUP system, we exhaustively predicted the colors produced by the halftoning mixture of every pair of primaries from the set of 330 hypercolor patches. We found that in all the IOCs, the predicted colors obtained by halftoning with each pair of primaries draw an almost straight line between them, as a consequence of the linear Eq. (1). This volume of colors is very close to the convex hull of the set of primaries used, i.e., the minimum convex volume that contains all the primaries in a given configuration. The color gamut in each of the geometries can there-fore be approximated in a simple manner as the convex hull defined by the primaries used. The extended color gamuts obtained for each of the six measurement configura-tions thanks to use of halftoning are presented in Fig. 9.

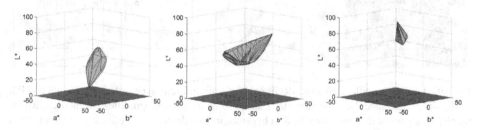

Fig. 9. Estimated color gamut volumes for the PICSLUP technology in the CIE 1976 L*a*b* color space for the 45°:0° off-specular reflection geometry (left), 15°:15° specular reflection geometry (center) and 0°:0° transmission geometry (right).

Despite the photometric constraints and limitations that exist for characterizing the PICSLUP technology, we demonstrated that line halftoning was possible in our system by obtaining a satisfactory accuracy in the prediction of the colors that can be produced by mixing different primaries. The worst accuracy was obtained in the off-specular reflection mode where the reflected radiance was very low, which made the measure-ments prone to errors due to stray light or diffraction effects. We can see by comparing Figs. 6 and 9 that the volume of producible colors notably increased and became more convex and continuous. This is important for color imaging, where a continuous sets of colors are necessary to produce gradients present in real images.

5   Multiview Imaging

Another advantage introduced by halftoning is that the amount of hypercolors is consid-erably increased, displaying each one a different set of colors in the different IOCs. It is then easier to obtain parameters to print areas that visually match a given color *A* in one geometry while matching another target color B in a different geometry. This opens the possibility for some interesting imaging design and security applications. For example, we can hide patterns in a background by selecting different sets of command parameters for the patterns and the background that display the same color in one geometry and reveal different colors in another geometry.

By way of illustration, we designed a 2-geometry pattern from samples measured by our hyperspectral imaging system. Figure 10 shows the colors produced in two different geometrical configurations by the four sets of parameters selected. These colors are then used to design the spatial arrangement of the areas that will be printed with each of the selected parameter sets. Figure 11 shows the spatial arrangement we designed to produce our 2-geometry pattern, as well as the resulting colors produced displayed in the two geometries.

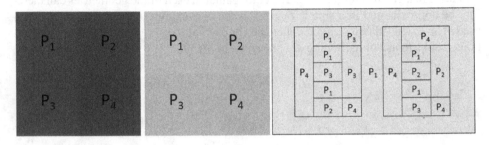

Fig. 10. Left and middle: Rendered sRGB color of four different hypercolors P1, P2, P3 and P4, in the 45°:0° off-specular reflection (left) and 0°:0° transmission (middle) geometries. Right: Spatial arrangement designed with the four hypercolors in order to produce the 2-geometry pattern displayed in Fig. 11.

Fig. 11. Rendered sRGB colors of a 2-geometry pattern observed in the 45°:0° off-specular reflection (left) and 0°:0° transmission (middle) geometries.

This approach can be extended to multicolor images, and it is probable that more than two different images can be displayed. The strong color variations that polarizing filters can generate is also a way of increasing the number of possible configurations [5]. However, multi-gamut mapping would be necessary to automatically determine the hypercolors, if any, that would be able to display the different targeted images, and no multi-gamut mapping technique is available today: a challenge for the incoming years.

6 Conclusions

In the paper, we presented a spectral and color characterization of glass plates coated with a layer containing composite layer nanostructured by laser irradiation, which exhibits different "hypercolors" (i.e., sets of colors displayed in different illumination/ observation configurations) in each point. Despite the difficulty of characterizing the color appearance of these strongly goniochromatic, transparent and specular samples, we could find a suitable measurement method thanks to hyperspectral imaging, where the camera is preceded by a telecentric lens. Several patches can thus be simultaneously measured, while being all viewed under the same angle independently of their position in the sample, thereby in the image. Special attention must be paid to the choice of the reference sample, which should have similar reflectance or transmittance as the studied sample in the considered measurement geometry in order to avoid a too low or excessive light signal detected. We then showed that, once knowing the spectral reflectance or transmittance of pure hypercolors (primaries), we can estimate, with rather good accuracy in this context, the spectral properties of halftone hypercolors obtained by juxtaposing thin lines of different primaries. This finally enables estimating to the color gamut of the printing technology in the considered illumination/observation geometry, and opens interesting perspectives for the production of multi-view still images.

Acknowledgement. This work was supported by the French National Research Agency (ANR) within the program "Investissements d'Avenir" (ANR-11-IDEX-0007), in the framework of project PHOTOFLEX n°ANR-12-NANO-0006 and the LABEX MANUTECH-SISE (ANR-10-LABX-0075) of Université de Lyon.

References

1. Martinez, J., Hébert, M., Trémeau, A., Destouches, N.: Multi-color properties of silver glaze images photo-engraved on glass plates. In: Color Imaging Conference, 19–23 October, Darmstadt, Germany (2015)
2. Tricot, F., Vocanson, F., Chaussy, D., Beneventi, D., Reynaud, S., Lefkir, Y., Destouches, N.: Flexible photochromic TiO2:Ag thin film elaborated by printing techniques. In: E-MRS 2015, Spring Meeting, symposium H, Nanoparticles in Dielectric Matrix for Electronics and Optics: From the Fabrication to the Devices (2015)
3. National Research Council: Photonics and the nanoworld. In: Controlling the Quantum World: The Science of Atoms, Molecules, and Photons. The National Academies Press, Washington, DC (2007)
4. Destouches, N., Martínez-García, J., Hébert, M., Crespo-Monteiro, N., Vitrant, G., Liu, Z., Trémeau, A., Vocanson, F., Pigeon, F., Reynaud, S., Lefkir, Y.: Dichroic colored luster of laser-induced silver nanoparticle gratings buried in dense inorganic films. J. Opt. Soc. Am. B **31**, C1–C7 (2014)
5. Destouches, N., Crespo-Monteiro, N., Epicier, T., Lefkir, Y., Vocanson, F., Reynaud, S., Charrière, R., Hébert, M.: Permanent dichroic coloring of surfaces by laser-induced formation of chain-like self-organized silver nanoparticles within crystalline titania films. In: Conference on Synthesis and Photonics of Nanoscale Materials X, Proceedings of SPIE, vol. 8609–860905 (2013)

6. Martinez, J., Hébert, M., Trémeau, A.: Color calibration of an RGB digital camera for the microscopic observation of highly specular materials. In: Proceedings of SPIE (SPIE/IS&T), Electronic Imaging Symposium, Measuring, Modeling, Reproduction Materials Appearance, vol. 9398, San Francisco, USA, 8–12 February (2015)
7. Lequime, M., Zerrad, M., Deumié, C., Amra, C.: A goniometric light scattering instrument with high-resolution imaging. Opt. Commun. **282**, 1265–1273 (2009)
8. Seroul, P., Hébert, M., Jomier, M.: Hyperspectral imaging system for in-vivo quantification of skin pigments. In: IFSCC, pp. 123–132 (2014)
9. Jolivot, R., Benezeth, Y., Marzani, F.: Skin parameter map retrieval from a dedicated multispectral imaging system applied to dermatology/cosmetology. J. Biomed. Imaging **2013**, 26 (2013)
10. Zhang, C., Rosenberger, M., Breitbarth,A., Notni, G.: A novel 3D multispectral vision system based on filter wheel cameras. In: Proceedings of IEEE International Conference on Imaging Systems and Techniques (IST), Chania, Greece, 4–6 October (2016)
11. Balasubramanian, R.: A spectral Neugebauer model for dot-on-dot printers. In: Proceedings of SPIE, vol. 2413 (1995)
12. Hébert, M., Hersch, R.: Review of spectral reflectance models for halftone prints: Principles, calibration, and prediction accuracy. Color Res. Appl. **40**(4), 383–397 (2015)

Fast-Calibration Reflectance-Transmittance Model to Compute Multiview Recto-Verso Prints

Serge Mazauric[✉], Thierry Fournel, and Mathieu Hébert

Univ Lyon, UJM-Saint-Etienne, CNRS, Institut d'Optique Graduate School,
Laboratoire Hubert Curien UMR 5516, 42023 Saint-Etienne, France
serge.mazauric@univ-st-etienne.fr

Abstract. Predicting simultaneously the spectral reflectance and transmittance of recto-verso prints is made easier thanks to a flux transfer matrix model. In the case where the printing support is symmetrical, i.e., its two sides are similar, the model can be calibrated from 44 halftone colors printed on the recto side, whose spectral reflectances and transmittance are measured. Color predictions are then allowed for any recto-verso halftone print illuminated on either side, and the inverse approach can be addressed: we can compute the digital layout for the recto and verso side that, once printed, can display different images according to the illuminated side.

Keywords: Computational printing · Flux transfer models · Duplex halftone print · Multiview images

1 Introduction

Spectral prediction models are key tools for fast and accurate color management in printing. They are also indispensable for designing advanced printing features such as those where the print displays different images according to the viewing conditions. Such multi-view effects can be obtained by using metallic inks [1] or a specular support [2] and observing the print in or out of the specular reflection direction. They can also be obtained by double-side printing with classical inks and supports, by observing one face in reflection mode or through both faces in transmission mode [3]. For these printing configurations, color management based on digital methods like ICC profile is almost impossible because the number of needed sample measurements, often beyond one thousand for single-mode observation, exponentially increases with the number of observation modes. The calibration time of the printing system thus becomes inacceptable, whereas a few tens of measurement often suffice to calibrate a prediction model, thus able to predict all reproducible colors in the different modes.

Among the most accurate models for the spectral reflectance of halftone prints, the physically-based models such as the Clapper-Yule model have high potential for extension to multilayer surfaces as they explicitly describe flux transfers between the layers. Some examples have been investigated in previous studies though stacks of printed films [4] and double-side printed papers [5, 6], configurations for which good prediction accuracy was achieved by means of acceptable number of calibration samples.

© Springer International Publishing AG 2017
S. Bianco et al. (Eds.): CCIW 2017, LNCS 10213, pp. 223–232, 2017.
DOI: 10.1007/978-3-319-56010-6_19

The main issues with these models where both reflectance and transmittance of prints are combined, it means that they need a calibration for the reflectance mode, and a separate calibration for the transmittance mode: one parameter may have different values in the two modes. This issue was recently solved thanks to the so-called Duplex Primary Reflectance-Transmittance (DPRT) model, a two-flux transfer matrix model predicting simultaneously the reflectance and transmittance of duplex halftone prints on both faces, whose parameters related to the primaries are deduced from both reflectance and transmittance measurements and therefore optimal for the two modes [8]. In the general case where the two faces of the support are different or printed with different inks, the DPRT model needs 256 spectral measurements. In the present paper, we show that in the special case where the support is symmetric, i.e., its two faces are identical and printed with the same ink set, the number of spectral measurements for calibration is reduced to 32, while keeping the optimal predictive performances in reflectance and transmittance modes.

The corresponding model, called Double-Layer Reflectance-Transmittance model, relies on the idea of separating the printed support into two sublayers, in which spectral flux transfers are described. We propose to present it and to show a few examples of multiview images that were designed by using the model in inversed mode.

2   Two-Flux Transfer Matrices

A flux transfer model is particularly adapted to the layered structure of printed supports. When the printing support is strongly scattering, like paper or white polymer, we can use a two-flux model. The model presented in Ref. [8] applies with a stack of layers of strongly materials and the interfaces between them. They are characterized by four *transfer factors*: the *front-side reflectance r*, the *back-side reflectance r'*, the *forward transmittance t* and the *backward transmittance t'*. The component is said to by symmetrical when $r = r'$, and $t = t'$. The angular distribution of the incident and transferred lights is to be considered in the definition of every transfer factor, which can be accordingly bi-hemispherical, directional-hemispherical, bi-directional and so on [9]. All fluxes and transfer factors may also depend upon wavelength.

When two components are on top of each other, interreflections of light occur between them, thus producing mutual exchanges between the fluxes propagating forwards (denoted as I_k in Fig. 1) and backwards (denoted as J_k). These exchanges can be easily described by using flux transfer matrices. For each component $k = 1$ or 2, assuming $t_k \neq 0$, the relations between incoming and outgoing fluxes is described by the following matrix equation:

$$\begin{pmatrix} I_{k-1} \\ J_{k-1} \end{pmatrix} = \frac{1}{t_k} \begin{pmatrix} 1 & -r'_k \\ r_k & t_k t'_k - r_k r'_k \end{pmatrix} \begin{pmatrix} I_k \\ J_k \end{pmatrix} \tag{1}$$

where the matrix is the transfer matrix attached to the component k, denoted as $\mathbf{M}_k$

$$\mathbf{M}_k = \frac{1}{t_k} \begin{pmatrix} 1 & -r'_k \\ r_k & t_k t'_k - r_k r'_k \end{pmatrix} \tag{2}$$

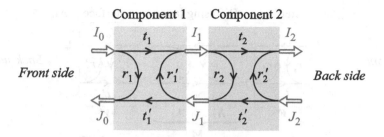

Fig. 1. Flux transfers between two flat components (arrows do not render orientation of light).

Grouping components 1 and 2 together, Eq. (1) can be repeated twice. One obtains:

$$\begin{pmatrix} I_0 \\ J_0 \end{pmatrix} = \mathbf{M}_1 \begin{pmatrix} I_1 \\ J_1 \end{pmatrix} = \mathbf{M}_1 \mathbf{M}_2 \begin{pmatrix} I_2 \\ J_2 \end{pmatrix} = \mathbf{M} \begin{pmatrix} I_2 \\ J_2 \end{pmatrix} \tag{3}$$

where $\mathbf{M}$, product of the transfer matrices of the individual components, is the transfer matrix representing the two layers together, similarly defined as Eq. (2) in terms of its transfer factors R, T, R' and T'. The multiplicative property of transfer matrices is true for any number of components, and the left-to-right position of the matrices in the product reproduces the front-to-back position of the corresponding components. Every transfer matrix has the structure displayed in Eq. (2) and from a given transfer matrix $\mathbf{M} = \{m_{ij}\}$, provided $m_{11} \neq 0$, one retrieves the transfer factors in the following way:

$$\begin{aligned} R &= m_{21}/m_{11} \\ T &= 1/m_{11} \\ R' &= -m_{12}/m_{11} \\ T' &= m_{22} - m_{21}m_{12}/m_{11} \end{aligned} \tag{4}$$

3 Double-Layer Reflectance-Transmittance (DLRT) Model

We will use flux transfer matrices to describe the reflection and transmission of light by recto-verso halftone prints. Let us first consider the support alone, by assuming it symmetrical and strongly scattering. Its structure is shown in Fig. 2: an effective diffusing medium of refractive index 1.5 is bordered by interfaces with the surrounding air. Since it is symmetrical, it has similar transfer factors $R(\lambda)$ and $T(\lambda)$ on its two sides, and is therefore represented by a transfer matrix, defined for each wavelength as:

$$\mathbf{P} = \frac{1}{T} \begin{pmatrix} 1 & -R \\ R & T^2 - R^2 \end{pmatrix} \tag{5}$$

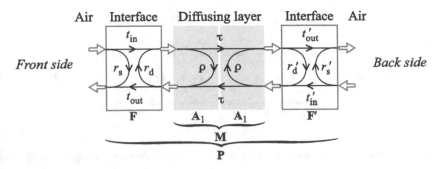

Fig. 2. Flux transfers between a diffusing layer (split into two identical sublayers) and its bordering interfaces, and corresponding flux transfer matrices.

The diffusing layer (considered without the interfaces) also has similar transfer factors $\rho(\lambda)$ and $\tau(\lambda)$ on its two sides. It is represented by the following transfer matrix:

$$\mathbf{M} = \frac{1}{\tau}\begin{pmatrix} 1 & -\rho \\ \rho & \tau^2 - \rho^2 \end{pmatrix} \tag{6}$$

The reflectances and transmittances of the interfaces depend on the measuring geometry. In the present study, measurements were done with the X-rite Color i7 spectrophotometer relying on the di:8° geometry in reflection mode (illumination with perfectly diffuse light over the hemisphere, and observation at 8° from the normal of the sample by including the specular reflection component), and the d:0° geometry in transmission mode (illumination with perfectly diffuse light over the hemisphere, and observation in the normal of the sample). The corresponding transfer factors are given in Fig. 2. For these geometries and the refractive index value 1.5, the transfer matrices representing the interfaces at the recto and verso sides are given by:

$$\mathbf{F} = \frac{1}{t_{in}}\begin{pmatrix} 1 & -r_d \\ r_s & t_{in}t_{out} - r_s r_d \end{pmatrix} = \begin{pmatrix} 1.111 & -0.667 \\ 0.044 & 0.403 \end{pmatrix}$$

$$\mathbf{F}' = \frac{1}{t_{out}}\begin{pmatrix} 1 & -r_s \\ r_d & t_{in}t_{out} - r_s r_d \end{pmatrix} = \begin{pmatrix} 1.111 & -0.044 \\ 0.667 & 0.403 \end{pmatrix} \tag{7}$$

In practice, the measurable quantities are the spectral reflectance $R(\lambda)$ and transmittance $T(\lambda)$ of the support *with interfaces*, therefore matrix **P**. The transfer matrix **M** for the diffusing layer *without interfaces* is then given by:

$$\mathbf{M} = \mathbf{F}^{-1} \cdot \mathbf{P} \cdot \mathbf{F}'^{-1} \tag{8}$$

Later, it will be convenient to decompose this diffusing layer into two similar sublayers (which justifies the appellation "double-layer reflectance-transmittance' model), thus represented by the transfer matrix:

$$\mathbf{A}_1 = \mathbf{M}^{1/2} = \left(\mathbf{F}^{-1} \cdot \mathbf{P} \cdot \mathbf{F}'^{-1}\right)^{1/2} \tag{9}$$

We can extend the model to the Neugebauer primaries, obtained when super-posing cyan, magenta and yellow halftone screens: white (surface with no ink, labelled $i = 1$) cyan, magenta, yellow, red (magenta + yellow), green (cyan + yellow), blue (cyan + magenta) and black (cyan + magenta + yellow). It is classical after Clapper and Yule [10] to consider the inked support as a four-compo-nent structure: the two interfaces, the ink layer and the diffusing layer. We proposed in [8] a different approach where the inked support without interfaces is one non-symmetrical layer of effective medium. According to the double-layer approach, we can then split it into two sublayers: one on the front side containing the inks repre-sented by a matrix $\mathbf{A}_i$, one with the matrix $\mathbf{A}_1$ given by (9) for the non-inked back side. Thus, the transfer matrix representing the support covered by primary i on the recto side only is written:

$$\mathbf{P}_{i1} = \mathbf{F} \cdot \mathbf{A}_i \cdot \mathbf{A}_1 \cdot \mathbf{F}'$$

We thus have, for each primary $i = 2, \ldots, 8$:

$$\mathbf{A}_i = \mathbf{M}_{i1} \cdot \mathbf{A}_1^{-1} = \left(\mathbf{F}^{-1} \cdot \mathbf{P}_{i1} \cdot \mathbf{F}'^{-1}\right) \cdot \left(\mathbf{F}^{-1} \cdot \mathbf{P}_{11} \cdot \mathbf{F}'^{-1}\right)^{-1/2} \equiv \frac{1}{\tau_i}\begin{pmatrix} 1 & -\rho_i' \\ \rho_i & \tau_i\tau_i' - \rho_i\rho_i' \end{pmatrix} \quad (10)$$

The transfer factors of the front sublayer, denoted ρ_i, ρ_i', τ_i, and τ_i', are obtained from (10) by applying formulas (4). Since the support is symmetrical, and the verso side is printed with the same inks as the recto side, we can create similar matrix as $\mathbf{A}_i$ for the verso side, by permuting ρ_i and ρ_i' on the one hand, and τ_i and τ_i' on the other hand, and finally replacing i with j:

$$\mathbf{A}_j' = \frac{1}{\tau_j'}\begin{pmatrix} 1 & -\rho_j \\ \rho_j' & \tau_j\tau_j' - \rho_j\rho_j' \end{pmatrix} \quad (11)$$

When a primary i is on the recto side and a primary j on the verso side, the matrix representing the whole inked support (interfaces excluded) is simply given by:

$$\mathbf{M}_{ij} = \mathbf{A}_i \cdot \mathbf{A}_j' \quad (12)$$

The model can be extended to halftone colors (Fig. 3). We denote as a_i $(i = 1, \ldots, 8)$ and a_j' $(j = 1, \ldots, 8)$ the surface coverages of the primaries on the recto side, respectively on the verso side. They are obtained from the surface coverages of the cyan, magenta and yellow inks using Demichel's equations, valable in case of typical stochastic or cluster dot halftoning techniques [11]. We use the transfer factors ρ_i, ρ_i', τ_i, and τ_i' issued from (4) and (10), and combine them according to the ink surface coverages a_i and a_j' present on each side of the support. By using the generic letter ξ for either ρ, ρ', τ, or τ', we have, for the recto side:

$$\xi_{\{a_i\}} = \sum_{i=1}^{8} a_i\xi_i \quad (13)$$

and for the verso side:

$$\xi_{\{a'_j\}} = \sum_{i=1}^{8} a_i \xi'_i \tag{14}$$

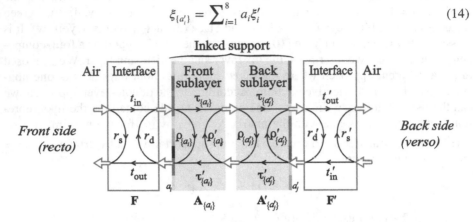

Fig. 3. Flux transfers within a homogeneous support printed with halftone on both sides: the inked support is split into two sublayers.

From these transfer factors given by (13) and (14), we create the transfer matrices representing the sublayers on the recto, respectively on the verso:

$$\begin{aligned}
\mathbf{A}_{\{a_i\}} &= \frac{1}{\tau_{\{a_i\}}} \begin{pmatrix} 1 & -\rho'_{\{a_i\}} \\ \rho_{\{a_i\}} & \tau_{\{a_i\}}\tau'_{\{a_i\}} - \rho_{\{a_i\}}\rho'_{\{a_i\}} \end{pmatrix} \\
\mathbf{A}'_{\{a'_j\}} &= \frac{1}{\tau_{\{a'_j\}}} \begin{pmatrix} 1 & -\rho'_{\{a'_j\}} \\ \rho_{\{a'_j\}} & \tau_{\{a'_j\}}\tau'_{\{a'_j\}} - \rho_{\{a'_j\}}\rho'_{\{a'_j\}} \end{pmatrix}
\end{aligned} \tag{15}$$

Finally, the duplex print *with* interfaces is represented by the transfer matrix:

$$\mathbf{M}_H = \mathbf{F} \cdot \mathbf{A}_{\{a_i\}} \cdot \mathbf{A}'_{\{a'_j\}} \cdot \mathbf{F}' \tag{16}$$

and its reflectances and transmittances are deduced from this matrix by using (4).

Note that we can also predict, without further calibration effort, the spectral reflectances and transmittances of a doubled printing support. The matrix $\mathbf{M}_H$ is simply computed as follows:

$$\mathbf{M}_H = \mathbf{F} \cdot \mathbf{A}_{\{a_i\}} \cdot \mathbf{A}_1 \cdot \mathbf{F}' \cdot \mathbf{F} \cdot \mathbf{A}_1 \cdot \mathbf{A}'_{\{a'_j\}} \cdot \mathbf{F}' \tag{17}$$

4   Calibration and Verification of the Model

The DPRT model introduced in [8], valid for any non-symmetrical diffusing support, needed $8 \times 8 = 64$ CMY patches for its calibration, corresponding to the different combinations of the eight primaries on the front side and the eight primaries on the back side. The present model, valid for homogenous diffusing supports, needs only 8 recto-only samples if the support is symmetrical and printed with the same set of inks on both sides. Since the four transfer factors of each sample must be measured, this makes an appreciable gain of time for the calibration of the DLRT model. The calibration of the model is made in two steps.

The first step is the determination of the matrices A_i, given by (10), for the eight Neugebauer primaries. For primary 1, the reflectance and transmittance of the unprinted support are measured on the recto side; for the other seven primaries, we print each primary with a coverage of 100% on the recto side, and measure the reflectances and transmittances of the printed support on its both sides. The reflectances and transmittances ρ_i, ρ_i', τ_i, and τ_i' for the front-side sublayer printed with each primary i are computed, then the matrices A_j representing the back-side sublayer printed with each primary j.

The second step is establishing the correspondence between the nominal ink surface coverages (those specified in the digital layout) and the effective ones, observed on the printed paper through the spectral reflectance and transmittance. We follow the very efficient method introduced by Hersch et al. [7], also detailed in [11], which yields 12 curves computed from 36 single-ink halftones printed on the recto side. For each halftone, the effective ink surface coverages is estimated by minimizing the difference between the measured and predicted spectra, according to a metric which may be the rms deviation between the spectral reflectances and/or transmittances, or the equivalent color distance (e.g. CIE ΔE_{94}^* computed from the spectra for a given illuminant and a given white reference).

Finally, for any recto-verso halftone defined by its nominal ink surfaces coverages (CMY values) on the recto and verso sides, the primary surface coverages a_i and a_i' are computed according to the Demichel equations, the transfer matrix M_H of the recto-verso print is obtained by using Eqs. (13) to (16), and the reflectances and transmittances by using formulas (4).

The model was verified over tens of recto-verso samples with CMY values randomly selected over the color gamut on both sides of the support. They were printed with both inkjet and electrophotography (laserjet) printer, each time on both high-quality supercalendered paper and usual office paper. The number of patches in each set is specified in Table 1. The prediction accuracy, in reflectance or transmittance mode, is assessed by the average CIE ΔE_{94}^* color distance between the predicted and measured spectra (see computation details in [11]).

Table 1. Average (Q95-Max) CIE ΔE_{94}^* value between predicted and measured spectra

Support	Printer	Samples	Model			
				DLRT	DCY	YN
Supercalendered paper	Inkjet	36	R	0.76 (1.66 – 1.77)	0.92 (1.87 – 1.96)	0.70 (1.40 – 1.50)
			T	0.75 (1.13 – 1.29)	1.01 (1.47 – 1.74)	0.94 (1.46 – 1.54)
	Laserjet	25	R	1.43 (2.54 – 2.98)	1.52 (2.66 – 2.75)	1.47 (2.62 – 2.74)
			T	0.87 (2.43 – 3.12)	1.50 (3.35 – 3.55)	1.27 (3.51 – 4.49)
Office paper	Inkjet	78	R	1.31 (3.11 – 3.43)	1.06 (2.88 – 3.53)	1.16 (3.11 – 3.62)
			T	1.17 (2.40 – 9.09)	1.58 (2.70 – 3.87)	1.33 (2.05 – 2.86)
	Laserjet	25	R	1.39 (2.78 – 3.10)	1.27 (2.21 – 2.45)	1.30 (2.53 – 2.84)
			T	0.89 (2.01 – 2.78)	2.31 (3.93 – 5.13)	1.42 (3.39 – 3.85)

The values presented in Table 1 show that the prediction accuracy is rather good, even though slightly poorer with the laserjet printer due to a low printing homogeneity, and with the office paper which is also less homogeneous than the supercalendered one. In most cases, the DLRT model is more accurate, and even much more accurate in transmittance mode, than previously proposed models: the Duplex Clapper-Yule model (DCY) [8], and the Yule-Nielsen model ([6, 7] for the extension to transmittance). Recall that the model is calibrated from only 44 recto-only color patches measured in reflectance and transmittance mode, and then that billions of recto-verso colors can be predicted.

5   Multiview Images

Once the model is calibrated and its prediction accuracy has been verified, we can use it in an inversed mode to produce *multiview prints*, i.e., prints displaying different images according to the illumination and observation configurations. For example, we can illuminate the print on the observer's side (reflection mode) or the opposite side (transmission mode). We can also consider a transmission mode where ambient light slightly illuminates the observer's side (with similar SPDs on both sides), which corresponds to an addition of α times the transmittance and $(1 - \alpha)$ times the reflectance, a configuration referred to as "α-transmission mode".

The ink quantities to print on the recto and verso sides are obtained by performing a brute-force optimization in order to obtain the targeted CIE 1976 $L * a * b *$ values, or the targeted spectral radiance, in the two selected illumination modes. We generally compute first the ink surface coverages on the recto side yielding the reflection-mode image, then the ones on the verso side so as to obtain the targeted image in α-transmission mode. The selection of the targeted colors for the two modes is critical since color matching is not always possible, a question addressed in [12].

Figure 4 shows an example of multi-view image printed by laserjet printer on doubled office paper. It displays (flipped) "10" patterns on the verso side in reflectance mode, and only part of these patterns remain visible in 0.9-transmittance mode, because the color of the other part matches the color of the background of the image. A second print is shown in Fig. 5, where randomly distributed squares of eight different colors are printed on the recto side, eight colors are correspondingly

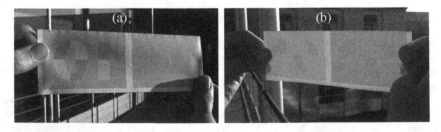

Fig. 4. Multiview recto-verso halftone print produced by laserjet printing on doubled office paper, displaying different images (a) on the verso side in reflection mode, and (b) on the recto side in transmission mode, under sunlight.

printed on the verso side in order to display, in 0.9-transmission mode, two patterns of homogenous color and a background with more contrasted texture. Registration of the recto and verso images, and perfect parallelism of the two paper sheet is crucial for a good rendering of the targeted visual effect.

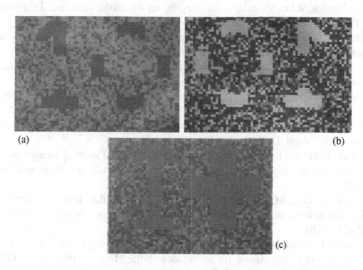

(a)   (b)

(c)

Fig. 5. Multiview recto-verso halftone print produced by laserjet printing on doubled office paper, displaying a mosaic of randomly distributed color squares on the recto side (a) and verso side (b), and homogenously colored patterns surrounded by a contrasted color mosaic in 0.9 transmission mode (c), with increased lightness.

6 Conclusions

The DLRT model is a two-flux transfer matrix model that allows the prediction of the reflectance and transmittance of duplex halftone prints with a better accuracy and no more halftone patches than previously proposed models such as the Duplex Clapper-Yule model and the Yule-Nielsen model extended to transmission. The model relies on the separation of the printing support into two sublayers, each one containing the inks of the recto halftone color, or accordingly the ones of the verso halftone color. The model should be limited to printing supports where the inks do not penetrate too much deeply, but a more exhaustive testing is needed to see the precise limitations in practice. The model showed its performance when multiview images are produced from layouts computed with it. Since these prints rely on color matching between different recto-verso halftones, the quality of the displayed images directly depends on the accuracy of the model.

References

1. Babaei, V., Hersch, R.D.: Yule-Nielsen based multi-angle reflectance prediction of metallic halftones. Proc. SPIE **9395**, 3023–3031 (2015). Paper 93950H
2. Pjanic, P., Hersch, R.D.: Specular color imaging on a metallic substrate. In: Proceedings of the IS&T 21st Color and Imaging Conference, pp. 61–68 (2013)
3. Hébert, M., Mazauric, S., Fournel, T.: Spectral mixing approach for modeling the coloration of surfaces. In: Workshop on Information Optics, Kyoto, 1–5 June 2015
4. Machizaud, J., Hébert, M.: Spectral transmittance model for stacks of transparencies printed with halftone colors. Proc. SPIE **8292**, 1537–1548 (2012). Paper 829240
5. Hébert, M., Hersch, R.D.: Reflectance and transmittance model for recto-verso halftone prints: spectral predictions with multi-ink halftones. J. Opt. Soc. Am. A **26**, 356–364 (2009)
6. Hébert, M., Hersch, R.D.: Yule-Nielsen based recto-verso color halftone transmittance prediction model. Appl. Opt. **50**, 519–525 (2011)
7. Hersch, R.D., Crété, F.: Improving the Yule-Nielsen modified spectral Neugebauer model by dot surface coverages depending on the ink superposition conditions. Proc. SPIE **5667**, 434–445 (2005)
8. Mazauric, S., Hebert, M., Simonot, L., Fournel, T.: Two-flux transfer matrix model for predicting the reflectance and transmittance of duplex halftone prints. J. Opt. Soc. Am. A **31**, 2775–2788 (2014)
9. Nicodemus, F.E., Richmond, J.C., Hsia, J.J., Ginsberg, I.W., Limperis, T.: Geometrical considerations and nomenclature for reflectance. NBS Monogr. **160**, 52 (1977). National Bureau of Standards, Washington, DC
10. Clapper, F.R., Yule, J.A.C.: The effect of multiple internal reflections on the densities of halftone prints on paper. J. Opt. Soc. Am. **43**, 600–603 (1953)
11. Hébert, M., Hersch, R.D.: Review of spectral reflectance prediction models for halftone prints: calibration, prediction and performance. Color Res. Appl. **40**, 383–397 (2015). Paper 21907
12. Dalloz, N., Mazauric, S., Fournel, T., Hébert, M.: How to design a recto-verso print displaying different images in various everyday-life lighting conditions. In: IS&T Electronic Imaging Symposium, Materials Appearance, Burlingame, 30 January–2 February 2017

Image Contrast Measure as a Gloss Material Descriptor

Jean-Baptiste Thomas[1](✉), Jon Yngve Hardeberg[1], and Gabriele Simone[2]

[1] The Norwegian Colour and Visual Computing Laboratory, NTNU,
The Norwegian University of Science and Technology, Gjøvik, Norway
jean.b.thomas@ntnu.no
[2] MIPS Lab, Department of Computer Science,
Universita degli Studi di Milano, Milano, Italy

Abstract. Bidirectional reflectance distribution function provides a physical description of material appearance. In particular, it helps to describe the gloss. We suggest that, at least, one attribute of gloss: Contrast gloss (luster), may be described directly from an image by using local image contrast measurement. In this article, we investigate the relation between image contrast measures, gloss perception and bidirectional reflectance distribution function based on the Ward's α model parameter. Although more investigation is required to provide stronger conclusions, it seems that image related contrast measures may provide an indication of gloss perception.

Keywords: Gloss perception · Contrast measurement · Gloss descriptor · Contrast gloss

1 Introduction

Total appearance of an object is described by its color, its gloss, its translucency and its texture, according to Hunter [1] and a subsequent CIE technical report on total appearance [2]. Within this context, the gloss of the material gives numerous cues about the object: It helps to understand in particular the structure of the illumination (*e.g.* spectral distribution as cue for color constancy, direction of light for scene understanding and also geometric properties that may help to assess invisible parts of the scene) and provide information on object properties (*e.g.* 3D shape, size and interaction within the scene). Although it is most probable that gloss must be combined with other attributes for material identification and scene understanding, it is, without a doubt, a determining and important factor [3].

The physical correlate of gloss perception is expressed within the bidirectional reflectance distribution function (BRDF). Huge progress has been achieved in the measurement of this correlate during the last decade. However, it is yet not very well understood how to correlate this measure to appearance perception. According to Hunter and others, six visual criteria may be necessary to evaluate

© Springer International Publishing AG 2017
S. Bianco et al. (Eds.): CCIW 2017, LNCS 10213, pp. 233–245, 2017.
DOI: 10.1007/978-3-319-56010-6_20

the perception of gloss: Specular gloss, contrast gloss, sheen, absence of bloom gloss (haze) and distinctness of image gloss [4–6].

Contrast gloss relates to the contrast perceived by the observer between the specular highlights and the diffuse area related to the same object and illumination condition. We propose that this *edge* between diffuse and specular may be partially representative of the perception of gloss to some extent and would be an indicator and a descriptor of near to specular area of the material. This indicator would necessarily be dependant on the size, magnitude and on other components of the scene. Consequently, we suggest that it could be characterized by a perceptual local image contrast measure of the specific related area of an image where specular reflection happens. This measure could be related to the BRDF measurement of the object and the gloss perceived by the observers.

We first introduce image contrast measurement and select specific *a priori* relevant metrics from the state of the art. We then generate simple objects that exhibit different surface properties. Focus is on roughness of object, which should significantly influence contrast gloss. We used an isotropic Ward model for that. In Sect. 4, we describe the visual experiment and categorization we performed, and in Sect. 5, we relate the physical model, the contrast measure and the perceptual categories together. Results suggest that some contrast measures may represent perceived gloss well, when gloss is perceived. However, it is not yet clear whether it is only contrast gloss that is evaluated, neither how robust is this indication.

2   Measures of Contrast for Digital Images

Studies have identified contrast as one of the fundamental perceptual attributes to describe the quality of an image [7]. So far there are still several definitions of contrast based on the field of research and target application. For example, in vision, contrast can be defined as the physical differences in luminance and color, as well as the perception of these differences [8], while in photography, contrast is typically related to the degree of information visible in the shadow areas [9].

In a century of contrast studies, different definitions led to development of different contrast measures. The very first contrast measures referred as global formulae are based on the highest and the lowest luminance in the scene [10–12]. Evolution of these measures embed more advanced global image statistics. In particular interest for this work is the measure proposed by King-Smith and Kulikowski [13] defined as $C^{KK} = \frac{L_{max}-L_{avg}}{L_{avg}}$, where L_{max} is the maximum luminance of the image and L_{avg} is the average luminance of the image.

Later studies have shown that perceived contrast can vary across the image due to different spatial frequencies [14,15] and to the presence of gloss and glare [16]. As a consequence, in the three last decades contrast measures based on local description of the image emerged, approaching the problem in various ways. We recall here a brief selection of them.

In 1983, Frankle and McCann [17] followed by Adelson *et al.* [18] proposed to use multilevel representation as feature to mimic the Human Visual System. The image is represented by a set of low-pass or band-pass copies, each representing information at a different scale. From this feature came the pioneering contrast measure of Peli [15] in 1990. This measure is commonly used in the following as benchmark of local contrast measurement.

Peli's local band-limited contrast c of each pixel location (x,y) is defined by $c_i(x, y) = \frac{a_i(x,y)}{l_i(x,y)}$, where $a_i(x, y)$ is the corresponding local luminance image and $l_i(x, y)$ is a low-pass-filtered version of the image containing all energy below the band i. The contrast image would then be the addition of $c_i(x, y)$ of each level. Then, C^P is computed as the average of the contrast image.

An optimization is later proposed by Lubin [19]. Following the multi-level representation, Iordache *et al.* [20] and Rizzi *et al.* [21], respectively, proposed a local contrast measure based on a weighted 8-neighborhood mask. Tadmor and Tolhurst [22] proposed a local contrast measure by modifying and adapting the Difference Of Gaussians (DOG) model from neurophysiological studies. Later Boccignone and Ferraro [23, 24] defined local contrast as a set of thermodynamical variables.

The local contrast measure proposed by Simone *et al.* [25], named Weighted Level Framework (WLF), combines and extends Rizzi *et al.* [21] and Tadmor and Tolhurst [22] measures. WLF has been shown to have high correlation with observers perceived contrast and is flexible to work in different color spaces and with color images. We consider this metric as being a potential good candidate to represent locally the visual effect of luster.

The WLF measure of contrast for greyscale images is defined by $C^{WLF} = \beta \cdot C$, where β is a scaling factor that is defined according to the image content and C the final multilevel average contrast of the image. This is defined as $C = \frac{1}{N_l}\sum_{l=1}^{N_l}\lambda_l \cdot \bar{c}_l$, where N_l is the number of levels, $\bar{c}_l$ is the average contrast at the level l and λ_l is the weight assigned to each level l that is defined according to the image content. Likewise in Rizzi *et al.* [21] the number of levels of N_l is image size independent and each level l is created reducing at each operation the previous level of a factor of 2 starting from the original image size.

At each level l, the contrast c of each pixel location (x,y) is calculated, using the DOG model proposed by Tadmor and Tolhurst [22] such as $c(x, y) = \frac{R_c(x,y)-R_s(x,y)}{R_c(x,y)+R_s(x,y)}$, where R_c and R_s are the center and surround components, respectively.

In the DOG model, the center component is described by a bi-dimensional Gaussian such as $Center(x,y) = \exp\left[-(x/r_c)^2 - (y/r_c)^2\right]$, where r_c is the radius of the center component. The surround component is represented by another Gaussian curve, with a larger radius, r_s, such as

$$Surround(x,y) = 0.85 \, (r_c/r_s)^2 \exp\left[-(x/r_s)^2 - (y/r_s)^2\right].$$

When the central component is placed at location (x,y), the output is calculated as $R_c(x,y) = \sum_{i=x-3r_c}^{i=x+3r_c} \sum_{j=y-3r_c}^{j=y+3r_c} Center(i-x, j-y)I(i,j)$. When the surround component is placed at location (x,y), the output is calculated as $R_s(x,y) = \sum_{i=x-3r_s}^{i=x+3r_s} \sum_{j=y-3r_s}^{j=y+3r_s} Surround(i-x, j-y)I(i,j)$. In both cases $I(i,j)$ is the image pixel value at position (i,j).

The rules of thumb for automatically choosing the various parameters are presented in Simone et al. [25]. In our experiment, we used two set of parameters for WLF, referred to as uniform (WLF-U, when $r_c = 1, r_s = 2, \lambda_l = 1$ and $\beta = 1$) and optimal (WLF-O, when $r_c = 2, r_s = 4, \lambda_l$ = variance of the level l and β = variance of the image).

3   Experimental Data

We propose to use one basic object, consistent setup and a simple model to investigate our proposal. We selected achromatic spheres, which surface is characterized by its BRDF defined by an isotropic Wards model [26]. In this sense, the only difference between these images lies in material properties defined by a single parameter. Images were generated with the software *BRDF Explorer*[1].

The Ward model for isotropic materials is defined as:

$$\rho_{isotropic}(\theta_i, \phi_i; \theta_r, \phi_r) = \frac{\rho_d}{\pi} + \rho_s \frac{1}{\sqrt{\cos\theta_i \cos\theta_r}} \frac{\exp(-tan^2\delta/\alpha^2)}{4\pi\alpha^2},$$

where ρ_d is the diffuse reflectance, ρ_s the specular reflectance. δ is the angle between the surface normal and the half angle between illumination and viewing angle. Viewing geometry remains the same. We set θ_i, the incident angle to $45°$. The planar incident angle ϕ_i remains also the same at $45°$. That gives the highlight in the upper right part of the sphere. The illumination remains the same and the gamma value for the imaging simulation was 2.2.

The only parameter that varies, α, the standard deviation of the surface slope, corresponds to material coarseness in our case. We vary it from 0 to 1. ρ_d and ρ_s are kept constant and simply set to 1. Also, Ward mentions that α is meaningful *as long as it is not much greater than 0.2*, we provide a span of values from 0 to 1 to investigate the contrast metrics, but perform visual experiments only on the area where Ward's model is more likely to represent some physical reality, arbitrarily between 0.1 and 0.4.

Examples of generated BRDFs are shown in Fig. 3. When $\alpha = 0.001$, the sphere is highly specular – we do not use this value after since only one pixel in the image would be white and it is quite unrealistic, after $\alpha = 0.3$, the specular direction does not saturate anymore the virtual sensor, and after 0.5, a more diffuse behavior is clearly observed. This is exemplified in Fig. 1. Images of the spheres used in the visual experiment are shown on Fig. 2.

---

[1] https://www.disneyanimation.com/technology/brdf.html.

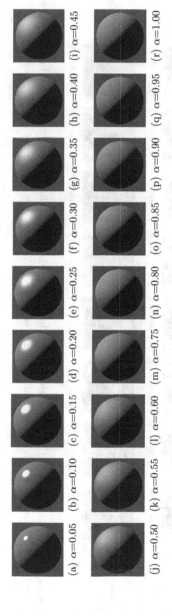

Fig. 1. Images of spheres showing BRDF properties defined by the Wards model. The parameter α defines how diffuse is the material. Here, $\alpha \in [0.05, 1.00]$.

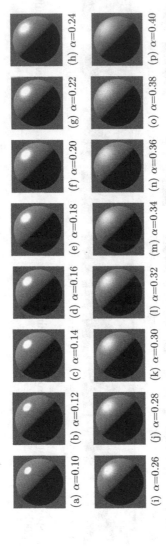

Fig. 2. Images of spheres showing BRDF properties defined by the Wards model. The parameter α defines how diffuse is the material. Here, $\alpha \in [0.10, 0.40]$. Note that for the experiment, we have added $\alpha = 0.05$ and $\alpha = 1.00$ as explained in Sect. 4.

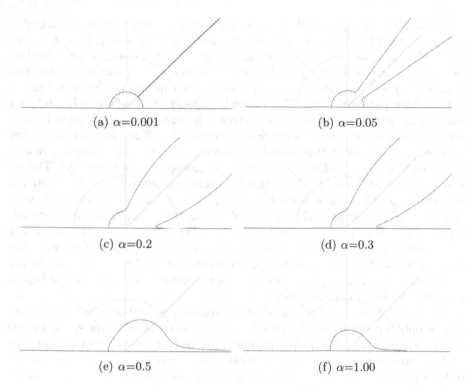

Fig. 3. Isotropic BRDFs considered in this work as instantiations of the Wards model, based on one parameter α.

4   Visual Experiment

We gathered a committee of experts for ranking and rating the images, 4 persons, including 2 of the authors, together in a dim room, and the images of spheres were displayed all at the same time on a screen by a video–projection system. Notice that the projected background was white, as this may be important in the following. One of the authors was chairing the discussion and giving a large degree of freedom to the participants to redesign the experiment and reach an unanimous decision on each tasks. The participants were able to interact freely with the images, to move around and to discuss, such that a collective decision could be made.

The task was first to rank the images of Fig. 2 from glossy to most glossy. Images were first presented in random order. This was done quite fast by the committee, the task was relatively easy and the ranking coincided perfectly with the increasing of the α parameter. There was no disagreement between the committee members. Since there is only one physical parameter that varies, it is not surprising that it was easy to rank the samples along a single dimension.

The next task was to rate the images. Through discussion, references of highly matte and highly specular images were included into the set-up ($\alpha = 1.00$ and $\alpha = 0.05$) to provide potential anchor for the judgment. Even with this addition, it was not possible to decide of rate values[2]. However, it was possible to categorize the images. A scale of seven steps: very matte (VM), matte (M), somewhat matte (SM), neither glossy or matte (N), somewhat glossy (SG), glossy (G), and very glossy (VG), was used to classify the images. The only image assumed to be very matte was the sample that is very close to a perfect diffuser ($\alpha = 1$). The three following samples ($\alpha = 0.40, 0.38, 0.36$) were considered as somewhat matte. The three next ($\alpha = 0.34, 0.32, 0.30$) were considered somewhat glossy. The six next ($\alpha = 0.28, 0.26, 0.24, 0.22, 0.20, 0.18$) were considered as glossy, and the remaining, including the other reference ($\alpha = 0.16, 0.14, 0.12, 0.10, 0.05$), were considered as very glossy. This is exemplified in the results later in color code (Fig. 5). No sphere was considered to be "neither glossy or matte", no sphere was considered "matte" within the range of our investigation. The scale was accepted within the context of this experiment, but doubt was emitted on the existence of an axis going from matte to glossy samples as it appears to be not perfectly correlated in some studies (e.g. [27]).

No specific questions were asked about contrast gloss/luster, as we consider α to be only representative of luster thanks to the stability of the scene and no difference in lighting conditions. This may limit our analysis as α would not only be the correlate of contrast gloss in more complex situations. However in this study, especially when $\alpha \leq 0.3$, only contrast gloss seems to change, according to the definition of contrast gloss.

5   Results

One aspect to take into account in our analysis, is that the images with an $\alpha \leq 0.3$ are most likely to contain a saturated pixel, so they would have all the same dynamic range. In order to identify the presence of a saturated pixel, *i.e.* that would represent dynamic range of the scene, we introduce, in addition to the contrast measures, a saturation index. This index is defined as $SI = \frac{L_{max}}{255}$, since our images are encoded into 8 bits.

Results for this indicator are shown in Fig. 4, i and j. These results are somewhat surprising in the sense that after that α value goes over 0.5, new brighter pixels appear at the edge of the sphere, which show then some sheen effects, *i.e.* gloss at grazing angles. This is out of the accepted validity of Ward's model and shows an aspect of gloss that we do not focus on in this paper, so it is hard to incorporate or discard these data into the discussion on solid ground.

We separate our analysis in two parts: first, we look at the behavior of the image contrast measures according to variation of BRDF parameter, and next we evaluate closely how we can relate that with the visual categorization.

---

[2] It might have been possible to rate by providing either a 50% patch or at least one example of number, which was not desired by the experimenters because we did not want to introduce weak priors.

5.1   Physical Aspects

We analyze the correlation between the Ward parameter α and a set of contrast measures, in addition to the saturation index just described. We chose the global image contrast measure proposed by King-Smith and Kulikowski [13] and two local image contrast measures, Peli [15] and Simone et al. [25] WLF.

The results of the different contrast measures investigated are shown in Fig. 4. On the right, the full range of samples is investigated, while on the left, only the oversampled area of visual interest is drawn.

The saturation index shows that no more saturated pixels are present in the image when $\alpha \geq 0.3$. The dynamic range reduces until $\alpha \geq 0.5$, and then increases again until $\alpha = 0.7$. This shows sheen effect.

A similar behavior is shown by the global measure of contrast King-Smith and Kulikowski, with more sensitivity to the amount of bright pixels due to the anchored average normalization. However, the score value drops down regularly according to evolution of the parameter, and then a change of slope is observed around $\alpha = 0.3$.

Peli local contrast measure does not seem to show strong tendency, and appears to be rather unstable. The curves that appear noisy must be related to the short range of scores, only approximately between $[0.235, 0.255]$. Thus, Peli local contrast measure does not seem to be highly sensitive to the changes of material properties. Similar conclusion could be pointed out for WLF-U local contrast measure (when WLF parameters are fixed).

On the contrary, WLF-O local contrast measure (WLF with optimal parameters, see Sect. 2) seems to perform a rather good ranking of the images for $0 \leq \alpha \leq 0.3$. Then for values greater than 0.3, a change in the function occurs, and it follows a descending behavior.

5.2   Visual Aspects

We incorporate here the observers categorization into the image contrast measures analysis. We remind to the reader that five images were categorized very glossy $\alpha \leq 0.16$ (Magenta), six glossy $0.18 \leq \alpha \leq 0.28$ (Green), three somewhat glossy $0.30 \leq \alpha \leq 0.34$ (Yellow), three somewhat matte $0.36 \leq \alpha \leq 0.40$ (light Blue) and one very matte $\alpha = 1$ (dark Blue), which color code correspond to Fig. 5.

As can be seen from Fig. 5(d), about when the saturation index starts to become lower than 1, meaning that there are no more saturated pixels in the image, the observers rate samples somewhat glossy. This behavior may be influenced by the white background and some adaptation process, which generates already a reference for the highest radiance in the visual field. However, this observation is consistent with other results, and whatever the reason, the metric indicates a similar trend as the observers: Gloss sensation reduces.

The global measure King-Smith and Kulikowski is shown on Fig. 5(c). In this case, observers perceived gloss until a similar point where the metric shows an inflexion. The interesting behavior here is that the values keep on going down

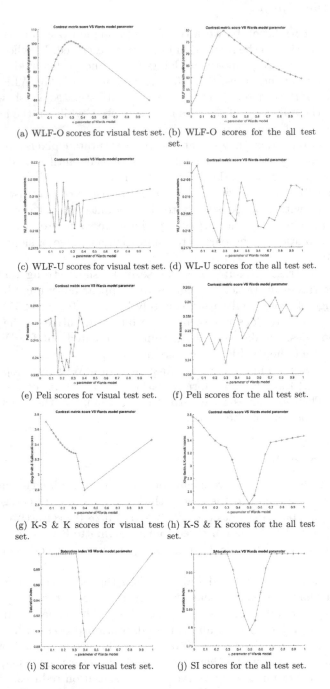

(a) WLF-O scores for visual test set. (b) WLF-O scores for the all test set.

(c) WLF-U scores for visual test set. (d) WL-U scores for the all test set.

(e) Peli scores for visual test set. (f) Peli scores for the all test set.

(g) K-S & K scores for visual test set. (h) K-S & K scores for the all test set.

(i) SI scores for visual test set. (j) SI scores for the all test set.

Fig. 4. Contrast metrics results versus Wards parameter α.

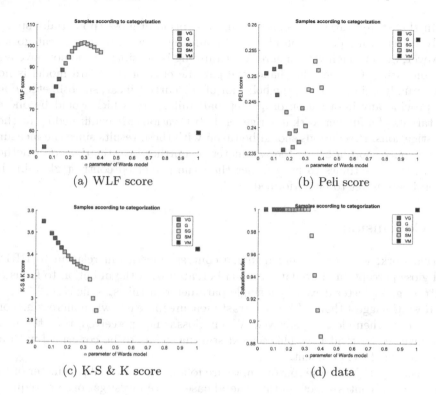

(a) WLF score

(b) Peli score

(c) K-S & K score

(d) data

Fig. 5. Perceptual categorization ordered in function of contrast measures score and Wards parameter. Legend stands for very matte (VM, dark blue), somewhat matte (SM, light blue), somewhat glossy (SG, yellow), glossy (G, green), and very glossy (VG, magenta). (Color figure online)

until $\alpha = 0.5$, which provide a potential ranking from very glossy to somewhat matte. However, after some sheen appears, matte material would show increasing values.

Peli local image contrast measure seems not following observers categorization as the categories exhibit a similar score as shown in Fig. 5(b). It seems that change in perceived contrast gloss/luster due to the changes in material properties cannot be adequately predicted in terms of perceived contrast by Peli measure in this case.

Of particular interest is the behavior of the WLF-O local image contrast measure. This measure shows a smooth curve, which increases within the range of gloss perception. When samples are rated somewhat glossy, the curves has changed its slope and started to decrease, which correlate with the observer categorizations. This agreement seems to be justified by the optimal parameters, which are not fixed but retrieved from statistics of the image, where variance has shown high correlation in terms of perceived contrast [25,28].

In this study, variance seems to link perception of gloss (potentially specifically luster) with perception of contrast and agree with observers categories. However, even though we can agree that ranking is possible, we do not have any clue on rating. On the other hand, the parameter α of the Ward model is not perceptually uniform. Thus, the behavior of the curve (linear, smooth, etc.) does not provide any information on perceptual uniformity, which would be one of the targets of a further work if our general observations are confirmed by further investigations. Precautions should be taken with these results since the measure may be only good in fitting the parameter α. Further investigations on whether the measure continues to fit α rather than the perceived contrast gloss in the general case is yet to be performed.

6   Conclusion

In this work, we have evaluated image contrast metrics in relation to BRDF and gloss perception. Two data sets were created with the intention to focus on contrast gloss/luster driven by a single parameter in this specific case.

Results suggest that WLF-O contrast measure increases when increasing contrast gloss, when gloss is perceived. When gloss is not perceived, then the measure inverses its tendency. This second statement has to be confirmed with an extension of the experiment.

It is not yet clear if the contrast measure follows the physical parameter or the perception of contrast gloss in the general case. More investigations are required in this direction. Further work would be performed with a more sophisticated model for BRDF and light simulation, which would permit to vary more parameters. The methodology for the visual experiment provides interesting qualitative results, but does not permit to rate quantitatively gloss perception. To this aim, more traditional psychometric methodology is required.

References

1. Hunter, R.S., Harold, R.W.: The measurement of appearance (1987)
2. CIE. TC 175:2006, a framework for the measurement of visual appearance (2006)
3. van Assen, J.J.R., Wijntjes, M.W.A., Pont, S.C.: Highlight shapes and perception of gloss for real and photographed objects. J. Vis. **16**(6), 6 (2016)
4. Hunter, R.S.: Methods of determining gloss. J. Res. National Bureau Stan. **18**, 19–39 (1937)
5. Leloup, F.B., Obein, G., Pointer, M.R., Hanselaer, P.: Toward the soft metrology of surface gloss: a review. Color Res. Appl. **39**(6), 559–570 (2014)
6. Chadwick, A.C., Kentridge, R.W.: The perception of gloss: a review. Vis. Res. **109**(Pt. B), 221–235 (2015). Perception of Material Properties (Part I)
7. Pedersen, M., Bonnier, N., Hardeberg, J.Y., Albregtsen, F.: Attributes of image quality for color prints. J. Electron. Imaging **19**(1), 011016-1–011016-13 (2010)
8. Valberg, A.: Light Vision Color. John Wiley & Sons, Chichester (2007)
9. Peres, M.R.: Focal Encyclopedia of Photography: Digital Imaging, Theory and Applications, History, and Science, 4th edn. Focal Press, Amsterdam (2007)

10. Michelson, A.: Studies in Optics. University of Chicago Press, Chicago (1927)
11. Burkhardt, D.A., Gottesman, J., Kersten, D., Legge, G.E.: Symmetry and constancy in the perception of negative and positive luminance contrast. J. Opt. Soc. Am. A **1**(3), 309–316 (1984)
12. Whittle, P.: Increments and decrements: luminance discrimination. Vision. Res. **26**(10), 1677–1691 (1986)
13. King-Smith, P.E., Kulikowski, J.J.: Pattern and flicker detection analysed by subthreshold summation. J. Physiol. **249**(3), 519–548 (1975)
14. Hess, R.F., Bradley, A., Piotrowski, L.: Contrast-coding in amblyopia i. differences in the neural basis of human amblyopia. Proc. R. Soc. Lond. B Biol. Sci. **217**(1208), 309–330 (1983)
15. Peli, E.: Contrast in complex images. J. Opt. Soc. Am. A **7**(10), 2032–2040 (1990)
16. McCann, J.J., Rizzi, A.: The Art and Science of HDR Imaging. John Wiley & Sons, New York (2012)
17. Frankle, J., McCann, J.J.: Method and apparatus for lightness imaging, patent US 4384336 a, May 1983
18. Adelson, E.H., Anderson, C.H., Bergen, J.R., Burt, P.J., Ogden, J.M.: Pyramid methods in image processing. RCA Eng. **29**(6), 33–41 (1984)
19. Lubin, J.: A visual discrimination model for imaging system design and evaluation. In: Visual Models for Target Detection and Recognition, chap. 10, pp. 245–283. World Scientific Publishers, River Edge (1995)
20. Iordache, R., Beghdadi, A., Viaris de Lesegno, P.: Pyramidal perceptual filtering using Moon and Spencer contrast. In: Proceedings 2001 International Conference on Image Processing (Cat. No.01CH37205), vol. 3, pp. 146–149 (2001)
21. Rizzi, A., Algeri, T., Medeghini, G., Marini, D.: A proposal for contrast measure in digital images. In: CGIV 2004 2nd European Conference on Color in Graphics, Imaging and Vision. IS&T Proceedings, Aachen, Germany, April 2004
22. Tadmor, Y., Tolhurst, D.J.: Calculating the contrasts that retinal ganglion cells and LGN neurones encounter in natural scenes. Vision. Res. **40**(22), 3145–3157 (2000)
23. Boccignone, G., Ferraro, M., Caelli, T.: Encoding visual information using anisotropic transformations. IEEE Trans. Pattern Anal. Mach. Intell **23**(2), 207–211 (2001)
24. Ferraro, M., Boccignone, G.: Image contrast enhancement via entropy production. Real-Time Imaging **10**(4), 229–238 (2004)
25. Simone, G., Pedersen, M., Hardeberg, J.Y.: Measuring perceptual contrast in digital images. J. Vis. Commun. Image Represent. **23**(3), 491–506 (2012)
26. Ward, G.J.: Measuring and modeling anisotropic reflection. SIGGRAPH Comput. Graph. **26**(2), 265–272 (1992)
27. Serrano, A., Gutierrez, D., Myszkowski, K., Seidel, H.-P., Masia, B.: An intuitive control space for material appearance. ACM Trans. Graph. **35**(6), 186:1–186:12 (2016)
28. Pedersen, M., Rizzi, A., Hardeberg, J.Y., Simone, G.: Evaluation of contrast measures in relation to observers perceived contrast. In: CGIV 2008 4th European Conference on Color in Graphics, Imaging and Vision. IS&T Proceedings, Terrassa, Spain, pp. 253–256, June 2008

Color Image Analysis

Artistic Photo Filtering Recognition Using CNNs

Simone Bianco[1]([✉]) ⓘ, Claudio Cusano[2], and Raimondo Schettini[1] ⓘ

[1] Department of Informatics, Systems and Communication,
University of Milano-Bicocca, Milano, Italy
{bianco,schettini}@disco.unimib.it
[2] Department of Electrical, Computer and Biomedical Engineering,
University of Pavia, Pavia, Italy
claudio.cusano@unipv.it

Abstract. In this paper we propose an approach based on deep Convolutional Neural Networks (CNNs) to recognize artistic photo filters applied to images. A total of 22 types of Instagram-like filters is considered. Different CNN architectures taken from the image recognition literature are compared on a dataset of more than 0.46 M images from the Places-205 dataset. Experimental results show that not only it is possible to reliably determine whether or not one of these filters has been applied, but also which one. Differently from other tasks, where the fine-tuning of a CNN trained on a different problem is usually good enough, here the fine-tuned AlexNet obtains an accuracy of only 67.5%. We show, instead, that an accuracy of about 99.0% can be obtained by training a CNN from scratch for this specific problem.

1 Introduction

Photo sharing services such as Flickr, Instagram etc. are continuously evolving with the progressive introduction of new features for their evergrowing user bases. One of the most popular features is the option to apply photographic filters which allow the user to adjust the mood of his pictures in a completely automatic way. Several preset filters are available corresponding to various image transformations, mostly related to shifts in the color distribution, variations in brightness and contrast, and the like.

In this work we investigate the problem of the automatic detection of the application photographic filters commonly used in the photo sharing services. We show how it is possible to reliably distinguish between original and processed images. Moreover, we also show how it is possible to identify with a very high confidence which filter has been used. The objective of this preliminary work is twofold. On one hand, it shows that it is possible to reliably identify certain kinds of distortions, paving the way for future investigation about the automatic classification of processed vs. unprocessed images; on the other hand, it would allow to take into account the influence of photographic filters in other computer vision tasks. In fact, Chen et al. [9] showed that state-of-the-art image recognition

© Springer International Publishing AG 2017
S. Bianco et al. (Eds.): CCIW 2017, LNCS 10213, pp. 249–258, 2017.
DOI: 10.1007/978-3-319-56010-6_21

approaches using Convolutional Neural Networks (CNN) fail to correctly classify social media photos (especially Instagram), where a lot of pictures have been edited with photographic filters.

The approach we investigate in this paper is based on the use of Convolutional Neural Networks trained on a large dataset of images processed with 22 different photographic filters designed to reproduce those available on Instagram. We experimented with different architectures taken from the image recognition literature and we show how they can be adapted to achieve a very high classification rate.

The paper is organized as follows: Sect. 2 reports all the information about the photographic filters and the data used in the experimentation; Sect. 3 illustrates the classification strategy; Sect. 4 reports the results obtained and discusses their implications; Sect. 5 concludes the paper by summarizing our findings and by suggesting future directions of research.

2 Photographic Filters

In this work we consider the following 22 types of Instagram-like filters (descriptions are taken from the Instagram website):

1. *1977*: the increased exposure with a red tint gives the photograph a rosy, brighter, faded look;
2. *Amaro*: adds light to an image, with the focus on the centre;
3. *Apollo*: lightly bleached, cyan-greenish color, some dusty texture;
4. *Brannan*: increases contrast and exposure and adds a metallic tint;
5. *Earlybird*: gives photographs an older look with a sepia tint and warm temperature;
6. *Gotham*: produce a black and white high contrast image, with bluish undertones;
7. *Hefe*: hight contrast and saturation, with a similar effect to Lo-Fi but not quite as dramatic;
8. *Hudson*: creates an "icy" illusion with heightened shadows, cool tint and dodged center;
9. *Inkwell*: direct shift to black and white — no extra editing;
10. *Kelvin*: increases saturation and temperature to give it a radiant "glow";
11. *Lo-Fi*: enriches color and adds strong shadows through the use of saturation and "warming" the temperature;
12. *Mayfair*: applies a warm pink tone, subtle vignetting to brighten the photograph center and a thin black border;
13. *Nashville*: warms the temperature, lowers contrast and increases exposure to give a light "pink" tint — making it feel "nostalgic";
14. *Poprocket*: adds a creamy vintage and retro color effect;
15. *Rise*: adds a "glow" to the image, with softer lighting of the subject;
16. *Sierra*: gives a faded, softer look;
17. *Sutro*: burns photo edges, increases highlights and shadows dramatically with a focus on purple and brown colors;

18. *Toaster*: ages the image by "burning" the centre and adds a dramatic vignette;
19. *Valencia*: fades the image by increasing exposure and warming the colors, to give it an antique feel;
20. *Walden*: increases exposure and adds a yellow tint;
21. *Willow*: a monochromatic filter with subtle purple tones and a translucent white border;
22. *X-Pro II*: increases color vibrance with a golden tint, high contrast and slight vignette added to the edges.

An example of the application of the 22 filters on an input image is reported in Fig. 1. Each filter is implemented by a sequence of basic image processing operations, such as: adjustment of color levels, adjustment of color curves (i.e. nonlinear channel transformation), brightness and contrast adjustment, addition of blur and/or noise, hue, saturation and lightness adjustment, addition of vignette, use of a color layer (to generate a color cast), use of a gradient layer, conversion to black & white, and addition of flare. A schematic view of which basic operations are used for each filter is reported in Table 1.

To generate a large scale dataset with filters, we randomly sampled 20 000 images from Places-205 [17]. After that, we applied the 22 filters to generate filtered images forming a dataset that contains 0.46 M images (original images included) in total. Original images are randomly divided into training, validation and test set with ratio 75%, 5%, and 20%.

3 Investigated Strategy

In the last years convolutional neural networks (CNNs) emerged as the *de facto* standard for image classification. According to the deep learning paradigm, networks are composed of several layers that progressively transform the raw data into high-level information [11]. The input consists in the image pixels, and the image features are learned, instead of being explicitly designed. The main drawback of CNNs is that their training require a large amount of annotated data and of computational time.

In most cases training a network from scratch is not really necessary. In fact it is possible to reuse a network previously trained on a different task by fine-tuning it with a relatively small amount of data. This strategy works because the features learned by the network tend to be quite general, providing information that can be exploited for various image classification domains (only the last layer need to be adapted to the actual classification task) [1, 16].

The baseline for image classification is represented by the AlexNet [10], a CNN that has been trained on more than one million images, distributed for the 2012 edition of the Imagenet Large Scale Visual Recognition Challenge [14]. Several other image classification tasks have been successfully addressed by fine-tuning AlexNet [13]. We argue that likewise to other similar computer vision tasks [5,6], the simple fine-tuning of a pre-trained network is not a viable solution to the problem of classifying Instagram-like filters. In fact, networks trained for

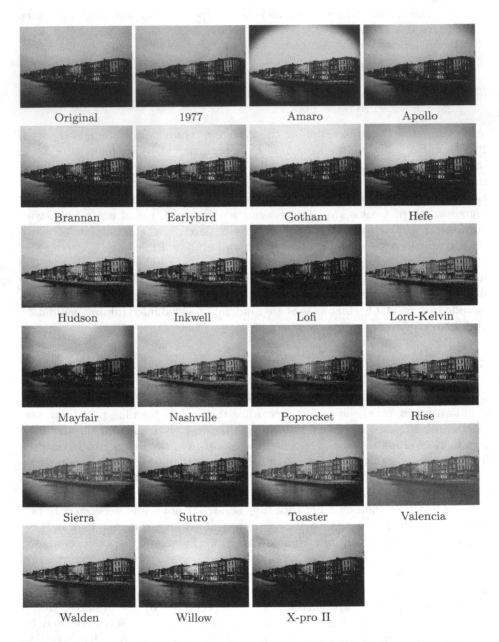

Fig. 1. Examples of the application of the 22 Instagram-like filters on one input image.

Table 1. Summary of the basic image processing operation used in each of the 22 Instagram-like filters.

Filter name	Color levels	Color curves	Brightness/ Contrast	Blur/ Noise	Hue/Sat/ Lightness	Vignette	Color layer	Gradient	Black & White	Flare
1977		•								
Amaro		•				•				
Apollo						•	•			
Brannan		•	•		•					
Earlybird		•	•		•	•	•			
Gotham		•		•					•	
Hefe			•		•	•				
Hudson		•					•			
Inkwell		•	•						•	
Lofi		•	•			•		•		
Lord Kelvin		•								
Mayfair	•	•		•	•					
Nashville	•	•	•							
Poprocket								•		
Rise				•	•	•	•	•		
Sierra		•				•		•		
Sutro		•	•		•	•	•			
Toaster		•				•	•	•		
Valencia	•	•								
Walden	•	•						•		
Willow				•		•		•	•	•
X-pro II		•								

object recognition tend to learn features that detect specific spatial patterns (i.e. those useful to discriminate the salient parts of the objects). For instance, the fist convolutional layer usually learns to extract features that resemble Gabor filters. The network learns to be as invariant as possible with respect to variations in color, contrast etc. In particular, it is expected that the network is able to recognize the same objects in images that have been modified by the application of the Instagram-like filters.

To address the problem of classifying the images into the 23 categories (22 filters + the original image) we experimented with three different networks derived from the AlexNet, the GoogLeNet and the LeNet architectures.

AlexNet is a network designed for the recognition of 1000 image categories. It includes three convolutional layers, followed by three fully-connected layers [10]. The input of the network is the image resampled to 227×227 pixels. The output of each convolutional layer is further processed by spatial max pooling, and rectified linear activations are applied to the output of both convolutional and fully connected layers. A final softmax layer maps the activation values to a vector of 1000 probability estimates.

GoogLeNet has a very complex architecture including a large number of different layers, the majority o which perform convolutions, pooling, and rectified linear activations. Groups of convolutions are used to form "Inception modules" that represent complex transformations of the data while requiring a relatively small number of parameters [15]. AlexNet and GoogLeNet have been designed for the same classification problem and, as a result, they have the same kind of inputs and outputs (with the minor difference that GoogLeNet accepts 224×224 input images).

LeNet is the first CNN proposed for an image classification task [12]. It has been designed for the recognition of handwritten digits and includes two convolutional and two fully connected layers. The network takes as input monochrome 32×32 images and produces as output a vector of probabilities (one for each of the ten symbols in the Arabic numeral system).

We adapted the three networks to our problem by resizing the last layer to 23 output units. In the case of the LeNet we also modified the input to 224×224 color images (note that this significantly increased the number of parameters). We trained each network by 450 000 iterations of the stochastic gradient descent algorithm, where each iteration processed a mini-batch of 256 images. For the AlexNet we also experimented with fine-tuning from the standard version trained on the Imagenet data (to do so, we allowed the training procedure to update only the coefficients of the last layer).

4   Experimental Results

The results we obtained on the test set are shown in Table 2. All the three network architectures allow to obtain high classification rates. Even for the simple LeNet we have more than 94% percent of accuracy. The best performing network is the AlexNet which obtained 99% of classification rate. GoogLeNet obtained slightly worse results (97.6%), but with little more than a tenth of the parameters. As expected, fine tuning of the original AlexNet trained for object recognition leads to quite poor results (67.5% of classification rate).

More details can be found in Table 3, that reports the confusion matrix obtained with AlexNet on the test set. The diagonal of the matrix shows how the network was able to detect with very high precision the 22 filters considered. For all of them we have more than 98% of correct classifications. The main difficulty for the network consists in detecting the absence of any filter. In fact, only 91.6% of the times the original images where recognizes as such. Instead, they are often classified as if the Hefe, Hudson or Mayfair filters would have been applied. These filters do not include any strong variation in the color distribution and, to human inspection, appear quite natural. Among the filters, the highest level of confusion (about 2%) occurs between the Inkwell and the Willow filters, which both produce gray-level images. In all the other cases, the off-diagonal entries of the confusion matrix are below 1%.

Table 2. Summary of the networks evaluated in the experiments. For each network are reported the training method (fine tuning or full training from scratch), the depth (numbers of learnable layers between input and output), the number of parameters, and the classification rates obtained on the test set (percentages of time in which the correct class is the predicted one, and in which it is among the five with the highest prediction scores).

Network	Training	Depth	Parameters	Top 1 (%)	Top 5 (%)
AlexNet	Fine tuning	8	57 M	67.52	93.92
AlexNet	Full training	8	57 M	**99.00**	**100.0**
GoogLeNet	Full training	22	6 M	97.64	99.92
LeNet	Full training	4	70 M	94.08	99.68

Table 3. Confusion matrix obtained on the test set by the AlexNet architecture retrained for the filter detection task. Results are reported as percentages.

	Original	1977	Amaro	Apollo	Brannan	Earlybird	Gotham	Hefe	Hudson	Inkwell	Lofi	Lord-K.	Mayfair	Nashville	Poprocket	Rise	Sierra	Sutro	Toaster	Valencia	Walden	Willow	X-pro II
Orig	91.6	0.6	0.1	0.2	0.3	0.5	0.0	1.9	1.3	0.1	0.2	-	1.2	0.1	0.0	0.8	-	0.4	-	0.0	0.2	0.1	0.3
1977	0.1	99.1	-	-	0.2	-	-	-	0.2	-	-	-	-	0.0	-	-	-	0.1	-	0.1	0.1	-	0.0
Amar	0.0	-	99.9	0.0	-	0.0	-	-	-	-	-	-	-	-	-	-	0.0	-	-	-	-	-	-
Apol	0.5	-	0.0	99.2	-	-	-	0.0	-	-	-	-	-	-	-	-	-	0.2	-	-	-	-	-
Bran	0.1	0.2	0.0	0.0	99.0	-	0.0	-	0.2	-	-	0.0	0.0	-	-	-	-	0.1	-	0.1	0.1	-	0.0
Earl	0.3	0.1	-	0.1	0.1	99.1	-	0.1	-	-	0.1	-	-	-	-	0.1	0.1	-	-	0.0	0.1	-	-
Goth	-	-	-	-	-	-	100	-	-	-	-	-	-	-	-	-	-	-	-	-	-	-	-
Hefe	0.9	-	-	0.1	-	-	-	98.5	-	0.1	0.2	-	0.1	-	0.0	0.0	-	0.1	-	0.0	-	-	-
Huds	0.9	0.2	0.0	-	0.2	-	-	-	98.2	-	-	-	-	0.1	0.0	0.1	0.0	0.0	-	0.1	0.2	-	0.1
Inkw	0.0	-	-	-	-	-	-	0.0	-	97.7	-	-	-	-	-	-	-	-	-	-	-	2.3	-
Lofi	0.1	-	-	0.1	-	-	-	0.0	-	-	99.8	-	-	-	0.0	-	-	-	-	0.0	-	-	-
Lord	-	-	-	-	-	-	-	-	-	-	-	99.9	-	0.1	-	-	-	0.0	-	0.0	0.0	-	-
Mayf	0.9	-	-	0.0	-	0.1	-	0.1	0.1	0.1	0.0	-	98.5	-	0.0	0.1	-	-	-	0.0	-	0.0	0.1
Nash	-	-	-	-	-	-	-	-	-	-	-	0.1	-	99.7	-	-	-	-	-	0.0	0.1	-	0.0
Popr	0.0	-	-	-	-	-	-	0.0	-	-	-	-	-	-	99.9	0.0	-	-	-	0.0	-	-	-
Rise	0.8	-	-	0.5	0.1	0.1	-	0.1	-	-	-	0.1	-	0.0	-	98.2	-	0.1	-	0.0	-	-	-
Sier	-	-	-	-	-	-	-	0.0	-	-	-	-	-	-	-	-	100	-	-	0.0	-	-	-
Sutr	0.2	0.1	-	0.0	0.1	-	-	0.0	0.1	-	0.1	-	-	-	-	-	-	99.3	-	0.1	0.1	-	-
Toas	-	-	-	-	-	-	-	-	-	-	-	-	-	-	-	-	-	-	100	-	-	-	-
Vale	0.0	-	-	-	-	-	-	0.0	-	-	-	-	-	-	-	-	-	-	-	99.9	-	-	-
Wald	-	0.1	-	0.1	-	-	-	0.1	-	-	0.1	-	0.2	-	-	-	-	0.1	-	0.0	99.3	-	0.1
Will	0.1	-	-	-	-	-	-	-	-	1.8	-	-	-	-	-	-	-	-	-	-	-	98.1	-
X-pr	0.1	-	-	0.0	0.1	-	-	-	-	-	-	-	0.1	-	-	0.0	-	-	0.0	0.1	-	-	99.6

The behavior of the GoogLeNet is very similar, as can be seen from the confusion matrix in Table 4. Results are in general slightly worse than those obtained by AlexNet, with the exception that the confusion among Willow and Inkwell filters raises up to 10.7%. For the sake of brevity we omit the confusion matrix of LeNet and of the fine-tuned AlexNet.

As we previously argued, the poor performance of the fine-tuned network can be explained by the fact that the original training forced the network to discard information about the color distribution that can be deceiving for image recognition, but useful for the classification of the filters. A qualitative evidence of this can be obtained by analyzing the coefficients learned by the first convolutional layer, that are reported in Fig. 2. For the standard AlexNet these coefficients form Gabor-like filters that are able to identify local features such as edges and corners. We obtained, instead, mostly low-pass filters sensitive to specific colors

Table 4. Confusion matrix obtained on the test set by the GoogLeNet architecture retrained for the filter detection task. Results are reported as percentages.

	Original	1977	Amaro	Apollo	Brannan	Earlybird	Gotham	Hefe	Hudson	Inkwell	Lofi	Lord-K.	Mayfair	Nashville	Poprocket	Rise	Sierra	Sutro	Toaster	Valencia	Walden	Willow	X-pro II
Orig	90.1	0.9	0.0	0.1	0.8	0.1	0.1	0.9	2.5	0.2	0.8	0.0	1.8	0.1	0.0	0.5	-	0.3	-	-	0.4	0.1	0.3
1977	0.2	98.5	-	-	0.1	-	-	-	0.7	-	0.0	0.0	0.0	-	-	-	0.0	0.1	-	0.1	0.1	0.0	-
Amar	0.0	-	99.9	-	-	-	-	-	-	-	-	-	-	-	-	-	0.1	-	-	-	-	-	-
Apol	1.4	-	0.1	97.6	-	-	-	0.1	0.0	-	0.2	-	0.3	-	-	0.2	0.1	0.1	-	-	-	-	0.0
Bran	0.1	0.2	-	-	99.2	-	-	0.0	0.3	-	-	0.0	-	-	-	0.0	0.1	0.0	0.1	0.1	-	-	-
Earl	1.7	0.1	0.2	0.1	0.2	95.9	-	0.1	0.1	-	0.2	-	0.2	0.0	0.0	0.3	0.3	0.2	-	0.0	0.3	-	0.1
Goth	0.0	-	-	-	-	-	100	-	-	-	-	-	-	-	-	-	-	-	-	-	0.0	-	-
Hefe	3.5	-	-	0.1	0.0	0.0	-	94.1	0.0	0.1	1.5	-	0.5	-	-	0.1	-	0.1	-	-	-	0.0	0.0
Huds	0.5	0.3	-	-	0.7	-	-	-	98.2	-	0.0	0.1	-	-	-	0.0	-	-	-	0.1	0.1	-	-
Inkw	0.1	0.0	-	-	-	-	-	0.0	-	99.0	-	0.0	-	-	-	-	-	-	-	-	-	0.8	-
Lofi	0.2	-	-	0.0	0.0	-	-	-	-	-	99.7	-	-	-	0.0	-	-	0.1	-	-	-	-	-
Lord	-	-	0.0	-	-	-	-	-	-	-	-	99.9	-	0.0	-	-	-	-	0.0	-	-	-	-
Mayf	3.8	-	0.0	0.0	0.0	0.1	-	0.2	0.1	0.2	0.1	-	95.2	-	0.1	0.1	-	0.0	-	-	0.1	-	0.0
Nash	-	-	-	-	-	-	-	-	-	-	-	0.5	-	99.4	-	-	-	-	0.0	0.0	-	-	-
Popr	0.6	-	-	-	0.1	0.0	-	0.0	0.9	-	0.8	-	0.2	0.0	97.0	0.0	-	0.1	-	-	0.1	-	0.1
Rise	2.3	-	0.1	0.4	0.4	0.1	-	0.1	0.4	-	0.1	-	0.2	-	-	95.7	0.1	0.2	0.0	-	-	-	-
Sier	-	-	-	-	-	-	-	-	-	0.1	-	-	-	-	-	-	100	-	-	-	-	-	-
Sutr	1.0	0.5	-	-	0.2	-	0.1	-	0.3	-	0.1	-	-	-	-	-	-	97.5	-	0.1	0.3	-	0.0
Toas	-	-	-	-	-	-	-	-	-	-	-	-	-	-	-	-	-	-	100	-	-	-	-
Vale	-	0.1	-	-	0.1	-	-	-	0.2	-	-	-	0.0	0.1	-	-	-	-	-	99.2	0.2	-	-
Wald	0.1	0.2	-	-	0.1	-	-	0.0	0.2	-	-	0.2	-	0.9	-	-	-	0.1	0.1	-	98.0	-	0.1
Will	-	-	-	-	-	-	-	0.0	-	10.7	-	-	-	-	-	-	-	-	-	-	-	89.3	-
X-pr	0.1	0.0	-	-	0.1	-	-	-	0.0	-	0.0	-	-	0.6	-	-	-	0.0	-	0.0	0.3	-	98.7

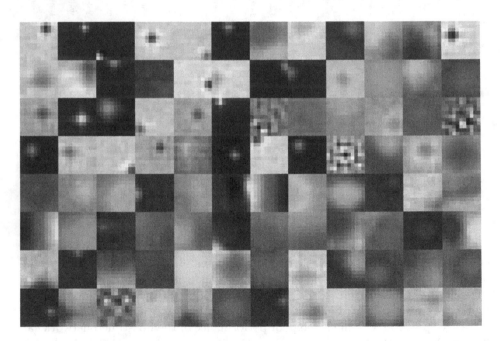

Fig. 2. Graphical representation of the coefficients learned for the 96 convolutions in the first level of the AlexNet architecture. (Color figure online)

(red, green, blue, purple, yellow, cyan among the others). A few filters seems able to detect edges at a particular orientation, often with opponent colors at the two sides. Only four filters have been learned for the detection of fine details.

5 Conclusions

In this paper we have investigated the problem of automatically detect the application of photographic filters commonly used in the photo sharing services. To this end, a total of 22 types of Instagram-like filters is considered to generate a dataset of more than 0.46 M images from the Places-205 dataset. Three different deep Convolutional Neural Networks (CNNs) have been compared: AlexNet, GoogLeNet, and LeNet. Experimental results show that it is both possible to determine with high accuracy whether or not one of these filters has been applied, and also which one. In particular, we showed that a recognition accuracy of about 99.0% can be obtained by training an AlexNet from scratch for this specific problem.

The contribution of this preliminary work is twofold: first, it shows that it is possible to reliably identify certain types of distortions, opening the possibility of future investigation about the automatic classification of processed vs. unprocessed images; second, it allows to take into account the influence of photographic filters in other computer vision tasks [2–4,7,8].

References

1. Bengio, Y.: Deep learning of representations for unsupervised and transfer learning. In: Unsupervised and Transfer Learning Challenges in Machine Learning, vol. 7, p. 19 (2012)
2. Bianco, S.: Reflectance spectra recovery from tristimulus values by adaptive estimation with metameric shape correction. J. Opt. Soc. Am. A **27**(8), 1868–1877 (2010)
3. Bianco, S., Ciocca, G., Marini, F., Schettini, R.: Image quality assessment by preprocessing and full reference model combination. In: IS&T/SPIE Electronic Imaging, p. 724200. International Society for Optics and Photonics (2009)
4. Bianco, S., Ciocca, G., Napoletano, P., Schettini, R.: An interactive tool for manual, semi-automatic and automatic video annotation. Comput. Vis. Image Underst. **131**, 88–99 (2015)
5. Bianco, S., Cusano, C., Schettini, R.: Color constancy using CNNs. In: Proceedings of the IEEE Conference on Computer Vision and Pattern Recognition Workshops, pp. 81–89 (2015)
6. Bianco, S., Cusano, C., Schettini, R.: Single and multiple illuminant estimation using convolutional neural networks. arXiv preprint (2015). arXiv:1508.00998
7. Bianco, S., Mazzini, D., Pau, D.P., Schettini, R.: Local detectors and compact descriptors for visual search: a quantitative comparison. Digital Signal Proc. **44**, 1–13 (2015)
8. Bianco, S., Schettini, R.: Computational color constancy. In: 2011 3rd European Workshop on, Visual Information Processing (EUVIP), pp. 1–7. IEEE (2011)
9. Chen, Y.H., Chao, T.H., Bai, S.Y., Lin, Y.L., Chen, W.C., Hsu, W.H.: Filter-invariant image classification on social media photos. In: Proceedings of the 23rd Annual ACM Conference on Multimedia Conference, pp. 855–858. ACM (2015)
10. Krizhevsky, A., Sutskever, I., Hinton, G.E.: Imagenet classification with deep convolutional neural networks. In: Advances in Neural Information Processing Systems, pp. 1097–1105 (2012)

11. LeCun, Y., Bengio, Y., Hinton, G.: Deep learning. Nature **521**(7553), 436–444 (2015)
12. LeCun, Y., Bottou, L., Bengio, Y., Haffner, P.: Gradient-based learning applied to document recognition. Proc. IEEE **86**(11), 2278–2324 (1998)
13. Razavian, A., Azizpour, H., Sullivan, J., Carlsson, S.: CNN features off-the-shelf: an astounding baseline for recognition. In: Proceedings of the IEEE Conference on Computer Vision and Pattern Recognition Workshops, pp. 806–813 (2014)
14. Russakovsky, O., Deng, J., Su, H., Krause, J., Satheesh, S., Ma, S., Huang, Z., Karpathy, A., Khosla, A., Bernstein, M., et al.: Imagenet large scale visual recognition challenge. Int. J. Comput. Vision **115**(3), 211–252 (2015)
15. Szegedy, C., Liu, W., Jia, Y., Sermanet, P., Reed, S., Anguelov, D., Erhan, D., Vanhoucke, V., Rabinovich, A.: Going deeper with convolutions. In: IEEE Conference on Computer Vision and Pattern Recognition (CVPR), pp. 1–9 (2015)
16. Yosinski, J., Clune, J., Bengio, Y., Lipson, H.: How transferable are features in deep neural networks?. In: Advances in Neural Information Processing Systems, pp. 3320–3328 (2014)
17. Zhou, B., Lapedriza, A., Xiao, J., Torralba, A., Oliva, A.: Learning deep features for scene recognition using places database. In: Advances in Neural Information Processing Systems, pp. 487–495 (2014)

Hand-Crafted vs Learned Descriptors for Color Texture Classification

Paolo Napoletano[✉]

DISCo (Dipartimento di Informatica, Sistemistica e Comunicazione),
Università degli Studi di Milano-Bicocca, Viale Sarca 336, 20126 Milano, Italy
napoletano@disco.unimib.it

Abstract. The paper presents a comparison between hand-crafted and learned descriptors for color texture classification. The comparison is performed on five color texture databases that include images under varying imaging conditions: scales, camera orientations, light orientations, light color temperatures, etc. Results demonstrate that learned descriptors, on average, significantly outperform hand-crafted descriptors. However, results obtained on the individual databases show that in the case of Outex 14, that includes training and test images taken under varying illuminant conditions, hand-crafted descriptors perform better than learned descriptors.

Keywords: Color texture classification · Hand-crafted descriptors · Global descriptors · Local descriptors · Learned descriptors · CNNs

1 Introduction

The problem of texture classification has been largely studied in computer vision and pattern recognition. Most of the works are focused on the definition of visual descriptors that are invariant, or at least robust, with respect to some variations in the acquisition conditions, such as rotations and scalings of the image, changes in brightness, contrast, and light color temperature [5,19].

Visual descriptors are often divided into two categories: traditional *hand-crafted* and *learned* features. Traditional hand-crafted descriptors are features extracted using a manually predefined algorithm based on the expert knowledge. These features can be *global* and *local*. Global features describe an image as a whole in terms of color, texture and shape distributions [33]. Some notable examples of global hand-crafted features are color histograms [36], Gabor filters [32], Local Binary Patterns (LBP) [38], Histogram of Oriented Gradients (HOG) [28], Dual Tree Complex Wavelet Transform (DT-CWT) [1,5] and GIST [39]. Readers who would wish to deepen the subject can refer to the following papers [34,42,50]. *Local* descriptors like Scale Invariant Feature Transform (SIFT) [30] provide a way to describe salient patches around properly chosen key points within the images. The dimension of the feature vector depends on the number of chosen key points in the image. The most common approach to

© Springer International Publishing AG 2017
S. Bianco et al. (Eds.): CCIW 2017, LNCS 10213, pp. 259–271, 2017.
DOI: 10.1007/978-3-319-56010-6_22

reduce the size of feature vectors is the *Bag-of-Visual Words* (BoVW) [46]. This approach has shown excellent performance in object recognition [26], image classification [17] and annotation [48]. The underlying idea is to quantize by clustering local descriptors into *visual words*. Words are then defined as the centroids of the learned clusters and are representative of several similar local regions. Given an image, for each key point the corresponding local descriptor is mapped to the most similar visual word. The final feature vector of the image is represented by the histogram of the visual words.

Learned descriptors are features extracted using Convolutional Neural Networks (CNNs). CNNs are a class of learnable architectures used in many domains such as image recognition, image annotation, image retrieval etc [43]. CNNs are usually composed of several layers of processing, each involving linear as well as non-linear operators, that are learned jointly, in an end-to-end manner, to solve a particular tasks. A typical CNN architecture for image classification consists of one or more convolutional layers followed by one or more fully connected layers. The result of the last full connected layer is the CNN output. The number of output nodes is equal to the number of image classes [29].

A CNN that has been trained for solving a given task can be also adapted to solve a different task. In practice, very few people train an entire CNN from scratch, because it is relatively rare to have a dataset of sufficient size. Instead, it is common to take a CNN that is pre-trained on a very large dataset (e.g. ImageNet, which contains 1.2 million images with 1000 categories [25]), and then use it either as an initialization or as a fixed feature extractor for the task of interest [41,49]. In the latter case, given an input image, the pre-trained CNN performs all the multilayered operations and the corresponding feature vector is the output of one of the fully connected layers [49]. This use of CNNs have demonstrated to be very effective in many pattern recognition applications [41].

In this paper we present a comparison between hand-crafted and learned descriptors for color texture classification. The comparison is performed on five color texture databases that include images under varying imaging conditions: scales, camera orientations, light orientations, light temperatures, etc. Each database allows to study the robustness of visual descriptors with respect to a given imaging condition. Results demonstrate that learned descriptors, on average, significantly outperform hand-crafted descriptors. However, results obtained on the individual databases show that in the case of Outex 14, that includes training and test images taken under varying illuminant conditions, hand-crafted descriptors perform better than learned descriptors.

2   Visual Descriptors

For the comparison we select a number of descriptors from hand-crafted and CNN-based approaches [5,9,33]. In some cases we consider both color and gray-scale images. The gray-scale image L is defined as follows: $L = 0.299R + 0.587G + 0.114B$. All feature vectors are L^2 normalized[1].

---
[1] The feature vector are divided by its L^2-norm.

Hand-Crafted Descriptors. As global descriptors we consider some variants of well known approaches such as Histogram, Local Binary Patterns, Wavelet and Gabor [22,34], in particular:

- 256-dimensional gray-scale histogram (Hist L) [36];
- 768-dimensional RGB histograms (Hist RGB) [40];
- 8-dimensional *Dual Tree Complex Wavelet Transform* features obtained considering four scales, mean and standard deviation, and three color channels (DT-CWT and DT-CWT L) [1,5];
- 512-dimensional *Gist* features obtained considering eight orientations and four scales for each channel (Gist RGB) [39];
- 32-dimensional *Gabor* features composed of mean and standard deviation of six orientations extracted at four frequencies for each color channel (Gabor L and Gabor RGB) [4,5];
- 243-dimensional *Local Binary Patterns* (LBP) feature vector for each channel. We consider LBP applied to gray images and to color images represented in RGB [31]. We select the LBP with a circular neighbourhood of radius 2 and 16 elements, and 18 uniform and no-rotation invariant patterns (LBP L and LBP RGB).
- 256-dimensional Local Color Contrast (LCC) obtained by using a quantized measure of color contrast [20];
- 499-dimensional LBP L combined with the LCC descriptor, as described in [3, 18,20,23].
- 729-dimensional LBP RGB combined with the LCC descriptor, as described in [20,21].

As local descriptor we consider the 1024-dimensional *Bag of Visual Words* (BoVW) of a 128-dimensional Scale Invariant Feature Transform (SIFT) calculated on the gray-scale image. The codebook of 1024 visual words is obtained by exploiting images from external sources.

Learned Descriptors. These descriptors are obtained as the intermediate representations of deep Convolutional Neural Networks originally trained for scene and object recognition. The networks are used to generate a visual descriptor by removing the final softmax nonlinearity and the last fully-connected layer. We select the most representative CNN architectures in the state of the art [49] by considering a different accuracy/speed trade-off. All the CNNs are trained on the ILSVRC-2012 dataset using the same protocol as in [29]. In particular we consider the following visual descriptors [41]:

- *BVLC AlexNet* (BVLC AlexNet): this is the AlexNet trained on ILSVRC 2012 [29].
- *BVLC Reference CaffeNet* (BVLC Ref): a AlexNet trained on ILSVRC 2012, with a minor variation [49] from the version as described in [29].
- *Fast CNN* (Vgg F): it is similar to the one presented in [29] with a reduced number of convolutional layers and the dense connectivity between convolutional layers. The last fully-connected layer is 4096-dimensional [9].

- *Medium CNN* (Vgg M): it is similar to the one presented in [51] with a reduced number of filters in the convolutional layer four. The last fully-connected layer is 4096-dimensional [9].
- *Medium CNN* (Vgg M-2048-1024-128): three modifications of the Vgg M network, with lower dimensional last fully-connected layer. In particular we use a feature vector of 2048, 1024 and 128 size [9].
- *Slow CNN* (Vgg S): it is similar to the one presented in [44] with a reduced number of convolutional layers, less filters in the layer five and the Local Response Normalization. The last fully-connected layer is 4096-dimensional [9].
- *Vgg Very Deep 19 and 16 layers* (Vgg VeryDeep 16 and 19): the configuration of these networks has been achieved by increasing the depth to 16 and 19 layers, that results in a substantially deeper network than the ones previously [45].
- *GoogleNet* [47] is a 22 layers deep network architecture that has been designed to improve the utilization of the computing resources inside the network.
- *ResNet 50* is Residual Network. Residual learning framework are designed to ease the training of networks that are substantially deeper than those used previously. This network has 50 layers [27].
- *ResNet 101* is Residual Network made of 101 layers [27].
- *ResNet 152* is Residual Network made of 101 layers [27].

3   Texture Databases

For the evaluation of visual descriptors we consider five texture databases. Each database allows to study the robustness of visual descriptors with respect to a given imaging condition. For instance, Outex 13 [37] and RawFooT [24] contain images with no variations in the imaging conditions between training and test images. KTH-TIPS2 [8] database contains images at different scales. Variations of the camera directions are included in the ALOT [7] database. Variations of the light temperature are included in the RawFooT and ALOT databases. Variations of the light direction are included in the RawFooT, KTH-TIPS2 and ALOT databases. Outex 14 [37] includes images taken under lights with different temperature and positioned differently. Table 1 summarizes all the imaging condition variations included in texture database.

3.1   Outex 13 and 14 Databases

Outex 13 and Outex 14 are parts of the Outex collection [37] (the data set is available at the address http://www.outex.oulu.fi). The Outex collection contains images that depict textures of 68 different classes acquired under three different light sources, each positioned differently: the 2856 K incandescent CIE A (denoted as 'inca'), the 2300 K horizon sunlight (denoted as 'horizon') and the 4000 K fluorescent TL84 (denoted as 'TL84'). An overview of the Outex collection is reported in Figs. 1 and 2. The photographs have been acquired with a Sony

Table 1. Variations of the imaging conditions included in the texture databases used in this paper.

Imaging conditions	Outex 13	Outex 14	RawFooT	KTH-TIPS2	ALOT
No variation	●	○	●	○	○
Image scale	○	○	○	●	○
Camera direction	○	○	○	○	●
Light temperature	○	○	●	○	●
Light direction	○	○	●	●	●
Light temp. & dir	○	●	●	○	○

Fig. 1. The 68 classes of the Outex collection under the light 'inca'.

DXC-755P camera calibrated using the 'inca' illuminant. Images are encoded in linear camera RGB space [31].

The Outex 13 database is composed of three different sets including images corresponding to each illuminant condition. The evaluation is performed on each single set independently and results are reported as average over the three results. Each set is made of 1360 images: 680 for training and 680 for test. Each set is made of training and test images acquired with no variations in the illuminant conditions.

To study the robustness of the proposed features to lighting variations we consider the Outex-14 test suite, that is obtained by considering all the possible combinations of illuminants for the training and the test sets. For instance, considering the training set from 'inca' and test set from 'horizon' and 'TL84' we obtain the subsets 'inca' vs 'horizon/TL84'. In this way, considering each light source as training, we obtain three different sets of images: 'inca' vs 'horizon/TL84', 'horizon' vs 'inca/TL84' and 'TL84' vs 'inca/horizon'. The evaluation is performed on each single set independently and results are reported as average over the three results. Each set is made of 2048 images: 680 for training

Fig. 2. Outex collection. Each row contains images from a different class. The first three columns contain images taken under the light 'inca'; the second three columns under the light 'horizon'; the last three columns under the light 'TL84'.

and 1360 for test. For both Outex 13 and 14, texture images are obtained by subdividing texture photographs in 20 sub-images of size 128×128 pixels.

3.2 RawFooT Database

The Raw Food Texture database (RawFooT), has been specially designed to investigate the robustness of descriptors and classification methods with respect to variations in the lighting conditions [24]. Classes correspond to 68 samples of raw food, including various kind of meat, fish, cereals, fruit etc. Samples taken under D65 at light direction $\theta = 24°$ are showed in Fig. 3. The database includes images of 68 samples of textures, acquired under 46 lighting conditions which may differ in:

1. the light direction: 24°, 30°, 36°, 42°, 48°, 54°, 60°, 66°, and 90°;
2. illuminant color: 9 outdoor illuminants: D40, D45, ..., D95; 6 indoor illuminants: 2700 K, 3000 K, 4000 K, 5000 K, 5700 K and 6500 K, we will refer to these as L27, L30, ..., L65;
3. intensity: 100%, 75%, 50% and 25% of the maximum achievable level;
4. combination of these factors.

Fig. 3. Overview of the 68 classes included in the Raw Food Texture database. For each class it is shown the image taken under D65 at direction $\theta = 24°$.

For each of the 68 classes we consider 16 patches obtained by dividing the original texture image, that is of size 800×800 pixels, in 16 non-overlapping squares of size 200×200 pixels. We select images taken under half of the imaging conditions for training (indicated as set1, a total of 10336 images) and the remaining for testing (set2, a total of 10336 images). For each class we select eight patches for training and eight for testing by following a chessboard pattern (white position is indicated as W, black position as B). As a result, we obtain four sets:

1. training: set1 at position W; test: set2 at position B;
2. training: set1 at position B; test: set2 at position W;
3. training: set2 at position W; test: set1 at position B;
4. training: set2 at position B; test: set1 at position W.

The evaluation is performed on each single set independently and results are reported as average over the four results.

Fig. 4. The 11 classes of the KTH-TIPS2b database.

3.3 KTH-TIPS2b Database

The KTH-TIPS (Textures under varying Illumination, Pose and Scale) image database was created to extend the CUReT database in two directions, by providing variations in scale as well as pose and illumination, and by imaging other samples of a subset of its materials in different settings [8].

The KTH-TIPS2 databases took this a step further by imaging 4 different samples of 11 materials (samples 1, 2, 3 and 4), each under varying pose, illumination and scale. Examples from the 11 classes is displayed in Fig. 4. Each sample has 108 patches acquired under different imaging conditions. We collect 4 sets of images composed as follow:

1. training: samples 1; test: samples 2,3,4;
2. training: samples 2; test: samples 1,3,4;
3. training: samples 3; test: samples 1,2,4;
4. training: samples 4; test: samples 1,2,3.

The evaluation is performed on each single set independently and results are reported as average over the four results.

3.4 ALOT Database

The Amsterdam Library of Textures (ALOT) is a color image collection of 250 rough textures. In order to capture the sensory variation in object recordings, the authors systematically varied viewing angle, illumination angle, and illumination color for each material. This collection is similar in spirit as the CURET collection [7]. Examples from the 250 classes is displayed in Fig. 5.

Fig. 5. The 250 classes of the ALOT database.

The textures were placed on a turn table, and recordings were made for aspects of 0°, 60°, 120°, and 180°. Four cameras were used, three perpendicular to the light bow at 0° azimuth and 80°, 60°, 40° altitude. Furthermore, one is mounted at 60° azimuth and 60° altitude. Combined with five illumination directions and one semi-hemispherical illumination, a sparse sampling of the BTF is obtained.

Each object was recorded with only one out of five lights turned on, yielding five different illumination angles. Furthermore, turning on all lights yields a sort of hemispherical illumination, although restricted to a more narrow illumination sector than true hemisphere. Each texture was recorded with 3075 K illumination color temperature, at which the cameras were white balanced. One image for each camera is recorded with all lights turned on, at a reddish spectrum of 2175 K color temperature.

For each of the 250 classes we consider 6 patches obtained by dividing the original texture image, in 6 non-overlapping squares of size 200×200 pixels. For each class we have 100 textures acquired under different imaging conditions. For each texture we select three patches for training and three for testing by following a chessboard pattern (white position is indicated as W, black position as B). As a result, we obtain a training set made of 75000 images (W position) and a test set made of 75000 images (B position).

4   Experiments

In all the experiments we use the nearest neighbor classification strategy: given a patch in the test set, its distance with respect to all the training patches is computed. The prediction of the classifier is the class of closest element in the training set. For this purpose, after some preliminary tests with several descriptors in which we evaluated the most common distance measures, we decided to use the $L1$ distance: $d(\mathbf{x}, \mathbf{y}) = \sum_{i=1}^{N} |\mathbf{x_i} - \mathbf{y_i}|$, where $\mathbf{x}$ and $\mathbf{y}$ are two feature vectors. All the experiments are conducted under the *maximum ignorance* assumption, that is, no information about the imaging conditions of the test patches is available for the classification method and for the descriptors. Performance is reported as classification rate (i.e., the ratio between the number of correctly classified images and the number of test images).

Table 2 reports the performance obtained by all the visual descriptors evaluated on each single texture database. The list of the visual descriptors is ordered by their average performance over databases.

It is almost clear that, on average, learned features are more powerful than hand-crafted ones. In particular, residual nets are the most powerful. Residual nets are expected to be more effective because contain many more layers than other networks. They are designed with the aim to be more accurate on the image/object recognition task. The less powerful networks are the shortest ones.

Amongst hand-crafted features, the most powerful are SIFT and some variants of LBP. On average, local descriptors are most performing than global ones [10]. Moreover, grayscale hand-crafted descriptors perform better than color ones (in Table 2 grayscale descriptors are denoted with the black bullet).

Table 2. Accuracy of selected color descriptors. For each column the best result is reported in bold. The visual descriptors are ordered by the last column, which is the average accuracy over the database. The black bullet stands for grayscale visual descriptors.

Features	Texture databases					Avg
	Outex 13	Outex 14	RawFooT	KTH-TIPS2	ALOT	
ResNet-101	88.09	66.67	98.12	**78.74**	98.13	**85.95**
ResNet-152	87.06	66.08	98.26	75.18	98.12	84.94
ResNet-50	88.09	63.92	**98.43**	75.71	**98.35**	84.90
Vgg VeryDeep 19	85.00	56.76	95.73	74.54	94.93	81.39
Vgg VeryDeep 16	85.59	53.90	96.18	73.57	95.51	80.95
Vgg M	86.03	59.29	94.25	69.37	94.14	80.62
Vgg M 2048	85.93	57.21	93.43	69.56	93.30	79.89
Vgg F	86.27	58.28	91.87	68.52	94.06	79.80
Vgg S	84.90	55.69	93.52	70.26	94.12	79.70
Vgg M 1024	85.64	57.50	93.01	69.62	92.58	79.67
GoogleNet	82.65	56.67	92.57	70.67	92.65	79.04
BVLC AlexNet	85.98	52.35	88.96	71.72	91.26	78.05
BVLC Ref	85.93	47.13	89.35	71.11	91.30	76.97
Vgg M 128	82.16	52.89	88.75	68.24	85.56	75.52
SIFT •	77.60	72.18	85.71	51.76	78.69	73.19
LBP L + LCC •	83.43	**72.25**	86.38	50.51	67.87	72.09
LBP RGB + LCC	88.63	38.97	79.77	53.91	76.06	67.47
Gist RGB	71.32	56.13	59.28	56.18	48.00	58.18
LBP L •	80.49	67.82	9.98	51.71	51.58	52.32
Gabor RGB	88.14	40.91	12.92	52.20	66.16	52.07
LBP RGB	87.75	36.18	13.20	54.47	65.64	51.45
DT-CWT	82.84	8.90	41.13	50.68	65.65	49.84
DT-CWT L •	61.08	53.19	53.15	49.64	30.67	49.54
Gabor L •	76.86	49.53	21.24	51.63	37.42	47.34
Hist. RGB	**90.15**	3.97	19.87	42.84	65.50	44.47
Gist	59.07	55.61	21.72	42.94	33.99	42.67
Hist. L •	74.31	42.23	7.09	34.41	30.53	37.72
LCC	25.98	12.50	9.68	29.52	18.43	19.22

Observing the results achieved on each single database, we discover that in the case of no-variations between training and test textures, histogram RGB works better than learned descriptors. In the case of simultaneously variation of light temperature and direction, the best performing visual descriptor is the LBP + LCC. This approach combines the powerful of grayscale LBP with a novel measure of the Local Color Contrast that is invariant with respect to rotations and translations of the image plane, and with respect to several transformations in the color space [20]. In the case of variations of image scale, light temperature, light direction and camera direction the learned descriptors outperform hand-crafted ones.

5   Conclusions

We focused, here, on texture classification under variable imaging conditions. To this purpose, several descriptors from hand-crafted and learned approaches on five state of the art texture databases are evaluated. Results show that learned descriptors, on average, perform better than hand-crafted ones. However, results show limit of learned descriptors when direction and temperature of the light change simultaneously. In this case, SIFT and some variants of LBP perform better than learned descriptors. As future works, we plan to evaluate recent hybrid [2,6,11] visual descriptors that combine local and learned descriptors [12–16,35].

References

1. Barilla, M., Spann, M.: Colour-based texture image classification using the complex wavelet transform. In: 2008 5th International Conference on Electrical Engineering, Computing Science and Automatic Control, CCE 2008, pp. 358–363, November 2008
2. Bianco, S., Ciocca, G., Napoletano, P., Schettini, R., Margherita, R., Marini, G., Pantaleo, G.: Cooking action recognition with iVAT: an Interactive video annotation tool. In: Petrosino, A. (ed.) ICIAP 2013. LNCS, vol. 8157, pp. 631–641. Springer, Heidelberg (2013). doi:10.1007/978-3-642-41184-7_64
3. Bianco, S., Cusano, C., Napoletano, P., Schettini, R.: On the robustness of color texture descriptors across illuminants. In: Petrosino, A. (ed.) ICIAP 2013. LNCS, vol. 8157, pp. 652–662. Springer, Heidelberg (2013). doi:10.1007/978-3-642-41184-7_66
4. Bianconi, F., Fernández, A.: Evaluation of the effects of gabor filter parameters on texture classification. Pattern Recogn. 40(12), 3325–3335 (2007)
5. Bianconi, F., Harvey, R., Southam, P., Fernández, A.: Theoretical and experimental comparison of different approaches for color texture classification. J. Electron. Imaging 20(4), 043006 (2011)
6. Boccignone, G., Napoletano, P., Ferraro, M.: Embedding diffusion in variational Bayes: a technique for segmenting images. Int. J. Pattern Recogn. Artif. Intell. 22(05), 811–827 (2008)
7. Burghouts, G.J., Geusebroek, J.M.: Material-specific adaptation of color invariant features. Pattern Recogn. Lett. 30(3), 306–313 (2009)
8. Caputo, B., Hayman, E., Mallikarjuna, P.: Class-specific material categorisation. In: 2005 Tenth IEEE International Conference on Computer Vision, ICCV 2005, vol. 2, pp. 1597–1604. IEEE (2005)
9. Chatfield, K., Simonyan, K., Vedaldi, A., Zisserman, A.: Return of the devil in the details: delving deep into convolutional nets. arXiv preprint arXiv:1405.3531 (2014)

10. Cimpoi, M., Maji, S., Kokkinos, I., Mohamed, S., Vedaldi, A.: Describing textures in the wild. In: 2014 IEEE Conference on Computer Vision and Pattern Recognition (CVPR), pp. 3606–3613 (2014)
11. Cimpoi, M., Maji, S., Kokkinos, I., Vedaldi, A.: Deep filter banks for texture recognition, description and segmentation. arXiv preprint arXiv:1507.02620 (2015)
12. Colace, F., Casaburi, L., De Santo, M., Greco, L.: Sentiment detection in social networks and in collaborative learning environments. Comput. Hum. Behav. **51**, 1061–1067 (2015)
13. Colace, F., De Santo, M., Greco, L.: An adaptive product configurator based on slow intelligence approach. Int. J. Metadata Seman. Ontol. **9**(2), 128–137 (2014)
14. Colace, F., De Santo, M., Greco, L., Napoletano, P.: Text classification using a graph of terms. In: 2012 Sixth International Conference on Complex, Intelligent and Software Intensive Systems (CISIS), pp. 1030–1035. IEEE (2012)
15. Colace, F., De Santo, M., Greco, L., Napoletano, P.: A query expansion method based on a weighted word pairs approach. In: Proceedings of the 3rd Italian Information Retrieval (IIR) 964, pp. 17–28 (2013)
16. Colace, F., De Santo, M., Greco, L., Napoletano, P.: Weighted word pairs for query expansion. Inf. Process. Manage. **51**(1), 179–193 (2015)
17. Csurka, G., Dance, C., Fan, L., Willamowski, J., Bray, C.: Visual categorization with bags of keypoints. In: Workshop on Statistical Learning in Computer Vision, ECCV, Prague, vol. 1, pp. 1–2 (2004)
18. Cusano, C., Napoletano, P., Schettini, R.: Illuminant invariant descriptors for color texture classification. In: Tominaga, S., Schettini, R., Trémeau, A. (eds.) CCIW 2013. LNCS, vol. 7786, pp. 239–249. Springer, Heidelberg (2013). doi:10.1007/978-3-642-36700-7_19
19. Cusano, C., Napoletano, P., Schettini, R.: Intensity and color descriptors for texture classification. In: Proceedings of the SPIE Image Processing: Machine Vision Applications VI, SPIE, vol. 8661, pp. 866113–866113-11 (2013)
20. Cusano, C., Napoletano, P., Schettini, R.: Combining local binary patterns and local color contrast for texture classification under varying illumination. JOSA A **31**(7), 1453–1461 (2014)
21. Cusano, C., Napoletano, P., Schettini, R.: Local angular patterns for color texture classification. In: Murino, V., Puppo, E., Sona, D., Cristani, M., Sansone, C. (eds.) ICIAP 2015. LNCS, vol. 9281, pp. 111–118. Springer, Cham (2015). doi:10.1007/978-3-319-23222-5_14
22. Cusano, C., Napoletano, P., Schettini, R.: Remote sensing image classification exploiting multiple kernel learning. IEEE Geosci. Remote Sens. Lett. **12**(11), 2331–2335 (2015)
23. Cusano, C., Napoletano, P., Schettini, R.: Combining multiple features for color texture classification. J. Electron. Imaging **25**(6), 061410 (2016)
24. Cusano, C., Napoletano, P., Schettini, R.: Evaluating color texture descriptors under large variations of controlled lighting conditions. J. Opt. Soc. Am. A **33**(1), 17–30 (2016)
25. Deng, J., Dong, W., Socher, R., Li, L.J., Li, K., Fei-Fei, L.: ImageNet: a large-scale hierarchical image database. In: IEEE Conference on Computer Vision and Pattern Recognition, pp. 248–255. IEEE (2009)
26. Grauman, K., Leibe, B.: Visual Object Recognition, No. 11. Morgan & Claypool Publishers (2010)
27. He, K., Zhang, X., Ren, S., Sun, J.: Deep residual learning for image recognition. In: Proceedings of the IEEE Conference on Computer Vision and Pattern Recognition, pp. 770–778 (2016)

28. Junior, O.L., Delgado, D., Gonçalves, V., Nunes, U.: Trainable classifier-fusion schemes: an application to pedestrian detection. In: Intelligent Transportation Systems (2009)

29. Krizhevsky, A., Sutskever, I., Hinton, G.E.: ImageNet classification with deep convolutional neural networks. In: Advances in neural information processing systems, pp. 1097–1105 (2012)

30. Lowe, D.: Distinctive image features from scale-invariant keypoints. Int. J. Comput. Vision 60(2), 91–110 (2004)

31. Mäenpää, T., Pietikäinen, M.: Classification with color and texture: jointly or separately? Pattern Recogn. 37(8), 1629–1640 (2004)

32. Manjunath, B.S., Ma, W.Y.: Texture features for browsing and retrieval of image data. IEEE Trans. Pattern Anal. Mach. Intell. 18(8), 837–842 (1996)

33. Mirmehdi, M., Xie, X., Suri, J.: Handbook of Texture Analysis. Imperial College Press, London (2008)

34. Napoletano, P.: Visual descriptors for content-based retrieval of remote sensing images. arXiv preprint arXiv:1602.00970 (2016)

35. Napoletano, P., Boccignone, G., Tisato, F.: Attentive monitoring of multiple video streams driven by a Bayesian foraging strategy. IEEE Trans. Image Process. 24(11), 3266–3281 (2015)

36. Novak, C.L., Shafer, S., et al.: Anatomy of a color histogram. In: 1992 Proceedings of IEEE Computer Society Conference on Computer Vision and Pattern Recognition, CVPR 1992, pp. 599–605. IEEE (1992)

37. Ojala, T., Mäenpää, T., Pietikäinen, M., Viertola, J., Kyllönen, J., Huovinen, S.: Outex-new framework for empirical evaluation of texture analysis algorithms. In: 16th International Conference on Pattern Recognition, vol. 1, pp. 701–706 (2002)

38. Ojala, T., Pietikäinen, M., Mänepää, T.: Multiresolution gray-scale and rotation invariant texture classification with local binary patterns. IEEE Trans. Pattern Anal. Mach. Intell. 24(7), 971–987 (2002)

39. Oliva, A., Torralba, A.: Modeling the shape of the scene: a holistic representation of the spatial envelope. Int. J. Comput. Vision 42(3), 145–175 (2001)

40. Pietikainen, M., Nieminen, S., Marszalec, E., Ojala, T.: Accurate color discrimination with classification based on feature distributions. In: 1996 Proceedings of the 13th International Conference on Pattern Recognition, vol. 3, pp. 833–838, August 1996

41. Razavian, A.S., Azizpour, H., Sullivan, J., Carlsson, S.: CNN features off-the-shelf: an astounding baseline for recognition. In: 2014 IEEE Conference on Computer Vision and Pattern Recognition Workshops (CVPRW), pp. 512–519 (2014)

42. Rui, Y., Huang, T.S., Chang, S.F.: Image retrieval: current techniques, promising directions, and open issues. J. Vis. Commun. Image Represent. 10(1), 39–62 (1999)

43. Schmidhuber, J.: Deep learning in neural networks: an overview. Neural Netw. 61, 85–117 (2015)

44. Sermanet, P., Eigen, D., Zhang, X., Mathieu, M., Fergus, R., LeCun, Y.: OverFeat: integrated recognition, localization and detection using convolutional networks. In: International Conference on Learning Representations (ICLR 2014), CBLS, April 2014

45. Simonyan, K., Zisserman, A.: Very deep convolutional networks for large-scale image recognition. arXiv preprint arXiv:1409.1556 (2014)

46. Sivic, J., Zisserman, A.: Video Google: a text retrieval approach to object matching in videos. In: 2003 Proceedings of the Ninth IEEE International Conference on Computer Vision, pp. 1470–1477. IEEE (2003)

47. Szegedy, C., Liu, W., Jia, Y., Sermanet, P., Reed, S., Anguelov, D., Erhan, D., Vanhoucke, V., Rabinovich, A.: Going deeper with convolutions. In: Proceedings of the IEEE Conference on Computer Vision and Pattern Recognition, pp. 1–9 (2015)
48. Tsai, C.F.: Bag-of-words representation in image annotation: a review. ISRN Artif. Intell. **2012** (2012)
49. Vedaldi, A., Lenc, K.: MatConvNet - convolutional neural networks for MATLAB. CoRR abs/1412.4564 (2014)
50. Veltkamp, R., Burkhardt, H., Kriegel, H.P.: State-of-the-Art in Content-based Image and Video Retrieval, vol. 22. Springer Science & Business Media, Heidelberg (2013)
51. Zeiler, M.D., Fergus, R.: Visualizing and understanding convolutional networks. In: Fleet, D., Pajdla, T., Schiele, B., Tuytelaars, T. (eds.) ECCV 2014. LNCS, vol. 8689, pp. 818–833. Springer, Cham (2014). doi:10.1007/978-3-319-10590-1_53

Improved Opponent Colour Local Binary Patterns for Colour Texture Classification

Francesco Bianconi[1]([✉]), Raquel Bello-Cerezo[1], Paolo Napoletano[2],
and Francesco Di Maria[1]

[1] Department of Engineering, Università degli Studi di Perugia,
Via G. Duranti 93, 06135 Perugia, Italy
bianco@ieee.org, raquel.bellocerezo@studenti.unipg.it,
francesco.dimaria@unipg.it
[2] Department of Informatics, Systems and Communication,
Università degli Studi di Milano–Bicocca, Viale Sarca 336, 20125 Milano, Italy
napoletano@disco.unimib.it

Abstract. In this paper we introduce Improved Opponent Colour Local Binary Patterns (IOCLBP), a conceptually simple yet effective descriptor for colour texture classification. The method was experimentally validated over eight datasets of colour texture images. The results show that IOCLBP outperformed other LBP variants and was at least as effective as last generation features from Convolutional Neural Networks.

Keywords: Local Binary Patterns · Image classification · Colour texture · Convolutional Neural Networks

1 Introduction

Texture is one of the fundamental visual properties of objects, materials and scenes. Understanding texture is therefore essential in a wide range of applications such as surface inspection and grading, content-based image retrieval, object recognition, material classification, remote sensing and medical image analysis. As a consequence, research on texture has been attracting significant attention for at least forty years, and a very large number of visual descriptors is now available in the literature – for an overview see for instance Refs. [9,33].

During the last two decades the 'bag of features' paradigm (BoF) has emerged as one of the most effective approaches to texture analysis. This scheme is best explained by resorting to a parallel with the 'bag of words' model (BoW), whereby a text is represented by the statistical, orderless distribution of its words over a predefined dictionary. Likewise, the BoF represents images by the distribution of local patterns regardless of their spatial distribution [2]. One possible implementations of the bag of features model is represented by a class of methods known as Histogram of Equivalent Patterns (HEP) [10]. Descriptors of this class sample the input images densely and assign each local image patch to one visual word among those in the dictionary. The image representation is the probability

© Springer International Publishing AG 2017
S. Bianco et al. (Eds.): CCIW 2017, LNCS 10213, pp. 272–281, 2017.
DOI: 10.1007/978-3-319-56010-6_23

distribution (histogram) of the visual words over the dictionary. In the HEP the mapping image patch → visual word is typically a function (usually referred to as the *kernel function*) of the grey-levels of pixels in the patch. In this approach the dictionary is defined 'a priori' and coincides with the codomain of the kernel function. Local Binary Patterns and related methods are all instances of this general scheme [2, 10].

Extensions of this approach to the colour domain involve comparing the colour (or multi-spectral) pixel values instead of the grey-levels. This area, however, has received significantly less attention than the grey-scale counterpart. One of the first extensions of LBP to colour images was Opponent Colour Local Binary Patterns (OCLBP) [25] in which, as we detail in Sect. 3, the LBP operator is applied to each colour channel separately as well as to pairs of colour channels. Herein we propose a conceptually simple yet effective improvement on this method. We denote our descriptor as Improved Opponent-colour LBP (IOCLBP) and show, experimentally, that it can significantly outperform OCLBP in colour texture classification.

In the remainder of the paper we first provide some background in Sect. 2 then introduce IOCLBP in Sect. 3; we discuss the experimental activity in Sect. 4 and summarise the results in Sect. 5. Some final considerations and directions for future studies conclude the paper (Sect. 6).

2 Background

Few would object that LBP is one the most prominent and widely investigated texture descriptors ever. Suffice it to say that Ojala and Pietikäinen's seminal work [27] has been cited no fewer than 5500 times[1] since it was first published in 2002. Keys to the success of this method are the ease of implementation, low computational demand and high discrimination accuracy. A lot of LBP variations also exist: so many, indeed, that in a recent review Liu *et al.* [21] noted that their number is so large that it is becoming more and more difficult – even to the expert in the field – to grasp them all.

In comparison, colour variants have received significantly less attention in the literature. A common strategy for extending LBP to the colour domain consists of applying the LBP operator to each colour channel separately (as for instance in [23]), and/or to pairs of channels jointly, as suggested by and Mäenpää and Pietikäinen [24, 25]. Alternatively, one can treat colour data as vectors in the three-dimensional space and compare them on the basis of their norm, relative orientation (e.g.: Local Angular Patterns [8]) or both (e.g. Local Color Vector Binary Patterns [20]). Another possible way consists of defining a suitable total ordering in the colour space, and use this as a replacement for the natural grey-level ordering in LBP definition. This strategy has been recently investigated extensively by Ledoux *et al.* [19].

---

[1] Source: Scopus®; visited on Nov. 29, 2016.

As we detail in Sect. 3, IOCLBP considers intra- and inter-channel features – just as OCLBP – but with a different local thresholding scheme. While in OCLBP the peripheral pixels are thresholded at the value of the central pixel, in IOCLBP thresholding is done against the average value. In the grey-scale domain the same approach has been used to define Improved Local Binary Patterns (ILBP) [16], which generally work better than LBP [11], but as far as we know this idea has not been extended to the colour domain yet. The method proposed here can be therefore considered an extension of ILBP to colour textures.

3   Improved Opponent Colour Local Binary Patterns

Let us consider a neighbourhood $\mathcal{N} = \{\mathbf{p}_0, \mathbf{p}_1, \ldots, \mathbf{p}_n\}$ composed of a central pixel $\mathbf{p}_0$ and n peripheral pixels $\mathbf{p}_i$, $i \in \{1, \ldots, n\}$. For the sake of simplicity we shall assume that the peripheral pixels be arranged circularly around the central one (Fig. 1), though this restriction is not essential (see Nanni et al. [26] on this point).

In Local Binary Patterns an instance $\mathcal{P}$ of $\mathcal{N}$ (i.e. a local image patch) is assigned a unique decimal code (or, equivalently, a visual word) in the following way:

$$f_{\text{LBP}}(\mathcal{P}) = \sum_{i=1}^{n} 2^{i-1} \phi\left[g\left(\mathbf{p}_0\right), g\left(\mathbf{p}_i\right)\right] \tag{1}$$

where

$$\phi(x, y) = \begin{cases} 0 & \text{if } x \leq y \\ 1 & \text{otherwise} \end{cases} \tag{2}$$

In Eq. 1 $g(\mathbf{p}_0)$ stands for a generic function which converts from colour into grey-scale; this is normally the standard NTSC/PAL grey-scale conversion [29, Sect. 4.3.1]. The resulting feature vector is the dense, orderless statistical distribution over the set of possible codes.

Mäenpää and Pietikäinen [25] proposed an extension of this scheme to the colour domain by considering intra- and inter-channel features. For a pair of channels (u, v) the resulting Opponent Colour Local Binary Patterns (OCLBP) can be defined as follows

$$f_{\text{OCLBP}_{u,v}}(\mathcal{P}) = \sum_{i=1}^{n} 2^{i-1} \phi\left(p_{0,u}, p_{i,v}\right) \tag{3}$$

where $\mathbf{p}_{i,v}$ indicates intensity of the i-th pixel in the v-th channel. In the RGB space the image representation is the concatenation of the feature vectors generated by $\text{OCLBP}_{R,R}$, $\text{OCLBP}_{G,G}$, $\text{OCLBP}_{B,B}$, $\text{OCLBP}_{R,G}$, $\text{OCLBP}_{R,B}$ and $\text{OCLBP}_{G,B}$. The resulting vector is therefore six times larger than LBP's.

Table 1. Summary table of the datasets used in the experiments.

ID	Name	No. of classes	No. of samples per class	Sample images
1	KTH-TIPS	10	81	
2	KTH-TIPS2b	11	432	
3	Outex-00013	68	20	
4	Outex-00014	68	60	
5	Plant Leaves	20	60	
6	RawFooT	68	184	
7	USPTex	191	12	
8	V×C TSG	42	12	

Improved Opponent Color Local Binary Patterns differ from OCLBP in that the thresholding is no longer point-to-point but point-to-average. In formulas we have:

$$f_{\text{IOCLBP}_{u,v}}(\mathcal{P}) = \sum_{i=0}^{n} 2^i \phi(\bar{p}_u, p_{i,v}) \tag{4}$$

where:

$$\bar{p}_u = \frac{1}{n} \sum_{i=0}^{n} \bar{p}_{i,u} \tag{5}$$

It is easy to see that the number of directional features generated by LBP, OCLBP and IOCLBP respectively is 2^{n-1}, $6 \times 2^{n-1}$ and 6×2^n. Variations of LBP such as the rotation invariant (LBP^{ri}) and the uniform, rotation invariant version (LBP^{riu2}) apply seamlessly to OCLBP and IOCLBP. The number of features in this case (see Table 2) can be computed through invariant theory as for instance shown by González et al. [12].

4   Experiments

We assessed the effectiveness of IOCLBP in a set of colour texture classification tasks. Datasets, classifier, accuracy evaluation procedure and methods used for comparison are detailed in the following subsections.

4.1   Datasets

We considered eight datasets of colour texture images as detailed below. The main features of each dataset along with sample images are also reported in Table 1.

KTH-TIPS includes images from the following 10 classes of materials: aluminum foil, bread, corduroy, cotton, cracker, linen, orange peel, sandpaper, sponge and styrofoam [14,18]. For each class one sample of the corresponding material was acquired at nine different scales, three poses and under three illumination conditions, resulting in 81 image samples per class. The dimension of the images is 200px × 200px.

KTH-TIPS2b extends KTH-TIPS by adding one class (i.e.: 11 instead of ten), three samples for each class (i.e.: four instead of one), and one illumination condition (i.e.: four instead of three). The overall dataset is therefore composed of 432 samples for each class [3,18]. The image dimension is the same as in KTH-TIPS.

Outex-00013 comprises the same 68 texture classes as Outex's test suite TC-00013. This is a collection of heterogeneous materials such as cardboard, fabric, natural stone, paper, sandpaper, wool, etc. [28]. The dataset contains 20 image samples of dimension 128px × 128px which have no variation in scale, rotation angle or illumination conditions.

Outex-00014 features the same classes as Outex-00013 – but in this case each sample was acquired under three different lighting sources, respectively a 2300 K horizon sunlight, a 2856 K incandescent CIE A and a 4000 K fluorescent TL84 lamp. There are therefore 60 samples for each class instead of 20, whereas the image dimension is the same as in Outex-00014.

It is important to point out that in order to maintain a uniform evaluation protocol (see Sect. 4.2) for all the datasets considered here, we used different subdivisions into train and test set than those provided with the TC-00013 and TC-00014 test suites.

Plant Leaves is composed of images of leaves from 20 different species of plants. There are 60 samples for each class, each of dimension 128px × 128px. The images were acquired under controlled imaging conditions through a planar scanner [4].

RawFooT is a dataset specifically designed for investigating the robustness of image descriptors against changes in the illumination conditions [9,30]. It includes 68 classes of different types of raw food such as grain, fish, fruit, meat, pasta and vegetables. There are 46 image samples for each class; each sample was acquired under 46 different lighting conditions which differ in the direction of light, colour, intensity and a combination of these. Other viewing conditions such as scale and rotation angle are invariable. In our experiments we subdivided each sample into four non-overlapping images of dimension 400px × 400px this way obtaining $46 \times 4 = 184$ samples for each class.

USPTex features 191 classes of colour textures with 12 samples per class [1,31]. The images are rather varied, representing materials such as seeds, rice and fabric, but also road scenes, vegetation, walls, clouds and soil. The images have been acquired 'in the wild' and have a dimension of 128px × 128px.

V × C TSG is based on 42 classes of ceramic tiles acquired under controlled and steady imaging conditions in the V × C laboratory at the Polytechnic University of Valencia, Spain [22,32]. The dataset is composed of 14 base classes and three grades for each class. Notably, the three grades are very similar and difficult to differentiate even to the trained eye. The original images come in different resolution, are either rectangular or square, and the number of samples varies from class to class. In our experiments we cropped in any case a maximal central square window and retained 12 samples for each class.

4.2 Classification and Accuracy Evaluation

Classification was based on the nearest-neighbour rule with L_1 ('cityblock') distance. Accuracy estimation was performed through split-sample validation with stratified sampling, i.e. half of the samples of each class was used to train the classifier and the remaining half to test it. The estimated accuracy was the fraction of samples of the test set that were classified correctly. For a stable estimation the results (Table 3) were averaged over 100 random splits into train and test set.

4.3 Comparison with Other Methods

We compared the performance of IOCLBP with that of the following closely related methods:

- Local Binary Patterns [27];
- Combination of Local Binary Patterns and Local Colour Contrast [7];
- Improved Local Binary Patterns [16]
- Completed Local Binary Patterns [13];
- Opponent-colour Local Binary Patterns [25];
- Local Colour Vector Binary Patterns [20];
- Texture Spectrum [15].

For each of the above descriptors a rotation-invariant, multi-resolution feature vector was obtained by concatenating the rotation-invariant feature vectors (e.g. LBP^{ri}) computed at resolution 1, 2 and 3 (Fig. 1). The number of features of each method is shown in Table 2.

For calibration purposes we also included off-the-shelf features from pre-trained CNN – specifically Caffe AlexNet and VGG-M as respectively described in Refs. [5,17]. We considered three different sets of features obtained by the following encoding systems [6]:

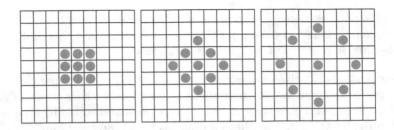

Fig. 1. Pixel neighbourhoods corresponding to resolutions 1, 2 and 3

- The output of the last fully-connected layer (FC);
- The output of the last convolutional layer pooled through a bag-of-words encoder (BoVW);
- The output of the last convolutional layer pooled through a vector of logically-aggregated descriptors encoder (VLAD).

Further post-processing involved L_2 normalisation of the FC and BoWV features, and individual L_2 normalisation of the VLAD subvectors. For a fair comparison we chose a number of clusters for the BoVW and VLAD encoders so as to guarantee that the three feature vectors (namely FC, BoVW and VLAD) had approximately the same length (see Table 2).

Table 2. Summary list of the methods included in the experiments

Method	Acronym	Reference	Year	No. of features
Texture Spectrum	TS	He and Wang [15]	1990	1494
Local Binary Patterns	LBP	Ojala *et al.* [27]	2002	108
Improved Local Binary Patterns	ILBP	Jin *et al.* [16]	2004	213
Opponent Col. Local Binary Patterns	OCLBP	Mäenpää & Pietikäinen [25]	2005	648
Completed Local Binary Patterns	CLBP	Guo *et al.* [13]	2010	432
Local Col. Vec. Local Binary Patterns	LCVBP	Lee *et al.* [20]	2012	324
LBP + Local Colour Contrast	LBP+LCC	Cusano *et al.* [7]	2014	876
Improved Opp. Col. Local Bin. Patt.	IOCLBP	This paper	2016	1287
Caffe-Alex fully connected	Caffe-Alex-FC	Krizhevsky *et al.* [17]	2012	4096
Caffe-Alex bag-of-words	Caffe-Alex-BoVW	Krizhevsky *et al.* [17]	2012	4096
Caffe-Alex vec. of loc. agg. desc.	Caffe-Alex-VLAD	Krizhevsky *et al.* [17]	2012	4224
VGG-M fully connected	VGG-M-FC	Chatfield *et al.* [5]	2016	4096
VGG-M bag-of-words	VGG-M-BoVW	Chatfield *et al.* [5]	2016	4096
VGG-M vector of locally agg. desc.	VGG-M-VLAD	Chatfield *et al.* [5]	2016	4096

5   Results and Discussion

Table 3 summarises the average classification accuracy by image descriptor and dataset. As can be seen, the performance of IOCLBP was superior to that of the methods of the same family (particularly OCLBP and LCVBP) in six datasets

Table 3. Overall accuracy by descriptor and dataset. Boldface figures indicate, for each dataset, the best among the hand-designed descriptors; boxed values the best among all descriptors.

Descriptor	ID datasets							
	1	2	3	4	5	6	7	8
Hand-designed local image descriptors								
CLBP	95.9	95.9	81.3	83.4	74.4	95.0	88.1	87.7
ILBP	95.6	95.1	85.7	88.5	77.0	97.1	86.9	90.0
IOCLBP	**96.3**	**98.5**	**91.1**	**91.7**	77.7	**97.7**	92.7	**94.8**
LBP	94.2	93.5	80.8	83.7	73.9	95.2	82.2	89.7
LBP+LCC	94.9	95.9	83.5	85.1	**79.5**	96.8	89.8	93.6
LCVBP	96.2	97.6	82.9	83.5	75.6	97.3	**93.7**	92.1
OCLBP	95.3	97.8	90.9	91.4	77.3	97.0	90.3	93.1
TS	92.9	94.6	81.1	83.9	76.0	96.6	85.3	91.1
CNN-based features								
Caffe-Alex-FC	**98.8**	99.0	82.8	83.8	71.6	97.6	95.8	79.7
Caffe-Alex-BoVW	95.2	96.3	76.5	74.7	53.0	94.0	89.1	72.2
Caffe-Alex-VLAD	97.4	98.5	76.4	76.6	59.3	94.7	91.5	78.3
VGG-M-FC	**98.8**	**99.3**	84.8	83.5	74.0	**98.4**	**97.7**	79.2
VGG-M-BoVW	94.5	96.3	76.9	74.1	59.2	93.7	91.9	70.9
VGG-M-VLAD	97.8	98.6	80.4	79.5	66.4	96.3	95.7	78.8

Datasets IDs: (1) KTH-TIPS; (2) KTH-TIPS2b; (3) Outex-13; (4) Outex-14; (5) Plant leaves (6) RawFooT; (7) USPTex; (8) V × C TSG

out of eight. Comparison with CNN-based features shows a perfectly split scenario, with IOCLBP performing better in four datasets out of eight and the reverse occurring in the remaining four. Particularly interesting was the result obtained with dataset V × C TSG: in this case IOCLBP outperformed all the other methods, and among them CNN-based features by a large margin (≈15% points). In fact, all the hand-designed methods performed better than CNN-based features with this dataset.

6 Conclusions

In this work we have introduced a variant of OCLBP which we called Improved Opponent Colour Local Binary Patterns. Experimentally we have shown the superiority of IOCLBP with respect to akin methods in texture classification tasks. In our experiments IOCLBP's accuracy was comparable to that of CNN-based features, but with the advantage that IOCLBP is conceptually much easier, training-free and less computationally demanding. Remarkably, IOCLBP showed clearly superior in the classification of texture images very similar to each other (e.g. dataset V × C TSG).

Acknowledgements. This work was partially supported by the Department of Engineering at the Università degli Studi di Perugia, Italy, under project *BioMeTron* – Fundamental research grant D.D. 20/2015 and by the Spanish Government under project AGL2014-56017-R.

References

1. Backes, A.R., Casanova, D., Bruno, O.M.: Color texture analysis based on fractal descriptors. Pattern Recogn. **45**(5), 1984–1992 (2012)
2. Bianconi, F., Fernández, A.: A unifying framework for LBP and related methods. In: Brahnam, S., Jain, L.C., Nanni, L., Lumini, A. (eds.) Local binary patterns: new variants and applications. Studies in computational intelligence, vol. 506, pp. 17–46. Springer, Heidelberg (2014). doi:10.1007/978-3-642-39289-4_2
3. Caputo, B., Hayman, E., Mallikarjuna, P.: Class-specific material categorisation. In: Proceedings of the IEEE International Conference on Computer Vision, Beijing, China, vol. 2, pp. 1597–1604, October 2005
4. Casanova, D., de Mesquita Sá Jr., J.J., Bruno, O.M.: Plant leaf identification using Gabor wavelets. Int. J. Imaging Syst. Technol. **19**(3), 236–243 (2009)
5. Chatfield, K., Simonyan, K., Vedaldi, A., Zisserman, A.: Return of the devil in the details: delving deep into convolutional nets. In: Proceedings of the British Machine Vision Conference 2014, Nottingham, United Kingdom, September 2014
6. Cimpoi, M., Maji, S., Vedaldi, A.: Deep filter banks for texture recognition and segmentation. In: Proceedings of the IEEE Computer Society Conference on Computer Vision and Pattern Recognition, Boston, USA, pp. 3828–3836, June 2015
7. Cusano, C., Napoletano, P., Schettini, R.: Combining local binary patterns and local color contrast for texture classification under varying illumination. J. Opt. Soc. Am. A Opt. Image Sci. Vis. **31**(7), 1453–1461 (2014)
8. Cusano, C., Napoletano, P., Schettini, R.: Local angular patterns for color texture classification. In: Murino, V., Puppo, E., Sona, D., Cristani, M., Sansone, C. (eds.) ICIAP 2015. LNCS, vol. 9281, pp. 111–118. Springer, Cham (2015). doi:10.1007/978-3-319-23222-5_14
9. Cusano, C., Napoletano, P., Schettini, R.: Evaluating color texture descriptors under large variations of controlled lighting conditions. J. Opt. Soc. Am. A **33**(1), 17–30 (2016)
10. Fernández, A., Álvarez, M.X., Bianconi, F.: Texture description through histograms of equivalent patterns. J. Math. Imaging Vis. **45**(1), 76–102 (2013)
11. Fernández, A., Ghita, O., González, E., Bianconi, F., Whelan, P.F.: Evaluation of robustness against rotation of LBP, CCR and ILBP features in granite texture classification. Mach. Vis. Appl. **22**(6), 913–926 (2011)
12. González, E., Bianconi, F., Fernández, A.: An investigation on the use of local multi-resolution patterns for image classification. Inf. Sci. **361–362**, 1–13 (2016)
13. Guo, Z., Zhang, L., Zhang, D.: A completed modeling of local binary pattern operator for texture classification. IEEE Trans. Image Process. **19**(6), 1657–1663 (2010)
14. Hayman, E., Caputo, B., Fritz, M., Eklundh, J.-O.: On the significance of real-world conditions for material classification. In: Pajdla, T., Matas, J. (eds.) ECCV 2004. LNCS, vol. 3024, pp. 253–266. Springer, Heidelberg (2004). doi:10.1007/978-3-540-24673-2_21
15. He, D.-C., Wang, L.: Texture unit, texture spectrum, and texture analysis. IEEE Trans. Geosci. Remote Sens. **28**(4), 509–512 (1990)

16. Jin, H., Liu, Q., Lu, H., Tong, X.: Face detection using improved LBP under Bayesian framework. In: Proceedings of the 3rd International Conference on Image and Graphics, Hong Kong, China, pp. 306–309, December 2004
17. Krizhevsky, A., Sutskever, I., Hinton, G.E.: ImageNet classification with deep convolutional neural networks. In: Proceedings of Advances in Neural Information Processing Systems, Lake Tahoe, USA, vol. 2, pp. 1097–1105, December 2012
18. The KTH-TIPS and KTH-TIPS2 image databases (2004). http://www.nada.kth.se/cvap/databases/kth-tips/. Accessed 16 Mar 2016
19. Ledoux, A., Losson, O., Macaire, L.: Color local binary patterns: compact descriptors for texture classification. J. Electron. Imaging 25(6) (2016)
20. Lee, S.H., Choi, J.Y., Ro, Y.M., Plataniotis, K.N.: Local color vector binary patterns from multichannel face images for face recognition. IEEE Trans. Image Process. 21(4), 2347–2353 (2012)
21. Liu, L., Fieguth, P., Guo, Y., Wang, X., Pietikäinen, M.: Local binary features for texture classification: taxonomy and experimental study. Pattern Recogn. 62, 135–160 (2017)
22. López, F., Valiente, J.M., Prats, J.M., Ferrer, A.: Performance evaluation of soft color texture descriptors for surface grading using experimental design and logistic regression. Pattern Recogn. 41(5), 1744–1755 (2008)
23. Losson, O., Macaire, L.: CFA local binary patterns for fast illuminant-invariant color texture classification. J. Real-Time Image Proc. 10(2), 387–401 (2015)
24. Mäenpää, T., Pietikäinen, M.: Classification with color and texture: jointly or separately? Pattern Recogn. 37(8), 1629–1640 (2004)
25. Mäenpää, T., Pietikäinen, M.: Texture analysis with local binary patterns. In: Chen, C.H., Wang, P.S.P. (eds.) Handbook of Pattern Recognition and Computer Vision, 3rd edn, pp. 197–216. World Scientific Publishing (2005)
26. Nanni, L., Lumini, A., Brahnam, S.: Local binary patterns variants as texture descriptors for medical image analysis. Artif. Intell. Med. 49(2), 117–125 (2010)
27. Ojala, T., Pietikäinen, M., Mäenpää, T.: Multiresolution gray-scale and rotation invariant texture classification with local binary patterns. IEEE Trans. Pattern Anal. Mach. Intell. 24(7), 971–987 (2002)
28. Ojala, T., Pietikäinen, M., Mäenpää, T., Viertola, J., Kyllönen, J., Huovinen, S.: Outex - new framework for empirical evaluation of texture analysis algorithms. In: Proceedings of the 16th International Conference on Pattern Recognition (ICPR 2002), Quebec, Canada, vol. 1, pp. 701–706. IEEE Computer Society (2002)
29. Palus, H.: Representations of colour images in different colour spaces. In: Sangwine, S.J., Horne, R.E.N. (eds.) The Colour Image Processing Handbook, pp. 67–90. Springer, New York (1998)
30. RawFooT, D.B.: Raw food texture database (2015). http://projects.ivl.disco.unimib.it/rawfoot/. Accessed 28 Dec 2015
31. USPTex dataset (2012). http://fractal.ifsc.usp.br/dataset/USPtex.php. Accessed 6 Jan 2016
32. V × C TSG image database for surface grading (2005). http://miron.disca.upv.es/vision/vxctsg. Accessed 4 July 2014
33. Xie, X., Mirmehdi, M.: A galaxy of texture features. In: Mirmehdi, M., Xie, X., Suri, J. (eds.) Handbook of Texture Analysis, pp. 375–406. Imperial College Press (2008)

Author Index

Printed in the United States
By Bookmasters